THE CERTIFIED SIX SIGMA
GREEN BELT HANDBOOK

Also available from ASQ Quality Press:

The Certified Six Sigma Black Belt Handbook, Second Edition
T. M. Kubiak and Donald W. Benbow

Applied Statistics for the Six Sigma Green Belt
Bhisham C. Gupta and H. Fred Walker

Statistical Quality Control for the Six Sigma Green Belt
Bhisham C. Gupta and H. Fred Walker

Six Sigma for the Office: A Pocket Guide
Roderick A. Munro

5S for Service Organizations and Offices: A Lean Look at Improvements
Debashis Sarkar

The Executive Guide to Understanding and Implementing Lean Six Sigma: The Financial Impact
Robert M. Meisel, Steven J. Babb, Steven F. Marsh, and James P. Schlichting

Transactional Six Sigma for Green Belts: Maximizing Service and Manufacturing Processes
Samuel E. Windsor

Defining and Analyzing a Business Process: A Six Sigma Pocket Guide
Jeffrey N. Lowenthal

Applying the Science of Six Sigma to the Art of Sales and Marketing
Michael J. Pestorius

Lean Kaizen: A Simplified Approach to Process Improvements
George Alukal and Anthony Manos

Business Performance Through Lean Six Sigma: Linking the Knowledge Worker, the Twelve Pillars, and Baldrige
James T. Schutta

The Certified Manager of Quality/Organizational Excellence Handbook, Third Edition
Russell T. Westcott, editor

Enabling Excellence: The Seven Elements Essential to Achieving Competitive Advantage
Timothy A. Pine

To request a complimentary catalog of ASQ Quality Press publications, call 800-248-1946, or visit our Web site at http://www.asq.org/quality-press.

THE CERTIFIED SIX SIGMA GREEN BELT HANDBOOK

*Roderick A. Munro, Matthew J. Maio,
Mohamed B. Nawaz, Govindarajan Ramu,
and Daniel J. Zrymiak*

ASQ Quality Press
Milwaukee, Wisconsin

American Society for Quality, Quality Press, Milwaukee 53203
© 2008 by ASQ
All rights reserved. Published 2007
Printed in the United States of America
16 15 14 13   8

Library of Congress Cataloging-in-Publication Data

The certified six sigma green belt handbook / Roderick A. Munro.
  p. cm.
  Includes bibliographical references and index.
  ISBN 978-0-87389-698-6 (hbk. : alk. paper)
  1. Six sigma (Quality control standard)—Handbooks, manuals, etc. 2. Production
management—Handbooks, manuals, etc. 3. Quality control—Statistical methods—
Handbooks, manuals, etc. I. Munro, Roderick A.

  TS156.C4235 2007
  658.4'013—dc22   2007043656

ISBN: 978-0-87389-698-6

Publisher: William A. Tony
Acquisitions Editor: Matt T. Meinholz
Project Editor: Paul O'Mara
Production Administrator: Randall Benson

ASQ Mission: The American Society for Quality advances individual, organizational, and community excellence worldwide through learning, quality improvement, and knowledge exchange.

Attention Bookstores, Wholesalers, Schools and Corporations: ASQ Quality Press books, videotapes, audiotapes, and software are available at quantity discounts with bulk purchases for business, educational, or instructional use. For information, please contact ASQ Quality Press at 800-248-1946, or write to ASQ Quality Press, P.O. Box 3005, Milwaukee, WI 53201-3005.

To place orders or to request a free copy of the ASQ Quality Press Publications Catalog, including ASQ membership information, call 800-248-1946. Visit our Web site at www.asq.org or http://www.asq.org/quality-press.

Printed in the United States of America

 Printed on acid-free paper

Quality Press
600 N. Plankinton Avenue
Milwaukee, Wisconsin 53203
Call toll free 800-248-1946
Fax 414-272-1734
www.asq.org
http://www.asq.org/quality-press
http://standardsgroup.asq.org
E-mail: authors@asq.org

To my wife Janna and daughters, Brianna and Hayley, thank you for your support, patience, and love. To my parents, John and Marge, thank you for challenging me to do better.

Matt

Special thanks for inspiration go to Dr. Jahan Baig, Professor and Dean, Kingdom University, Bahrain, for her enthusiastic input and support. I would also like to thank my daughters Shahana and Sofia for their patience.

Mohamed

I thank my mom Vasantha and dad Ramu for providing me with the right educational foundation and morals and my wife Anitha and daughter Vibha for their unconditional love and support.

Govind

To my wife Susan and my children, Ryan and Brooke, and to my late parents John and Angie. My passion for quality, Six Sigma, and operational excellence emanates from the positive examples of my employer Accenture, my prior employers and clients, and the universities and colleges where I have taught. Finally to ASQ and ASQ Quality Press, which have enabled me to expand my horizons beyond expectation— ASQ allows members to stand on the shoulders of giants in their pursuit of ideals.

Dan

I would like to dedicate this book to Matt, Mohamed, Govind, and Dan. They had to put up with a lot from me in trying to bring this project to completion, and I do thank them a lot for their support and patience as we went through this exercise. I know it became frustrating for them at times as we moved through the process and hopefully we will be able to achieve a high level of quality in maintaining this reference handbook for the Six Sigma community. Thus we do request your help, the reader, to give us feedback through the live Web page that ASQ has so generously set up for this effort: http://asqgroups.asq.org/cssgbhandbook/.

As in any work of substance, there are a lot of people involved. The authors would like to also thank all these people for their time and support. Of special note, thanks goes to ASQ Quality Press, especially Paul O'Mara as he tried to herd this group into some form of timing on this project. Another helpful ASQ staff person was Sally Harthun of the Certification Committee who along with the ASQ volunteers from the Green Belt Committee were as open about the CSSGB BoK as our ASQ Policies and Procedures allows. We also had many individuals assist this project, from helping to develop practice exam questions (we actually duplicated the same process used by the ASQ National Certification Committee) to developing white papers and other tools for Green Belt use, as well as a college class from Davenport College in Grand Rapids, Michigan who, along with their instructor, Mr. Don Brecken, worked on creating a paper for the CD-ROM. We want to acknowledge everyone for their time, effort, and assistance in helping to bring this handbook to potential Green Belts everywhere.

Rod

Table of Contents

CD-ROM Contents

How to Use This CD

Appendices to Handbook

ASQ Materials

Blank Forms

Case Studies and Papers

Dataplot Software Handbook

Exam Question Samples

Figures

Odds and Ends

Presentation Sample Formats

Standards and Specifications

Tools

List of Figures and Tables

Acknowledgments

Rod Munro would like to acknowledge the following people for their participation and contribution's to this book's content and CD-ROM: Trisha Balazovic, Pam Bethune, Edward Blackman, Steven Bonacorsi, John Bower, Don Brecken, Scott Burnside, Laura Burr Busse, David Carosella, William "Rob" Cushard, Sheila Deporter, Grace Duffy, Brenda Dusek, Arland Eilert, Ed Faylo, Kevin Hankins, Elizabeth Hanna, Mark Havens, Mark Hehl, William John Hindelang, Rita Ita, Chad Johnson, Rajinder Kapur, Terry L. Kozlowski, Bob Kukla, Mike La Dolcetta, Steve Leggett, Joe Lucido, Janet MacDonald, William Maholick, Tariq Malik, Marcia Martin, Cecelia McCain, Ryan McCleary, F. Leland McClue, Max Moore, Scott Neal, Peter Picketts, Salil Raje, Roger Rau, John Roberts Jr., Ibzahima Sall, Abhijit Sengupta, Kush Shah, Mogda Shin, Steven Sibrel, Deepan Sivaraj, Mary Beth Soloy, Maria C. Staab, Andrea Stamps, Rita Stockman, Peter Vadhanasindhu, John Vandenbemden, Michael Walmsley, Xiaobo Wang, Eric Zink.

Govindarajan (Govind) Ramu would like to acknowledge a number of students who participated in the ASQ Ottawa section certification courses, JDS Uniphase Corporation Black Belt and Green Belt courses, and quality professionals from ASQ and Elsmar discussion boards who have triggered many thought provoking questions. Practical solutions addressed in this book were inspired by such questions.

Introduction:
The ASQ Certification Process

Welcome to *The Certified Six Sigma Green Belt Handbook*. This reference manual is designed to help those interested in passing the American Society for Quality's (ASQ) certification exam for Six Sigma Green Belts and others who want a handy reference to the appropriate materials needed to conduct successful Green Belt projects. This handbook consists of an introduction to the exam process, the Body of Knowledge (BoK) materials used in the ASQ exam with appropriate references, handy tips for taking exams, useful tables and formulas, and a CD-ROM disk with sample exam questions that can be used for practice. *Note: you will not be allowed to take the exam questions with you into the ASQ-proctored exam.*

This introduction contains information about the exam process itself. This material is not considered part of the exam, so if your only interest is in learning the BoK, you may choose to skip this section.

THE TEST DEVELOPMENT PROCESS

Many exams, whether tests or certifications, are written by a very few people (sometimes only one person) based on what they think an examinee should know to meet the criteria of some training materials (like nearly all college exams). The American Society for Quality Control (ASQC changed its name to ASQ in 1997) started developing the Certified Quality Engineer (CQE) program in 1967, making it the oldest professional quality certification in the United States. ASQC gathered a small number of quality professionals together for the development cycle of the exam. The first CQE exam developers and a few others were grandfathered in, bypassing the taking of the first exam, which was offered in 1968.

Throughout the 1970s and early 1980s ASQC and others developed more certification exams. During this time, the issue of what the difference is between a professional certification and a state license (for example, the Professional Engineers exam process) was being raised as some U.S. states and Canada started questioning the professional community about what they were doing. ASQC and other professional organizations started trying to distinguish certifications given by their organizations from state or other governmental certifications. Basically, one is granted by peer recognition (professional organizations), the other by a governmental licensing process.

In response to this growing concern and the possibility of legal litigation as to the fairness of the exam process, ASQC wanted to become proactive about their certification process. After a benchmarking exercise and a search for what was considered the very best exam development process, ASQC partnered with the Educational Testing Service (ETS is the organization that creates and maintains the SAT exams for college-bound students).

The two organizations worked together to develop an exam development process that would be both legally defensible in court and to the various governmental organizations who might choose to challenge the process. The ASQC CQE exam was the first to be redesigned with the new development process. The basic steps include:

- Design of a survey to identify the current tools and methodologies being used in a wide breadth of industries across the United States.

- Targeting ASQ members who are currently certified in a particular discipline, as well as managers and industry leaders who are aware of the needs in the various industry sectors across the country.

- Tabulating the results of the most widely used tools, techniques, and methodologies to create a basic Body of Knowledge (BoK) for the new or redeveloped exam.

- Coordinating exam-writing workshops around the BoK, paying special attention to the demographics of the exam question writers. Each industry and all parts of the country are ensured some participation in the exam-writing process.

- During the exam-writing process the participants are broken up into teams. Each person writes a few questions based on their assigned portion of the BoK and then has two or more other team members review the question for accuracy, references, and fairness.

- The team leader submits the questions to the exam-writing workshop lead person, who also reviews the questions. Others will then review anything that raises any issue at the workshop.

- The questions are then entered into a proposed exam bank based on their relevance to the specified exam's BoK.

- As enough questions are identified in the proposed exam bank, another workshop is called with new reviewers to look over each question. The questions are accepted, reworked, or rejected for the BoK exam bank.

- About six months before an exam is to be given, a sort of the exam bank is conducted to select a new exam (each exam is different from all other exams) with some alternate questions for each area of the BoK. This exam mockup is then presented to an exam review workshop. These participants review every question and discuss their attributes related to the BoK. At the end of this process the exam is set for the next offering.

- Exams are prepared and distributed to ASQ sections or at ASQ conferences where they will be administered to participants.

- After the day of the exam, exams and relevant materials are returned to ASQ for grading. All exams are graded using the identified answers from the exam bank. Once all exams are graded, a statistical cut score is developed to maintain a predetermined level of ongoing knowledge for the BoK field of experience (this is not just a simple 70 percent or some other numerical pass score).

- With the cut score established for a given exam sequence, all exams are then reviewed to determine those who passed. Any examinee that falls below the cut score will receive a Pareto diagram of their exam identifying where they had problems. Those that pass the exam will receive a certification and exam card for their wallet or purse.

- Once an exam has been given, the exam questions are statistically reviewed for how well they discerned the knowledge of the applicants. Any questions that were generally missed or passed by a significant portion of the audience will be discarded. Only a very few of the questions will return to the exam bank for possible use on a future exam.

- Every five years this cycle is repeated for each exam that ASQ offers.

This process is long and tedious, and ASQ spends a lot of time, resources, and volunteer effort to maintain this process to ensure the highest level of professionalism possible for the certifications offered by the Society. Once you pass an exam, you are encouraged to join in this process to help ensure that future exams will be meaningful to the participants.

ONGOING MAINTENANCE

As can be seen in the previous section, ASQ maintains a comprehensive process for ensuring that exams are reviewed every five years and that the exams are of the highest professionalism possible. To this end, security is tight for the entire process, and very few individuals know the entire history of an exam question's life to ensure that questions are not released to exam participants prior to an exam being given.

Some of the general activities that ASQ uses to maintain exam processes are:

- If you are a local section volunteer helping to administer a refresher program or teach a refresher course or other training process, you are not allowed to proctor an exam for the same BoK.

- If you proctor an exam for a section or conference, you are not allowed to teach that BoK.

- If you volunteer to assist with any of the activities listed in the previous section on the exam development cycle, you are not allowed to teach or publish anything related to that BoK (for example, Roderick Munro was a volunteer refresher course leader and instructor from 1985 through 1991, then on the ASQ National Certification Committee for CQE from 1991 to 1998, then waited several years before working on *The Certified Quality Engineer Handbook* and teaching refresher courses again).

- ASQ maintains an ASQ National Certification Committee for each exam that is offered through the Society. Each exam is either coordinated through an ASQ division (based on their field of expertise) and/or the ASQ National Headquarters, who coordinates with all ASQ divisions that might have a stake in a specific exam.

- These ASQ National Certification Committees are made up of ASQ member volunteers who meet on a regular basis to ensure that the processes listed above, the ASQ national activities, and other issues related to their specific exam are maintained at the highest possible level of professionalism. This includes recertification activities for those exams that have that requirement.

- These ASQ National Certification Committees ensure that the process listed in the previous section is followed (usually by participating in and/or coordinating the various events) as well as ensure that the BoK is positioned for reevaluation every five years.

Once an exam has been given, most of the questions will be put into an archival file with notes on each as to when it was used and statistical results of how the question performed on the exam. In future exam-writing workshops, these old files can occasionally be used as a basis for writing new or variations of questions. Thus it would be very rare to see exactly the same question show up on a future exam. That is why although using practice exams (as included on the CD-ROM accompanying this handbook) can be useful, the user should realize that these are not real questions that will be used on the exam by ASQ.

THE EXAMINATION PROCESS

Given the aforementioned process, the Green Belt candidate should realize that anyone saying that they have inside information as to what will be on any given exam is either violating the ASQ Code of Ethics (by stealing information, in which case ASQ will prosecute if found out) or stretching the truth in the way that they are presenting the information. The ASQ certification exam process is always evolving and will rarely ever have a question in the same format on any two given exams. The candidate must be prepared to answer questions (you are allowed to have reference questions with you) that could be reasonably extracted from the ASQ Certified Six Sigma Green Belt BoK (see Appendix B).

Also, given the number of various industries in the marketplace today, general questions can be asked about a given topic in any number of ways. One example here is the FMEA (note: acronyms are very rarely used in the actual exam). If you are in the automotive industry you might use the *AIAG Potential Failure Mode and Effects Analysis (FMEA) Reference Manual,* Third Edition or the SAE J1739:2000 standard. On the other hand, if you are in the medical devices industry, you would have to use BS EN ISO 14971:2001 "Medical devices—Application of risk management to medical devices." Still other industries might use the book *Failure Mode Effect Analysis: FMEA from Theory to Execution*, Second Edition. Either way, any question related to FMEA might focus on what the primary function of FMEA is, which is to manage the risk of the product or service that your organization offers to a customer (either internal or external). So you should not be shaken if a question sounds as if it comes from an industry other than the one in which you work. The point is whether you can decipher the intent of the question as it relates to the Green Belt BoK and answer the question using facts and reason. The sample questions on the CD-ROM have been developed by a group of Black Belts for you to use for practice. They are not part of the ASQ exam bank and any duplicated questions on the exam are by coincidence.

The *ASQ Certified Six Sigma Green Belt Guidelines* booklet starts off the explanation of the BoK with:

> Included in this body of knowledge (BoK) are explanations (subtext) and cognitive levels for each topic or subtopic in the test. These details will be used by the Examination Development Committee as guidelines for writing test questions and are designed to help candidates prepare for the exam by identifying specific content within each topic that can be tested. Except where specified, the subtext is not intended to limit the subject or be all-inclusive of what might be covered in an exam but is intended to clarify how topics are related to the role of the Certified Six Sigma Green Belt (SSGB). The descriptor in parentheses at the end of each subtext entry refers to the highest cognitive level at which the topic will be tested. A complete description of cognitive levels is provided at the end of this document.[1]

After the BoK is listed, a description of the meanings of *remember, understand, apply, analyze, evaluate,* and *create* is given. This is important as it tells you the examinee what level of knowledge you will need for that category of the BoK. The ASQ booklet lists the levels of cognition as:

Based on Bloom's Taxonomy—Revised (2001)

In addition to content specifics, the subtext for each topic in this BoK also indicates the intended complexity level of the test questions for that topic. These levels are based on "Levels of Cognition" and are presented below in rank order, from least complex to most complex.

Remember (Knowledge Level)

Recall or recognize terms, definitions, facts, ideas, materials, patterns, sequences, methods, principles, and so on.

Understand (Comprehension Level)

Read and understand descriptions, communications, reports, tables, diagrams, directions, regulations, and so on.

Apply (Application Level)

Know when and how to use ideas, procedures, methods, formulas, principles, theories, and so on.

Analyze (Analysis Level)

Break down information into its constituent parts and recognize their relationship to one another and how they are organized; identify sublevel factors or salient data from a complex scenario.

Evaluate (Evaluation Level)

Make judgments about the value of proposed ideas, solutions, and so on, by comparing the proposal to specific criteria or standards.

Create (Synthesis Level)

Put parts or elements together in such a way as to reveal a pattern or structure not clearly there before; identify which data or information from a complex set are appropriate to examine further or from which supported conclusions can be drawn.[2]

These words can be kept in mind while reviewing the chapters in this book to get a better sense of the detail of questions that could be asked in that section. This is also why it may appear that some material may be covered in more than one section of the BoK.

In preparing for the actual exam, we suggest that you do the following:

- Follow the list of "What Can and Can Not Be Brought into the Exam Site" found on the ASQ certification Web site—Frequently Asked Questions—"Taking the Exam."

- Select the reference that you have used in preparing for the exam. You should be familiar with how the reference is laid out and how you will use it.

- Create an index of your planned references—you are allowed to use self-prepared information as long as there are no practice exam questions in the material.

- Consider having a good Standard English dictionary available. Sometimes a word might be used in the questions that you may not be familiar with.

- Arrive at the exam site early so that you can set up your materials in a manner that best fits your needs. You might even call the chief proctor ahead of time to learn the room layout if you have not been to the particular exam site before.

- Remember that anything that you write on during the exam (scratch paper, exam pages, answer sheets, and so on) must be turned in to the proctor at the end of the exam. Thus, do not write in any of your references that you want to take home with you.

- Relax and breathe.

Additional advice given in the *ASQ Certified Six Sigma Green Belt* brochure includes:

Test takers are also advised to keep in mind these general pointers about standardized exams:

- *Read all of the questions on the first page of the test so you realize that you do know the material. In other words, relax.*

- *Read each question thoroughly. Don't assume you know what's being asked.*

- *Eliminate implausible answers and move quickly past the obviously wrong choices.*

- *Keep in mind that an answer may be a correct statement in itself but may not answer the question.*

- *Two answers may say exactly the opposite things or may be very similar. Read them again to decide what makes one correct and the other wrong.*

- *ASQ does not subtract points for incorrect answers. Answer every question. There is no penalty for guessing, so you have a minimum 25 percent chance of getting it right, and even higher if you are successful in eliminating one or two of the answers as incorrect.*

- *Go through and answer the questions you know. Then go through and read the ones you're unsure of.*

- *Mark those you are still uncomfortable with. You will narrow the field down to just a few questions you will need to spend more time on. These are the questions you might want to use your reference books for.*

- *Be aware of the time available for the exam and the remaining time as you work through the exam.*

- *Do not select more than one answer for a question. If you do, it will be scored as a "blank." For example, you think that both A and C are correct answers. Select only one answer and use the comment sheet supplied with your test to point out why you think both A and C are correct. Your comments will be reviewed before results are reported.*[3]

Taking an exam (offered by ASQ or any other organization) is a matter of preparation on the participant's part, and your results will show how well you achieved the exam requirements. We have seen people who, based on overall education, should pass an exam not do well and the other extreme where a person who we thought might struggle, but studied very hard, actually passed the exam. Study and use your reference materials and know where and how to find information when you need it. Few people can memorize everything, so the next best thing is knowing how to find information quickly when needed so that you can finish the exam in a timely manner.

The remainder of this introduction shows the linkage between the ASQ Certified Six Sigma Green Belt BoK (note the number of questions for each section) and the ASQ Certified Six Sigma Black Belt BoK, and suggested further readings to help you understand the makeup of the ASQ exam process better.

Further suggested readings from *Quality Progress* magazine in exam development and preparation:

Table i.1 Certified Six Sigma Green Belt BoK mapped to Certified Six Sigma Black Belt BoK.

Six Sigma Green Belt BoK	SSBB BoK
I. Overview: Six Sigma and the Organization (15 questions)	
A. Six Sigma and organizational goals	
1. *Value of Six Sigma.* Recognize why organizations use Six Sigma, how they apply its philosophy and goals, and the origins of Six Sigma (Juran, Deming, Shewhart, and so on). Describe how process inputs, outputs, and feedback impact the larger organization. (Understand)	I.A.2, I.A.5
2. *Organizational drivers and metrics.* Recognize key drivers for business (profit, market share, customer satisfaction, efficiency, product differentiation) and how key metrics and scorecards are developed and impact the entire organization. (Understand)	II.D
3. *Organizational goals and Six Sigma projects.* Describe the project selection process, including knowing when to use Six Sigma improvement methodology (DMAIC) as opposed to other problem-solving tools, and confirm that the project supports and is linked to organizational goals. (Understand)	I.B.4, I.B.5
B. Lean principles in the organization	
1. *Lean concepts and tools.* Define and describe concepts such as value chain, flow, pull, perfection, and so on, and tools commonly used to eliminate waste, including kaizen, 5S, error-proofing, value stream mapping, and so on. (Understand)	I.A.3, I.A.4
2. *Value-added and non-value-added activities.* Identify waste in terms of excess inventory, space, test inspection, rework, transportation, storage, and so on, and reduce cycle time to improve throughput. (Understand)	V.A.2, V.A.3 IX.A.4
3. *Theory of constraints.* Describe the theory of constraints. (Understand)	VII.E
C. Design for Six Sigma (DFSS) in the organization	
1. *Quality function deployment (QFD).* Describe how QFD fits into the overall DFSS process. (Understand) (Note: the application of QFD is covered in II.A.6.)	IV.A.3
2. *Design and process failure mode and effects analysis (DFMEA and PFMEA).* Define and distinguish between design FMEA (DFMEA) and process FMEA (PFMEA) and interpret associated data. (Analyze) (Note: the application of FMEA is covered in II.D.2.)	VI.C
3. *Road maps for DFSS.* Describe and distinguish between DMADV (define, measure, analyze, design, verify) and IDOV (identify, design, optimize, verify), identify how they relate to DMAIC and how they help close the loop on improving the end product/process during the design for Six Sigma (DFSS) phase. (Understand)	IX.B, IX.D

Continued

Table i.1   Certified Six Sigma Green Belt BoK mapped to Certified Six Sigma Black Belt BoK. (Continued)

Six Sigma Green Belt BoK	SSBB BoK
II. Six Sigma—*Define* (25 Questions)	
A. Process management for projects	
1. *Process elements.* Define and describe process components and boundaries. Recognize how processes cross various functional areas and the challenges that result for process improvement efforts. (Analyze)	I.A.5
2. *Owners and stakeholders.* Identify process owners, internal and external customers, and other stakeholders in a project. (Apply)	I.B.1, II.A
3. *Identify customers.* Identify and classify internal and external customers as applicable to a particular project, and show how projects impact customers. (Apply)	II.A, IV.A.1
4. *Collect customer data.* Use various methods to collect customer feedback (for example, surveys, focus groups, interviews, observation) and identify the key elements that make these tools effective. Review survey questions to eliminate bias, vagueness, and so on. (Apply)	IV.A.2
5. *Analyze customer data.* Use graphical, statistical, and qualitative tools to analyze customer feedback. (Analyze)	IV.A.2
6. *Translate customer requirements.* Assist in translating customer feedback into project goals and objectives, including critical to quality (CTQ) attributes and requirements statements. Use voice of the customer analysis tools such as quality function deployment (QFD) to translate customer requirements into performance measures. (Apply)	IV.A.3
B. Project management basics	
1. *Project charter and problem statement.* Define and describe elements of a project charter and develop a problem statement, including baseline and improvement goals. (Apply)	IV.B.1
2. *Project scope.* Assist with the development of project definition/scope using Pareto charts, process maps, and so on. (Apply)	IV.B.2
3. *Project metrics.* Assist with the development of primary and consequential metrics (for example, quality, cycle time, cost) and establish key project metrics that relate to the voice of the customer. (Apply)	IV.B.4
4. *Project planning tools.* Use project tools such as Gantt charts, critical path method (CPM), and program evaluation and review technique (PERT) charts, and so on. (Apply)	IV.C
5. *Project documentation.* Provide input and select the proper vehicle for presenting project documentation (for example, spreadsheet output, storyboards) at phase reviews, management reviews, and other presentations. (Apply)	N/A
6. *Project risk analysis.* Describe the purpose and benefit of project risk analysis, including resources, financials, impact on customers and other stakeholders, and so on. (Understand)	N/A

Continued

Table i.1   Certified Six Sigma Green Belt BoK mapped to Certified Six Sigma Black Belt BoK. *(Continued)*

Six Sigma Green Belt BoK	SSBB BoK
7. *Project closure.* Describe the objectives achieved and apply the lessons learned to identify additional opportunities. (Apply)	N/A
C. *Management and planning tools.* Define, select, and use 1) affinity diagrams, 2) interrelationship digraphs, 3) tree diagrams, 4) prioritization matrices, 5) matrix diagrams, 6) process decision program charts (PDPC), and 7) activity network diagrams. (Apply)	III.F
D. *Business results for projects*	
1. *Process performance.* Calculate process performance metrics such as defects per unit (DPU), rolled throughput yield (RTY), cost of poor quality (COPQ), defects per million opportunities (DPMO) sigma levels, and process capability indices. Track process performance measures to drive project decisions. (Analyze)	II.E, V.F.1, V.F.2, V.F.7
2. *Failure mode and effects analysis (FMEA).* Define and describe failure mode and effects analysis (FMEA). Describe the purpose and use of scale criteria and calculate the risk priority number (RPN). (Analyze)	VI.C
E. *Team dynamics and performance*	
1. *Team stages and dynamics.* Define and describe the stages of team evolution, including forming, storming, norming, performing, adjourning, and recognition. Identify and help resolve negative dynamics such as overbearing, dominant, or reluctant participants, the unquestioned acceptance of opinions as facts, groupthink, feuding, floundering, the rush to accomplishment, attribution, discounts, plops, digressions, tangents, and so on. (Understand)	III.B.1, III.B.2
2. *Six Sigma and other team roles and responsibilities.* Describe and define the roles and responsibilities of participants on Six Sigma and other teams, including Black Belt, Master Black Belt, Green Belt, champion, executive, coach, facilitator, team member, sponsor, process owner, and so on. (Apply)	I.B.5
3. *Team tools.* Define and apply team tools such as brainstorming, nominal group technique, multivoting, and so on. (Apply)	III.E
4. *Communication.* Use effective and appropriate communication techniques for different situations to overcome barriers to project success. (Apply)	III.B.3
III. Six Sigma—*Measure* (30 Questions)	
A. *Process analysis and documentation*	
1. *Process modeling.* Develop and review process maps, written procedures, work instructions, flowcharts, and so on. (Analyze)	V.A.3
2. *Process inputs and outputs.* Identify process input variables and process output variables (SIPOC), and document their relationships through cause-and-effect diagrams, relational matrices, and so on. (Analyze)	V.A.1

Continued

Table i.1   Certified Six Sigma Green Belt BoK mapped to Certified Six Sigma Black Belt BoK. *(Continued)*

Six Sigma Green Belt BoK	SSBB BoK
B. *Probability and statistics*	
1. *Drawing valid statistical conclusions.* Distinguish between enumerative (descriptive) and analytical (inferential) studies, and distinguish between a population parameter and a sample statistic. (Apply)	V.D.1, V.D.5
2. *Central limit theorem and sampling distribution of the mean.* Define the central limit theorem and describe its significance in the application of inferential statistics for confidence intervals, control charts, and so on. (Apply)	V.D.2
3. *Basic probability concepts.* Describe and apply concepts such as independence, mutually exclusive, multiplication rules, and so on. (Apply)	V.E.1
C. *Collecting and summarizing data*	
1. *Types of data and measurement scales.* Identify and classify continuous (variables) and discrete (attributes) data. Describe and define nominal, ordinal, interval, and ratio measurement scales. (Analyze)	V.B.1, V.B.2
2. *Data collection methods.* Define and apply methods for collecting data such as check sheets, coded data, and so on. (Apply)	V.B.4
3. *Techniques for assuring data accuracy and integrity.* Define and apply techniques such as random sampling, stratified sampling, sample homogeneity, and so on. (Apply)	V.B.3
4. *Descriptive statistics.* Define, compute, and interpret measures of dispersion and central tendency, and construct and interpret frequency distributions and cumulative frequency distributions. (Analyze)	V.D.3
5. *Graphical methods.* Depict relationships by constructing, applying, and interpreting diagrams and charts such as stem-and-leaf plots, box-and-whisker plots, run charts, scatter diagrams, Pareto charts, and so on. Depict distributions by constructing, applying, and interpreting diagrams such as histograms, normal probability plots, and so on. (Create)	V.D.4
D. *Probability distributions.* Describe and interpret normal, binomial, and Poisson, chi square, Student's t, and F distributions. (Apply)	V.E.2
E. *Measurement system analysis.* Calculate, analyze, and interpret measurement system capability using repeatability and reproducibility (GR&R), measurement correlation, bias, linearity, percent agreement, and precision/tolerance (P/T). (Evaluate)	V.C.2
F. *Process capability and performance*	
1. *Process capability studies.* Identify, describe, and apply the elements of designing and conducting process capability studies, including identifying characteristics, identifying specifications and tolerances, developing sampling plans, and verifying stability and normality. (Evaluate)	V.F.6
2. *Process performance versus specification.* Distinguish between natural process limits and specification limits, and calculate process performance metrics such as percent defective. (Evaluate)	V.F.7

Continued

Table i.1 Certified Six Sigma Green Belt BoK mapped to Certified Six Sigma Black Belt BoK. *(Continued)*

Six Sigma Green Belt BoK	SSBB BoK
3. *Process capability indices.* Define, select, and calculate C_p and C_{pk}, and assess process capability. (Evaluate)	V.F.2
4. *Process performance indices.* Define, select, and calculate P_p, P_{pk}, C_{pm}, and assess process performance. (Evaluate)	V.F.2
5. *Short-term versus long-term capability.* Describe the assumptions and conventions that are appropriate when only short-term data are collected and when only attributes data are available. Describe the changes in relationships that occur when long-term data are used, and interpret the relationship between long- and short-term capability as it relates to a 1.5 sigma shift. (Evaluate)	V.F.3
6. *Process capability for attributes data.* Compute the sigma level for a process and describe its relationship to P_{pk}. (Apply)	V.F.5
IV. Six Sigma—*Analyze* (15 Questions)	
A. *Exploratory data analysis*	
1. *Multi-vari studies.* Create and interpret multi-vari studies to interpret the difference between positional, cyclical, and temporal variation; apply sampling plans to investigate the largest sources of variation. (Create)	VI.A.4
2. *Simple linear correlation and regression.* Interpret the correlation coefficient and determine its statistical significance (p-value); recognize the difference between correlation and causation. Interpret the linear regression equation and determine its statistical significance (p-value); use regression models for estimation and prediction. (Evaluate)	VI.A.1, VI.A.2
B. *Hypothesis testing*	
1. *Basics.* Define and distinguish between statistical and practical significance and apply tests for significance level, power, type I and type II errors. Determine appropriate sample size for various tests. (Apply)	VI.B.1
2. *Tests for means, variances, and proportions.* Define, compare, and contrast statistical and practical significance. (Apply)	VI.B.5
3. *Paired-comparison tests.* Define and describe paired-comparison parametric hypothesis tests. (Understand)	VI.B.5
4. *Single-factor analysis of variance (ANOVA).* Define terms related to one-way ANOVAs and interpret their results and data plots. (Apply)	VI.B.6
5. *Chi square.* Define and interpret chi square and use it to determine statistical significance. (Analyze)	VI.B.7
V. Six Sigma—*Improve and Control* (15 Questions)	
A. *Design of experiments (DOE)*	
1. *Basic terms.* Define and describe basic DOE terms such as independent and dependent variables, factors and levels, response, treatment, error, repetition, and replication. (Understand)	VII.A.1

Continued

Table i.1   Certified Six Sigma Green Belt BoK mapped to Certified Six Sigma Black Belt BoK. *(Continued)*

Six Sigma Green Belt BoK	SSBB BoK
2. *Main effects.* Interpret main effects and interaction plots. (Apply)	VII.A.5
B. *Statistical process control (SPC)*	
1. *Objectives and benefits.* Describe the objectives and benefits of SPC, including controlling process performance, identifying special and common causes, and so on. (Analyze)	VIII.A.1
2. *Rational subgrouping.* Define and describe how rational subgrouping is used. (Understand)	VIII.A.3
3. *Selection and application of control charts.* Identify, select, construct, and apply the following types of control charts: $\bar{X}$ and R, $\bar{X}$ and s, individuals and moving range (IMR/XmR), median (X), p, np, c, and u. (Apply)	VIII.A.4
4. *Analysis of control charts.* Interpret control charts and distinguish between common and special causes using rules for determining statistical control. (Analyze)	VIII.A.5
C. *Implement and validate solutions.* Use various improvement methods such as brainstorming, main effects analysis, multi-vari studies, FMEA, measurement system capability reanalysis, and post-improvement capability analysis to identify, implement, and validate solutions through F-test, t-test, and so on. (Create)	VII.C.1, VIII.D
D. *Control plan.* Assist in developing a control plan to document and hold the gains, and assist in implementing controls and monitoring systems. (Apply)	VII.C.2

Black, Sam P. "Internal Certification: The Key to Continuous Quality Success." *Quality Progress* 26, no. 1 (January 1993): 67.

Brown, John O. "A Practical Approach to Service-Supplier Certification." *Quality Progress* 31, no. 1 (January 1998): 35.

"Certified Quality Engineer Examination." (Reprint from June 1981.) *Quality Progress* 17, no. 7 (July 1984): 35.

Cochrane, Don. "ASQ's Black Belt Certification—A Personal Experience." *Quality Progress* 35, no. 5 (May 2002): 33.

Hartman, Melissa G. "Developing a New Kind of Certification." *Quality Progress* 35, no. 5 (May 2002): 24.

Heinrich, George. "Use CMI Certification to Achieve Strategic Initiatives." *Quality Progress* 36, no. 5 (May 2003): 56.

Landon, Tammy. "13 Steps to Certification in Less Than a Year." *Quality Progress* 36, no. 3 (March 2003): 32

Maass, Richard A. "Supplier Certification—A Positive Response to Just-in-Time." *Quality Progress* 21, no. 9 (September 1988): 75.

Maness, Thomas C. "New Industry-Specific Quality Certification." *Quality Progress* 35, no. 6 (June 2002): 65.

Moran, John W. "ASQ Certification Program Gains Wider Recognition." *Quality Progress* 33, no. 4 (April 2000): 29.

Rayman, Deborah A. "The Quest for CMI Certification." *Quality Progress* 25, no. 8 (August 1992): 101.

Rooney, James J. "Certification Exam Tips, Trips, and Traps." *Quality Progress* 37, no. 10 (October 2004): 41.

Spindler, Garold R. "Managing in Uncertainty: Lessons from the Underground." *Quality Progress* 34, no. 1 (January 2001): 83.

Vora, Manu K., Sally M. Harthun, and Ronald G. Kingen. "ASQC Certification Committee Practices What It Preaches." *Quality Progress* 26, no. 11 (November 1993): 99.

Ware, Paul A. "A Cooperative Approach to Vendor Certification." *Quality Progress* 17, no. 11 (November 1984): 26.

Part I

Overview: Six Sigma and the Organization

Part I

Chapter 1

A. Six Sigma and Organizational Goals

1. VALUE OF SIX SIGMA

> Recognize why organizations use six sigma, how they apply its philosophy and goals, and the origins of six sigma (Juran, Deming, Shewhart, etc.). Describe how process inputs, outputs, and feedback impact the larger organization. (Understand)
>
> **Body of Knowledge I.A.1**

Every company or organization (even so-called not-for-profits) must make money in some form or another to stay in business. If an organization spends more than it takes in, then it will be out of business. Thus, the challenge for every organization is to become profitable at whatever it does so that it can continue to do what it does. Managers, employees, suppliers, and customers all have their wants and needs that the business must satisfy in an efficient manner so profit can be achieved. Thus the first formula that every Six Sigma Green Belt must learn is the S-bar calculation: $!

History

Over the centuries, managers have tried to find ways to keep their organization in business. Many different techniques have been employed over the years to keep customers coming back time and time again. Unfortunately for many organizations, people's wants and needs change over time, leaving the organization with the challenge of finding new and better ways of satisfying those needs and wants. The concept of setting standards of work goes back many centuries and was the foundation of the guilds and crafts trades that developed over the years. During the mid-1800s to early 1900s, separation of work was developed to speed up the process of development and production. Innovators like Frederick Taylor and Henry Ford developed ideas and techniques that are still with us today.

Given these new methods of doing business, the quality control/quality assurance (QC/QA) specialist was created to ensure that standards were established and maintained so that customers would be satisfied. In many organizations, however, this also created a separation of tasks, and many people in organizations came to think of the responsibility for satisfying customers as only in the hands of the people in the QC/QA groups/departments instead of in the hands of the people who actually did the work of making the product or providing the service. This was especially true in the United States during the decades of the 1950s, 1960s, and 1970s as managers looked for better ways to try to manage all the resources of the organization. Many organizations still struggle with customer satisfaction!

In the mid-1920s a young engineer named Walter Shewhart devised a technique of using graphs to monitor a process to identify whether that process was acting in a predicable manner or if what he termed *special causes* were affecting the process. These charts became known as *quality control charts;* however, today we sometimes call them *process behavior charts,* as we want to look at what the process is doing in relation to statistical probabilities. Many other tools and techniques have been developed since then, known by a long list of names. Quality developments over the years are summarized in Table 1.1.

Table 1.1   Some approaches to quality over the years.

Quality approach	Approximate time frame	Short description
Quality circles	1979–1981	Quality improvement or self-improvement study groups composed of a small number of employees (10 or fewer) and their supervisor. Quality circles originated in Japan, where they are called "quality control circles."
Statistical process control (SPC)	Mid-1980s	The application of statistical techniques to control a process. Also called "statistical quality control."
ISO 9000	1987–present	A set of international standards on quality management and quality assurance developed to help companies effectively document the quality system elements to be implemented to maintain an efficient quality system. The standards, initially published in 1987, are not specific to any particular industry, product, or service. The standards were developed by the International Organization for Standardization (ISO), a specialized international agency for standardization composed of the national standards bodies of 91 countries. The standards underwent revisions in 2000 and 2008, and now include ISO 9000:2000 (definitions), ISO 9001:2000 (requirements), and ISO 9004:2000 (continuous improvement).
Reengineering	1996–1997	A breakthrough approach involving the restructuring of an entire organization and its processes.

Continued

Table 1.1   Some approaches to quality over the years. *(Continued)*

Quality approach	Approximate time frame	Short description
Benchmarking	1988–1996	An improvement process in which a company measures its performance against that of best-in-class companies, determines how those companies achieved their performance levels, and uses the information to improve its own performance. The subjects that can be benchmarked include strategies, operations, processes, and procedures.
Balanced scorecard	1990s–present	A management concept that helps managers at all levels monitor their results in their key areas.
Baldrige Award criteria	1987–present	An award established by the U.S. Congress in 1987 to raise awareness of quality management and recognize U.S. companies that have implemented successful quality management systems. Two awards may be given annually in each of five categories: manufacturing company, service company, small business, education, and health care. The award is named after the late Secretary of Commerce Malcolm Baldrige, a proponent of quality management. The U.S. Commerce Department's National Institute of Standards and Technology manages the award, and ASQ administers it.
Six Sigma	1995–present	As described in Chapter 1.
Lean manufacturing	2000–present	As described in Chapter 2.

Six Sigma

Six Sigma is a structured and disciplined process designed to deliver perfect products and services on a consistent basis. It aims at improving the bottom line by finding and eliminating the causes of mistakes and defects in business processes. Usually, Six Sigma is associated with process capabilities of $C_{pk} > 1.5$, which are considered world-class performance. *Sigma* is a statistical term that refers to the standard deviation of a process about its mean.

A wide range of companies have found that when the Six Sigma philosophy is fully embraced, the enterprise thrives. What is this Six Sigma philosophy? Several definitions have been proposed. The threads common to these definitions are:

- Use of teams that are assigned well-defined projects that have direct impact on the organization's bottom line.

- Training in "statistical thinking" at all levels and providing key people with extensive training in advanced statistics and project management. These key people are designated "Black Belts."

- Emphasis on the DMAIC approach to problem solving: define, measure, analyze, improve, and control.

- A management environment that supports these initiatives as a business strategy.

Opinions on the definition of Six Sigma can differ:

- *Philosophy.* The philosophical perspective views all work as processes that can be defined, measured, analyzed, improved, and controlled (DMAIC). Processes require inputs and produce outputs. If you control the inputs, you will control the outputs. This is generally expressed as the $y = f(x)$ concept.

- *Set of tools.* Six Sigma as a set of tools includes all the qualitative and quantitative techniques used by the Six Sigma expert to drive process improvement. A few such tools include SPC, control charts, failure mode and effects analysis, and process mapping. There is probably little agreement among Six Sigma professionals as to what constitutes the tool set.

- *Methodology.* This view of Six Sigma recognizes the underlying and rigorous approach known as DMAIC. DMAIC defines the steps a Six Sigma practitioner is expected to follow, starting with identifying the problem and ending with the implementation of long-lasting solutions. While DMAIC is not the only Six Sigma methodology in use, it is certainly the most widely adopted and recognized.

- *Metrics.* In simple terms, Six Sigma quality performance means 3.4 defects per million opportunities (accounting for a 1.5-sigma shift in the mean).

At this point, Six Sigma purists will be quick to say, "You're not just talking about Six Sigma; you're talking about lean too." Today, the demarcation between Six Sigma and lean has blurred. With greater frequency, we are hearing about terms such as "sigma-lean," because process improvement requires aspects of both approaches to attain positive results.

Six Sigma focuses on reducing process variation and enhancing process control, while lean—also known as lean manufacturing—drives out waste (non-value-added activites) and promotes work standardization and value stream mapping. Six Sigma practitioners should be well versed in both.

Quality Pioneers

Most of the techniques found in the Six Sigma toolbox have been available for some time thanks to the groundbreaking work of several professionals in the quality sciences.

Walter Shewhart worked at the Hawthorne plant of Western Electric where he developed and used control charts. He is sometimes referred to as the father of statistical quality control because he brought together the disciplines of statistics, engineering, and economics. He described the basic principles of this new discipline in his book *Economic Control of Quality of Manufactured Product.* He was ASQ's first honorary member.

W. Edwards Deming emphasized the need for changes in management structure and attitudes. He developed a list of "Fourteen Points." As stated in his book *Out of the Crisis*[1] they are:

1. Create constancy of purpose for improvement of product and service.

2. Adopt a new philosophy.

3. Cease dependence on inspection to achieve quality.

4. End the practice of awarding business on the basis of price tag alone; instead, minimize total cost by working with a single supplier.

5. Improve constantly and forever every process for planning, production, and service.

6. Institute training on the job.

7. Adopt and institute leadership.

8. Drive out fear.

9. Break down barriers between staff areas.

10. Eliminate slogans, exhortations, and targets for the workforce.

11. Eliminate numerical quotas for the workforce and numerical goals for management.

12. Remove barriers that rob people of pride of workmanship. Eliminate the annual rating or merit system.

13. Institute a vigorous program of education and self-improvement for everyone.

14. Put everybody in the company to work to accomplish the transformation.

Joseph M. Juran since 1924 has pursued a varied career in management as an engineer, executive, government administrator, university professor, labor arbitrator, corporate director, and consultant. He developed the Juran trilogy, three managerial processes for use in managing for quality: quality planning, quality control, and quality improvement. Juran wrote hundreds of papers and 12 books, including *Juran's Quality Control Handbook, Quality Planning and Analysis* (with F. M. Gryna), and *Juran on Leadership for Quality.* His approach to quality improvement includes the following points:

1. Create awareness of the need and opportunity for improvement.

2. Mandate quality improvement; make it a part of every job description.

3. Create the infrastructure: establish a quality council, select projects for improvement, appoint teams, provide facilitators.

4. Provide training in how to improve quality.

5. Review progress regularly.

6. Give recognition to the winning teams.

7. Propagandize the results.

8. Revise the reward system to enforce the rate of improvement.

9. Maintain momentum by enlarging the business plan to include goals for quality improvement.

Deming and Juran worked in both the United States and Japan to help businesses understand the importance of continuous process improvement.

Philip Crosby wrote many books including *Quality Is Free, Quality without Tears, Let's Talk Quality,* and *Leading: The Art of Becoming an Executive.* Crosby, who originated the zero defects concept, was an ASQ honorary member and past president. Crosby's fourteen steps to quality improvement as noted in the *Certified Manager of Quality/Organizational Excellence Handbook*[2] are:

1. Make it clear that management is committed to quality.

2. Form quality improvement teams with representatives from each department.

3. Determine how to measure where current and potential quality problems lie.

4. Evaluate the cost of quality and explain its use as a management tool.

5. Raise the quality awareness and personal concern of all employees.

6. Take formal actions to correct problems identified through previous steps.

7. Establish a committee for the zero defects program.

8. Train all employees to actively carry out their part of the quality improvement program.

9. Hold a "zero defects day" to let all employees realize that there has been a change.

10. Encourage individuals to establish improvement goals for themselves and their groups.

11. Encourage employees to communicate to management the obstacles they face in attaining their improvement goals.

12. Recognize and appreciate those who participate.

13. Establish quality councils to communicate on a regular basis.

14. Do it all over again to emphasize that the quality improvement program never ends.

Armand Feigenbaum originated the concept of total quality control in his book *Total Quality Control,* published in 1951. The book has been translated into many languages, including Japanese, Chinese, French, and Spanish. Feigenbaum is an ASQ honorary member and served as ASQ president for two consecutive terms. He lists three steps to quality:

1. Quality leadership

2. Modern quality technology

3. Organizational commitment

Kaoru Ishikawa developed the cause-and-effect diagram. He worked with Deming through the Union of Japanese Scientists and Engineers (JUSE). The *Certified Manager of Quality/Organizational Excellence Handbook*[3] summarizes his philosophy with the following points:

1. Quality first—not short-term profit first.

2. Consumer orientation—not producer orientation. Think from the standpoint of the other party.

3. The next process is your customer—breaking down the barrier of sectionalism.

4. Using facts and data to make presentations—utilization of statistical methods.

5. Respect for humanity as a management philosophy—full participatory management.

6. Cross-functional management.

Genichi Taguchi taught that any departure from the nominal or target value for a characteristic represents a loss to society. He also popularized the use of fractional factorial designed experiments and stressed the concept of robustness

Toyota Motor Company provided leadership in lean manufacturing systems. This will be covered in Chapter 2.

Processes

A process is a series of steps designed to produce products and/or services. A process is often diagrammed with a flowchart depicting inputs, a path that material or information follows, and outputs. An example of a process flowchart is shown in Figure 1.1. Understanding and improving processes is a key part of every Six Sigma project.

The basic strategy of Six Sigma is contained in the acronym DMAIC, which stands for *define, measure, analyze, improve,* and *control.* These steps constitute the cycle used by Six Sigma practitioners to manage problem-solving projects. The individual parts of the DMAIC cycle are explained in subsequent chapters.

Business Systems

A business system is designed to implement a process or, more commonly, a set of processes. Business systems make certain that process inputs are in the right place at the right time so that each step of the process has the resources it needs. Perhaps most importantly, a business system must have as its goal the continual improvement of its processes, products, and services. To this end the business system is responsible for collecting and analyzing data from the processes and other sources that will help in the continual improvement of process outputs. Figure 1.2 illustrates the relationships between systems, processes, subprocesses, and steps.

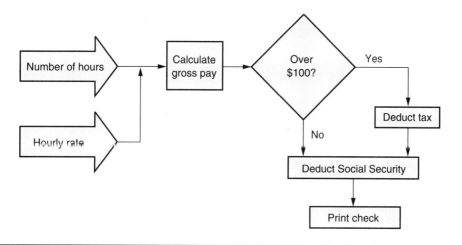

Figure 1.1   Example of a process flowchart.

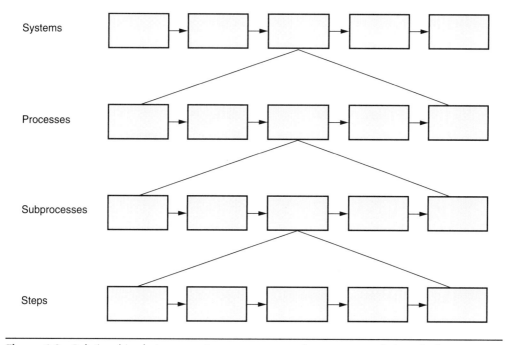

Figure 1.2   Relationships between systems, processes, subprocesses, and steps. Each part of a system can be broken into a series of processes, each of which may have subprocesses. The subprocesses may be further broken into steps.

Process Inputs, Outputs, and Feedback

Figure 1.3 illustrates the application of a feedback loop to help in process control. It is often useful to expand on a process flowchart with more elaborate diagrams. Various versions of these diagrams are called process maps, value stream maps, and so on. Their common feature is an emphasis on inputs and outputs for each process step, the output from one step being the input to the next step. Each step acts as the customer of the previous step and supplier to the next step. The value to the parent enterprise system lies in the quality of these inputs and outputs and the efficiency with which they are managed. There are two ways to look at the method by which efficient use of inputs/resources is implemented to produce quality outputs:

- Some would state that a function of process management is the collection and analysis of data about inputs and outputs, using the information as feedback to the process for adjustment and improvement.

- Another way of thinking about this is that the process should be designed so that data collection, analysis, and feedback for adjustment and improvement are a part of the process itself.

Either approach shows the importance of the design of an appropriate data collection, analysis, and feedback system. This begins with decisions about the points at which data should be collected. The next decisions encompass the measurement systems to be used. Details of measurement system analysis are discussed in later chapters. The third set of decisions entails the analysis of the data. The fourth set of decisions pertain to the use of the information gleaned from the data:

- Sometimes the information is used as real-time feedback to the process, triggering adjustment of inputs. A typical example would involve the use of a control chart. Data are collected and recorded on the chart. The charting process acts as the data analysis tool. The proper use of the chart sometimes suggests that a process input be adjusted.

- Another use for the information would be in the formation of plans for process improvement. If a stable process is found to be incapable, for instance, designed experiments may be required. Any enterprise system must perform process improvement as part of its day-to-day operation. Only in this way can the enterprise prosper.

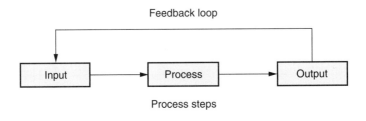

Figure 1.3   A feedback loop.

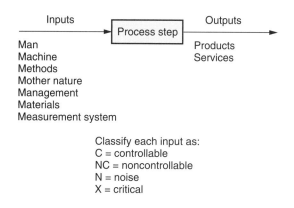

Figure 1.4   Categories of inputs to a process step.

Figure 1.4 shows the categories of inputs to a process step. It is helpful to list inputs in the various categories and then classify each input as indicated.

Significance of Six Sigma

Six Sigma is just the latest term for the more general concept of continual improvement. Continual improvement can be defined as the use of problem-solving techniques and quick deployment to implement improvements and then use process behavioral studies (Wheeler) to maintain the gains. Six Sigma has been described as a breakthrough system (Juran) and is being used in many organizations today in a variety of applications. Basically, Six Sigma is about collecting data on a process and using that data to analyze and interpret what is happening in that process so that the process can be improved to satisfy the customer (Kano and Taguchi). A basic process can be defined as an input, transformation, and output.

Six Sigma was first started at Motorola, Inc. and was then developed more into what we know today at General Electric. By following a prescribed process, the entire organization starts to look at everything that it does in the light of reducing variation and reducing waste with the result of increasing customer satisfaction. Customers could be anyone from the next person who uses the work we do (internal customer) to the ultimate customer who uses the products or services that our organization produces (external customer). To assist in this process, sometimes the supplier and customer will be added to the basic process definition listed above, creating the SIPOC identification: supplier, input, process, output, customer. This is used especially to help define the boundaries of what is to be studied.

For some, the idea of improving a process is a waste of time that should not be bothered with ("we are already working the hardest that we can"). But as Juran once said: "Changes creep up on us week by week, a little bit at a time. Over a year or two, there are 50 or 100 of these bits, which amounts to quite a bit. The skills of the men have not necessarily kept pace, and we wake up to the existence of a wide gap."[4] This is one explanation for why accidents and product rejections happen in our shops. If the root cause is actually found for any accident or rejection of product or service, it will usually be traced back to many small changes that occurred either within our own organization or at our supplier.

By using Six Sigma methodologies, we will be able to find those bits of changes and decide which ones should be changed for process improvement and which ones need to be corrected. This process is not meant to be a quick fix (magic bullet) approach. The logical use of the tools over time will save us resources and effort in doing our daily jobs.

A Green Belt's Role

You will find in this process for solving problems a number of tools and methods that you may already be familiar with and a few that may be new to you. You may very well ask: "How is this any different from what we have been doing before?" The direct answer will need to be answered by your organization depending on the various programs that have already been tried. For many of us, this process will be part of an ongoing evolution of how we do our work. One of the main things that you should notice is that upper management will be more involved with your problem-solving efforts and in the everyday problems that are found in your work areas.

During the process, and while using this book, you will be able to reference the Six Sigma model for improvement. It has been shown and demonstrated that by using a model or road map, we can usually accomplish something much quicker than without a guide. Some organizations today use something called the *MAIC model*. They refer to this process as being able to do "magic" without the "garbage" (G) that we find in most operations. Many organizations have added a *define* (D) stage, identifying the process customers, thus making for the DMAIC model.

You may already have control plans, process sheets, standard operating procedures, or any number of other things that you use in your daily work. The use of the Six Sigma model for improvement should not replace anything that you are currently doing, but be used to review daily work to look for areas or methods of improving the process in light of what your customers want and need. Just because we are doing the same things that we might have done before, do our customers still want the same things from us?

We are entering a journey of continual improvement that can involve our work and our lives. Some of us have been on this journey for some time while others may be just starting. The process involves using what Deming refers to as *profound knowledge:* appreciation for a system, knowledge about variation, theory of knowledge, and psychology. Through the Six Sigma methodology and using the Six Sigma model for improvement, we should see things around us work better and satisfy our customers more.

Potential Tasks

Your organization may already be using something called Six Sigma or some other method (for example, quality operating system [QOS], continuous improvement [CI], total quality management [TQM], or some other name). As an operator of a process, you will be asked by your supervisors or management to help implement improvement of the process(es) that you work with. Your challenge will be to look at the process for both the simple improvements that you may already know need to be made (preventive maintenance, cleanliness, parts wearing out, and so on.) as well as to assist in measuring certain factors about the process to investigate better ways of performing the process.

You will be asked to use the tools in this book, and maybe others, to study your work and process(es) to look for improvement ideas and to implement those ideas. You may already be familiar with some of these tools, and the challenge will be how to use them, possibly in new ways, to make the changes that will help your company stay in business in today's fiercely competitive world. We no longer compete only against others within our own country, but against others from countries around the world. How can they do a better job than us, ship the parts that we make, and sell them to our customers faster, better, and cheaper than us? This is the question that should be on your team's mind.

Many of us have found that by using a model or framework we can do things simpler—a picture is worth a thousand words. This is also true when trying to improve processes. Dr. Ishikawa (yes, the guy who created the fishbone chart) gave us a road map to follow when first looking at a process that needs to be improved. The words may not make much sense right now, but as you work with process improvement, you will come to understand the importance of what is said here:

1. Determine the assurance unit (what is to be measured).

2. Determine the measuring method (how it will be measured).

3. Determine the relative importance of quality characteristics (is this key to our process?).

4. Arrive at a consensus on defects and flaws (does everyone agree on good and bad quality?).

5. Expose latent defects (look at the process over time).

6. Observe quality statistically (use process behavior charting).

7. Distinguish between "quality of design" and "quality of conformance."

After we know what we can change (quality of conformance) versus what we can not change right now (quality of design—this is left to *design for Six Sigma* [DFSS]), we can start working on our processes. Many operators start out viewing this effort as only more work, but many will find that doing these studies will actually save them a lot of time and grief in the future as things start to improve and machines start to work better. One question to ask yourself now is, How often does your process slow down or stop due to something not working the way it should? Or, Is the output ever scrapped by someone down the line (including at your external customers) because something did not happen right at your operation?

Be willing to experiment with the tools and look for ways of applying them to the work and processes to learn as much as you can about how a process operates so that you can modify it as appropriate to give the customers the best possible output that is possible.

DMAIC Model

The DMAIC model stands for: *define, measure, analyze, improve,* and *control* and is very similar to the PDSA or PDCA model that you may already be using.

A key factor in each step is for management to allow the time and resources to accomplish each of the phases to strive for continual improvement. This is one of the driving forces that makes Six Sigma different from other quality improvement programs. The other driving forces include: getting everyone in the organization involved, getting the information technology group to assist in supplying data more quickly for everyone, and getting financial data in the form of cost of quality analysis.

Everyone will be asked to get involved with the Six Sigma model to look for continual improvement opportunities in their work areas. Basically, you will do the following in each step:

Define: identify the issue causing decreased customer satisfaction

Measure: collect data from the process

Analysis: study the process and data for clues to what is going on

Improve: act on the data to change the process for improvement

Control: monitor the system to sustain the gains

A number of tools and methods can be used in each of the steps of the DMAIC model. This is only a quick overview of many of these items. More detailed information can be found in the references, on the Internet, or probably in the quality office of your organization. The DMAIC model uses the following:

Define

Management commitment—PDSA

SIPOC (supplier, input, process, output, customer)

Define the problem—five whys and how

Systems thinking

Process identification

Flowchart

Project management

Measure

Management commitment—PDSA

Identify a data collection plan

Measurement systems analysis (MSA)

Collect data—check sheets, histograms, Pareto charts, run charts, scatter diagrams

Identify variability—instability, variation, off-target

Benchmark—start by setting the current baseline for the process

Start cost of quality

Analyze

Management commitment—PDSA

Continual improvement

Preventive maintenance

Cleanliness

Benchmark—continue process

Central limit theorem

Geometric dimensioning and tolerancing (GD&T)

Shop audit

Experiments

Improve

Management commitment—PDSA

Process improvement

Organizational development

Variation reduction

Problem solving

Brainstorm alternatives

Create "should be" flowcharts

Conduct FMEA

Cost of quality

Design of Experiments

Control

Management commitment—PDCA

Control plan

Dynamic control plan (DCP)

Long-term MSA

Mistake-proofing

Process behavior charts

Update lessons learned

Many will find this process very exciting as they will have the tools and methods to demonstrate the improvements that they are helping the organization to achieve. There have been times in the past when an employee tried to tell a supervisor that something was wrong with a machine or process. Now we have the means to not only tell but show and demonstrate what needs to be done. Following this process creates a road map for continual improvement and once started, is a never-ending journey. These tools and methods have proven themselves to be useful everywhere: from shop floors to front offices, from schools to hospitals, and even in churches or at home.

The Six Sigma Road Map

As we prepare for the Six Sigma journey, here is a quick view of the suggested map that we can follow:

1. Recognize that variation exists in everything that we do; standardize your work.

2. Identify what the customer wants and needs. Reduce variation.

3. Use a problem-solving methodology to plan improvements.

4. Follow the DMAIC model to deploy the improvement.

5. Monitor the process using process behavior charts.

6. Update standard operating procedures and lessons learned.

7. Celebrate successes.

8. Start over again for continual improvement—PDSA/SDCA.

Cost–Benefit Analysis (Cost of Quality–Quality Cost)

This is a financial tool that should be used to report how quality levels are being sustained on the shop floor within an organization. Many things that are worked on throughout the shop can be classified into one of four categories: *prevention costs, appraisal costs, internal failure costs,* or *external failure costs.* However, not all expenses of the company are used, only those that relate in some way to the products or services that are shipped to customers. The real power of this tool is not so much that you use the exact or "right" measures for each expense, but that you look at trends over time to see what you are doing. You want to find out what the *total cost* is to provide your customers with products and services (see Figure 1.5).

Traditionally, when cost of quality is first calculated for an organization, a picture such as Figure 1.5 emerges. Part of the reason for this is that many accountants and managers have not been taught about this tool in their formal education nor does any governmental or professional organization require the reporting of financial data in this format.

On the other hand, organizations that have learned to use the cost–benefit analysis of quality cost, as called for in Six Sigma, are typically very surprised at the amount of waste that is being produced. By focusing on reducing prevention and appraisal costs, failure costs will slowly start to come down. This will not happen overnight and may take years, in stubborn cases, to show improvement as old products work their way out of the customer system.

No one should be blamed for the poor results of the first measurement. It is important to look at these numbers as a benchmark to measure improvement from. The results of the numbers should be made available to everyone so that ideas can be generated as to what can be done and how. Remember the old adage: "What gets measured, gets done!" Thus, if everyone knows that management is watching the numbers on cost of quality, things should start to improve.

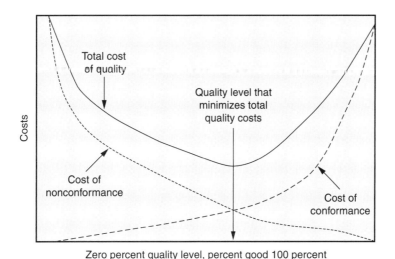

Figure 1.5   Traditional quality cost curves.

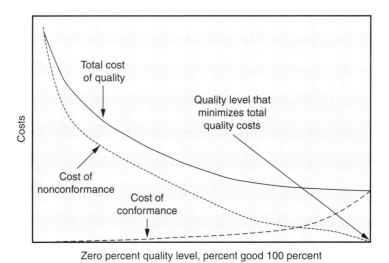

Figure 1.6   Modern quality cost curves.

The ultimate goal is to change the overall picture to look like Figure 1.6. As an organization continually improves their products and services, they will see an overall reduction in total cost to manufacture and produce products and services.

2. ORGANIZATIONAL DRIVERS AND METRICS

> Recognize key drivers for business (profit, market share, customer satisfaction, efficiency, product differentiation) and how key metrics and scorecards are developed and impact the entire organization. (Understand)
>
> **Body of Knowledge I.A.2**

Key Drivers

All organizations depend heavily on the measurement and analysis of performance. Such measurements should not only derive from business needs and strategy, but they should also provide critical data and information about key processes, outputs, and results. Several types of data and information are needed for performance management. A number of key drivers form the backbone of any business's effort to present performance information to executives and staff. These include customer, product, service, operational, market, competitive, supplier, workforce, cost, financial, governance, and compliance performance. A major consideration in performance improvement and change management involves the selection and use of performance measures or indicators. The measures or indicator that one selects must best represent the factors that lead to improved customer, operational, financial, and ethical performance. A comprehensive set of measures or indicators tied to customer and organizational performance requirements provides a clear basis for aligning all processes with one's organizational goals.

Voice of the Customer (VOC)

One of the key organizational drivers is customer and market knowledge—the ability of an organization to determine the requirements, needs, expectations, and preferences of customers and markets. Also necessary are the relationships with customers and the ability to determine the key factors that lead to customer acquisition, satisfaction, loyalty, and retention, and to business expansion and sustainability. The *voice of the customer* (VOC) is the process for capturing customer-related information. This process is proactive and continuously innovative to capture stated, unstated, and anticipated customer requirements, needs, and desires. The goal is to achieve customer loyalty and to build customer relationships, as appropriate. The VOC might include gathering and integrating survey data, focus group findings, Web-based data, warranty data, complaint logs and field reports, and any other data and information that affect the customer's purchasing and relationship decisions.

Balanced Scorecard

Many business professionals advocate the use of a balanced scorecard type of approach for the selection of project metrics as a method for ensuring that the project meets both customer and business needs. The balanced scorecard approach includes both financial and nonfinancial metrics, as well as lagging and leading measures across four areas or perspectives: financial, customer, internal processes, and employee learning and growth. Lagging measures are those that are measured at the end of an event, while leading measures are measures that help achieve objectives and are measured upstream of the event.

This new approach to strategic management was developed in the early 1990s to help managers monitor results in key areas. The concept was illustrated by Drs. Robert Kaplan and David Norton, who named this system the *balanced scorecard.* Recognizing some of the weaknesses and vagueness of previous management approaches, the balanced scorecard approach provides a clear prescription as to what companies should measure in order to "balance" financial results.

The balanced scorecard is not only a measurement system, but also a management system that enables organizations to focus on their vision and strategy and translate them into actions. It provides feedback on both internal business processes and external outcomes in order to continuously improve strategic performance and results. When fully deployed, the balanced scorecard transforms strategic planning from an academic exercise into the nerve center of the enterprise.

Most balanced scorecard metrics are based on brainstorming; however, the approach of brainstorming can have limited success in establishing sound metrics that maintain a good balance between lagging and leading measures.

3. ORGANIZATIONAL GOALS AND SIX SIGMA PROJECTS

Describe the project selection process including knowing when to use six sigma improvement methodology (DMAIC) as opposed to other problem-solving tools, and confirm that the project supports and is linked to organizational goals. (Understand)

Body of Knowledge I.A.3

Linking Projects to Organizational Goals

Organizational goals must be consistent with the long-term strategies of the enterprise. One technique for developing such strategies is called *hoshin* planning. This is a planning process in which a company develops up to four vision statements that indicate where the company should be in the next five years. Company goals and work plans are developed based on the vision statements. Periodic audits are then conducted to monitor progress.

Once Six Sigma projects have shown some successes there will usually be more project ideas than it is possible to undertake at one time. Some sort of project proposal format may be needed along with an associated process for project selection. It is common to require that project proposals include precise statements of the problem definition and some preliminary measures of the seriousness of the problem, including its impact on the goals of the enterprise.

A project selection group, including Master Black Belts, Black Belts, organizational champions, and key executive supporters, establishes a set of criteria for project selection and team assignments. In some companies the project selection group assigns some projects to Six Sigma teams and others to teams using other methodologies. For example, problems involving extensive data analysis and improvements using designed experiments would likely be assigned to a Six Sigma team while a process improvement not involving these techniques might be assigned to a lean manufacturing team. New-product design should follow DFSS guidelines.

The project selection criteria is always a key element to furthering of organizational goals. One key to gauging both the performance and health of an organization and its processes lies with its selection and use of metrics. These are usually converted to financial terms such as return on investment, cost reduction, and increases in sales and/or profit. Other things being approximately equal,

---

EXAMPLE

A gambler is considering whether to bet $1.00 on red at a roulette table. If the ball falls into a red cell, the gambler will receive a $1.00 profit. Otherwise the gambler will lose the $1.00 bet. The wheel has 38 cells, 18 being red.

Analysis: Assuming a fair wheel, the probability of winning is $18/38 \approx 0.474$ and the probability of losing is $20/38 \approx 0.526$. In table form:

Outcome	Profit	Probability	Profit × Probability
Win	$1	.474	$0.474
Loss	−$1	.526	−$0.526
	Expected outcome = −$0.052		

In this case the gambler can expect to lose an average of about a nickel (−$0.052) for each $1.00 bet. Risk analysis for real-life problems tends to be less precise primarily because the probabilities are usually not known and must be estimated.

EXAMPLE

A proposed Six Sigma project is aimed at improving quality enough to attract one or two new customers. The project will cost $3M. Previous experience indicates that the probability of getting customer A only is between 60 percent and 70 percent and the probability of getting customer B only is between 10 percent and 20 percent. The probability of getting both A and B is between 5 percent and 10 percent.

One way to analyze this problem is to make two tables, one for the worst case and the other for the best case, as shown in Table 1.2.

Assuming that the data are correct, the project will improve enterprise profits between $1M and $2.5M.

When estimating the values for these tables, the project team should list the strengths, weaknesses, opportunities, and threats (SWOT) that the proposal implies. A thorough study of this list will help provide the best estimates (see Figure 1.7).

Table 1.2   Risk analysis table.

Outcome	Worst case profit			Best case profit		
		Probability	Profit × Probability		Probability	Profit × Probability
A only	$2 M	.60	$1.2 M	$2 M	.70	$1.4 M
B only	$2 M	.10	$0.2 M	$2 M	.20	$0.4 M
A & B	$7 M	.05	$0.35 M	$7 M	.10	$0.7 M
None	−$3 M	.25	−$0.75 M	−$3 M	0	$0 M
	Expected profit = $1 M			Expected profit = $2.5 M		

Strengths:	Weaknesses:
High-quality product	Pricing
Monthly quantity commitment	Union plant
Tooling cost by customer	High employee turnover
Just-in-time concepts	Aging equipment—downtime
Online interface	issues
Product mix	
Opportunities:	**Threats:**
Potential industry leadership	Competition from startups
More growth	Labor force
Long-term contract	Union plant
	Unstable market
	Unstable labor force

Figure 1.7   A format for SWOT analysis.

the projects with the greatest contributions to the bottom line receive the highest priority.

The formula for expected profit is

$$EP = \Sigma \, \text{Profit} \times \text{Probability}$$

A *system* may be thought of as the set of processes that make up an enterprise. When improvements are proposed it is important to take a systems approach. This means that consideration be given to the effect the proposed changes will have on other processes within the system and therefore on the enterprise as a whole. Operating a system at less than its best is called *suboptimization*. Changes in a system may optimize individual process but suboptimize the system as a whole.

Examples:

- The resources invested in improving process A might be more profitably invested in process B.

- The throughput rate of a process increases far beyond the ability of the subsequent process to handle it.

- A distribution center loads its trucks in a manner that minimizes its work. However, this method requires the receiving organization to expend more time, energy, resources, and dollars unloading the truck. A different loading style/arrangement might be more expensive to the distribution center but would result in significant cost reduction for the entire system.

Chapter 2

B. Lean Principles in the Organization

1. LEAN CONCEPTS AND TOOLS

Define and describe concepts such as value chain, flow, pull, perfection, etc., and tools commonly used to eliminate waste, including kaizen, 5S, error-proofing, value-stream mapping, etc. (Understand)

Body of Knowledge I.B.1.

Value

The single most important concept that has been brought to awareness in the business community in recent years is *value*. Value is defined by the customer based on their perception of the usefulness and necessity of a given product or service.

While Japanese-made cars and German-made cars are sold in the same market, some customers prefer Japanese-made for their quality, reliability, resale value, and fuel efficiency. German-made cars can satisfy some of those expectations and additionally offer a pride of ownership attached to the car maker. There is a segment of customer who prefers German-made cars for these very reasons. Thus, customers define the value of the product. American car makers build trucks and vans sturdy enough to handle tough jobs. Some American cars, trucks, and vans are comparable in quality and reliability to the Japanese and German competition. They also have built-in customer loyalty. There is a segment of customer who will buy American-made vehicles for these very reasons.

Once the concept of value is understood, the target cost for the product or service can be determined. According to Womack, this target cost is a mixture of current selling prices of competitors and examination of elimination of waste by lean methods.

Value Stream

A value stream is the series of activities that an organization performs such as order, design, produce, and deliver products and services. A value stream often starts from a supplier's supplier and ends at the customer's customer. Wastes are both explicit and hidden along this value stream.

The three main components of a value stream are:

1. Flow of materials from receipt of supplier material to delivery of finished goods and services to customers. Examples:

   • Raw material shipped weekly from supplier to the organization by truck

   • Movement of material from raw material storage to production process through to finished goods warehouse

   • Shipping of the finished goods to overseas customer via customs

2. The transformation of raw materials into finished goods or inputs into outputs. Example:

   • Production steps like cutting, shaping, forging, welding, polishing, and assembly

3. The flow of information required to support the flow of material and transformation of goods and services. Example:

   • Purchase order to supplier, internal work order, shipping notice

This concept is visually illustrated via a lean tool called the *value stream map.* This map uses simple graphics and icons to illustrate the movement of material, information, inventory, work-in-progress, operators, and so on. Value stream mapping is a very powerful tool. The analysis subsequent to value stream mapping called *value stream analysis* can help uncover hidden wastes within the organization. An organization that effectively uses lean thinking and applies lean tools to reduce waste throughout the value stream and offer value to their customers is a *lean enterprise* organization.

Achieving a lean enterprise requires a change in attitudes, procedures, processes, and systems. It is necessary to zoom out and look at the flow of information, knowledge, and material throughout the organization. In any organization there are multiple paths through which products, documents, and ideas flow. The process of applying lean thinking to such a path can be divided into the following steps:

1. Produce a value stream map. This is also referred to as a *value chain diagram.* This diagram is described in detail by Rother and Shook.[1] It has boxes labeled with each step in the process. Information about timing and inventory is provided near each process box. Some symbols that are used on value stream maps are shown in Figure 2.1. Figure 2.2 shows an example of a value stream map.

2. Analyze all inventory notes with an eye toward reduction or elimination. Inventory tends to increase costs because:

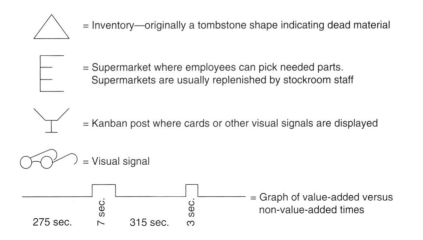

△ = Inventory—originally a tombstone shape indicating dead material

= Supermarket where employees can pick needed parts. Supermarkets are usually replenished by stockroom staff

= Kanban post where cards or other visual signals are displayed

= Visual signal

= Graph of value-added versus non-value-added times

275 sec.   7 sec.   315 sec.   3 sec.

Figure 2.1   Symbols used in value stream mapping.

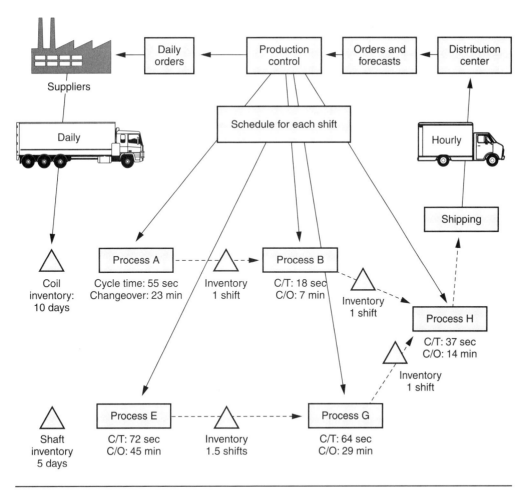

Figure 2.2   Value stream map example.

- Storage space may be expensive (rubber awaiting use in a tire factory is stored at 120°F, wood inventory may need to be humidity-controlled).

- Quality may deteriorate (rust, spoilage, and so on).

- Design changes may be delayed as they work their way through the inventory.

- Money invested in inventory could be used more productively elsewhere.

- Quality problems that are not detected until a later stage in the process will be more expensive to correct if an inventory of defective products has accumulated.

One company refers to its racks of safety stock as the "wall of shame."

3. Analyze the entire value stream for unneeded steps. These steps are called non-value-added activities and are discussed in detail later in this chapter.

4. Determine how the flow is driven. Strive to move toward value streams in which production decisions are based on the pull of customer demand. In a process where pull-based flow has reached perfection, a customer order for an item will trigger the production of all the component parts for that item. These components would arrive, be assembled, and delivered in a time interval that would satisfy the customer. In many situations this ideal has not been reached and the customer order will be filled from finished goods inventory. The order should still, however, trigger activities back through the value chain that produce a replacement item in finished goods inventory before it is needed by a customer.

5. Extend the value stream map upstream into suppliers' plants. New challenges continue to occur regarding compatibility of communication systems. The flows of information, material, knowledge, and money are all potential targets for lean improvements.

When beginning the process, pick a narrow focus—don't try to boil the ocean, as the saying goes.

5S

5S is a workplace organization method that can help improve the efficiency and management of operations. A process is impacted by its environment, as is the ability of personnel to respond to process change. Improvements in the general state of the work area, including access to hand tools, and so on, are an aid to process control. Especially critical here are the cleanliness, lighting, and general housekeeping status of any area where measurements are conducted since process control data are filtered through the measurement system. Example: A workbench cluttered with tools and accessories wastes the valuable time of skilled workers and causes distraction from work resulting in poor quality. Similarly, an office table covered with disorganized files and papers can cause clerical errors and delays in processing. 5S is the one of the first tools to apply in the path to achieving lean enterprise organizations.

The sequence for 5s is:

Sort. Remove unneeded items. Be it in the office or home, we tend to collect items that are very rarely needed or not needed at all. Over a period of time these items accumulate into a mess and make it less efficient to search for needed items, and sometimes even cause safety issues. The first step is sorting through the items as required and cleaning up the work area. Never-used items should be discarded immediately.

Set-in-Order. Arrange the required and rarely-required items for ease of accessibility. The items that are required more often like drawings, instructions, tools, safety goggles, and so on, are placed in designated and marked locations so that they can not be placed elsewhere. In short, a place for everything and everything in its place. The rarely-required items like machine manuals, shop floor layout plans, and so on, can be kept out of the way.

Shine. This involves cleaning the work area and equipment. As simple as this may sound, many quality issues are uncovered through effective cleaning of the work area. Example: cleaning of the inspection surface plate provides better measurement results, cleaning of the equipment work table provides for better movement, cleaning of the floor prevents accidents. For some industries, like semiconductor manufacturing, cleanliness is mandatory and is measured in particle count.

Standardize. This involves developing checklists, standards, and work instructions to keep the work area in a clean and orderly condition.

Sustain. This is the most difficult sequence in 5S. Most organizations are initially successful in the first four steps but sustaining the efforts and continuing them require support from management and empowerment of employees. Management needs to realize that this time is well spent and be willing to invest in the time. The time invested in 5S improves productivity and overall efficiency, and reduces accidents. Management should also empower the employees by allowing them to take ownership of their work areas.

Visual Factory

Visual factory provides visual identification of the status of material and information throughout the value stream. Examples of visual factory include providing status of material in/out at a raw material warehouse, showing units produced, units to complete order, and total produced by shift or day on a production display board, and indicating machine status with red, yellow, and green lights on the machine. Imagine that we need to find out the current status of a work order for a given customer. Often this is achieved by talking to line supervisors, referring to logbooks, conducting internal meetings, and so on.

In short, if an employee can walk onto a shop floor and can tell which machines are running, what product is being produced, how many more are to be produced by customer, follow posted safety instructions, and report to management, that is an effective visual workplace.

Kaizen versus Kaizen Events

Kaizen is a Japanese term for change for improvement, or improving processes through small incremental steps. Breakthrough improvement is referred to by another Japanese term, *kaikakku*.

Kaikakku is referred to in North America as a *kaizen event* or *kaizen blitz*. Hence, many practitioners often get confused with the interchangeable usage of kaizen and kaizen event. In lean implementation, kaizen events are used to provide quicker implementation results. Kaizen events are conducted by assembling a cross-functional team for three to five days and reviewing all possible options for improvement in a breakthrough effort. Management support is required for such initiatives. If the employees can't afford taking three to five days to improve a process constraint, then either the problem is unimportant or the organization requires more fundamental cultural adjustment before implementing lean.

Pull System

This is a vital component of the *just in time* (JIT) concept and lean implementation. Traditionally, organizations produce more than the customer wants and store the excess as inventory or work-in-progress, and tend to push the finished goods to the next process. This is done with the idea of optimizing the subprocess and not looking at the value stream as a whole. In a pull system, the process produces only when there is a pull from the subsequent process. This is signaled as either an empty bin or kanban card. The pull system links accurate information with the process to minimize waiting and overproduction.

Kanban

A system is best controlled when material and information flows into and out of the process in a smooth and rational manner. If process inputs arrive before they are needed, unnecessary confusion, inventory, and costs generally occur. If process outputs are not synchronized with downstream processes, delays, disappointed customers, and associated costs may occur. A properly administered kanban system will improve system control by assuring timely movement of products and information. Kanban is implemented using a visual indicator called kanban cards. The card indicates the quantity to be replenished once the minimum level is reached.

An empty bin with a kanban card is the signal for production to pull material from the previous step. The kanban quantity is mathematically calculated and fine-tuned during practical implementation. Typically, organizations take a while to perfect the kanban. Kanban is a more mature concept. It is important that other fundamentals of lean (5S, standard work, total productive maintenance [TPM], variation reduction) are put in place before venturing into kanban. If not, frequent equipment failure and unstable or inconsistent processes will defeat the purpose of kanban, resulting in huge kanban sizes to shield against these uncertainties.

Poka-Yoke

Poka-yoke, a Japanese term for mistake-proofing or error-proofing, is a method used to prevent errors. There are a number of examples in day-to-day life that use the mistake-proofing concept, such as electrical plugs and sockets that prevent plugging the wrong way, valves that shut once the maximum pressure is reached, fixtures that prevent loading the component in a wrong orientation, and so on. A window envelope is also a mistake-proofing method that allows users to see the letter with the right address sealed in. Similarly, there is detection-type mistake-proofing that alerts a user immediately after an error is made (to prevent further errors). Examples: car alarms when the driver closes the door with the lights on, an automatic gauging machine that alarms when an oversize or undersize part is produced.

Total Productive Maintenance

If the lean enterprise implementation is to be sustained, the manufacturing or service equipment has to be reliable. In order to have reliable equipment an organization has to maintain the equipment periodically. Preventive maintenance examples include changing oil at the required frequency, tightening loose parts, and watching for any visible or audible symptoms of failure. A comprehensive maintenance program may need a battery of maintenance technicians. This can be impractical and expensive. Hence, a total productive maintenance (TPM) program partners the maintenance technicians and line workers as a team to help each other reduce machine downtime. Management support is required to cross-train line workers to perform simple, basic maintenance and repairs. As the operators are trained to watch for symptoms of common failures, communication reaches maintenance technicians faster, thereby reducing downtime. Mature TPM programs use metrics like overall equipment effectiveness (OEE), which is a product of equipment availability, performance, and quality of output.

Standard Work

Basically, standard work is a tool that defines the interaction between man and machine in producing a part. It has three components: standard time, standard inventory, and standard sequence. Standard work helps in training new operators and reducing the variation in the process.

The basic idea is to make manufacturing methods and/or service process consistent. Quality management systems like ISO 9001 provide a basic foundation to lean implementation by incorporating standard work as part of the controlled documentation. Further, by having standard work, equipment, tools, layout, methods, and materials are standardized and thus reduce variation in processes. A detailed process work instruction with all of the above can be a very useful standard work document.

2. VALUE-ADDED AND NON-VALUE-ADDED ACTIVITIES

> Identify waste in terms of excess inventory, space, test inspection, rework, transportation, storage, etc., and reduce cycle time to improve throughput. (Understand)
>
> **Body of Knowledge I.B.2**

Lean experts define a process step as value-added if:

- The customer recognizes the value

- It changes (transforms) the product

- It is done right the first time

Some activities perform functions that do not change the form or function of the product or service, and the customer is not willing to pay for these activities. These activities are labeled non-value-added. A classic example is rework. The customer expects to pay for the printing of a document, for instance, but does not want to pay for corrections caused by errors of the supplier. A key step in making an organization more lean is the detection and elimination of non-valued-added activities.

In searching for non-value-added activities, the operative guideline should be "question everything." Steps that are assumed to be necessary are often ripe with opportunities for improvement. Team members not associated with a process will often provide a fresh eye and ask the impertinent questions.

There are, of course, gray areas where the line between valued-added and non-value-added may not be obvious. One such area is inspection and testing. A process may be so incapable that its output needs to be inspected to prevent defective parts from entering downstream processes. It could be argued that this inspection is a value-added activity because the customer doesn't want defective products. The obvious solution is to work on the process, making it capable and rendering the inspection activity unnecessary. Most authorities would agree that this inspection is non-value-added. On the other hand, a gas furnace manufacturer must fire-test every furnace in order to comply with CSA requirements. Customers are willing to pay for the CSA listing so this test step is a value-added activity.

Studies have shown that an overwhelming percent of lead time is non-value-added, much of it spent waiting for the next step. Yet over the years, efforts to decrease lead time have often focused on accelerating value-added functions rather than reducing or eliminating non-value-added functions.

Some authors list seven or eight categories of waste, or *muda* as it is referred to in some sources. These lists usually include overproduction, excess motion, waiting, inventory, excess movement of material, defect correction (rework), excess processing, and lost creativity (underutilization of resource skills). The following paragraphs examine the causes and results of each of these wastes.

Overproduction

Defined as making more than is needed or making it earlier or faster than is needed by the next process, the principal symptom of overproduction is excess work-in-progress (WIP). Companies adopt overproduction for various reasons including long setup times, unbalanced workload, and a just-in-case philosophy. One company maintains a six-month supply of a particular small part because the machine that produces it is unreliable. In some cases accounting methods have dictated that machines overproduce to amortize their capital costs. All WIP should be continuously scrutinized for possible reduction or elimination.

Excess Motion

This can be caused by poor workplace layout including awkward positioning of supplies and equipment. This results in ergonomic problems, time wasted searching for or moving supplies or equipment, and often in reduced quality levels. Kaizen events are effectively used to focus a small short-term team on improvements in a particular work area. The team must include personnel with experience in the positions involved as well as those with similar functions elsewhere. In addition it is essential to include people with the authority to make decisions. Such teams have made startling changes in two to five days of intense activity.

Waiting

Typically caused by such events as delayed shipments, long setup time, or missing people, waiting results in waste of resources and perhaps more importantly, demoralization of personnel. Setup time reduction efforts and total productive maintenance are partial answers to this problem. Cross-training of personnel so that they can be effectively moved to other positions is also helpful in some cases. Most important, of course, is carefully planned and executed scheduling.

Inventory

When inventories of raw materials, finished goods, or work-in-progress are maintained, costs are incurred for environmental control, record keeping, storage and retrieval, and so on. These functions add no value to the customer. Of course, some inventory may be necessary, but if a competitor finds ways to reduce costs by reducing inventory, business may be lost. One of the most tempting times to let inventory levels rise is when a business cycle is in the economic recovery phase. Instead of increasing inventories based on forecasts, the proper strategy is to synchronize production to increase with actual demand. Similarly, production or administrative functions that use more space or other resources than necessary increase costs without adding value. The common analogy of the sea of inventory, shown in Figure 2.3, illustrates how excess inventory makes it possible to avoid solving other problems. As the level of inventory is lowered, some problems will rear their ugly heads and need to be solved before further progress is possible.

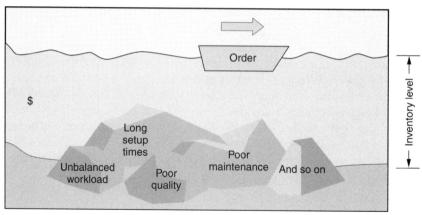

a) The order floats through the system protected from unresolved problems by excess inventory.

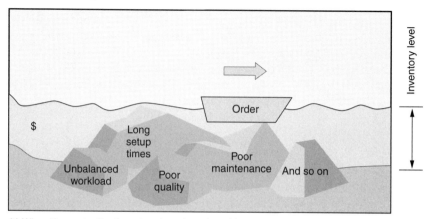

b) When the protective inventory is reduced, problems emerge that must be solved. To reduce cost, we must fix the problems.

Figure 2.3   A sea of inventory often hides unresolved problems.

Excess Movement of Material

Large conveyor systems, huge fleets of forklifts, and so on, make production more costly and complex, and often reduce quality through handling and storing. Poor plant layout is usually to blame. Plants with function-oriented departments (all lathes together, all presses together, and so on) require excessive material movement. A better plan is to gather equipment together that is used for one product or product family. This may mean having a manufacturing cell contain several types of equipment requiring personnel with multiple skills. Many companies have had success with cells that form a C shape, as shown in Figure 2.4, because they can be staffed in several ways. If demand for the cell's output is high, six people could

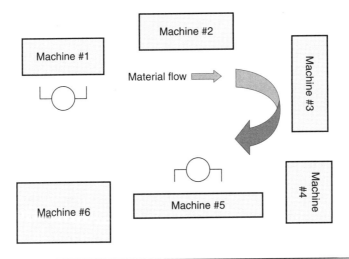

Figure 2.4   C-shaped manufacturing cell.

be assigned, one per machine. If demand is very low, one person could move from machine to machine, producing parts one at a time.

Defect Correction

This activity is non-value-added because the effort to fix the defective part is wasted. Typical causes of defects are poor equipment maintenance, poor quality system, poor training/work instructions, and poor product design. Lean thinking demands a vigorous look at these and other causes in order to continuously reduce defect levels.

Excess Processing

This form of waste is often difficult to recognize. Sometimes entire steps in the value chain are non-value-added. A steel stamping operation produces a large volume of parts before they are scheduled for painting. This may require the practice of dipping the parts in an oil solution to prevent rust as they wait to be painted. As the paint schedule permits, the parts are degreased and painted. The customer is unwilling to pay for the dip/degrease activities because they do not enhance the product. The best solution in this case is to schedule the pre-paint activities so that the parts are painted immediately upon production. This may require smaller batch sizes and improved communication procedures, among other things.

The purpose of the grinding step that often follows a welding operation is to remove some of the weld imperfections. Improving the welding process may reduce or eliminate the need for grinding. The unnecessary grinding would be classified as excessive processing. Excess processing can occur in the office as well as on the plant floor. Information from customer purchase orders is sometimes entered into a database and the order itself is filed as a backup hard copy to resolve any later disagreements. A recent study by one company revealed the fact that the hard copies, although they are occasionally pulled from files and initialed, stamped, stapled, and so on, really serve no useful purpose. The company now discards the PO once the information has been entered. The processes of filing, storing, and maintaining these records required one-half person performing non-value-added activity.

Lost Creativity

This is perhaps the most unfortunate waste. Most manufacturing employees have ideas that would improve processes if implemented. Standard organizational structures sometime seem designed to suppress such ideas. Union/management divides seem almost impossible to bridge. Lean thinking recognizes the need to involve employees in teams that welcome and reward their input. These teams must be empowered to make changes in an atmosphere that accepts mistakes as learning experiences. The resulting improved morale and reduced personnel turnover impact the bottom line in ways that no accountant has yet calculated. These are the nontangible benefits of lean thinking.

Perfection

You now understand value-added activities. You also learned about various wastes both hidden and explicit in processes. By optimizing value-added activities and eliminating waste, your organization can aim toward achieving "perfection" in lean. This is not a one-time effort. This is a continual learning process.

3. THEORY OF CONSTRAINTS

> Describe the theory of constraints.
> (Understand)
>
> **Body of Knowledge I.B.3**

Theory of constraints is a problem-solving methodology that focuses on the weakest link in a chain of processes. Usually the constraint is the process that is slowest. Flow rate through the system can not increase unless the rate at the constraint increases. The theory of constraints lists five steps to system improvement:

- *Identify.* Find the process that limits the effectiveness of the system. If throughput is the concern, then the constraint will often have work-in-progress (WIP) awaiting action.

- *Exploit.* Use kaizen or other methods to improve the rate of the constraining process.

- *Subordinate.* Adjust (or subordinate) the rates of other processes in the chain to match that of the constraint.

- *Elevate.* If the system rate needs further improvement, the constraint may require extensive revision (or elevation) This could mean investment in additional equipment or new technology.

- *Repeat.* If these steps have improved the process to the point where it is no longer the constraint, the system rate can be further improved by repeating these steps with the new constraint.

The strength of the theory of constraints is that it employs a systems approach, emphasizing that improvements to individual processes will not improve the rate of the system unless they improve the constraining process.

Drum–Buffer–Rope (DBR)

Goldratt[2] introduced a squad of soldiers walking in single file as an analogy of a string of production processes. As the first soldier moves forward he receives unprocessed material, the fresh ground. Each succeeding soldier performs another process by walking on that same ground. As the last soldier passes over the ground it becomes finished goods. So the individual processes are moving over fixed material rather than the other way around. Lead time is the time that it takes for the squad to pass over a certain point. If each soldier moves as fast as he can, the lead time tends to lengthen, with the slower soldiers falling behind and holding up those behind them since passing is not permitted.

The system constraint is the slowest soldier. The ground can't be processed faster than this soldier can move. This soldier sets the drumbeat for the entire system. To avoid lengthening the lead time, a rope connects the lead soldier to the slowest soldier.

Now the squad moves along as a unit with minimum lead time and minimum work-in-progress (WIP). If a soldier that is behind the slowest soldier happens to drop his rifle he'll fall behind a little (especially if the sergeant notices it) but will be able to catch up since he is not the slowest soldier. This is analogous to a minor process problem at one station. If a soldier in front of the slowest soldier drops his rifle the squad will not have to stop unless the slowest soldier catches up with the one in front of him. So if the squad has a high tendency to drop their rifles the rope must be longer. The length of the rope is the size of the buffer. In summary, to avoid long lead times and excess work-in-progress, all system processes should be slowed down (via the rope) to the speed of the slowest process (the drum), with the amount of WIP (or buffer) determined by the dependability of the individual processes. For further explanation of these concepts see Goldratt's *Critical Chain*.

Chapter 3

C. Design for Six Sigma (DFSS) in the Organization

1. QUALITY FUNCTION DEPLOYMENT (QFD)

> Describe how QFD fits into the overall DFSS process. (Understand) (Note: the application of QFD is covered in II.A.6.)
>
> **Body of Knowledge I.C.1**

Some of the most important applications of Six Sigma are in the design and redesign of processes and products. The ideal design meets or exceeds customer requirements at the lowest possible cost. Key steps in achieving this ideal are:

1. Link customer requirements to features of products and processes. Quality function deployment (QFD) provides a valuable approach to this activity.

2. Design a product and processes that will result in the desired quality at the lowest possible cost.

3. Employ design tools that will result in entirely new approaches to problem solving.

QFD provides a process for planning new or redesigned products and services. The input to the process is the voice of the customer (VOC). The QFD process requires that a team discover the needs and desires of their customer and study the organization's response to these needs and desires. The QFD matrix aids in illustrating the linkage between the VOC and the resulting technical requirements.

A quality function deployment matrix consists of several parts. There is no standard format matrix or key for the symbols, but the example shown in Figure 3.1 is typical. A map of the various parts of Figure 3.1 is shown in Figure 3.2. The matrix is formed by first filling in the customer requirements ①, which are developed from analysis of the voice of the customer (VOC). This section often includes a scale reflecting the importance of the individual entries. The technical requirements are established in response to the customer requirements and placed in

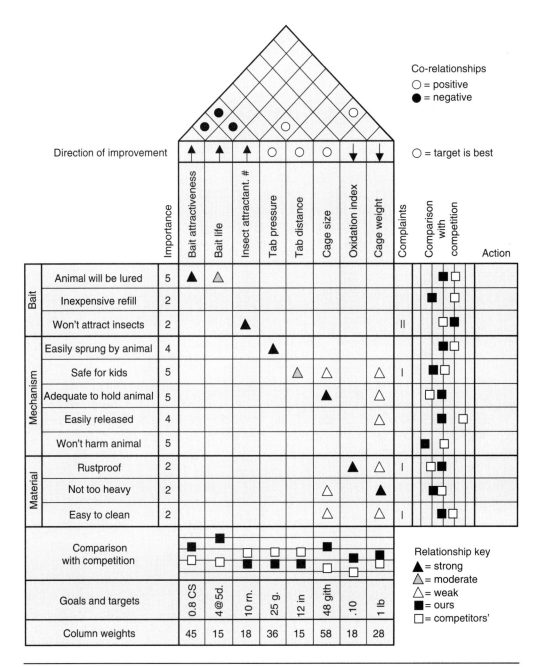

Figure 3.1   Example of a QFD matrix for an animal trap.

area ②. The symbols on the top line in this section indicate whether lower (↓) or higher (↑) is better. A circle indicates that target is better. The relationship area ③ displays the connection between the technical requirements and the customer requirements. Various symbols can be used here. The most common are shown in Figure 3.1. Area ④ is not shown on all QFD matrices. It plots comparison with

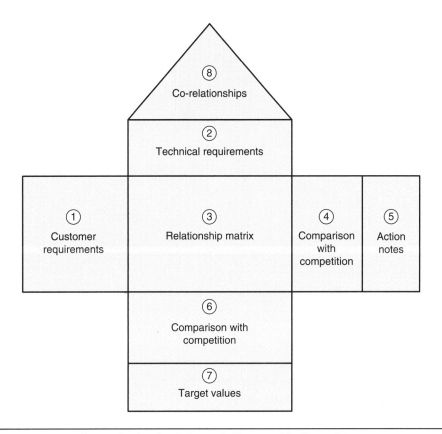

Figure 3.2   Map to the entries for the QFD matrix illustrated in Figure 3.1.

competition of the customer requirements. Area ⑤ provides an index to documentation concerning improvement activities. Area ⑥ is not shown on all QFD matrices. It plots comparison with competition of the technical requirements. Area ⑦ lists the target values for the technical requirements. Area ⑧ shows the co-relationships between the technical requirements. A positive co-relationship indicates that both technical requirements can be improved at the same time. A negative co-relationship indicates that improving one of the technical requirements will make the other one worse. The column weights shown at the bottom of the figure are optional. They indicate the importance of the technical requirements in meeting customer requirements. The value in the column weights row is obtained by multiplying the value in the "importance" column in the customer requirements section by values assigned to the symbols in the relationship matrix. These assigned values are arbitrary; in the example, a strong relationship is assigned a 9, moderate 3, and weak 1.

The completed matrix can provide a database for product development, serve as a basis for planning product or process improvements, and suggest opportunities for new or revised product or process introductions.

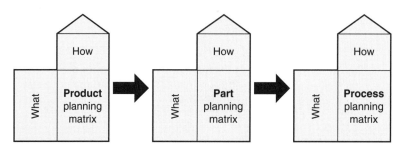

Figure 3.3   Sequence of QFD matrices for product, part, and process planning.

The customer requirements section is sometimes called the "what" information, while the technical requirements section is referred to as the "how" area. The basic QFD product-planning matrix can be followed with similar matrices for planning the parts that make up the product and for planning the processes that will produce the parts (see Figure 3.3).

If a matrix has more than 25 customer voice lines, it tends to become unmanageable. In such a situation, a convergent tool such as the affinity diagram (see page 92) may be used to condense the list.

2. DESIGN AND PROCESS FAILURE MODE AND EFFECTS ANALYSIS (DFMEA AND PFMEA)

> Define and distinguish between design FMEA (DFMEA) and process (PFMEA) and interpret associated data. (Analyze) (Note: the application of FMEA is covered in II.D.2.)
>
> **Body of Knowledge I.C.2**

The failure mode and effects analysis (FMEA) process is a systemic approach to evaluating a process or product (for example, design) to determine how the process or product could fail and the failure effects. Items are identified through various methods like brainstorming and evaluated to determine severity, occurrence, and detection. The evaluations assign a number to each category and then a risk priority number (RPN) is generated. The RPN helps to provide focus—what should be addressed first—and then actions are identified to mitigate or reduce the RPN. An FMEA should be considered a living document and process, to be reviewed and reevaluated on a periodic basis and particularly if significant events occur like a design change, introduction of new equipment, significant change in personnel or assembly methods, and so on. The goals of an FMEA should be to recognize the potential effects of failure occurrence and to identify actions that will reduce or eliminate the probability of the failure occurring. Documenting the analysis and FMEA results, maintaining them, and periodically reviewing the results, actions, and the analysis, can help improve process or design costs and reliability.

As noted, there are two primary focuses for an FMEA—*design* and *process.*

Design FMEA

A design FMEA (DFMEA) is performed during the initial design or when significant design changes are considered. The focus of a design FMEA is to ensure that the design is producible in a cost-effective manner, will meet its intended performance in the intended environment, and that the potential for failure is identified and actions (for example, design changes, material changes, performance specification updates) are implemented to improve the design and reduce or eliminate the probability of failure occurrence. Design FMEA is usually conducted by a cross-functional team that includes representation of downstream stakeholders (for example, manufacturing, test) and the engineering design team.

Benefits of performing a DFMEA include: objective analysis, synergy (new thoughts or potential failures and actions are identified based on experience and other's ideas), and increased probability that failure modes and their associated effects have been identified and evaluated for impact on the design, system, and so on. Understanding the potential failures and their effects allows the organization to prioritize actions to reduce the potential for catastrophic failure or personal injury and improve manufacturability and reliability.

Process FMEA

A process FMEA (PFMEA) is performed to assess the impacts of the process (manufacturing, service, support, engineering, and so on) on producing the desired outcome. For example, if the desired outcome is to complete processing of a purchase requisition and placement of a purchase order within one business day, the organization would review the process for the potential failures that would impact this goal and identify action to reduce or eliminate these failures. To take this example further, the potential failures could include limited user access to systems, insufficient information on the purchase requisition, system (for example, computer) failure, unplanned personnel absences (that is, no buyers were available to place the order), and so on. Like the DFMEA, the PFMEA identifies potential failures, the likelihood of occurrence, the severity or impact of their occurrence, and actions that can be taken to reduce or eliminate the potential failures.

However, the process FMEA is focused on the processes and changes to them (consider man, machine, and so on) that can influence the probability of failure—in other words, for manufacturing environments, focus is primarily on the process and not product design changes. The PFMEA is a powerful tool; a potential challenge is ensuring that personnel are appropriately trained in the PFMEA process and that the right personnel are involved in the PFMEA. Benefits to performing a PFMEA include reducing bottom-line costs, improved employee morale, improved customer satisfaction (especially for service industries where the product is usually process related), and so on.

In summary, the FMEA is a powerful, structured, and flexible tool that can be applied in any industry. FMEA, whether design or process, should be documented, reviewed, and updated to continue to be of value to the organization. Given appropriate focus, openness, and passion, the FMEA can be completed in a reasonable time and be very effective in improving the design or process being assessed and providing lessons learned and improvement opportunities for related designs and processes.

3. ROAD MAPS FOR DFSS

> Describe and distinguish between DMADV (define, measure, analyze, design, verify) and IDOV (identify, design, optimize, verify), identify how they relate to DMAIC and how they help close the loop on improving the end product/process during the design (DFSS) phase. (Understand)
>
> **Body of Knowledge I.C.3**

Organizations must extend their design beyond simple functionality and customer wishes to consider fulfilling other attributes and expectations. This holistic approach to design will result in a more stable and robust product that not only reflects customer preferences, but is capable of being used and applied in the specified environment by the intended user.

DMADV (define, measure, analyze, design, verify) and IDOV (identify, design, optimize, verify), relate to DMAIC and help close the loop on improving the end product/process during the design for Six Sigma (DFSS) phase.

IDOV

Woodford[1] refers to IDOV as a four-phase process that consists of *identify, design, optimize,* and *verify.* These four phases parallel the four phases of the traditional Six Sigma improvement methodology, MAIC—*measure, analyze, improve,* and *control.* The similarities can be seen below.

Identify Phase. The identify phase tasks link the design to the voice of the customer:

- Identify customer and product requirements
- Establish the business case

- Identify technical requirements, critical to quality (CTQ) variables, and specification limits
- Roles and responsibilities
- Milestones

Design Phase. The design phase tasks emphasize CTQ variables and attributes:

- Formulate concept design
- Identify potential risks using failure mode and effects analysis (FMEA)
- For each technical requirement, identify design parameters
- Plan procurement, raw materials, manufacturing, and integration
- Use DOE (design of experiments) and other analysis tools to determine CTQs and their influence on the technical requirements (transfer functions)

Optimize Phase. The optimize phase develops detailed design elements to predict performance and optimize design:

- Assess process capabilities to achieve critical design parameters and meet CTQ limits
- Optimize design to minimize sensitivity of CTQs to process parameters
- Design for robust performance and reliability
- Error-proofing
- Establish statistical tolerancing
- Optimize sigma and cost

Validate Phase. The validate phase consists of testing and validating the design and recording information for design improvements:

- Prototype test and validation
- Assess performance, failure modes, reliability, and risks
- Design iteration
- Final phase review

DMADV

Breyfogle[2] refers to the approach known as DMADV (for define, measure, analyze, design, verify), which he says "is appropriate, instead of the DMAIC approach, when a product or process is not in existence and one needs to be developed. Or the current product/process exists and has been optimized but still doesn't meet customer and/or business needs."

Historically, the redesign process has been found to be a common source of waste that can be reduced by enhancing the original design process. Design for Six Sigma is the process of designing with a particular attribute in mind.

1. Define. Before beginning a design initiative, the Six Sigma team needs to evaluate and prioritize the primary design objectives for the organization. By targeting the primary priorities, the design efforts will have the most significant impact possible on achieving Six Sigma targets.

2. Measure. This requires a combination of technical and competitive product management analysis, specifying the design criteria most valued by the industry and customer. In addition, there are expectations imposed by regulators, partners, and other stakeholders.

3. Analyze. The statistical and investigative approaches used for Six Sigma can identify design priorities with significance and confidence.

4. Design. Having obtained a clear direction for design objectives, it is incumbent on the Six Sigma team to collaborate with designers to ensure that the final design outputs include the desired attributes. If these are treated as requirements or specifications, the fulfillment of Six Sigma design objectives will be incorporated into the development and testing activities, and embedded into the overall solution. Without this approach, the Six Sigma design objectives will have to be an additional layer, which is potentially expensive and wasteful.

4.01 Design for Cost (also known as Design to Cost). In most markets, cost has become a major consideration in the design process. This requires a constant search for alternative processes, materials, and methods. People with cost accounting and purchasing backgrounds can assist the design team in this quest.

4.02 Design for Manufacturing/Design for Producibility/Design for Assembly. Many companies have found that minor design changes can make the product easier and less costly to produce. Tolerance design can result in savings in machining processes, tooling, and gauging. Designers should be familiar with existing manufacturing equipment and processes and strive to design products that don't require additional capability. Some manufacturers have found that drastic reductions in the number of parts in a product is an effective way to reduce manufacturing costs. As a general rule, the earlier that manufacturing personnel are involved in the design process, the more producible the design.

4.03 Design for Test (also known as Design for Testability). In products where in-process testing is critical, designers must make provision for performing tests earlier in the production cycle rather than relying entirely on functional tests of a finished assembly or subassembly.

4.04 Design for Maintainability. The ability to perform routine maintenance must be considered in the design process. Products that require long downtimes for diagnosis and repair can cause the user to miss deadlines and alienate customers. Maintainability includes modularity, decoupling, and component standardization.

4.05 Design for Robustness. Adequate time must be allowed during the design process to conduct lifecycle tests of all parts, subassemblies, and assemblies. Suppliers of purchased parts should be required to document the mean time to failure (MTTF) or mean time between failures (MTBF) for all products they supply. MTTF is used for nonrepairable items and MTBF is used for repairable items. A basic relationship in this area is that between failure rate λ and MTTF or MTBF:

$$MTTF = 1/\lambda \text{ or } MTBF = 1/\ \lambda \text{ and, of course, } \lambda = 1/MTTF \text{ or } \lambda = 1/MTBF$$

4.06 Design for Usability. The quality of a product is determined by validation, where it is applied for its prescribed purpose by its intended users in its specified environment. The ability of a user to work comfortably with the product, system, or service to obtain value can be measured and improved.

4.07 Design for Extended Functionality. Many products initially designed and intended for a single purpose can have their features applied to extended functionality beyond the initial vision of the designers. Computer software applications are good examples of products that were initially developed for quick mathematical calculation and numerical tracking, but are now preferred tools for graphic design, word processing, and database management.

4.08 Design for Efficiency. The product or system must be designed in a way that consumes minimal resources. This is correlated with design for cost, except the criteria for evaluation are time, resources, and consumption of critical components. Efficiency will have positive effects on long-term cost and reliability.

4.09 Design for Performance. Performance refers to the achievement of aggressive benchmarks or breakthroughs on a consistent basis. Terms like "cutting edge" or "latest and greatest" reflect the constant challenge of exceeding once unachievable levels of delivery. Historical examples include the design of aircraft faster than the speed of sound, and the continuous increase in processing power of microchips.

4.10 Design for Security. Security is becoming a bigger threat as maladies like computer viruses, identity theft, and product misuse increase in scope and complexity. Security will preserve product integrity, and protect the intellectual property and privacy of users and designers.

4.11 Design for Scalability. Products or systems deployed for use in a growth market should anticipate expansion or rapid adoption. Without this attribute, quality will be compromised when the product surpasses the threshold of users or scope. An example is the auction Web site that suddenly has a blank screen during peak periods because it cannot handle the load of 100,000 concurrent users at month-end.

4.12 Design for Agility. Many organizations compete on their ability to deliver customized solutions within a short time. This requires a nimble approach to rapid development, a robust architecture or structural foundation, and a ready array of components or vendors who can augment the core product with unique touches. An example is a hot tub manufacturer who incorporates the basic hot tub into the style and design of a building or landscape to create a seamless effect.

Table 3.1   Design objectives and outputs traceability matrix.

Design objective	Design output	Status
Extended functionality	Business user can apply software to their operations	Achieved functionality
Maintainability	Modular approach with minimal coupling	Replacement of modules results in quicker diagnosis and maintenance
Efficiency	Point-of-sale transaction system allows sale to be completed within five minutes	Design supports the application of the product to make customers more efficient
Security	Password encryption for user access	Security achieved to prevent unauthorized product use
Compliance to Kyoto standards for emissions	Product did not pass mandated emissions standards	Redesign is required for marketability

4.13 Design for Compliance. Designers have regulations imposed on them that must be fulfilled in order for the product to be marketed. Compliance requirements can range from achieving specific product performance capabilities to demonstrating that suitable design processes were followed and recorded. If the DFSS initiative is operating in a highly regulated environment, cost-benefit can be derived by the penalties and opportunity costs of noncompliance. An example is designing a process that requires configuration management updates every time the product is changed, to ensure proper and accurate documentation.

5. Verify. Having completed the design, it is necessary to ensure that the outcome fulfills the design objectives. This can be demonstrated with a traceability matrix linking the design objectives to the design outputs (see Table 3.1).

Part II
Six Sigma—*Define*

Part II

Where are we? Or, what is the problem? Where do we want to be? How will we get there? How will we know when we are there?

These are critical questions that are asked and answered during the define–measure–analyze–improve–control (DMAIC) *define* phase. Without understanding these basic tenets, the activity (or project) to resolve the problem or improve performance can flounder aimlessly, wasting needed resources and frustrating personnel to the point of not supporting an improvement culture.

This section of *The Certified Six Sigma Green Belt Handbook* will provide:

1. An overview of the define phase that includes process flows and guidelines to help ensure that a project is on track. Here the difference between defining the "improvement project" and defining the "issue or problem" will be discussed. We will also discuss how these two items, "project" and "problem," differ and how they are similar. Finally, the overview will close out with guidance on tailoring the define phase intensity to the specific activity to be worked, in other words, how to keep this simple.

2. A review of each area of the American Society for Quality's Certified Six Sigma Green Belt Body of Knowledge. The goal here is to provide information that can help you successfully pass a certification exam, but more importantly to ensure that this handbook is a tool that helps you execute improvement projects. In this review, tools that can be used will be discussed at a high level, with more in-depth explanations provided later in the section.

3. A tools section to provide detailed information regarding applicable define phase tools—how they work and how and when to use them. This section also lists additional resources in different media (that is, in print, on the included CD-ROM, or on the Web). The purpose of listing these additional resources is to ensure a balanced view of the tools and to provide useable templates and resources to execute a Green Belt project.

4. A summary of the items discussed that highlights the most commonly used tools, key resources, critical factors to success, and general process flows for successful execution of a project.

OVERVIEW

The define phase of the DMAIC model serves two purposes: to define the project management process for the Green Belt improvement project and to define the problem or issue to be worked on by the Green Belt project team. This overview will outline these two focus areas by detailing basic processes and recommended items for each area and annotating potential pitfalls to avoid.

As noted, when we execute the define phase, two primary deliverables are the project plan and detailed knowledge of the current state of the problem. The project plan outlines several aspects of the project to assure that the Green Belt project team and key stakeholders understand what needs to be done, what resources (for example, people, financial, tools and equipment, infrastructure) are anticipated, and when things will be completed. The documentation associated with gaining knowledge of the problem and the current state of the process varies widely based on the problem or issue being worked on. The primary goal is to have sufficient detail on what is happening to cause the undesirable performance or nonconformance to keep the project focused through the remaining DMAIC phases.

An organization that has an improvement culture based on a proven methodology, such as DMAIC, will be able to consistently improve performance and eliminate problems. However, if the organization allows itself to become mired in bureaucracy, it could lose this edge and reduce the overall effectiveness and motivation to improve. One method to avoid this pitfall is to ensure that the improvement culture process (based on a methodology like DMAIC) allows for flexibility in the level of project detail and tool selection. For example, some projects may only need a short charter approved by a process owner, champion, Black Belt, or Master Black Belt. Yet others, especially larger projects, may require a more detailed plan, coordination with multiple process owners, intra-phase reviews, and so on. Keep things simple, adjust based on the process, but stay true to the basic methodology—this should lead to a successful improvement program embraced across the entire organization. One caution: be aware not to focus on sub-area/process optimization to the detriment of the whole process or "system."

As noted above, the first chapter of this section will follow the outline of the ASQ Six Sigma Green Belt Certification Body of Knowledge. Although this makes the most sense for the handbook and as a certification resource, note that in many cases it is better to outline the project management aspects and get stakeholder buy-in prior to spending too many resources on defining the problem and fully understanding the current state of the problem or process.

Key Point: Ensure that the management and money are lined up before starting any project—and check in often.

Key Point: The more time you spend up front in good planning, the higher probability of a successful project.

Part II

Chapter 4

A. Process Management for Projects

1. PROCESS ELEMENTS

> Define and describe process components
> and boundaries. Recognize how processes
> cross various functional areas and
> the challenges that result for process
> improvement efforts. (Analyze)
>
> **Body of Knowledge II.A.1**

A process is a step or sequence of steps that uses inputs and produces a product or service as an output. Every process has inputs and outputs. Inputs are traditionally categorized as man (used here to allow for five to eight M's—we do include women), material, methods/machines, Mother Nature, management, money, and measurement system (as the measurement system may have an impact on the output). Outputs are usually products (hardware, software, systems, and so on) or services. Figure 4.1 depicts the model of a process.

Processes often are made up of smaller subprocesses. For example, a part may be produced through a process that has a machining step. This machining step

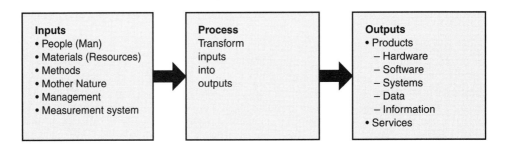

Inputs
- People (Man)
- Materials (Resources)
- Methods
- Mother Nature
- Management
- Measurement system

Process
Transform
inputs
into
outputs

Outputs
- Products
  - Hardware
  - Software
  - Systems
  - Data
  - Information
- Services

Figure 4.1 Process diagram/model.

may be thought of as a process whose steps might include clamping, turning, plunging, facing, and so on. In addition, the plunging step is a process in itself. In a similar manner, a payroll process has subprocesses, which include gathering time clock information, making deductions, and so on. The deduction process itself could be thought of as having subprocesses for tax deductions, insurance, and so on.

When defining a process it is important to define its start and end points—its boundaries. If, for example, a team is charged with improving a process, they need to know these process boundaries. Cross-functional processes may incur subprocess boundaries defined by the organizational structure, geography, and so on.

Process Identification

Everything we do can be defined in terms of a process or system. Many of the tools discussed in this book can help identify the causes and effects, the frequency and distribution of measures, the most frequently occurring data, the process flow as it is occurring, and other factors about the process or system. When planning to study a process or system, it is very important to first identify the boundaries to work within. There are many ways to identify the process boundaries; most are not complex and can be implemented easily with common process knowledge and some investigation.

The two primary tools used to identify process boundaries are the basic process model identified in Figure 4.1 and the supplier–input–process–output–customer (SIPOC) diagram in Figure 4.2. The basic process model provides a quick high-level look at the process, but, in some cases, may be too simplistic to provide an improvement team with a clear understanding of the process/problem to work on and the boundaries of where and when to stop.

The SIPOC diagram can be enhanced by also capturing the requirements of the process and customer, as shown in Figure 9.23, page 125.

Remember, understanding the boundaries of the improvement project and/or process does not prevent outside-of-the-box thinking; it just provides clear guidelines of what to deal with as daily activities and improvement activities are performed. Taking the time to actually list or draw the components of the process will assist in visualizing and being able to find issues quicker than might have otherwise been possible.

Key Point: Many projects flounder due to the lack of clear boundaries for the project.

When identifying the process it is important to recognize that processes usually affect multiple departments and organizations. Crossing functional areas (departments) and organizations (suppliers, intercompany, teammate company, and so on) can add challenges to an improvement project. The first step in recognizing the challenges is to understand the organizations and functional areas involved with the process. As noted, the SIPOC diagram can help in identifying these organizations and functional areas as process suppliers and customers. The flowchart (especially the "swim-lane" style) and process map are other tools that can be used

Part II.A.1

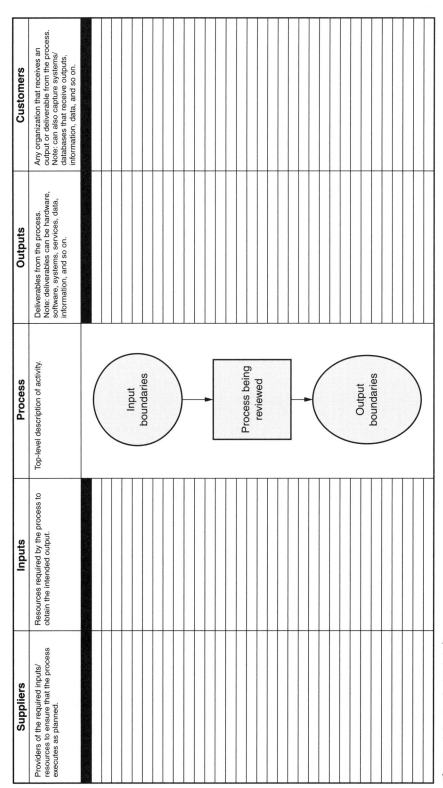

Suppliers	Inputs	Process	Outputs	Customers
Providers of the required inputs/ resources to ensure that the process executes as planned.	Resources required by the process to obtain the intended output.	Top-level description of activity.	Deliverables from the process. Note: deliverables can be hardware, software, systems, services, data, information, and so on.	Any organization that receives an output or deliverable from the process. Note: can also capture systems/ databases that receive outputs, information, data, and so on.

Figure 4.2 Basic SIPOC diagram.

to help recognize these interactions. Challenges associated with these interactions include, but are not limited to:

- Process ownership (two or more areas may think they own the process and have final decision authority on changes)

- Sharing of information (for example, proprietary issues, hiding poor performance)

- Commonality of measures (for example, finance usually measures things in dollars, production may use defects or productivity, engineering considers productivity and design completion)

- Process knowledge or expertise (that is, manufacturing may not fully understand how the supply chain works or the requirements)

If the challenges identified are significant, it is recommended that the challenges be included as potential risks for the project so associated mitigation activities can be performed. Risk identification and mitigation are discussed in more detail in Chapter 5.

The details of how to use and implement the basic process model diagram and SIPOC diagrams are provided in Chapter 9. SIPOC templates are provided on the accompanying CD-ROM for both the basic SIPOC diagram and the SIPOC diagram with requirements capture formats.

Systems Thinking

According to Rice, the recognition/identification and consideration of all the various individual elements that interrelate with a common purpose toward a whole function of a unit is considered *systems thinking*. Systems thinking is using tools and methods available to understand what is being done at a specific operation and how that activity affects tasks and products further downstream and how prior tasks and products affect the process being reviewed. Far too often a change made in one part of an operation causes new problems somewhere else—this type of change is effected without applying systems thinking.[1]

Using systems thinking, we strive to understand the process and know that if one factor is changed or influenced in some particular way, then something different might happen downstream in the process. For example, if a supplier ships a material with a higher than normal moisture content, how do processes that use that product need to adjust to ensure that the end product meets requirements? All of this is part of systems thinking and we are able to use the tools and processes in this book to assist us in reducing variation and satisfying the customer.

Note: For those who received training in continuous improvement during the 1980s and early 1990s, please note that in order to actually improve the process, sometimes the *process behavior charts* (called *control charts* back then) will sometimes have to go out of control to show an improvement in the system. Thinking that we can have both continuous improvement and control charts that are always in control is *not* systems thinking!

2. OWNERS AND STAKEHOLDERS

> Identify process owners, internal and
> external customers, and other stakeholders
> in a project. (Apply)
>
> **Body of Knowledge II.A.2**

Process owners are those who have responsibility for the execution and implementation of a specific process. Process owners are usually formally recognized in this role through related documentation (for example, procedures, work instructions, documentation approval authority), through their job/position description, or through the organization chart.

Stakeholders are those who have a vested interest in the process and/or its products and outputs. Generally, stakeholders of an organization include customers, suppliers, employees, investors, and communities. Stakeholder interest and involvement with the process may change over time depending on economic, contractual, and other influences. Process owners are those that are responsible for the definition, execution, maintenance, and improvement of the process; in some cases process owners may also be referred to as subject matter experts. Personnel involved with process design usually have a specific interest in systems, subprocesses, and individual steps within processes.

The most effective methods of process improvement utilize teams representing process owners *and* all stakeholders because:

- Stakeholders have the best knowledge base about the process

- Stakeholders tend to have the best ideas for process improvement

- Stakeholders are often the most aware of unintended consequences of process changes

- Stakeholders' buy-in is usually necessary to implement real process improvement

The stakeholders in a process are:

- Process operators and managers from all shifts

- Process customers, internal and external

- Process suppliers, internal and external

- Process design personnel

- Maintenance personnel

- Others impacted in some way by process changes

3. IDENTIFY CUSTOMERS

> Identify and classify internal and external customers as applicable to a particular project, and show how projects impact customers. (Apply)
>
> **Body of Knowledge II.A.3**

It is important to identify and understand a project or process's customers. Depending on the maturity of the product or process, the customers may be known. Even if the customers are known, it is always good practice to identify the customers, using some of the tools in this book. Methods used to identify customers include:

- Brainstorming

- SIPOC

- Marketing analysis data

- Tracking a product or service to delivery

Internal and external customers should be identified when applicable. Customers can be grouped into segments, with this segmentation driven by customer requirements, and often includes the following categories:

- Internal and external

- Age groups, especially for consumer products

- Geographical location, including climate, language, ethnicity, and so on

- Industry type (for example, construction, agricultural)

Where possible, a listing of customers within a segment should be constructed. When a project team proposes changes of any type, customers, internal and external, must be consulted, or at minimum the customers' concerns must be represented.

4. COLLECT CUSTOMER DATA

> Use various methods to collect customer
> feedback (e.g., surveys, focus groups,
> interviews, observation) and identify the key
> elements that make these tools effective.
> Review survey questions to eliminate bias,
> vagueness, etc. (Apply)
>
> **Body of Knowledge II.A.4**

Once identified, the next step is to understand the wants, requirements, and expectations of the customer. One of W. E. Deming's more famous statements is that some of the most important numbers are unknown and unknowable. He was referring to such things as the financial value of customer goodwill. And if a supplier/employee disappoints a customer, the customer will ". . . tell all his friends and some of his enemies . . . " in Deming's words. His point, of course, is that it is easy to underestimate the value of understanding and providing for customers' needs. Without customers we have nothing![2]

There are several tools available for capturing customer data. The most widely used tools include:

- The voice of the customer (VOC)
- Surveys
- Quality function deployment (QFD)
- Interviews
- Focus groups

Statistically, the most valid procedure for collecting customer data is to randomly select a reasonably large group of customers and obtain complete and accurate data on each one selected. Since this procedure is not possible in many situations, various other methods are employed. Each method usually comprises "statistically valid" procedures in one or more ways.

The data collected should be objective and designed to shed light on customer requirements. It is important to use several independent resources to obtain this information. The results can be played against each other to determine patterns of reinforcement or contradiction of conclusions. After customer data has been collected, the accuracy and consistency of the data should be verified; it is important to resolve conflicts or ambiguous data.

5. ANALYZE CUSTOMER DATA

> Use graphical, statistical, and qualitative tools
> to analyze customer feedback. (Analyze)
>
> **Body of Knowledge II.A.5**

The purpose of analyzing customer data is to understand customer needs and requirements and prioritize the data collected to enable effective change. The analysis process uses the collected customer data, utilizing typical tools such as affinity diagrams, FMEA, Pareto diagrams, interrelationship digraphs, matrix diagrams, and priority matrices, to identify group issues and determine which issues can be addressed that will have the greatest impact for the resources expended.

6. TRANSLATE CUSTOMER REQUIREMENTS

> Assist in translating customer feedback
> into project goals and objectives, including
> critical to quality (CTQ) attributes and
> requirements statements. Use voice of
> the customer analysis tools such as quality
> function deployment (QFD) to translate
> customer requirements into performance
> measures. (Apply)
>
> **Body of Knowledge II.A.6**

The best customer data collection and analysis is useless unless there is a system to use the data to effect changes. This system should study each item of customer feedback to determine which processes, products, and/or services will be impacted. One such tool is called *quality function deployment* (QFD)—reference QFD in Chapters 3 and 9 for details. The volume and/or urgency of customer concerns will help determine the requirements that customers deem critical. Some type of criticality rating system should be applied to the feedback data, with phone calls from customers given a higher rating than responses to a questionnaire. Suppose, for example, that analysis of customer data identifies six areas where product quality is compromised. With the help of the criticality rating scale perhaps two of the six would be deemed important enough to motivate immediate improvement projects.

Chapter 5

B. Project Management Basics

1. PROJECT CHARTER AND PROBLEM STATEMENT

> Define and describe elements of a project charter and develop a problem statement, including baseline and improvement goals. (Apply)
>
> **Body of Knowledge II.B.1**

A charter is a document stating the purposes of the project. It serves as an informal contract that helps the team stay on track with the goals of the organization. Each charter should contain the following points:

- *Problem statement.* This is a statement of what needs to be improved

- *Purpose.* Establishes goals and objectives of the team

- *Benefits.* States how the enterprise will fare better when the project reaches its goals

- *Scope.* Provides project limitations in terms of budget, time, and other resources

- *Results.* Defines the criteria and metrics for project success—including the baseline measures and improvement expectations

The problem statement is a summation of what requires improvement. Examples include:

"The computer modem circuit card assembly takes too long to produce"

"The response time to Internet inquires from potential customers is too long and the responses are not adequate based on customer survey responses"

Project Planning

Project planning is a disciplined approach to monitoring how and when a project will be accomplished, with recognition of the system that the project is working in. If you want to go on a long trip, do you just jump in a car and go? Most of us plan the trip, some to more detail than others, so that we know what needs to be taken, how long we will be gone, and any number of other details that have to be handled.

As with many of the tools and processes listed in this book, there is a lot of information available in various references on project planning and project management. There is even a professional certification available just for project management. Here, only the basics involved are discussed to assist in daily work.

Effective project planning requires skills in the following areas:

- Information processing

- Communication

- Resource negotiations

- Securing commitments

- Incremental and modular planning

- Assuring measurable milestones

- Facilitating top management involvement[1]

2. PROJECT SCOPE

> Assist with the development of project definition/scope using Pareto charts, process maps, etc. (Apply)
>
> **Body of Knowledge II.B.2**

As noted above, the purpose of documenting the project scope, or boundaries, is to ensure a common understanding of what the project team, and its associated resources, will work on and what is outside those defined boundaries. The scope is usually defined, at least in part, based on the problem statement, which gives the project its initial focus. Using the problem statement, experience, and tools like SIPOC, brainstorming, Pareto charts, and so on, the scope of the project can be defined and documented.

Part II.B.2

3. PROJECT METRICS

> Assist with the development of primary and consequential metrics (e.g., quality, cycle time, cost) and establish key project metrics that relate to the voice of the customer. (Apply)
>
> **Body of Knowledge II.B.3**

Project timelines and activity plans can become little more than paperwork if meaningful performance measurements are not included. These measurements or metrics should link directly to the project goals and through them to the benefits for the enterprise. For example, if a goal is to increase process throughput by 25 percent, a key metric might be cycle time. The project's intermediate objectives and documentation need to include incremental cycle time reduction measures. Project measures typically are linked to a specific project, usually for the life of just that specific project, and they are often manifested as:

- Percent of work accomplished on time (schedule performance index)

- Percent of work accomplished on budget (cost performance index)

- Other similar measures (for example, availability of resources, quality of key deliverables)

4. PROJECT PLANNING TOOLS

> Use project tools such as Gantt charts, critical path method (CPM), and program evaluation and review technique (PERT) charts, etc. (Apply)
>
> **Body of Knowledge II.B.4**

Project planning tools include project charters, project management plans, milestone charts, Gantt charts, project schedules, goal and objective statements or bullets, and so on. The number of tools used and depth of data contained in the tools varies based on the project size and scope. Usually, larger projects have more documentation as they take more time and expend more resources. Project documentation is controlled and maintained (that is, updated) during the lifecycle of the improvement project.

5. PROJECT DOCUMENTATION

> Provide input and select the proper vehicle for presenting project documentation (e.g., spreadsheet output, storyboards, etc.) at phase reviews, management reviews, and other presentations. (Apply)
>
> **Body of Knowledge II.B.5**

Failure to provide project documentation leads to miscommunication and misunderstanding. Examples abound of projects that solved a problem other than the one they were intended to solve or answered a question no one was asking.

Project documentation usually includes:

- Goals and objectives

- Project sponsors and stakeholders

- Project plans and schedules—usually for larger projects

- Key project milestones

- Project budget

- Project boundaries

- Roles and responsibilities of project team members

- List of deliverables

- Metrics to be used to assess the project's performance

Smaller projects include these critical areas in the project charter; larger projects may require more detailed documentation and plans. A project charter can be in many formats but is usually limited to one or two pages to serve as a top-level, quick overview of the project.

In addition to the project charter and project management plan, additional charts and diagrams can be produced for each of the activities listed. These graphical tools are also useful for tracking and evaluating the project at various phases and at final management reviews. Storyboards are sometimes used to convey project information involving changes that are easier to draw or photograph than to explain in words. A common application of storyboards is before-and-after pictures, often called *current state* and *future state,* for a proposed project. This approach is appropriate for facility or product redesign projects. Storyboards for Six Sigma projects are often formatted into five sections labeled *define, measure, analyze, improve,* and *control* (DMAIC) with charts, figures, and documents illustrating the activity in each area.

6. PROJECT RISK ANALYSIS

> Describe the purpose and benefit of project risk analysis, including resources, financials, impact on customers and other stakeholders, etc. (Understand)
>
> **Body of Knowledge II.B.6**

Project risk analysis is initially performed early in the project's lifecycle—usually during the planning stage—to identify potential risks, the associated impacts, and potential mitigation plans. In addition to performing the initial risk analysis, it is recommended that the analysis be periodically reviewed and updated—especially if an identified risk is realized. Risk analysis is a formal process that can be performed using dedicated tools such as:

- Strength–weakness–opportunity–threat (SWOT) analysis
- Risk priority number (RPN) or risk priority matrix
- Failure mode and effects analysis (FMEA)
- Formula for expected profit

These tools can be combined with other tools like brainstorming to ensure effective coverage for risk identification, analysis of potential impact if the risk is realized, and potential mitigation plans.

Successful risk analysis depends, in part, on ensuring that appropriate organizations are represented during risk analysis meetings and that all aspects of potential risk are considered. Aspects of risk to consider include, but are not limited to, the potential impact on:

- Meeting established goals or objectives
- The planned schedule
- Identified resources
- Safety
- Produceability
- Serviceability
- Reliability
- Meeting customer expectations and requirements

Risk assessment involves determining the impact severity if the risk occurs and the probability that the risk will occur. Determining the impact severity is usually done by performing analysis of like risks from other projects, historical data, and through the use of brainstorming, as well as other methods. Risk probability is determined based on the likelihood that the risk will occur during the execution of the project. A risk assessment assignment matrix, as shown in Figure 5.1, helps the project by having each risk individually ranked on a scale from 1 to 3 for severity and probability. The assignment number (a simpler version of the risk priority number [RPN] derived from FMEA data) is calculated as the severity rating multiplied by the probability rating. Risks with the highest assignment number require the most attention from the project team and the organization's leadership.

After identification of the risks, risk mitigation and verification are performed throughout the project's lifecycle. Risk mitigation begins with identifying activities the team or organization can perform to reduce the likelihood that an identified risk will occur and/or to reduce its impact (that is, reduce the delay in the schedule or the cost in dollars, product quality, or customer satisfaction) if the identified risk is realized. For example, if a risk is associated with a key supplier not delivering on time, mitigation activities might include developing another supplier, providing additional supplier oversight, colocation of personnel, shared design information, and so on, to help the supplier deliver on time.

Once risk mitigation planning occurs, the plans are implemented during the project and should be reviewed on a regular basis (usually weekly or monthly) to assess the status of existing risks (that is, are mitigation activities working?) and determine whether new risks have been identified or if identified risks were realized (that is, occurred). In some cases, mitigation is not always possible and the risk is realized; the risk identification, mitigation, and review processes provide the team with knowledge of the worst-case scenario and what they should

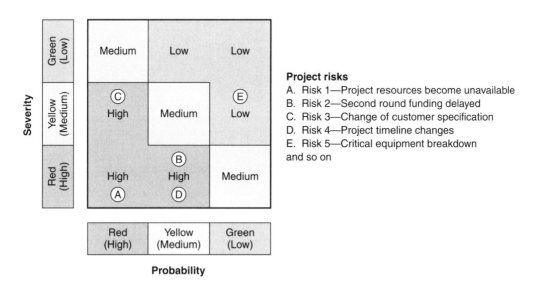

Project risks
A. Risk 1—Project resources become unavailable
B. Risk 2—Second round funding delayed
C. Risk 3—Change of customer specification
D. Risk 4—Project timeline changes
E. Risk 5—Critical equipment breakdown
and so on

Figure 5.1   Risk assessment assignment matrix.

do. Risk verification is the process of ensuring that the risk mitigation activities reasonably prevent the risk from occurring. An example is the security risk for an automated teller machine. The risk is that someone else can improperly access your bank account. The mitigation is the additional requirement of a secured six- to 10-digit numeric password, along with a restriction of three false attempts before freezing the account. The verification is the attempt to access a secured account with an invalid or null password.

A risk management system will curtail the potential losses arising from quality problems and build quality into designs and processes more effectively than a reactive, trial-and-error approach of finding and fixing problems as they occur.

7. PROJECT CLOSURE

Describe the objectives achieved and apply the lessons learned to identify additional opportunities. (Apply)

Body of Knowledge II.B.7

It is important to note that project closure is not a negotiation, it is a final step performed based on proving that the project met established goals and objectives, ensuring that required documentation is completed and appropriately stored, and conducting a closure meeting with the project sponsors to ensure agreement that the project is completed.

The project charter is an excellent tool to use as a measure of project completion as it established the scope, goals and objectives, and time frame for the project. Usually a review of the charter against documented project results is sufficient for closing a project. At times, the project sponsor may want an independent review or assessment prior to formal project closure. Typically, this is done using an audit approach. Another method of proving that the project achieved its intent is analysis of project measures.

Chapter 6

C. Management and Planning Tools

> Define, select, and use 1) affinity diagrams,
> 2) interrelationship digraphs, 3) tree diagrams,
> 4) prioritization matrices, 5) matrix diagrams,
> 6) process decision program charts (PDPC),
> and 7) activity network diagrams. (Apply)
>
> **Body of Knowledge II.C**

Important elements of any improvement project are defining the problem, selecting the most appropriate tools for the specific project, and using those tools to measure the current state, perform analysis, and make recommendations for change (that is, improvement), and then monitoring the results. As noted above, there are many tools used for managing the project and helping define the problem and current state. Key tools for defining the problem and current state include 1) affinity diagrams, 2) interrelationship diagrams (also referred to as digraphs), 3) tree diagrams, 4) prioritization matrices, 5) matrix diagrams, 6) process decision program charts (PDPC), and 7) activity network diagrams. Details on each of these tools are provided in Chapter 9.

The objective here is to ensure an understanding that the tools exist and that selection is driven by the project, data available (known or thought to be available), and the application of the simplest tool(s) to provide the most reliable data.

Key Point: Not every tool should be used on every Six Sigma project!

Key Point: There is not one tool that has to be used on every Six Sigma project!

Chapter 7

D. Business Results for Projects

Business results can be shown in many forms and at many levels of detail. The measures for project results should be identified during the initial planning stages and be refined as the project progresses. Results, also known as performance measures, are usually related to the business, project, or process. Business performance measures are usually expressed through tools known as:

- Balanced scorecard

- Performance to established goals

To provide an approach to measuring multiple aspects of a business, not just the financial aspect, Dr. Robert Kaplan and Dr. David Norton developed the *balanced scorecard* in the early 1990s. Their research indicated that the financial aspect of measurement is restricted to past events and is only one part of the business. The balanced scorecard requires the organization to look at its performance in four primary areas: financial, customer, internal processes, and learning and growth. This approach helps the organization align its vision and goals with the objective of ensuring that no single area far outweighs the others—thus providing a balanced method of results measurement. Kaplan has written several books on activity-based costs and activity-based management, both central to the profitability emphasis of Six Sigma. These topics also provide other approaches for establishing business results for projects.

Performance to established goals is that simple. The organization establishes goals and periodically measures its performance against them. The goals usually reflect desired results such as:

Increase revenue (for example, sales) 10 percent over last year

Improve net profit by eight percent over last quarter

Ensure that all employees receive 40 hours of job-related training

Project performance measures usually include:

- *Cost performance index (CPI).* Measures the project's performance in dollar terms (for example, the ratio of value earned [budgeted cost of work performed] versus the actual cost of work performed). A ratio of 1 or higher is the desirable condition.

- *Schedule performance index (SPI).* Measure of the project's efficiency to schedule as expressed in the ratio of earned value to planned value.

- Other measures based on project or organizational requirements such as:

  - Defects per single line of code (SLOC) for software projects

  - Customer complaints or corrective action requests

  - Inquiry response time

  - Defect containment

1. PROCESS PERFORMANCE

> Calculate process performance metrics such as defects per unit (DPU), rolled throughput yield (RTY), cost of poor quality (COPQ), defects per million opportunities (DPMO), sigma levels, and process capability indices. Track process performance measures to drive project decisions. (Analyze)
>
> **Body of Knowledge II.D.1**

Process performance is usually a measure of how the process is executing against some established goals or statistical measure.

Process performance measures usually include:

- *Defects (deficiencies) per unit (DPU).* Calculated as the total number of defects divided by the total number of products produced in some time period (for example, per day).

- *Defects (deficiencies) per million opportunities (DPMO).*[1] To calculate the number of opportunities, it is necessary to find the number of ways each defect can occur on each item. In a hypothetical product, blurred printing occurs in only one way (the pencil slips in the fixture), so in the batch there are 40,000 opportunities for this defect to occur. There are three independent places where dimensions are checked, so in the batch there are $3 \times 40,000 = 120,000$ opportunities for dimensional defects. Rolled ends can occur at the top and/or the bottom of the pencil, so there are $40,000 \times 2 = 80,000$ opportunities for this defect to occur. The total number of opportunities for defects is $40,000 + 120,000 + 80,000 = 240,000$. Let us consider this product has an average 165 defects/unit:

$$DPO = DPU \div (\text{total number of opportunities})$$
$$DPMO = DPO \times 10^6 = (165 \div 240,000) \times 10^6 = 687.5$$

- *Rolled throughput yield (RTY).*[2] RTY applies to the yield from a series of processes and is found by multiplying the individual process yields (Throughput yield = e^{-DPU}). If a product goes through four processes whose yields are .994, .987, .951, and .990, then RTY = .994 × .987 × .951 × .990 ≈ .924

- *Sigma Levels.*[3] Suppose the tolerance limits on a dimension are 5.000 ± 0.012, that is, 4.988 to 5.012. Data collected from the process during second shift indicates that the process mean is 5.000 and its standard deviation $\sigma = 0.004$. Note that ±3σ fits inside the tolerance because ±3σ = ±3 × 0.004 = ±0.012. A capability calculation would show $C_p = C_{pk} = 1$. The traditional way to calculate yield in this situation is to use a standard normal table to determine the area under the normal curve between ±3σ. This gives a yield of about 0.9973. Experience indicates, however, that the process mean doesn't remain constant. There is general agreement on the somewhat arbitrary rule that the process mean may shift 1.5σ to the right or 1.5σ to the left. If we assume a 1.5σ shift to the right, the yield is the area under the normal curve to the right of –1.5σ or about 0.9332. Suppose, now, that process variation is reduced so that $\sigma = 0.002$. There is now ±6σ between the tolerance limits, and the process can be called a 6σ process. To calculate the yield for a Six Sigma process, we allow the mean to shift ±1.5σ. Suppose the mean shifts 1.5σ to the right so the yield is the area under a normal curve to the right of –4.5σ. This turns out to be 0.9999966. The defect level is 1 – 0.9999966, which is 0.0000034 or 3.4 ppm, the oft-quoted defect level for Six Sigma processes. At best this is a rather theoretical number, because the mean may not shift exactly 1.5σ on each side and no process is truly normal to the sixth decimal place.

- *Process capability indices.* There are various process capability indices, the most common being C_p, C_{pk}, and C_r.

  C_p is the ratio of tolerance to six sigma, or the upper specification limit (USL) minus the lower specification limit (LSL) divided by six sigma.

  C_{pk} is the lesser of the USL minus the mean divided by three sigma (or the mean) minus the LSL divided by three sigma. The greater the C_{pk} value, the better.

  Capability ratio (C_r) is the ratio of 1 divided by C_p. The lower the value of C_r, the better, with 1 being the historical maximum.

if centered, $C_{pk} = C_p = \dfrac{\sigma}{3}$

2. FAILURE MODE AND EFFECTS ANALYSIS (FMEA)

> Define and describe failure mode and effects analysis (FMEA). Describe the purpose and use of scale criteria and calculate the risk priority number (RPN). (Analyze)
>
> **Body of Knowledge II.D.2**

See Chapter 9 (page 100) for detailed information on FMEA and an example.

Part II.D.2

Chapter 8

E. Team Dynamics and Performance

TEAM BASICS

Remember the famous quote, "there is no 'I' in 'team' "? The essence of it is to imply that a team is a collective effort of individuals. To harness the best of each individual, the team members need to understand each other's strengths, roles, responsibilities, and the scope of the task. There are several books that go into detail about how to form a team, organize meetings, manage projects, and accomplish the desired goals. In the context of Six Sigma, we will cover areas important to a Green Belt. Protocols such as setting the team agenda, recording the minutes of the meeting with actions, sticking to meeting time, and enforcing meeting attendance need to be followed for an effective team meeting. An initial meeting to kick off the team with introductions and high-level discussion on the goal, objective, milestones, and so on, will provide an opportunity for the team to get to know each other and understand the expectations. A team agenda can be flexible but you need to have one.

Some teams have their team goals, objective, and scope/boundaries visibly displayed in every meeting to keep the members on track. Management presence during kickoff and with regular frequency during the project helps enforce the importance of the team objective.

TEAM FORMATION

A team usually comprises five to nine members (seven is considered an ideal size) with complementary skills to achieve the goals and objectives of the team. Team composition should be driven by the size and scope of the project; it is possible to have a team of one or two for a smaller project and a large team with subteams for a big project. The team includes subject matter experts and stakeholders. Subject matter experts sometimes remain outside the team as resource or extended team members. Stakeholders are always part of the team. The team will not be able to implement their ideas and solutions without having stakeholders or their representation on the team. Teams smaller than five reduce the opportunity for interaction problems and are easier to manage, whereas teams greater than nine produce a lot of interaction that can be counterproductive to a team's progress. Teams with greater diversity tend to produce better interaction between team members. Some teams also bring in individuals who are neither subject matter experts nor stakeholders but are outsiders to the team. The outsider helps the team ask questions that were never explored by the team members closer to the process. This needs to be moderated as the outsider might ask too many questions and frustrate the core members. Typically, Six Sigma teams are cross-functional to address the issues from every angle.

VIRTUAL TEAMS

This is an interesting innovation that has evolved in the last decade due to the development of technology in communication tools and the Internet, which have led to the ability to meet and share data virtually. Virtual teams enable people from all over the globe to meet via teleconferences, videoconferences, and Internet tools such as shared computers. There are many benefits to virtual teaming, the most prevalent being reduced costs and real-time data sharing and updating. However, virtual teams also face challenges that include slowing of the progression of normal team-building, inability to get true commitment and buy-in, and the potential for miscommunication—especially with teleconferencing, as the important factor of nonverbal communication is lost. Virtual teaming has its place in every organization and can be very effective, especially if team members are familiar with each other.

1. TEAM STAGES AND DYNAMICS

> Define and describe the stages of team evolution, including forming, storming, norming, performing, adjourning, and recognition. Identify and help resolve negative dynamics such as overbearing, dominant, or reluctant participants, the unquestioned acceptance of opinions as facts, groupthink, feuding, floundering, the rush to accomplishment, attribution, discounts, plops, digressions, tangents, etc. (Understand)
>
> **Body of Knowledge II.E.1**

It is important to understand team dynamics and performance. There are many projects that have failed miserably because of lack of teamwork and not understanding the roles and responsibilities of the team members. It is important to note that the team members were technically competent and had complementary skill sets to succeed in those projects.

According to B. W. Tuckman's "Developmental Sequence in Small Groups," teams typically go through the stages of *forming, storming, norming,* and *performing.* Let us explore each stage and identify the appropriate management approach required for that stage.[1]

Stage 1: Forming

1. Team members getting to know each other
2. Group is immature
3. Sense of belonging to the group
4. Take pride in membership with the group
5. Trying to please each other
6. May tend to agree too much on initial discussion topics
7. Not much work is accomplished
8. Members' orientation on the team goals
9. Members understand the roles and responsibilities
10. Group is going through the "honeymoon" period

Stage 2: Storming

1. Team members voice their ideas
2. Understanding of the scope and members' roles, responsibilities will be put to test
3. Ideas and understanding start to conflict
4. Disagreements start to slow down the team
5. Not much work is accomplished
6. Necessary evil that every team member has to go through to position themselves on the team
7. Caution to be aware of as too much disagreement can completely stall the team progress

Stage 3: Norming

1. Team members resolve their conflicts
2. Team members agree on mutually acceptable ideas to move forward
3. Some amount of work gets accomplished
4. Start to function as a team
5. Team members start to trust each other and share their ideas and work products without hesitation

Stage 4: Performing

1. Team is effective, skills complement, synergy is created
2. Team members realize interdependence

3. Develop ability to solve problem as a team

4. Large amount of work gets accomplished

Stage 5: Transitioning

1. Team is disbanded

2. Team members go on with other activities of their work

3. If the project is continued with additional scope, may be that some team members are changed

4. Team dynamic changes and tends to go back to one of the earlier stages

5. Major changes can result in going back to forming stage

Recognition

The often forgotten piece of team dynamics, or rather, taken for granted. Even though team members are salaried or compensated monetarily for their time and skill, it does not mean that the team is already recognized. Teams can be recognized in many ways, from a simple pat on the back by senior management, to thank-you notes, bulletin boards, organizationwide e-mails, newsletters, all-employee meetings, certificates of accomplishment, bonuses, stock options, and many other ways.

This is the typical evolution of team stages. Depending on organizational cultural issues some stages may shorten or lengthen, but the team still goes through them. It is healthy for the team to go through these stages as they set ground rules and expectations for themselves. These stages also depend on team maturity, complexity of the task (project), and team leadership.

Team Leadership

The team leadership may vary depending on the maturity of the team and the stage the team is at based on the leader's perception. Examples of leadership activities during these stages include:

Forming. Appropriate leadership style during this stage is *directing:*

- Leader provides close supervision, exhibits directive behavior

- Leader instructs the team as to what to do when, where, and how

- Leader also listens to team's feedback

- Encourages and welcomes the team

- Leader explains the roles, responsibilities, and goals of team members

- Leader identifies opportunities for developing skills to meet team goals

Storming. Appropriate leadership style is *coaching:*

- Leader still continues close supervision, exhibits directive behavior
- Leader also starts some supportive behavior
- Leader increases the listening level to solicit the team's feedback

As discussed earlier, to keep the storming at an acceptable level (not detrimental to the task at hand) the leader may use conflict resolution approaches.

Norming. Appropriate leadership style is *supporting*:

- Leader reduces the level of directive behavior and increases the supportive behavior
- Leader encourages the team on decision-taking responsibilities
- Helps move to a performing stage before the team reverts to earlier stages
- Emphasizes ground rules, scope, roles and responsibilities

Performing. Appropriate leadership style is *delegating:*

- Since the team is mature, the leader reduces the level of being directive and supportive in day-to-day functions
- Team leader still monitors the goals and performance of the team
- Watches for any change in dynamics due to major changes

Negative Team Dynamics

Several negative team dynamics are pretty much reflective of the organizational culture rather than personalities of individuals. If something is "acceptable" within the organization as a norm, that becomes the way of running the business. In other words, the organizational culture becomes the "enabler" of the many team problems that organizations face.

Negative dynamics in the team can:

- Have a negative impact on team member motivation
- Hurt a team member's ego and self-esteem
- Intimidate team members
- Reduce the self-confidence of others
- Increase stress and exhaust patience
- Increase feelings of insecurity
- Foster a lack of morale

As a result, unchecked or unaddressed negative team dynamics may cause:

- Goals and objectives of the project/task to not be met

- Targets to be frequently revised to team's advantage

- The project to be cancelled

- The team to miss project milestones and deadlines

- Project resources to not be effectively utilized

- The project to overrun its cost targets

Table 8.1 outlines common negative team dynamics and possible countermeasures. There are more facilitation tactics discussed in *The Certified Six Sigma Black Belt Handbook* and the *Team Handbook*.

Table 8.1   Common negative team dynamics and potential countermeasures.

Negative dynamic	Symptoms	Probable causes	Potential countermeasures
Overbearing member(s)	Team interaction is limited to a few individuals. The rest of the team is always in listening mode rather than participating in the discussion.	Team is composed of a few influential members (senior management staff, founders, inventors), members with legitimate authority (investor, major shareholder, owner), subject matter experts, and so on. This may intimidate other team members, who hesitate to voice their opinions.	With the support of the influential team member, the team leader reinforces round-robin voicing of opinions, using methods like nominal group technique, conducting the meeting in a more informal setting, keeping experts and influential members as an extended team, and so on.
Dominant member(s)	Meeting discussion getting chaotic and difficult to listen to or understand. Only a few members dominating the entire discussion.	Dominant team members keep interrupting the conversation of other team members.	Structure the agenda to provide equal participation for all team members. Effective moderation by team leader that allows other team members to finish their thoughts. Team leader initiates round-robin to provide opportunity for every team member.

Continued

Table 8.1   Common negative team dynamics and potential countermeasures. *(Continued)*

Negative dynamic	Symptoms	Probable causes	Potential countermeasures
Floundering	Team is currently proceeding or performing in an unsteady, faltering manner.	Lack of team direction. Some teams have high-profile team leaders from the organization but they hardly ever attend meetings or team discussions. There are situations where the organizations are going through major changes and no one is clear about the future of the team. Team members are overwhelmed. This can be due to multiple reasons. Organization going through a major change: leadership, downsizing, new mergers and acquisitions, offshore transfers, and so on. Postponing of team decisions. This is related to lack of direction from the team leadership. If there is no clear direction, decision-making gets difficult.	During early stages of the team more direction is required. Team leadership should be visibly present during the team meetings and decisions. Team leadership should keep the team focused by not getting distracted by events happening within the organization. Team leaders should address the concerns of the team members but not allow the team agenda to be hijacked by other events. Reinforce management support and commitment when team starts to challenge the purpose of the team.
Reluctant participants	Lack of participation, noncommittal feedback. Basically showing disinterest.	Team member may not have any stake in the team's outcome. Intimidated by other team members or leaders. In the process of moving out of the current job function or organization. Fear of losing job or position by voicing opinions.	Team leaders support the team members' active participation and protect the team members voicing their opinions.

Continued

Table 8.1   Common negative team dynamics and potential countermeasures. *(Continued)*

Negative dynamic	Symptoms	Probable causes	Potential countermeasures
Unquestioned acceptance of opinions as facts	Members present information without backing up data or analysis. Members present unfounded assumptions, and so on.	Mainly organization cultural reasons. Lack of management by facts.	Team leader requests supporting data, analysis, and conclusions that are statistically valid. Question the assumptions behind the analysis.
Groupthink	No public disagreements. Doubts expressed in private discussions. There are several other classical symptoms identified by researchers.	Members fear group cohesiveness will be at stake if there are any disagreements. Putting group harmony as paramount.	Bring independent members from outside to participate. Rotate roles and responsibilities of members at milestones. Management by fact.
Feuding	Hostilities resulting in heated arguments, slowed progress, low morale of the team.	Conflict resolution not effectively handled by the team leadership. Lack of mutual respect between team members. Team operating ground rules not enforced.	Confront the adversaries offline and not in the team meeting. Confronting in public can worsen the situation. Enforce discipline and emphasize mutual respect among team members. Restate the objective of the team as main focus.
Rush to accomplishment	Incomplete data collection. Inconsistent analysis. Trying to get conclusion faster.	Team under unrealistic deadline. Untrained team members. Looking for short-term gains.	Team leadership asks for data collection, analysis, and statistical significance. Ask for alternate solutions. Revise the deadline to a more realistic one based on resources.

Continued

Table 8.1 Common negative team dynamics and potential countermeasures. *(Continued)*

Negative dynamic	Symptoms	Probable causes	Potential countermeasures
Attribution	Members make casual references. Members don't seek explanations, preferring psychological and emotional judgments.	Similar to "rush to accomplishment" causes.	Team leaders challenge the assumptions made by team members. Use devil's advocate approach. Ask for analysis behind the conclusions drawn.
Discounts	Members' opinions are ignored. Members do not seem to listen to each other. Sarcasm, low team morale.		Encourage mutual respect. Enforce discipline. Ask for clarification from the members providing opinions.
Digressions and tangents	Discussion straying out of the scope/agenda of the meetings. Distractions. Meeting time not properly utilized. Not much achieved from the meetings.	Organization going through major change. Cultural issues. Lack of focus from leadership.	Enforce compliance to agenda items and time allotment. Restate meeting ground rules. Redirect the discussions.

2. SIX SIGMA AND OTHER TEAM ROLES AND RESPONSIBILITIES

> Describe and define the roles and responsibilities of participants on six sigma and other teams, including black belt, master black belt, green belt, champion, executive, coach, facilitator, team member, sponsor, process owner, etc. (Apply)
>
> **Body of Knowledge II.E.2**

Six Sigma successes are not just about application of statistical tools. A strong Six Sigma organization is necessary for sustainable success. Without this organiza-

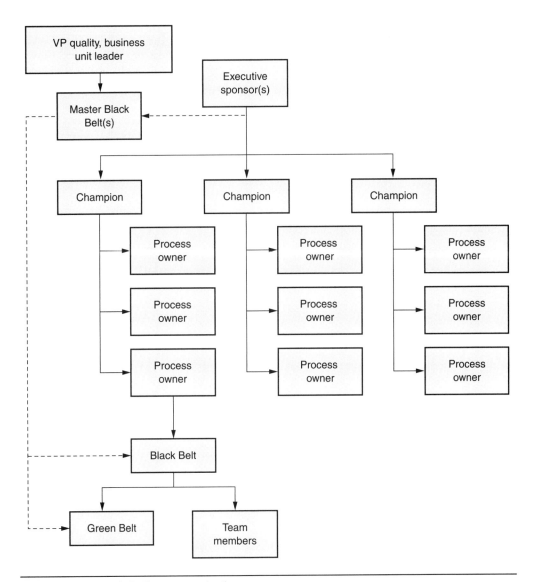

Figure 8.1   Typical Six Sigma organization.

tion, there will be no accountability to the investment made in employees in terms of training, resources spent, and consistent approach of methodologies. Smaller organizations may combine some roles; however, the responsibilities should be maintained. A typical Six Sigma organization is shown in Figure 8.1.

One factor that has helped Six Sigma be successful is the structure it demands of organizations. Table 8.2 shows typical Six Sigma roles, the organizational mem-

Table 8.2 Typical Six Sigma roles.

Role	Candidate	Training/background	Primary responsibilities
Executive sponsor	Business unit leader responsible for profit and loss (usually at director level or above)	Six Sigma concepts, strategies, overview, operational definitions.	• Set direction and priorities for the Six Sigma organization • Allocation of resources for projects • Set Six Sigma vision, overall objectives for the program • Monitor the progress of the overall program • Initiate incentive programs • Reward successful projects
Champion	Typically upper-level managers	Six Sigma concepts, strategies, tools and methods, operational definitions. Emphasis on management tools.	• Liaison with senior management • Allocation of resources for projects • Determine project selection criteria • Remove barriers hindering the success of the project • Approve completed projects • Implement change
Process owner	An individual responsible and accountable for the execution and results of the process. The sponsor or champion could also be a process owner.	Six Sigma concepts, strategies, tools and methods, operational definitions. Emphasis on statistical tools.	• Select team members • Allocation of resources for projects • Provide process knowledge • Review process changes • Approve changes/ support change management • Implement change • Ensure that improvements are sustained

Continued

Table 8.2   Typical Six Sigma roles. *(Continued)*

Role	Candidate	Training/background	Primary responsibilities
Master Black Belt	Individuals trained in Six Sigma methodologies, statistical tools, basic financial tools, change management, risk assessment, project management, executive communication, and well experienced in teaching, coaching, and mentoring Black Belts and Green Belts. This is always a full-time position.	Six Sigma Body of Knowledge, lean enterprise synergy, finance for nonfinancial managers, risk assessment, project management, change agent skills, Master Black Belt train the trainer, presentation skills, communication skills, leadership skills, facilitation skills.	• Coach Six Sigma Black Belts and Green Belts • Utilize the resources provided by management effectively • Formulate overall business strategy linking to Six Sigma program • Monitor project progress closely • Typically between 15–20 projects overseen at a time • Provide coaching, mentoring for new Black Belts and Green Belts • Work with champions and process owners for selection of projects • Address issues of project stagnation • Remove barriers hindering the success of the project • Support as a subject matter expert for the organization • Review and approve completed projects • Share lessons learned with the extended team • Provide inputs to rewards committee

Continued

Part II.E.2

Table 8.2 Typical Six Sigma roles. *(Continued)*

Role	Candidate	Training/background	Primary responsibilities
Black Belt	Individuals trained in Six Sigma methodologies, statistical tools, basic financial tools, change management, risk assessment, project management, and well experienced in managing Black Belt projects. This is always a full-time position.	Six Sigma Black Belt Body of Knowledge, lean enterprise synergy, finance for nonfinancial managers, risk assessment, project management, change agent skills, presentation skills, communication skills, leadership and facilitation skills. Certified as Six Sigma Black Belt.	• Lead and manage Six Sigma projects • Utilize the resources provided by management effectively • Provide net present value, return on investment (ROI), payback calculations on projects • Work full-time on four to six projects per year • Monitor project progress closely • Follow DMAIC process, apply appropriate statistical methods • Work with champions, Master Black Belt, and process owners for selection of projects • Address issues of project stagnation/consult Master Black Belt • Remove barriers hindering the success of the project • Update and present project progress to management • Review completed projects • Share lessons learned with the extended team

Continued

Table 8.2 Typical Six Sigma roles. *(Continued)*

Role	Candidate	Training/background	Primary responsibilities
Green Belt	Individuals trained in Six Sigma methodologies, basic statistical tools, and process improvement techniques. This is typically a full-time position. However, some organizations make this part of an existing job responsibility.	Six Sigma Green Belt Body of Knowledge, lean enterprise synergy, presentation skills, communication skills. Certified as Six Sigma Green Belt.	• Support Six Sigma projects with higher ROI • Lead smaller projects with moderate savings and ROI • Follow DMAIC process, apply appropriate statistical methods • Review the approach periodically with the experienced Black Belt and Master Black Belt • Provide inputs to Master Black Belt and Black Belt and process owners during selection of projects • Identify issues of project stagnation/ consult Black Belt, Master Black Belt • Identify and report barriers hindering the success of the project • Share lessons learned with the extended team
Project team member	Selected by process owner and trained in Six Sigma methodologies, quality, basic statistical tools, and process improvement techniques.	Six Sigma methodologies, quality tools, process improvement, teamwork.	• Support and contribute to Six Sigma projects • Participate in charter and scope definition • Provide inputs during project meeting, brainstorm ideas • Help collect data where responsible • Follow DMAIC process, apply appropriate tools • Review the approach periodically with the Green Belt and experienced Black Belt • Provide inputs to Green Belt and Black Belt and process owners during project

Part II.E.2

bers that typically fill the roles, their expected training or background, and the primary responsibilities for each role.

3. TEAM TOOLS

Define and apply team tools such as brainstorming, nominal group technique, multi-voting, etc. (Apply)

Body of Knowledge II.E.3

As we discussed earlier, teams go through several stages before performing and may face obstacles due to human interactions. Hence, soliciting ideas from all team members by providing an equal opportunity and arriving at sound conclusions requires the use of a systematic and proven approach.

Team tools are useful for guiding team interaction in a systematic way. There are times when the topic of discussion is sensitive or controversial. There are times when a problem has not been explored enough and the team leader is looking for as many ideas as possible. Also there are times when team members have multiple ideas and want to explore everything. These scenarios are not uncommon in a typical team setting. We will be discussing in this section some of the team tools and their application to solving these issues.

Brainstorming

Brainstorming is a method of generating a large number of creative ideas in a short period of time. This tool is used when broad ranges of options and creative and original ideas are desired. This tool also encourages team participation.

The team identifies the subject or problem at hand and writes it down on a whiteboard. It is important to clearly define the problem. This will keep the ideas on topic. Sometimes for a totally unfamiliar issue, it is acceptable to keep it open so that we get a very wide range of ideas. The team leader explains the problem or subject to the team members.

Examples with scope defined to facilitate majority of ideas focusing in defined area:

- Contamination of polished surface before optical subassembly
- Low attendance at ASQ section program meetings
- Food menu for Thanksgiving dinner

Examples with scope wide open:

- Global warming
- Unemployment

• Organizational culture

The team is given few minutes to think about the subject. In structured brainstorming the team leader opens up a round-robin discussion. This way everyone gets the opportunity to contribute. If someone doesn't have an idea at this time, they are allowed to pass and contribute during the next round. The team members are not allowed to criticize each other or evaluate the ideas at this stage. The recording individual can ask for clarity on an idea and phrases it the same way as the idea contributor. Rephrasing without the consent of the idea owner is not allowed. Everyone is allowed one idea at a time. Some members will have the urge to provide multiple ideas during their turn. The team leader should facilitate such situations. Members are allowed to develop an idea already cited by a fellow member. Quantity is more important than quality so that the ideas keep flowing. All ideas are recorded on the whiteboard or flip-chart.

Let us examine an example of defined-scope brainstorming: How to improve member attendance of ASQ section programs? (Problem rephrased as a question.)

Every major city in North America has a local ASQ section run by volunteers. One of the main benefits of this section is the monthly program meeting. Unfortunately, the section monthly program meetings draw a very low attendance (about seven to 10 percent) of members from the region, with at least 20 percent of the members attending once throughout the year.

The program chair (responsible for ASQ section monthly meetings) chairs the brainstorming session as a team leader. The section chair may act as a facilitator.

A team has been assembled with other section executives, past section chairs, and/or executives, section senior members, and members who were randomly selected from the membership database.

One of the members volunteered as a recorder and the team was given three minutes to think about the subject in a focused manner, then the session was started in a round-robin style.

Ideas started flowing. Keep in mind it is about quantity and not quality at this point! No judgment or evaluation is allowed.

How to improve member attendance of ASQ section programs?

1. Bring in reputed speakers.

2. Present topics that are current.

3. Provide value for time and money.

4. Keep program interactive; debate, quiz.

5. Survey members for desired topics.

6. Rotate program locations based on member concentration.

7. Conduct some programs in the organizations with most members.

8. Not charge for meeting.

9. Offer pizza, snacks, sandwiches, and coffee.

10. Offer time for networking.

11. Section chair and executives mix with members and attendees during break (rather than talking to themselves as a small group).

12. Check weather forecast before planning meetings.

13. Update members on other section events.

14. Conduct less frequent but more effective meetings.

15. Not waste meeting time with logistics issues—be prepared.

16. Offer the meeting virtually—Webcast, teleconference.

17. Draw name cards from fishbowl and offer a small gift.

18. Make the process easier for program attendance, recertification units claim.

19. Present two diverse topics so that members do not choose to attend only some meetings.

20. Active members provide carpool to meeting location for new or potential members.

21. Liaise with other professional organizations to offer combined program meeting.

22. Attract more students from universities.

23. Conduct some meetings on the local community college or university campus to attract students.

24. Provide "back to basics" programs with applications for students and small business owners.

25. Interview random sample of members who never attended a single meeting and find out why.

26. Interview random sample of members who always attend every meeting and find out why.

27. Introduce first-time attendee members/nonmembers in the group to make them feel wanted.

28. Program chair to survey every program for attendee satisfaction and review feedback.

29. Appoint marketing chair to reach wider member base and potential new members.

30. Keep the section Web site updated and easily accessible.

31. Upload archive presentations to the Web site.

32. Communicate at least twice about monthly program—three weeks before and one week before.

33. Announce and recognize newly certified professionals.

34. Record and archive the program events on DVD/VHS and issue to
    local libraries for free and also make available online.

Wow, isn't this quite a collection of ideas? Now the team leader looks for any
redundancy or any ideas that require further expansion for clarity.

Some teams will break after a few rounds and revisit the list with any additional thoughts. However, this should not be prolonged as the team may get bored
and ideas will start to be counterproductive or too critical.

There are other team tools used to take these ideas to the next step:

- *Multivoting* to short-list the ideas as a group.

- *Cause-and-effect diagram* to assign each idea under one category, namely
  person–machine–material–method–measurement–environment and
  further analyze why.

Nominal Group Technique

This is also a type of brainstorming but with limited team vocal interaction. The
tool is thus named "nominal" group technique. This technique is applied when
some group members are much more vocal then others, to encourage equal participation from all members, or with a controversial or sensitive topic, and so on. This
technique helps to alleviate peer pressure and reduces the impact of such pressure
on the generation of ideas.

Similarly to brainstorming, the facilitator explains the rules and the team
leader presents the topic to the assembled members. The team is given a good 10
to 15 minutes so that they can silently sit, think, and generate ideas.

No verbal interactions are allowed during the session. The member ideas are
collected and posted in a space where all can read them. The members may also
read the ideas aloud one by one in a round-robin format. At this stage no judgment or criticism is passed. The ideas are simply written down. The members are
allowed to expand on existing ideas, provide clarity, and eliminate redundancy
during the consolidation. For a controversial or sensitive subject the team leader
may opt to collect the ideas and write them down on the board, maintaining anonymity of the contributors.

Multivoting

Multivoting complements nominal group technique (NGT). This can also be successfully used with brainstorming results. Even though this tool is typically used
in combination with NGT, it can be a technique on its own. The consolidated ideas
are numbered or identified by an alphabetical letter and the team members are
asked to prioritize the top five or 10 items that can be of significant influence on
the problem.

The team members are given five to 10 minutes to prioritize and the results
are tabulated. Let us extend the previous example of "How to improve member
attendance of ASQ section programs?" The members were asked to submit and
prioritize ideas. As we see there were 34 ideas provided from the diversified member group. Even though many of these ideas are good, the section may not have

resources to address them all at one time. The section chair wants to select the five most important ideas to address in the next three years and implement them in order of priority.

Every team member selects the five most important ideas by placing check marks by the idea. It is important for the facilitator to restate the objective and refocus the team to select ideas from the ASQ section point of view. If this facilitation is not done, you may end up with multiple ideas with an equal number of check marks. Once this is done and you have the five ideas that most team members have selected as significant to improving the attendance of a section program, the prioritization process is begun. This can be done through either a non-weighted (ranking) or weighted approach.

The members selected the following five ideas as having the most significant impact on improving section attendance:

A. *Value.* Bring in reputed speakers and present topics that are current.

B. *Logistics.* Rotate program locations based on member concentration.

C. *Affordability.* Not charge for meeting and offer pizza, snacks, sandwiches, and coffee.

D. *Outreach.* Conduct some meetings on the local community college or university campus to attract students.

E. *Communication.* E-mails twice per month, updated section calendar event Web page.

The multivoting ranked approach outcome is shown in Figure 8.2.

In the weighted multivoting approach the team rates rather than ranks the choices. This is like the $100 or 100 points approach where the team member is asked to split $100 or 100 points between five choices. The multivoting weighted approach outcome is shown in Figure 8.3.

As can be seen by examining the data in Figure 8.2 and Figure 8.3, the two approaches in this example produced similar ranking. However, this is not always the case, which is why using both approaches can help a team to focus on the most

Venue: Caribou meeting room
Date: 3-Feb-07
Subject: How to improve member attendance of ASQ section programs?
Scale: 1 (least important) to 5 (most important)

	Member 1	Member 2	Member 3	Member 4	Member 5	Member 6	Member 7	Member 8	Member 9	Total
A	5	3	4	5	5	3	4	5	5	39
B	2	4	3	3	4	4	3	3	4	30
C	1	5	5	4	3	5	5	4	3	35
D	3	3	1	2	2	3	1	2	2	19
E	4	1	2	1	1	1	2	1	1	14

Figure 8.2 Multivoting ranked approach example.

Venue: Caribou meeting room
Date: 3-Feb-07
Subject: How to improve member attendance of ASQ section programs?

	Member 1	Member 2	Member 3	Member 4	Member 5	Member 6	Member 7	Member 8	Member 9	Total
A	30	20	25	35	20	25	25	35	30	245
B	15	25	20	20	25	20	20	20	15	180
C	10	30	30	25	30	30	30	25	10	220
D	20	15	10	15	15	10	10	15	20	130
E	25	10	15	5	10	15	15	5	25	125

There is NO ranking scale applicable to this approach. The column total should add up to 100 for all individual columns and the relative importance of A to E to be understood by the points allotted by each member (from that member's point of view). Overall relative importance is understood from reviewing the "Total" column. Based on consolidated input from all members, in this example, A is most important, followed by C, B, D and E.

Figure 8.3   Multivoting weighted approach example.

Part II.E.4

critical items. If the values get too close to each other, another round of voting can be conducted between the close choices to select a clear winner.

Note: The problem chosen for this example and ideas generated are realities for most ASQ sections. However, this example is not targeted on a specific ASQ section. The top choices and ranking were created to demonstrate the example rather than to provide solutions to the existing problem.

4. COMMUNICATION

> Use effective and appropriate communication techniques for different situations to overcome barriers to project success. (Apply)
>
> **Body of Knowledge II.E.4**

A message is sent to convey *information;* information is meant to change *behavior.* Hence, the effectiveness of a communication is vital if we expect desired action to happen. Communication is a key skill that is required for any individual be they an operator on the assembly line or the CEO of an organization. The skill-level expectation increases as the individual moves up to higher positions and communicates information that can literally change the lives of employees, the future of the organization, and the consequences to society. For situations that can make an impact of this magnitude, it is important to "plan to communicate." In a project setting with a matrix organization structure, the importance of communication can not be stressed enough. Go/no-go decisions for the project and support from stakeholders require effective communication.

There are several types of communication flow that are used in different situations:

- *Top-down flow or downward flow.* Used when top management or the executive sponsor of the project is providing instructions, communicating policies, or providing feedback on project performance. If this communication is passed from executive sponsor to champion to process owner to Black Belt to team members, there is a possibility of losing some information as the message may get filtered or distorted. It is better for the top manager to send a written communication to the team and/or convene a meeting to communicate to the entire chain of command. Management may leave sensitive information to be communicated through the chain of command. This will help make the middle-level managers feel they are not losing their importance.

- *Bottom-up flow or upward flow.* When a line operator or front desk personnel want to provide feedback to the management or a team member wants to communicate to the executive sponsor of the project, a bottom-up flow of communication occurs. Similar to top-down, the bottom-up method may also see information distorted as it reaches the higher level. Top management should encourage an open-door policy, survey employees, and set up suggestion boxes and stand-up meetings. Luncheon meetings are good for providing bottom-up communication opportunities. All these ideas have to be planned and executed correctly or they will become a mockery of the system. Examples of poor implementation include: suggestion boxes turning into complaint boxes, open-door policy being misused to disrupt work or point fingers.

- *Horizontal communication.* This is more effectively used in "flatter" organizations. This is very effective and quicker to get results. However, where there is a process to be followed for authorization and approval of management, horizontal communication is not suitable as it may tend to shortcut the process. In a vertical organization, the middle and higher management personnel may feel that they have been surpassed due to horizontal communication. It is better for management to provide guidelines as to where horizontal communication is encouraged.

Communication delivery method and meeting room setting are helpful to the effectiveness of the message as well. Reprimanding must be done in private whereas appreciation has to be given in public. Sensitive issues have to be communicated in person as body language plays a key role between the sender and receiver of the message. E-mails are not good at communicating emotions and hence disagreements are best handled face to face.

Chapter 9

Commonly Used Define Phase Tools

I

n this chapter, the typical tools used during the *define* phase are highlighted. Many of these tools have templates and additional information available on the accompanying CD-ROM. Other highly recommended resources include:

Part II

- www.asq.org. See the "Quality Tools" page in the Knowledge Center for tools and explanations of their use.

- *The Quality Toolbox,* Second Edition, by Nancy R. Tague, ASQ Quality Press, 2005.

- *Customer Driven Company*, by Richard C. Whiteley, The Forum Corporation, 1991.

- www.iSixSigma.com. An improvement-based Web site that has numerous templates and tool guides, as well as case studies.

- www.freequality.org. This Web site has several free templates available for download.

ACTIVITY NETWORK DIAGRAMS

The activity network diagram (AND) is similar to the PERT chart discussed later in this chapter because it graphically shows interdependencies between tasks. An AND highlights key tasks, the time to accomplish the tasks, flow paths (serial or parallel), and so on. This tool, like PERT and critical path analysis, can provide a top-level overview or detailed data depending on the project need. An example of an AND is shown in Figure 9.1.

ADVANCED QUALITY PLANNING

Advanced quality planning (AQP) is founded on the idea that solid planning helps prevent surprises and saves valuable resources. Anything that is to be done can be first thought out, or written plans can actually be made to lay out a pattern or blueprint of what you are going to do.

AQP is a process where we first look at the parameters of what we are going to do. Do we have the right amount of material available? Do we have the right people to do the job or provide the service needed? Do we have the right tools to do the job well? Do we know the correct way of using everything we have

91

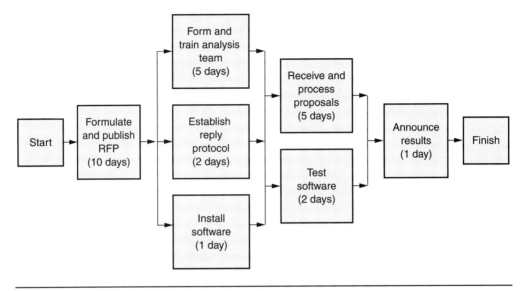

Figure 9.1   Example of an activity network diagram.

to provide a safe working environment? All of these questions and many more should be answered before we start work! One of several tools that could be used here to help answer these questions is the cause-and-effect diagram. This forces us to ensure that we have thought of all the elements (causes) that will give us the desired output (effect). You can also think of AQP as the first step of the plan–do–study–act (PDSA) cycle where the plan is done before work actually starts.

AFFINITY DIAGRAMS

Affinity diagrams are used to produce many possible answers to an open-ended question such as "What are some of the ways to reduce cycle time for process A?" The first step is to brainstorm to obtain two to three dozen responses. Each response is clearly written on self-adhesive note paper. The next step is to move the notes around until they fall into five to 10 natural groups. Some suggest this be done in silence with all team members participating, as they prefer. If a note gets moved back and forth between two groups several times, a duplicate may be made so that one can be placed in each group. The next step is to find a name for each group. This may take several iterations before team consensus is reached. The last step is to draw lines containing all the notes in a group with the group name. An example of an affinity diagram is shown in Figure 9.2.

AUDITING

Auditing is an independent assessment of processes and/or projects against established plans and goals. This checking process is sometimes called "quality" auditing and is commonly performed in organizations with established quality

Problem: What are some of the ways to reduce cycle time for process A?

Machine	Personnel	Infrastructure
• Run machine faster • Get a new machine • Apply new controls • Reduce setup time • Simplify machine operations	• Assign more people • Provide additional training • Let Joe run the process/ machine • Provide help during setup	• Reduce paperwork • Improve forklift uptime • Better conveyor • New overhead crane • Prompt deliver of route sheets

Vendor	Maintenance
• Improve vendor communication • Use cell phone to contact vendor • Have additional sources • Work with vendor to improve quality and delivery • Reduce resupply time	• Better lubricant • Reliability-centered maintenance • More frequent lubrication • More prompt response to maintenance calls

Figure 9.2   Example of an affinity diagram.

management systems (for example, AS9100, ISO 9001, ISO/TS 16949) or those that have applied for a quality award (Malcolm Baldrige National Quality Award or state-level quality awards).

The first thing to know when planning to audit something is what the standard or criteria are that we will be auditing against. If it is a process audit, the auditor needs to know what applicable standard operating procedures or other process sheets are used to ensure that things are done in a standardized manner. If conducting a safety audit, then having the written safety rules would be important. Some other items that could be audited include: project closure, cleanliness, product quality, system knowledge, emergency procedures, and so on.

An individual audit, like most other activities, is a sequence of processes and typically includes: audit planning (or preparation), audit performance, audit reporting, and audit closure. Audit planning is the auditor's preparation phase to ensure familiarity with the item being audited, to schedule the audit, and to notify the auditee. The audit performance phase is where the auditor gathers the evidence of performance through interviews, observations, and so on. This phase also includes reconciliation to ensure the validity of any potential findings (that is, noncompliances or nonconformances) or opportunities for improvement (that is, items that could lead to a finding). The audit report phase includes drafting the report, which summarizes the audit scope, activities, and results, and the generation of associated corrective actions (findings) or preventive actions (opportunities for improvement). The audit closure phase includes any necessary follow-up activities to ensure that action plans were implemented and effective in eliminating their associated causes.

It should be noted that there are several types of audits including first-party, second-party, third-party, internal (most likely used for Six Sigma), and external. Audits typically focus on products, systems, suppliers, or regulatory compliance. There are numerous books available through ASQ Quality Press and other publishers related to auditing.

When asked to be part of an audit team, there are some basic things to be aware of and know in conducting an audit:

- Be pleasant to the person being audited; you are not a cop looking to catch them doing something wrong.

- Be prepared. Understand the process to be audited and associated documentation, and verify document availability, revision, and references prior to audit conduct.

- Be factual in what you observe. Hiding things does not help the company to improve and being too critical may harm personal objectivity.

- Be thorough in looking at the process as it relates to the standard. If you miss something, customer satisfaction may suffer or worse yet, someone might get hurt.

- Ask questions for clarity. We want to be as positive as possible given the situation.

- Record your observations for the record and the next person who will audit the area.

- Follow what the internal lead auditor directs you to do.

Being an internal auditor for your organization can be both challenging and informative as we usually get a better view of what our companies are doing if we have a chance to look at other operations. For some of us it will also break the routine of what we do every day and give us a chance to see how others might be doing things and benchmark (see the following section) that against what we do.

BENCHMARKING

Benchmarking is the process of looking at one system(s) and applying the concepts observed to another system. This usually involves some give and take between the organization doing the benchmarking and the organization that is the benchmark. The idea is to make it a win/win situation—how can the organizations learn from each other? Another critical point about benchmarking is that it can be done internally and externally. When performed internally, different departments assess each other's processes and take the best from each process to improve their own process. When external benchmarking is performed, it can be done within the same industry or with an organization from another industry. Usually, benchmarking against an organization in another industry is easier as it removes the competitive aspects of reviewing processes. All information gained during the benchmarking process should be considered protected—for internal use only.

The basic process steps of benchmarking are:

1. Flowchart the current process

2. Identify the areas to be improved

3. Brainstorm ideas

4. Investigate how others (internal and external) perform similar processes

5. Develop plans for application of ideas

6. Pilot test ideas

7. Initiate the new process

8. Evaluate the new process

Before starting a benchmarking project, it is advisable to ensure that you know exactly how your current process works. This may sound funny, but it has been shown that when people actually flowchart a process, there is usually a lot of disagreement as to the exact steps and/or the order of those steps. Thus, any time that there is more than one person who works on or around a machine, the process should be flowcharted.

Then it is time to do some research into how others (internal or external to the organization) do similar things. Once you have seen other ways of doing things, it is time to try to figure out how you can do things differently in your own operations. Establish a plan for the changes and acquire the needed resources from management. The plan should list what materials are needed, when and where new operations will be installed, identification and planning of any training that may be needed, and other details that will allow for a changeover to the new idea. Then prepare and run a pilot test to ensure that the plan will work. It is usually unwise to just jump right into the new idea without testing it first. Even the best-laid plans may have unforeseen bugs that cause problems, so run a small test first.

BRAINSTORMING

Brainstorming is a process where an individual or team develops as many ideas concerning a topic as they can using various creativity techniques or methods. There are two basic phases to brainstorming: the creative phase, which is used to generate a large number of ideas, and the evaluation phase, where the ideas generated are looked at for usefulness or applicability. There should be a time break between the two phases as different parts of the brain are used in each phase. At minimum, a ten-minute stretch break should be taken versus going directly into evaluation after being creative.

During the creative phase there should be no criticism or other distractions allowed. During this phase, the team should maintain open minds to all the possibilities no matter how wild the idea—the goal is to get as many ideas as possible. If ideas are being put on a flip-chart with a large group, you should have two or more available to capture all of the ideas as they develop. Otherwise you could have each person say what they are thinking and have them or someone else record the idea on a sticky note and put it on the wall. Facilitation can be used during the creative phase, but free-wheeling also works well. Some basic guidelines that should be followed in the creativity phase of brainstorming include:

- No criticism, compliments, or questions

- Wild ideas are welcome

- Don't wait

- Quantity is important (versus quality)

- Hitchhike—build on previous ideas

During the evaluation phase, at some point after the creativity phase, it is best to have a facilitator work with the group to look over the ideas in a sequence. There are many ways to go about evaluating the ideas generated. One good starting point is to organize the list of things into like groups or categories (that is, build an affinity diagram) to help in the evaluation process. The caution here is not to get overly critical, as there may be something in one of those "crazy" ideas that might actually work for the given situation. This is often true because of new technology or different ways of doing things that are not common in our organizations.

To make brainstorming most effective, prior to starting the activity review, help the team understand the importance of avoiding these idea-stopping thoughts or behaviors:

- Don't be ridiculous

- Let's shelve it for right now

- It won't work here

- Our business is different

- Let's think about it some more

- We did all right without it

- It's too radical a change

- Management won't like it

- Where did you dig up that idea?

- It's not practical

- It's too expensive

- You can't be serious

- You can't do that

- The technology will not allow that

- Were will you get . . .

- We've never done it before

- I have something better
- It's too risky
- Let's be sensible
- We'll never get it approved
- The employees won't like it
- It's good, but . . .
- Let's check on it later
- Too much work
- Let's get back to reality
- That's been tried before
- That's not my job
- You do not know how we do things around here
- That's too high-tech for us
- It will never work

See the brainstorming example in Chapter 8 for additional information.

CAUSE-AND-EFFECT DIAGRAM (FISHBONE DIAGRAM OR ISHIKAWA DIAGRAM)

Originally developed in the 1940s by Kaoru Ishikawa in Japan, the *cause-and-effect diagram* is a graphical analysis tool that allows the user to display the factors involved in a given situation. Cause-and-effect diagrams are drawn to clearly illustrate the various causes (x) affecting the item being investigated. "A good cause-and-effect diagram is one that fits the purpose, and there is no one definite form."[1]

These causes can be any item or occurrence that is related to the effect (Y) that is being studied. Thus the effect of a situation is the result of the function of the causes [$Y = f(x)$]. Other names for this tool that are sometimes used include: *Ishikawa diagram, fishbone diagram,* or even *feather diagram* given the shape of the graphic.

Key Point: Cause-and-effect diagrams can be used to analyze positive effects as well as undesirable ones.

Asking the five W's and one H (what, why, when, where, who, and how) can be effective in developing the elements of the cause-and-effect diagram. Besides using the five W's and one H in creating the cause-and-effect diagram, consider starting with the six M's:

- Man (people/operator)
- Machine (equipment)

- Methods (operating procedures)

- Materials

- Measurement

- Mother Nature (environment)

- Money (optional—but an important consideration)

- Management (optional)

This tool is relatively simple to use and yet very powerful. Once it is completed, it is able to show graphically the factors of the system or process to management and other teams.

Figure 9.3 is a cause-and-effect diagram example in which a manufacturing team tries to understand the source of periodic iron contamination in product. The team used the six generic headings to prompt ideas. Layers of branches show thorough thinking about the causes of the problem.

For example, under the heading "Machines," the idea "materials of construction" shows four kinds of equipment and then several specific machine numbers.

Note that some ideas appear in two different places. "Calibration" shows up under "Methods" as a factor in the analytical procedure, and also under "Measurement" as a cause of lab error. "Iron tools" can be considered a "Methods" problem when taking samples or a "Manpower" problem with maintenance personnel.

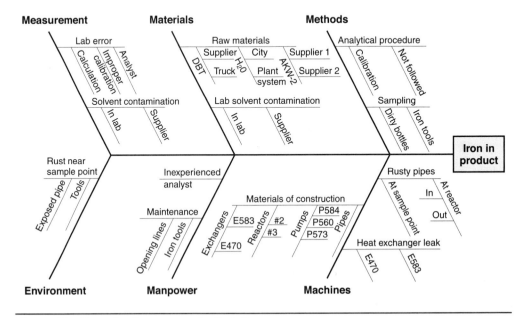

Figure 9.3   Example of a cause-and-effect diagram.
Source: N. R. Tague, *The Quality Toolbox*, 2nd ed. (Milwaukee: ASQ Quality Press, 2005): 87.

Paint color defect causes

Reason	Day of the week							Weekly total
	Mon	Tue	Wed	Thu	Fri	Sat	Sun	
Operator misread instructions	I	I	0	II	卌	卌 II	III	19
Wrong pigment used	III	I	卌	III	IIII	IIII	卌 卌	30
Wrong color code from customer	II	I	II	0	0	卌	0	10
Outdated base paint	0	0	I	0	III	0	IIII	8
Daily total	6	3	8	5	12	16	17	67

Figure 9.4   Example of a check sheet.

CHECK SHEETS

Check sheets are used to observe or review a process, usually during execution of the process. Check sheets precategorize potential outcomes for data collection using sets of words, tally lists, or graphics. Figure 9.4 is an example of a completed check sheet, in tabular format, used to collect data related to a paint mixing process. This simple tool provides a method of easy collection of the data. By collecting data on a check sheet, common patterns or trends can be identified.

The basic steps in making a check sheet are:

1. Identify and agree to the causes or conditions that are to be collected.

2. Decide who will collect the data, over what time period(s), and how the data will be collected.

3. Create a check sheet that will work within the operation where it will be used.

4. Collect the data as designed to ensure consistency and accuracy of the information.

Check sheets can be the basis for other analytical tools and are incorporated into attribute process behavior charts. Creating and using a check sheet can help focus on continual improvement and may foster changes just because the check sheet is being used.

CUSTOMER FEEDBACK

Feedback is a method or process of finding out what the customer actually thinks of your products or services. Finding out what the customer thinks, wants, and needs is a very time-consuming effort and many customers are getting tired of filling out paper surveys. Sometimes when customers (internal or external) do tell us something, we either can't do anything about it, do not want to hear what they are saying, or they expect something other than what we offer.

There are many traditional techniques for talking with customers and, with the advent of e-mail and the Internet, even more so today. The problem with many surveys is that we really do not know how many or which customers actually bothered to send them back. Also, paper surveys tend to have a very low return rate so we really do not get a very good overall picture. The point is that we must keep trying to talk with customers as often as possible to ensure that we know what their wants and needs are. The most effective method still seems to be actually getting out into the world with the customers to experience what they do and to interact with them as they use your products and services.

FAILURE MODE AND EFFECTS ANALYSIS

The concepts of failure mode effects analysis (FMEA) have been around a long time. In the past, inventors and product developers thought about possible ways that a product could fail during extreme conditions, handling, and usage. They started to provide countermeasures in the design and manufacturing process to prevent these failure modes. FMEA thus started to evolve informally. The military standard MIL-STD-1629A (now obsolete) was a formal document used for FMEA by aerospace and defense applications. This is probably the earliest known FMEA document.

The idea behind identifying the failure modes in system, design, and process started to evolve during the last half-century with changes to how risks were weighted, categorized, and calculated. Ford Motor Company used this FMEA approach for design and manufacturing to safeguard against safety- and regulatory-related failure modes. Eventually they started to see benefit in reducing the risks confronting product quality.

In 1993, Chrysler, Ford, and General Motors, with inputs from several other technical professionals, created a document, "potential failure mode and effects analysis," that encompassed design and process FMEA. This document became part of the QS-9000 (now ISO/TS 16949) standard's expectations for automotive suppliers. This document, currently in its third edition, has been revised with significant inputs from the SAEJ1739 work group and other automotive product–related organizations.

The Automotive Industry Action Group (AIAG) described FMEA as a systematic group of activities intended to:

- Recognize and evaluate the potential failure of a product/process and the effects of that failure

- Identify actions that could eliminate or reduce the chance of the potential failure occurring

- Document the entire process[2]

The purpose of FMEA is to understand the opportunities for failure and the impact of risks in a product or process design, prioritize the risks, and take actions to eliminate or reduce the impact of these risks. FMEA is a front-end tool. Successful product/process development requires anticipating failure modes and taking actions to eliminate or reduce failure during deployment and lifecycle. FMEA is not a one-time event; the product/process design team needs to periodically review and update the failure modes. During the early stages of product/process development, the team identifies the risks based on existing data from similar processes, knowledge, and experience. As the product/process is deployed, new unforeseen risks and failures may show up. Hence, reviewing the FMEA on a continual basis ensures sustainable success.

FMEA needs to be documented and revision-controlled and should be part of the existing quality management system (QMS). In a well-designed QMS, FMEA is linked to quality function deployment in the design and process "houses of quality" and linked to control plans in the production house of quality. FMEA is not just confined to manufacturing applications. FMEA has been successfully used in service/transactional processes, software development, the medical field, and so on.

Although in principle FMEA is conducted to address the potential failures in product design and process design, FMEA is identified separately as design FMEA and process FMEA. (There is also a system FMEA that is beyond the scope of this BoK).

Please see the Glossary for some of the fundamental terms used in FMEA such as *failure mode, cause, effect, failure mechanism, severity, occurrence, detection, risk priority number,* and so on.

An evolution of FMEA is FMECA, which includes provisions for assessing and charting the probability of a failure mode occurring versus the severity of the consequences of realizing the failure mode. This is referred to as a *criticality analysis*— the "C" in FMECA.

Steps in Performing FMEA

The team approach is most effective for conducting an FMEA, so it is discussed here. Assemble a cross-functional team with diverse knowledge about the process, product, or service, and customer needs. Functions often included are: design, manufacturing, quality, testing, reliability, maintenance, purchasing (and suppliers), sales, marketing (and customers), and customer service. It is important to have process experts' presence in design FMEA and design experts in process FMEA. For effective interaction, the team is typically five to seven people. If additional experts are needed to provide inputs on safety, regulatory, or legal issues, they are included in the team as subject matter experts.

Identify the scope of the FMEA. Is it for concept, system, design, process, or service? What are the boundaries? How detailed should we be? See Table 9.1 for steps in performing an FMEA.

Do's

- Always provide FMEA training to team members before assigning to an FMEA team.
- Always use the team approach.
- Ask for subject matter expertise if required.
- Talk to your customer about how they intend to use the product.

Table 9.1 Steps in performing a design or process FMEA.

	Steps	Design FMEA	Process FMEA
1	Review the design/process	Use schematic diagram and functional block diagram to identify each of the main components of the design and determine the function or functions of those components and interfaces between them. Make sure you are studying all components defined in the scope of the DFMEA. Some components may have more than one function.	Use flowcharts to identify the scope and to make sure every team member understands it in detail. It is also recommended that the team perform a walk-through of the process and understand the process steps firsthand.
2	Brainstorm potential failure modes	A potential failure mode represents any manner in which the product component could fail to perform its intended function or functions.	A potential failure mode represents any manner in which the process step could fail to perform its intended function or functions.
3	List potential effects of failure	The potential effect at interim (local) and end effects are both identified. The effect is the ability of the component to perform its intended function due to the failure mode.	The potential effect at interim (local) and end effects are both identified. The effect is the impact on the process outcome and product quality due to the failure mode.
4	Assign severity rating (S)	Severity rating corresponds to each effect the failure mode can cause. Typically the scale is 1 to 10. Higher severity is rated at the high end, lower severity at the low end of the scale.	
5	List potential causes	For every failure mode, list possible cause(s). Use team tools like brainstorming, cause-and-effect charts, NGT, multivoting, and so on. Where applicable use a pilot experiment, past data, expert knowledge.	
6	Assign occurrence rating (O)	Occurrence rating corresponds to the likelihood or frequency at which the cause can occur. Typically the scale is 1 to 10. Higher occurrence is rated at the high end, lower occurrence at the low end of the scale.	
7	Current controls	For each cause, current process controls are identified. Controls can be of different types. They may just detect the failure or prevent the failure from happening. The controls range from work instructions to AQL sampling, SPC, alarms, mistake-proofing fixture, and so on.	
8	Assign detection rating (D)	Detection rating corresponds to the ability to detect the occurrence of the failure mode. Typically the scale is 1 to 10. Higher detectability is rated at the low end, lower detectability at the high end of the scale.	
9	Calculate RPN	Product of severity (S), occurrence (O), and detection (D). $S \times O \times D =$ risk priority number (RPN). Severity × occurrence = criticality is also important in some industries.	

Continued

Table 9.1   Steps in performing a design or process FMEA. *(Continued)*

	Steps	Design FMEA	Process FMEA
10	Develop action plan	Action plan may contain tasks to improve the current controls or reduce the frequency of the occurrence of the cause. In order to reduce the severity, the team may have to think of redesigning the product or process. Assign a realistic completion date and responsibility for tasks.	
11	Take action	This is a step where many FMEAs fall apart due to lack of management support, conflicting priorities, lack of resources, and lack of team leadership. The actions have to be implemented and results should be validated. Building a prototype and testing the action and piloting the process in small scale before mass producing are recommended.	
12	Recalculate the RPN	Bring the team back and objectively recalculate the RPN. Use objective evidence like customer feedback, reliability tests, warranty return rate, yield tracking, and so on, to reassess the score.	
13	Periodically review and update new risks	Carefully evaluate customer feedback, warranty analysis, internal nonconformance reports, ongoing reliability test reports, and so on, to explore new risks and update the FMEA. Keep the FMEA as a living document.	

- Take time as a team to standardize the scales (for the nature of business or the organization). This helps when comparing the overall risks between FMEAs and helps set up a cutoff score.

- Brainstorm all possible failure modes if they can happen occasionally.

- When two risks have the same overall score, the risk with the higher severity rating is escalated.

- Complete the action and reassess the risks as a team.

- Update the FMEA with new learned risks.

Don'ts

- Try not to copy the S-O-D scales from another industry or from a different organization. The description of the scale levels and impact may be different.

- Try not to force-fit into a 1 to 10 scale. If there are not many levels of severity, occurrence, and detection in your industry, try a 1 to 5 scale.

- Discourage creating customized scales within the organization unless absolutely essential.

- Don't fight over ratings of small difference, such as between 4 and 5 or 6 and 7. Analyze the impact thoroughly if the team is divided by two or three rating points, for example 4 and 7.

- Don't get hung up on a numbers game; the objective is to create a reduced-risk product and/or service.

- Don't perform FMEA to comply with the procedures or standards. FMEA is a business risk management tool. It has to be used with commitment to make it work.

Successful FMEA implementation requires leadership and management commitment. Few tools can test the patience of team members as finishing an FMEA; tackle multiple process steps for the product as a team in several meetings. In these cases split the process into major process blocks and perform FMEA by block. Maintain a good FMEA database. This will significantly reduce the time spent on successive FMEAs.

Once the initial RPN scores are tabulated, the team may decide on a cutoff score. For most organizations, the cutoff score is standardized. The cutoff score of one organization may not be directly applicable to another. Too low a cutoff score

Before taking action					After taking action				
Risk ID	S	O	D	Initial RPN	Risk ID	S	O	D	Recalc RPN
Risk 7	5	8	7	280	Risk 7	5	5	3	75
Risk 1	8	8	4	256	Risk 1	8	4	3	96
Risk 3	5	5	7	175	Risk 3	5	4	4	80
Risk 9	7	5	4	140	Risk 9	7	3	4	84
Risk 5	8	4	4	128	Risk 5	8	3	3	72
Risk 2	7	4	3	84	Risk 2	7	4	3	84
Risk 4	5	5	3	75	Risk 4	5	5	3	75
Risk 6	3	7	2	42	Risk 6	3	7	2	42
Risk 8	5	3	2	30	Risk 8	5	3	2	30
Risk 10	3	3	3	27	Risk 10	3	3	3	27

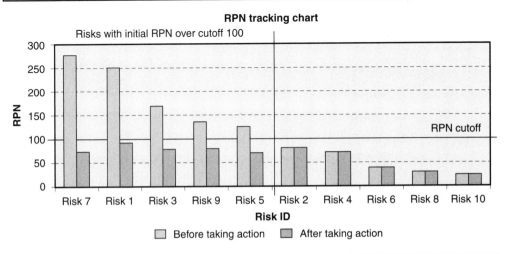

Figure 9.5   Example FMEA reporting and RPN chart.

Risk ID		Jan 07	Feb 07	Mar 07	Apr 07	May 07	Jun 07
Risk 7	Planned						
	Actual						
Risk 1	Planned						
	Actual						
Risk 3	Planned						
	Actual						
Risk 9	Planned						
	Actual						
Risk 5	Planned						
	Actual						

Figure 9.6   A typical risk action plan Gantt chart.

XYZ Corporation

Management Review Report—FMEA Implementation Progress

No. of FMEA risks over cutoff 100 = 245

Total no. of FMEA risks identified = 550

No. of risks to be reduced below cutoff by end of quarter* = 60

*Organizations review their performance by end of Q1, Q2, Q3, and Q4.

Figure 9.7   A typical top-level management review report for FMEA progress.

can result in spending lots of resources to eliminate or reduce several risks. Too high a cutoff can result in not addressing important risks. Management needs to review and agree on a score.

Figures 9.5 through 9.8 show various FMEA implementation tools and examples.

Note: FMEA is a powerful tool, but requires in-depth knowledge to successfully execute. It is recommended that guidance be sought from others who have performed an FMEA prior to or during the application of an FMEA to an improvement project.

FLOWCHART

According to Nancy Tague in *The Quality Toolbox*, a flowchart is a picture of the separate steps of a process in sequential order, including materials or services entering or leaving the process (inputs and outputs), decisions that must be made, people who become involved, time involved at each step, and/or process measurements.

Tague describes the basic procedure for development of a flowchart as:

Part II

Function	Potential failure mode	Potential effect(s) of failure	S	Potential cause(s) of failure	O	Current process controls	D	RPN	CRIT	Recommended action(s)	Responsibility and target completion date	Action taken	Action results S	O	D	RPN	CRIT
Dispense amount of cash requested by customer	Does not dispense cash	Customer very dissatisfied	8	Out of cash	5	Internal low-cash alert	5	200	40								
		Incorrect entry to demand deposit system		Machine jams	3	Internal jam alert	10	240	24								
		Discrepancy in cash balancing		Power failure during transaction	2	None	10	160	16								
	Dispenses too much cash	Bank loses money	6	Bills stuck together	2	Loading procedure (riffle ends of stack)	7	84	12								
		Discrepancy in cash balancing		Denominations in wrong trays	3	Two-person visual verification	4	72	18								
	Takes too long to dispense cash	Customer somewhat annoyed	3	Heavy computer network traffic	7	None	10	210	21								
				Power interruption during transaction	2	None	10	60	6								

Figure 9.8 An example of FMEA.

1. Define the process to be diagrammed. Write its title at the top of the work surface.

2. Discuss and decide on the boundaries of your process: Where or when does the process start? Where or when does it end? Discuss and decide on the level of detail to be included in the diagram.

3. Brainstorm the activities that take place. Write each on a card or sticky note. Sequence is not important at this point, although thinking in sequence may help people remember all the steps.

4. Arrange the activities in proper sequence.

5. When all activities are included and everyone agrees that the sequence is correct, draw arrows to show the flow of the process.

6. Review the flowchart with others involved in the process (workers, supervisors, suppliers, customers) to see if they agree that the process is drawn accurately.[3]

Figures 9.9 and 9.10 depict typical flowchart examples.

FOCUS GROUPS

Focus groups are an attempt to improve the depth and accuracy of customer responses. Focus groups generally provide more accurate answers with more depth than other techniques. However, the sample is often nonrandom and too small. As statisticians say, "The plural of *anecdote* is not *data*." Understanding the limitations of focus groups, they can still be effective in gaining knowledge related to product quality and perceptions of the organization's ability to satisfy its customers (internal and external). Prior to conducting focus group sessions, planning for the sessions must occur. Focus group planning includes:

- Identifying the goals of the session

- Developing actual or prototype products

- Determining how the sessions will be conducted: brainstorming, survey, cause-and-effect (or question–response)

Once the planning is completed, the focus groups can be identified, the focus group sessions conducted, the data collected, and the data analyzed to determine how the process or product should be adjusted to better meet the expectations

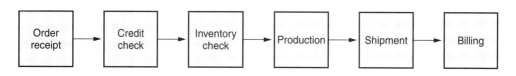

Figure 9.9   High-level flowchart for an order-filling process.
Source: N. R. Tague, *The Quality Toolbox*, 2nd ed. (Milwaukee: ASQ Quality Press, 2005): 257.

Part II

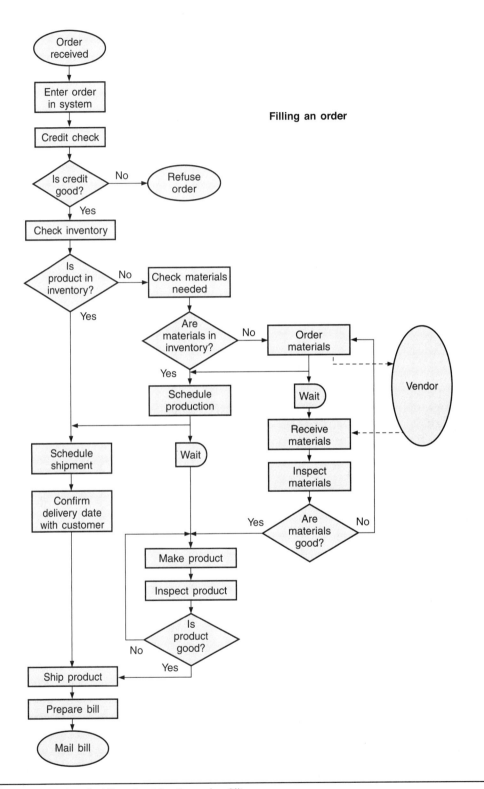

Figure 9.10   Detailed flowchart for the order-filling process.
Source: N. R. Tague, *The Quality Toolbox,* 2nd ed. (Milwaukee: ASQ Quality Press, 2005): 261.

Future state: number of errors is less than three per hundred documents.	
Driving forces	**Restraining forces**
Pressure from customer A	Ambient noise level
Group incentive system	Weak spell-checker
Operator enthusiasm	Lack of training
Use of control charts	Inertia
Supportive management	Poor input data

Figure 9.11   Example of force-field analysis.

	Date											
	July				August				September			
Objective	7	14	21	28	4	11	18	25	1	8	15	22
A. Construct survey questionnaire	▨											
C. Print and mail questionnaire			▨									
B. Make software decision: buy/build	▨											
D. Buy/build software			▨▨									
E. Test software						▨▨						
F. Enter data into database						▨▨						
G. Use software to analyze results								▨▨				
H. Interpret results and write report									▨▨▨			

Figure 9.12   Gantt chart example.

of the targeted groups. Focus group techniques are usually limited to consumer product–related activities.

FORCE-FIELD ANALYSIS

Force-field analysis is illustrated in Figure 9.11. A goal or objective is first listed as the future or desired state. Then two columns are produced from brainstorming or a similar technique to determine the driving and restraining forces on achieving the future or desired state. The "driving forces" column lists the things that help make the future state occur while the items in the "restraining forces" column are those that prevent the future state from occurring. The team then ranks the two lists using nominal group technique (NGT) or a similar tool. The team consensus provides guidance on how to proceed. It is often more useful to reduce or remove restraining forces than to focus entirely on driving forces.

GANTT CHART

A Gantt chart, as shown in Figure 9.12, is used to graphically display a project's key activities and the duration associated with those activities. These are then overlaid on a calendar to show when the activities occur. In addition to showing the key activities, the Gantt chart also shows the task milestones and the task relationships between predecessor and successor tasks. This provides a visual representation and allows for quick identification of the impact on schedule (that is, delay or pull-in to tasks or the entire project) based on the delay or pull-in of a single task. The Gantt chart provides a quick look at the project planned activities and schedule, allows for assessment of key resources against the plan, and also allows for the assessment of the project's performance against the plan.

GRAPHICAL CHARTS, CONTROL CHARTS, AND OTHER STATISTICAL TOOLS

This information on control charts is provided as a quick overview; details are available in Parts III and V of this handbook.

A control chart is a graph used to study how a process changes over time. Comparing current data to historical control limits leads to conclusions about whether the process variation is consistent (in control) or is unpredictable (out of control—affected by special causes of variation).

Different types of control charts can be used, depending on the type of data. The two broadest groupings are for variable data and attribute data.

- *Variable data* are measured on a continuous scale. For example: time, weight, distance, or temperature can be measured in fractions or decimals. The possibility of measuring to greater precision defines variable data.

[handwritten margin note: continuous]

- *Attribute data* are counted and can not have fractions or decimals. Attribute data are used when you are determining only the presence or absence of something: success or failure, accept or reject, correct or not correct. For example, a report can have four errors or five errors, but it cannot have four and a half errors.

[handwritten margin note: discrete]

Variables Charts

- $\bar{X}$ and R chart (also called averages and range chart)

- $\bar{X}$ and s chart

- Chart of individuals (also called X chart, $\bar{X}$ and R chart, *IX-MR* chart, *XmR* chart, moving range chart)

- Moving average–moving range chart (also called *MA–MR* chart)

- Target charts (also called difference charts, deviation charts, and nominal charts)

- CUSUM (also called cumulative sum chart)

- EWMA (also called exponentially weighted moving average chart)

- Multivariate chart (also called hotelling T2)

Attributes Charts

- *p* chart (also called proportion chart)
- *np* chart
- *c* chart (also called count chart)
- *u* chart
- *D* chart (weighted deficiencies)
- *U* chart (weighted deficiencies)

Charts for Other Kind of Data

- Short-run charts (also called stabilized charts or *Z* charts)
- Group charts (also called multiple characteristic charts)
- Paynter charts[4]

More details are available in Part III of this handbook.

Graphical tools are an effective way to understand and convey customer feedback, process performance, defect data, and so on. The examples shown in Figure 9.13 are less complex graphical data representations.

The use of statistical tools to analyze data is explained in detail in other chapters in this book. One cautionary note: analysis of customer data almost always falls in the general category of "observational studies," which means that high

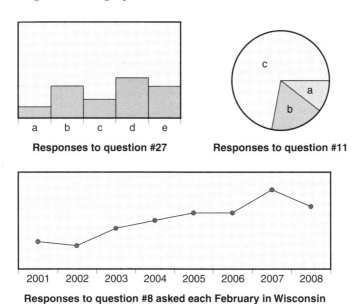

Responses to question #27

Responses to question #11

Responses to question #8 asked each February in Wisconsin

Figure 9.13   Graphical representations of question responses.

correlation between variables doesn't imply cause-and-effect relationships. For example, suppose a survey shows a correlation coefficient of $r = 0.83$ between the number of television advertisements watched and the amount of money spent on product W. The analyst is not statistically justified in concluding that watching the ad causes an increase in the amount spent on the product.

It is useful to compare internal predictive metrics with customer feedback data. This helps shape internal prediction methods and procedures.

INTERRELATIONSHIP DIGRAPHS

Interrelationship digraphs are used to identify cause-and-effect relationships. A typical application would begin with the listing of a half dozen to a dozen concerns one to a note sheet and arranged in no particular order around the perimeter of a flip-chart or a whiteboard. For each pair of concerns draw an arrow from the one that is most influential on the other. Draw no arrow if there is no influential relationship. This is most easily accomplished by starting at the twelve o'clock position and comparing the item to the next item in a clockwise direc-

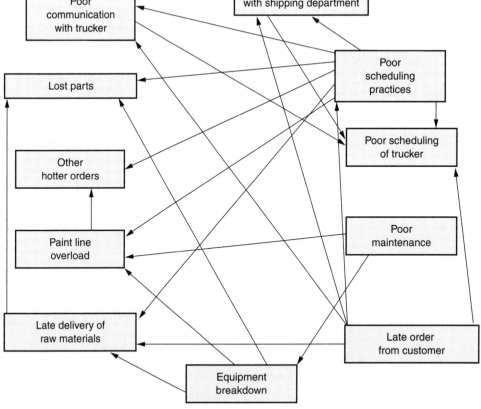

Figure 9.14   Example interrelationship digraph.

tion. Draw the appropriate arrow (or no arrow). Then compare the twelve o'clock note with the next note, again moving clockwise. After the twelve o'clock note has been compared to all other notes, begin with the note clockwise from the twelve o'clock note and compare it to all other notes that it has not been compared to. Repeat this process until all pairs of notes have been compared. In each case ask, "Does A influence B more than B influences A?" Revise this diagram as necessary using additional information or data if needed. An example of an interrelationship digraph at this stage is shown in Figure 9.14. The next step is to find the note that has the most outgoing arrows. This note is called the driver. In the example shown in Figure 9.14 "poor scheduling practices" is the driver. The driver, or drivers if there is a tie or near tie, is often a key cause of the problem. The note with the greatest number of incoming arrows, "poor scheduling of trucker" in the example, is called the outcome and can often be used as a source of a metric for determining project success

INTERVIEWS

Interviews by phone or in person permit a higher response rate than written surveys. Although interviews take more effort, the effort is usually returned with more accurate data gathered and additional information provided by the interviewee that may not be captured in written (hard copy or electronic) surveys. A skillful interviewer can record customer feelings that written surveys would not detect by noting interviewee emotions, body language, other nonverbal clues, and so on.

		Unit								
		1	2	3	4	5	6	7	8	9
Objectives	Review basics	⊙		⊙	O			Δ		
	Math skills	O	Δ	⊙			⊙	O		
	Communication skills						O		Δ	
	Attitude/motivation								Δ	
	Sketching			⊙			O			
	Ohm's law				⊙	O	Δ			
	Kirkoff's law					⊙	O			
	Thevinev's law						Δ		O	
	Heisenberg's uncertainty principle									

⊙ = strong relationship   O = moderate relationship   Δ = weak relationship

Conclusions: Thevinev's law and communication skills covered only weakly
Attitude/motivation barely covered
Heisenberg's uncertainty principle not covered
Unit 2 contributes very little toward objectives
Unit 9 contributes nothing toward objectives

Figure 9.15   Example matrix diagram.

MATRIX DIAGRAM

A matrix diagram is typically used to discover and illustrate relationships between two groups of items. In Figure 9.15 the two groups are the units of a training course and the objectives of the course. The items in one group are listed across the top of the chart and the items in the other group are listed down one side. The team examines each square in the matrix and enters one of three symbols or leaves it blank depending on the relationship between the items in the row and column represented by the square. The most conventional symbols are shown in the example although letters and numbers are sometimes used. The team then examines the completed matrix and discusses possible conclusions.

MULTIVOTING

As discussed in Chapter 8, multivoting complements the nominal group technique (NGT). Even though this tool is typically used in combination with NGT, it can be used independently (for example, to prioritize brainstorming results). Please reference Chapter 8 for details on multivoting.

NOMINAL GROUP TECHNIQUE

This is also a type of brainstorming but with limited team vocal interaction. The tool is hence named "nominal" group technique (NGT). This technique has its application when some group members are much more vocal then others, to encourage equal participation from all members, or with controversial or sensitive topics, and so on. This technique helps to alleviate peer pressure and reduces the impact of such pressure on the generation of ideas.

Similarly to brainstorming, the facilitator explains the rules. The team leader presents the topic to the assembled members. The team is given a good 10 to 15 minutes so that they can silently sit, think, and generate ideas.

No verbal interactions are allowed during the session. The members' ideas are collected and posted in a space where all can read them. The members may also read the ideas aloud one by one in a round-robin format. At this stage no judgment or criticism is passed. The ideas are simply written down. The members are allowed to expand on existing ideas, provide clarity, and eliminate redundancy during the consolidation. For a controversial or sensitive subject the team leader may opt to collect the ideas and write them down on the board, maintaining anonymity of the contributors.

PRIORITIZATION MATRIX

A prioritization matrix is used to aid in deciding among options. In the example shown in Figure 9.16 the options are four different software packages, A, B, C, and D. The team determines by consensus the criteria against which the options will be measured (for example, requirements document) and the relative importance of each of the criteria items. In the example, the criteria and their relative importance are compatibility (.25), cost (.30), ease of use (.40), and training time (.05).

Step1: Each option is ranked against the criteria with the **desirable numbers being larger. (For cost, smaller the desireable).**

Determine the most suitable software package

		Lowest is most desirable.	Criteria		
		Compatibility	Cost	Ease of use	Training time	Total
Options	Package A	1.00	0.45	1.20	0.15	2.80
	Package B	0.25	1.20	0.80	0.05	2.30
	Package C	0.75	0.45	1.60	0.20	3.00
	Package D	0.50	0.90	0.40	0.10	1.90

Step2: Assign ranking, 4 to 1, 4 being most desirable, 1 least desirable. Apply averages for tie. Package A and C tied for lowest cost.

Determine the most suitable software package

		Criteria				
		Compatibility	Cost	Ease of use	Training time	Total
Options	Package A	4	3.5	3	3	
	Package B	1	1	2	1	
	Package C	3	3.5	4	4	
	Package D	2	2	1	2	

Step3: Assign Weights based on relative importance. Multiply each of the option values by criteria weights at the top of the column and calculate row totals.

Determine the most suitable software package

		Criteria				
		Compatibility (0.25)	Cost (0.3)	Ease of use (0.40)	Training time (0.05)	Total
Options	Package A	1.00	1.05	1.20	0.15	3.40
	Package B	0.25	0.30	0.80	0.05	1.40
	Package C	0.75	1.05	1.60	0.20	3.60
	Package D	0.50	0.60	0.40	0.10	1.60

Step4: Option with the highest total is the one most favored by the prioritization matrix. (Highlighted)

Figure 9.16 Prioritization matrix example.

Each option is ranked against the criteria with the desirable numbers being larger. In the example, since there are four options, the highest-ranking option would be assigned a value of four, the second place item would be assigned a three, and so on. Assigning each option the average values for the two places designates a tie. For example, if two options are tied for third place, the two places are third and fourth, which have values of 2 and 1 respectively, so each of the options would receive a value of 1.5. In the example in Figure 9.16, option A and C are the most desirable (Lowest) cost so it is assigned 3.5 both (A and C are tied). The package withthe next lowest cost is option D and is assigned 3. Option B has the highest cost and is assigned 1.

Once the values are assigned, the next step is to multiply each of the option values by the criteria weights at the top of the column and calculate the row totals. The option with the highest total is the one most favored by the prioritization matrix.

PROBLEM SOLVING

Some of the most successful attempts to solve problems have been through the use of a model or tools that outline the steps that should be followed in investigating, containing issues, and fixing the problems so that they will not return. Unfortunately, many of us have seen situations where someone or even a group or team will fix a problem, only for the same issue to crop up again in a week, month, or year. The question is, how do we permanently solve problems?

One common approach to problem solving is called the *eight discipline approach* (8D). The steps usually associated with this process are:

1. *Use a team approach.* Organize a small group (note we did not say team) of people with the process/product knowledge, allocated line authority, and skill in the required technical disciplines to solve the problem and implement corrective actions. The group must have a designated champion.

2. *Describe the problem.* Specify the internal/external customer problem by identifying the quantifiable terms for who, what, when, where, why, how, and how many (5W2H) for the problem. Use such methods as SIPOC, brainstorming, flowcharts, and any other methods that the group feels are appropriate.

3. *Start and check interim (containment) actions.* Define and implement containment actions to isolate the effect or problem from the current problem. Verify the effectiveness of this containment action to ensure that the internal or external customer does not see further problems.

4. *Define and check root causes.* Identify all potential causes that could explain why the problem occurred (a cause-and-effect chart is useful here). Isolate and verify the root cause by testing each potential cause (sampling is used here) against the problem description and test data (individual test or a design of experiments if needed). Identify alternative corrective actions to eliminate root causes using a process behavior chart to ensure that the process remains stable.

5. *Check corrective action.* Through a sampling plan, quantitatively confirm that the selected corrective actions will resolve the problem for the customer, and will not cause undesirable issues (FMEA and control plans).

6. *Start permanent corrective action.* Once it is verified that corrective action is working, update all procedures and processes to incorporate the new process. This should include training where appropriate.

7. *Stop future problems.* Modify the management systems, operating systems, preventive maintenance, practices and procedures, and documentation to prevent recurrence of this and all similar problems. Note: if similar processes are found in the shop, look closely at them also to ensure that they do not develop the same issue.

8. *Congratulate your team.* Improvements happen only because many people work together. Everyone deserves credit.[5]

Besides the method described above, your external customers may have a prescribed problem-solving methodology that they want the shop to use. Other methods that can be used in problem solving are the plan–do–study–act (PDSA) cycle or, although not recommended, the scientific method that you probably learned in high school.

PROCESS DECISION PROGRAM CHART

The process decision program chart (PDPC) is a tree diagram that is used to illustrate anticipated problems and list possible solutions. It may be used as a dynamic document to be updated as the project proceeds. An example PDPC is shown in Figure 9.17.

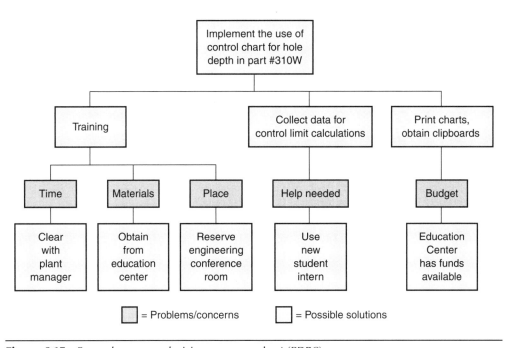

Figure 9.17   Example process decision program chart (PDPC).

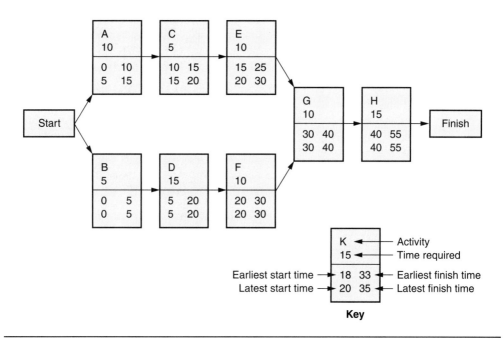

Figure 9.18 PERT/critical path chart example.

PROJECT EVALUATION AND REVIEW TECHNIQUE AND CRITICAL PATH METHOD

The project evaluation and review technique (PERT) and critical path method (CPM) have become essentially merged in current software packages. The critical path is the path from start to finish that requires the most time. In Figure 9.18 there are just two paths: ACEGH and BDFGH. Path ACEGH requires 10 + 5 + 10 + 10 + 15 = 50 days and path BDFGH requires 5 + 15 + 10 + 10 + 15 = 55 days. Therefore BDFGH is the critical path. Software packages are available to identify and calculate the critical path for projects with multiple paths. If activities on the critical path are delayed, the entire project will be delayed. The critical path time is the time required to complete the project. The only way to complete the project in less time is to decrease the time for at least one of the activities. This is usually accomplished by putting more resources into one or more activities on the critical path. This is sometimes referred to as "crashing" the project.

QUALITY FUNCTION DEPLOYMENT

Quality function deployment (QFD), also known as the *house of quality*, organizes customer requirements and desires (wants) and allows them to be traced to specifications. By providing a clear link from the *voice of the customer* (VOC), there is increased assurance that fulfilling the linked specifications will result in customer satisfaction.

QFD provides a process for planning new or redesigned products and services, reflecting the preferences of the voice of the customer. The QFD process requires that a team discover the needs and desires of their customer and study the organization's response to these needs and desires. The QFD matrix aids in illustrating the linkages between the VOC and the resulting technical requirements.

QFD is a powerful planning technique, particularly suited for large-scale products and projects that have complex interactions and diverse components.

Description

The QFD approach can be summarized to the following steps:

1. Plan—determine objectives and data

2. Collect data

3. Analyze and understand data using QFD to generate the technical targets of opportunity for innovation

4. Deploy and apply the information to improve designs and achieve customer value

5. Evaluate and improve the QFD process

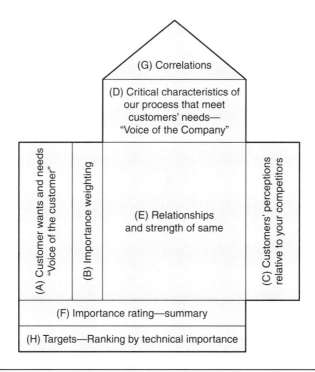

Figure 9.19   QFD matrix elements.

Source: R. T. Westcott, *The Certified Manager of Quality/Organizational Excellence Handbook*, 3rd ed. (Milwaukee: ASQ Quality Press, 2006): 475.

A quality function deployment matrix consists of several parts or elements, as shown in Figure 9.19.

Specific descriptions of the data sources used to populate the QFD include:

- Data for customer wants and needs are obtained from several sources including customer experience, focus groups, surveys, and joint development.

- Wants should be quantified and weighted by importance to prioritize and ensure that the most important criteria are defined.

- Customer perceptions relative to competitors can be obtained through research and actual customer experience or by neutral agents with an independent perspective.

- Critical process characteristics describe how things are done and should specify design requirements, operational factors, and human factors.

Relationships are tracked and the key links are determined to find out which customer wants are correlated with a specific design approach. These relationships are ranked to determine the targets of opportunity by technical importance, and areas of focus for improvement or innovation.

The completed matrix, as depicted in Figure 9.20, can provide a database for product development, serve as a basis for planning product and/or process improvements, and suggest opportunities for new or revised product and/or process introductions.

QFD can be applied to other processes to improve quality. In a staged environment, the outcomes of one stage are the inputs of the succeeding stages, as shown in Figure 9.21. QFD is a useful technique to entrench the customer requirements into the earliest stages and allow the captured information to cascade to subsequent stages to ensure that there are no gaps to customer satisfaction.

Application

QFD is applied to improve customer satisfaction at acceptable cost. The basic relationship is captured in the input–output matrix (see Figure 9.22). "Whats" can be expressed as required (must have), necessary (expected to have), and optional (nice to have). "Hows" refer to the technical details, and should be defined to address—at minimum—the specific requirements of the customer.

Quality function deployment supports the adoption of customer value within the product. Table 9.2 shows product and service value characteristics.

QFD supports customer-driven quality and the total customer experience by providing an objective and traceable matrix linking customer wants and expectations to technical details and acceptance criteria. This reinforces the robustness of the design, and will more accurately define the terms of product development, delivery, maintenance, and fulfillment.

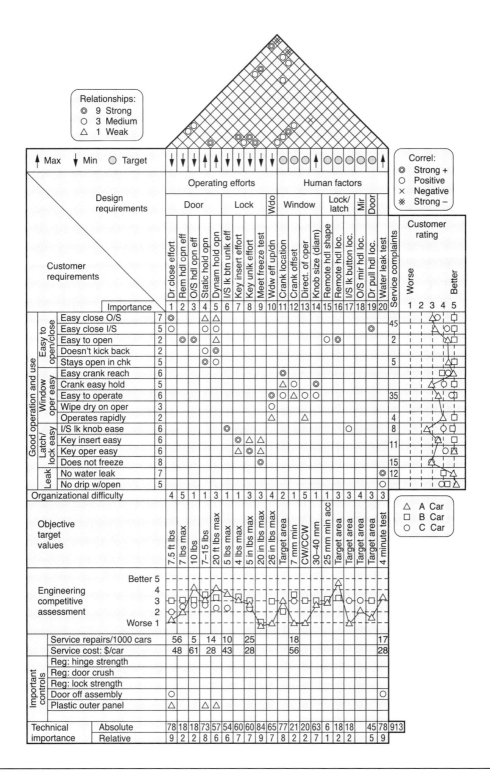

Figure 9.20   Example of a completed QFD matrix.

Source: R. T. Westcott, *The Certified Manager of Quality/Organizational Excellence Handbook,* 3rd ed. (Milwaukee: ASQ Quality Press, 2006): 477.

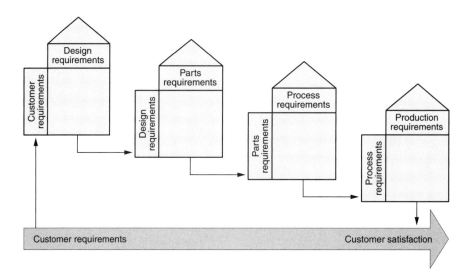

Figure 9.21 QFD stage flow and relationships.

Source: R. T. Westcott, *The Certified Manager of Quality/Organizational Excellence Handbook,* 3rd ed. (Milwaukee: ASQ Quality Press, 2006): 478.

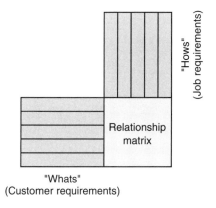

Figure 9.22 QFD input–output matrix.

Source: R. W. Berger et al., *The Certified Quality Engineer Handbook,* 2nd ed. (Milwaukee: ASQ Quality Press, 2006): 67.

RISK PRIORITY NUMBER/MATRIX

The risk priority number (RPN) is calculated from FMEA data, specifically the severity rating (S), occurrence rating (O), and detection rating (D). RPN = S × O × D. The RPN is used to help determine the potentially highest-risk items to aid a project team in prioritizing the items to work on most aggressively.

Table 9.2   QFD value characteristics.

Product value characteristics	Service value characteristics
Performance	Responsiveness
Benefit relative to cost	Reliability
Durability	Competence
Safety	Access
Serviceability	Communication
Usability/ease of use	Credibility/image
Simplicity of design	Confidentiality/security
Functionality	Understanding the customer
Availability	Accuracy/completeness
Performance	Timeliness

Part II

RPN is covered in more detail in the FMEA section of this chapter and Part III of this handbook.

Key Point: The RPN is a factor of the process, not some external goal or prescribed numeral listing. The intent of the RPN is to use the full range (typically: $10 \times 10 \times 10 = 1000$) to distinguish the most important risks for the team to work on!

SAMPLING PLAN

Dr. Joseph Juran said that 100 percent inspection is only 80 percent effective: "Collectively, these inspector errors result in a performance of about 80 percent accuracy."[6] Whenever we try to inspect large quantities, any number of things can happen to distract us from the task at hand or cause problems in correctly identifying the items to be addressed. One solution to this is to take samples (preferably randomly) from the population in question to get an idea of what the population contains.

Usually, the quality organization will assist in developing a sampling plan for inspecting products. These plans take into account the various factors, for example, line speed, technology available, number of personnel available, customer expectations, and so on, to establish a sampling plan to ensure that the process, product, and customer requirements are met.

Randomness in sampling is when every part that could be measured has an equal chance or probability of actually being selected by the operator. Instead of saying "we only check the first parts after setup," we might say that we will check the first piece and then every x (specified number) part after that. Or we could say that once each hour we will check a certain number of parts. Then the operator must pick a random time each hour that fits into the production cycle to check the parts (versus doing it only at 15 minutes past each hour).

A check sheet to demonstrate that the checks were actually done and to simplify the collecting of the data will usually accompany sampling plans. An operator using a check sheet can quickly see if they are following the sample plan and when the next part(s) should be evaluated.

Sampling is a useful tool, and the sampling plan gives us a guide as to how and when we are to do the sampling. The sampling plan should be designed ahead of actual use and be available for inspection itself at any time.

SUPPLIER–INPUTS–PROCESS–OUTPUTS–CUSTOMERS (SIPOC) DIAGRAM

To develop a supplier–inputs–process–outputs–customer (SIPOC) diagram, start by defining the process and its boundaries (center of the diagram shown in Figure 9.23). Next, identify the outputs of the process, including data, services, products, information, records, and so on. For each identified output, identify all of the associated inputs. Then, move on to the internal and external customers—those that receive the identified outputs. Finally, move back to the supplier column to identify the internal and external suppliers for each identified input. Although it may seem odd to bounce back and forth from side to side on the chart, this is done to help stimulate thinking. For example, new outputs are often identified when discussing inputs or customers.

External suppliers to a process are those outside the enterprise that provide process inputs including materials, purchased parts, contracted services, electrical power, and so on. Internal suppliers to a process are departments or processes inside the enterprise that provide process inputs. Similarly, a process's external customers are those outside the enterprise who receive process outputs while internal customers are those inside the enterprise who receive process outputs.

Suppliers of either type are responsible for meeting the requirements of their customers. Customers of either type are responsible for communicating their requirements to their suppliers.

TREE DIAGRAMS

Tree diagrams help to break a general topic into a number of activities that contribute to it. This is accomplished through a series of steps, each one digging deeper into detail than the previous one. A note listing the general topic is posted at the top of a flip-chart or whiteboard. Have the team suggest two to five slightly more specific topics that contribute to the general topic and write these on individual notes and post them in a horizontal row beneath the original general topic. For each of these new topics, have the team suggest two to five even more specific topics and post these on the next level down. Continue each branch of the tree as far as seems practical. Draw appropriate connecting lines. Review the tree by making sure that each item actually contributes to the item above it. The resulting diagram should provide specific activities that, when they occur, contribute to the general topic. An example is shown in Figure 9.24.

Suppliers	Inputs	Process	Outputs	Customers
Providers of the required inputs/resources to ensure that the process executes as planned.	Resources required by the process to obtain the intended output.	Top-level description of activity.	Deliverables from the process. Note: deliverables can be hardware, software, systems, services, data, information, and so on.	Any organization that receives an output or deliverable from the process. Note: can also capture systems/databases that receive outputs, information, data, and so on.
		Requirements		**Requirements**
Development team	S/W size estimating guide	S/W size estimation methods/formulas		
External customer/ program manager	System specifications • Prime item development specification • System requirements doc • And so on	Total count of requirements allocated to S/W Preferred soft copy with requirements identified ("shall")	• New SLOC • Modified SLOC • Reused SLOC • Auto-generated SLOC	SLOC formatted for entry into price estimating software and organizational metrics collection system. — Project/pursuit software lead
S/W development leads of past and current projects	Legacy systems knowledge	Legacy SLOC data from project assessment library and organizational metrics	Basis of estimate (BOE) for quote	Rational for SLOC estimates Information for fact finding — Proposal manager
Organization subject matter experts	Identification of most applicable/similar legacy S/W	Determine scope of similarities (number of requirements new, modified, reused, or deleted)	Legacy code product information	Reused S/W development information • Documentation • Version • Qualification test/results • Standards (498, DO178B, and so on) — Proposal manager

Process flow (center of diagram):

Customer requirements → Identify customer requirements impact to code → Software lines of code (SLOC) estimate

Part II

Figure 9.23 SIPOC diagram with requirements capture.

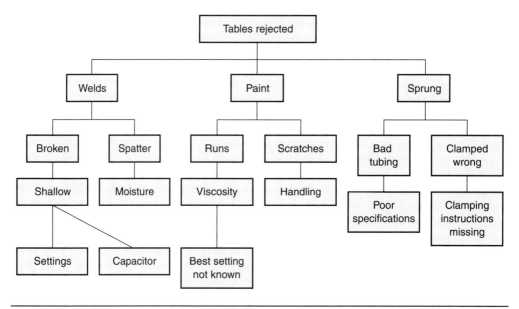

Figure 9.24   This example of a tree diagram is a fault tree (used to study defects and failures).

WRITTEN SURVEYS

Written surveys can be sent to a randomly selected group of customers or potential customers, but getting responses from all those selected almost never occurs. In addition, the accuracy of the responses is questionable. A carefully worded and analyzed survey can, however, shed significant light on customer reactions.

SUMMARY

The *define* phase focuses on determining the scope of the improvement project and the resources and schedule needed to execute the project. There are many tools to aid in the definition and management of the project, including the charter and Gantt chart. The tools and level of detail should be selected based on the size of the project and organization requirements. Additionally, the tools used to scope the problem and define the current state vary in detail, focus, and complexity. During the initial project planning, an initial determination of the tools to be used for the problem/current state definition should be identified, allowing for adjustment as the project matures. The primary goal of the define phase is to ensure that the problem and project are defined to provide focus for the remaining phases—measure, analyze, improve, and control.

Part III
Six Sigma—*Measure*

Part III

Chapter 10

A. Process Analysis and Documentation

1. PROCESS MODELING

Develop and review process maps, written procedures, work instructions, flowcharts, etc. (Analyze)

Body of Knowledge III.A.1

Process Maps and Flowcharts

ISO 9000:2000 defines a process as a set of interrelated or interacting activities that transforms inputs into outputs. A process is easily understood by visually showing the process using common shapes and symbols. This helps to depict processes, both simple and complex, more effectively than through written descriptions. Organizations often send their process information in the form of process map documentation to their suppliers and customers for contractual reasons. Using consistent mapping icons helps different individuals to interpret the maps in the same way. Process mapping is often the first step in improving a process. Risk analysis tools such as failure mode and effects analysis (FMEA) start with process mapping. Value stream mapping, used in lean enterprise projects, is also a type of process mapping but uses different mapping icons.

Flowcharts show each step in a process, decision points, inputs, and outputs. Process maps usually contain additional information about the steps including costs, setup time, cycle time, inventory, types of defects that can occur, probability of defects, and other appropriate information.

Process maps and flowcharts enable a broader perspective of potential problems and opportunities for process improvement. Teams using these tools get a better understanding of individual and group goals.

Figure 10.1 shows some of the most frequently used process mapping symbols. Figure 10.2 gives a basic flowchart example.

There are a number of mapping icons available within software applications such as Microsoft Visio, iGrafx, and All Clear, to a name a few.

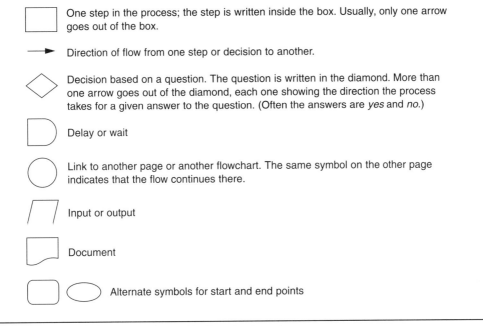

One step in the process; the step is written inside the box. Usually, only one arrow goes out of the box.

Direction of flow from one step or decision to another.

Decision based on a question. The question is written in the diamond. More than one arrow goes out of the diamond, each one showing the direction the process takes for a given answer to the question. (Often the answers are *yes* and *no*.)

Delay or wait

Link to another page or another flowchart. The same symbol on the other page indicates that the flow continues there.

Input or output

Document

Alternate symbols for start and end points

Figure 10.1   Symbols commonly used in flowcharts and process maps.
Source: N. R. Tague, *The Quality Toolbox*, 2nd ed. (Milwaukee: ASQ Quality Press, 2005): 262.

Part III.A.1

Process mapping involving multiple departments or functions is more easily understood using "swim lane" mapping. A swim lane process map is similar to a typical process map except that the process blocks are arranged aligned with the department or functions that perform a given process step.

Let us re-map the previous example using the swim lane flowchart approach. For simplicity we have taken out the decision loops from the previous chart. In a real business scenario, the swim lane flowchart (see Figure 10.3) contains all the components presented in a basic flowchart. It uses the same flowchart symbols and guidelines (Figure 10.1) for creating the chart.

Creating a Flowchart (Process Map or Process Flow Diagram). When creating a flowchart, we are creating a picture of the actual steps in a process or system as it actually operates or is supposed to operate. Given the old adage that a picture is worth a thousand words, this tool allows us to communicate using standard symbols. The flowchart is very useful when looking at a machine or process that we want to improve.

We can follow some basic steps to create the flowchart:

1. Create the boundaries of the process that we intend to flowchart. These might be the inputs and outputs of the process or the suppliers and customers of the process.

2. Determine the various steps in the process. (At this point, we are not worried about sequence, only collecting all of the steps.)

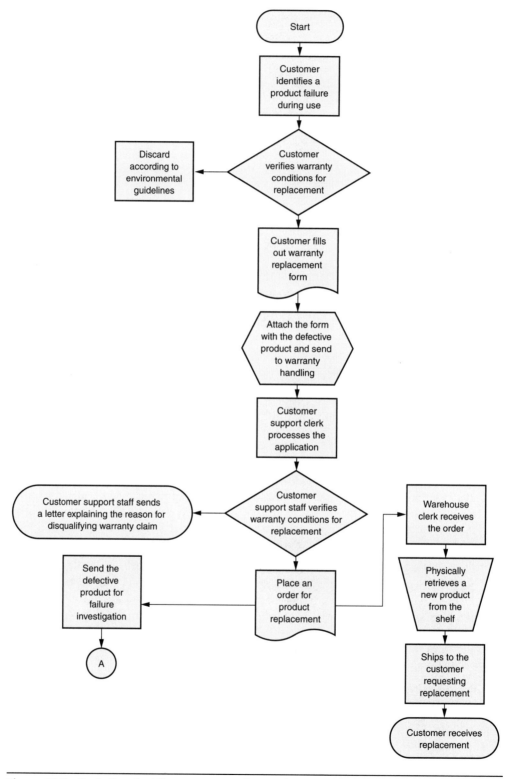

Figure 10.2   Basic flowchart for warranty product replacement.

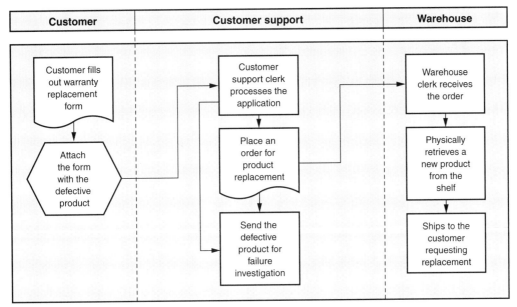

Customer	Customer support	Warehouse

Figure 10.3   Cross-functional or swim lane flowchart.

3. Build the sequence of the process, putting everything into the appropriate order. We have to also make sure we understand that some process steps happen in parallel, and the chart should reflect this accordingly. There are also alternative paths identified in some charts.

4. Draw the flowchart using the appropriate mapping symbols.

5. Verify that the flowchart is complete and appropriate for the given operation. This can be very important if more than one group is working on a similar process. Overlaps or deletions may occur between processes. Hence, this activity is best performed as a team.

Flowcharts are a good analytical tool for monitoring a process over time and also for conducting training of new operators or supervisors. By referencing the flowcharts on a regular basis, we will be able to use them as visual standards to help ensure that things are still running as they are supposed to. Note that if there is a change made to the process, it is important to update the flowchart to reflect the change. Regular audits may be done in a given area for any number of reasons (safety, quality, environmental, and so on) so having the flowcharts readily available helps everyone involved.

Process mapping can help visualize redundancy in the process, non-value-added steps, and unnecessary complexities. Process mapping can be used to identify and eliminate those process issues and improve the process.

For some common mistakes in process mapping, refer to either www.isixsigma.com/library/content/c030217a.asp or the video *Time: The Next Dimension of Quality* (CRM Films).

Key Point: The biggest mistake of all in process mapping is not trying to do one!

Written Procedures and Work Instructions

Due to worldwide demand for ISO 9001 compliance, the necessity for written procedures and work instructions has become very important. Irrespective of whether or not an organization pursues ISO 9001 registration, having written procedures and work instructions for business and manufacturing processes helps drive consistency. A consistent approach to process management helps with yield improvement, root cause analysis, traceability, and so on.

Procedures are written to describe:

- What is done during the process

- Why it is done (business reason)

- Where it is done (location/process step)

- When it is done (trigger)

Work instructions explain two other important aspects:

- Who does what (personnel with specific skill set)

- How it is done (step by step)

There are certain processes for which the ISO standards require a documented procedure and/or work instruction with a "shall" requirement.

Where the organization has no specific internal procedure for a particular activity, and is not required to by a standard, it is acceptable for this activity to be conducted as a "method." A method is an unwritten process but must be followed consistently. In determining which processes should be documented, the organization may wish to consider factors such as:

- Effect on quality

- Risk of customer dissatisfaction

- Statutory and/or regulatory requirements

- Economic risk

- Effectiveness and efficiency

- Competence of personnel

- Complexity of processes

Work instructions can be documented as:

- Written instructions

- Checklists

- Flowcharts

- Photographs

- Drawn pictures

- Videos

- Electronic screen shots

- Electronic software-driven process steps

Examples of procedures and work instructions can be found on the CSSGB handbook share point. (See back cover for Web address.)

2. PROCESS INPUTS AND OUTPUTS

> Identify process input variables and process output variables (SIPOC), and document their relationships through cause and effect diagrams, relational matrices, etc. (Analyze)
>
> **Body of Knowledge III.A.2**

Every process has input variables, output responses, and feedback loops. The feedback is used to improve the process.

Examples of inputs include:

- Needs

- Ideas

- Expectations

- Requirements

- Information

- Data

- Documents

- Resources

Examples of outputs include:

- Designs

- Decisions

- Results

- Measurements

- Products

- Services

- Proposals
- Solutions
- Authorizations
- Action

Identification of inputs and outputs is important before we start with analysis of relationships. Earlier we dealt with process mapping, which provides a clear visual view of inputs to processes, interrelated process steps, and outputs of the process. They provide a detailed view of the process. If we had to create a process map for a value stream or product line or at the organizational level, we might end up creating a complex map with several hundreds of process blocks, decision boxes, inspection points, and storage locations. Hence, it is important to create a high-level process map that can encompass suppliers, inputs, processes, outputs, and customers. This high-level map, called SIPOC for short, provides a bird's-eye view at an enterprise level. It is recommended that in the process portion of a SIPOC chart you limit the number of process blocks to between four and seven high-level process steps to ease the complexity.

A SIPOC chart helps a team to quickly familiarize themselves with the process at an organizational level and visually understand the scope of the project.

The process input variables are measured and variations are controlled so that variations in output response results are correspondingly reduced. The effects of variations of input on output are explored through quality tools like cause-and-effect diagrams, cause-and-effect diagrams with addition of cards (CEDAC), relationship matrices, cause-and-effect matrices, scatter diagrams, and so on.

A thorough understanding of process inputs and outputs and their relationships is a key step in process improvement. The cause-and-effect diagram (also

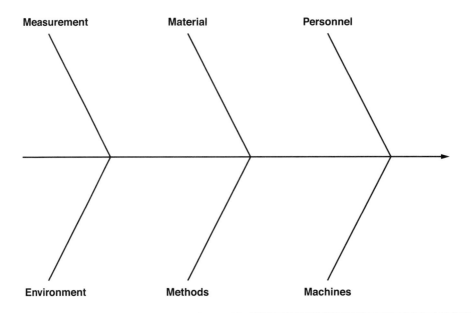

Figure 10.4 Empty cause-and-effect diagram.

called the Ishikawa diagram or fishbone diagram) traditionally divides causes into several generic categories. In use, a large empty diagram is often drawn on a whiteboard or flip-chart as shown in Figure 10.4.

This diagram is then used as a next step to document the final list of causes from the brainstorming session. The participants in the session should include people with a working knowledge of the process as well as those with a theoretical background. For example, suppose a machining operation is producing surface defects. After a few steps of typical brainstorming, the cause-and-effect diagram would look like Figure 10.5.

Brainstorming is a powerful technique for soliciting ideas. Brainstorming intentionally encourages divergent thinking through which, hopefully, all possible causes are identified. This is a team exercise and requires a good facilitator to get the ideas flowing without hesitation. The facilitator's job is to enforce ground rules during brainstorming and encourage ideas. A common tendency among the brainstorming team is to criticize the ideas instantly and discard them during the session. This will discourage team members from contributing for fear of being rejected. There are no bad ideas. At this stage, quantity of ideas is given priority. A typical brainstorming session can generate between 25 to 40 ideas. Once the ideas are collected, the team can review them for redundancy and feasibility and prioritize the ideas. The selected ideas are categorized under personnel–machine–material–methods–measurement–environment. Sometimes the team includes measurement under methods. Cause-and-effect diagrams are flexible to the operation (for example, software development uses people–processes–products–resources–miscellaneous).

It is not uncommon for the team to continue the brainstorming in a second sitting to add more ideas to the existing list. There are other variations of brainstorming, like nominal group technique, idea mapping, and mind mapping,

Part III.A.2

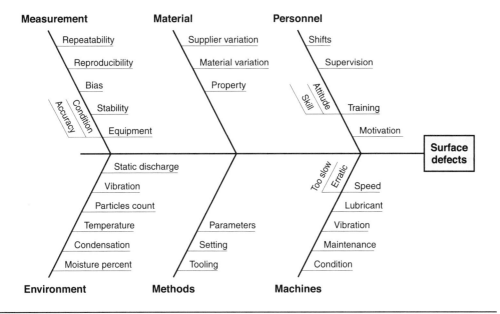

Figure 10.5   Cause-and-effect diagram after a few steps of a brainstorming session.

that are used in different scenarios. CEDAC (cause-and-effect diagram with addition of cards) is an alternative approach tried out by some organizations where the fishbone diagram is displayed on a huge wall or board and employees are encouraged to identify causes by writing on it or using sticky notes. Success of this approach depends on organizational culture and communication.

Once the ideas are collected by performing brainstorming, the next step is to condense the list into those causes most likely to impact the effect. Multivoting and nominal group technique (NGT) are two convergence tools that also rank the priorities. NGT is particularly effective when the issue being discussed is sensitive and emotional or when the team is composed of members from several layers of the organization (rank and file to senior management), and encourages quiet team members to contribute, think without pressure, and so on. Once the ideas are collected, redundant items are removed, and the rest are displayed, the team silently ranks the items. The ranks are tallied and priority items to work on are identified. The prioritization obtained by this approach is not swayed by dominant members (typical in some teams). Hence, this provides better team ownership of the identified items. Multivoting is similar to this approach; 100 points are divided between the choices based on relative importance. Brainstorming, NGT, and multivoting are explained in Chapter 8 under Team Tools. The affinity diagram (explained in more detail in Chapter 9) also complements brainstorming. The affinity diagram organizes a large number of ideas into their natural relationships. When the team is confronted with overwhelming facts and ideas, issues seem too large and complex to grasp, or when group consensus is necessary, the team arranges the ideas in the form of an affinity diagram. This tool is very helpful in analyzing customer qualitative data and feedback.

Convergence can also be accomplished by asking brainstorming participants to collect data on the various causes for a future reporting session. In some cases the data might come directly from the process, for example, "I used two different coolants and found no difference in the surface defects." In other situations the sources of the data might be exterior to the process, for example, "We found that the manufacturer recommends a relative humidity of 55 to 60 percent." As data are collected, the various causes might be prioritized on a Pareto chart as shown in Figure 10.6.

The Pareto chart has been so widely used in recent years that "Pareto" is sometimes used as a verb. It is not uncommon to hear from managers to "Pareto" data for presentation. Some people who are not familiar with Pareto charts interchangeably use a bar graph to "Pareto" data. The true Pareto chart, however, has uniqueness to it. It shows the data arranged in descending order of frequency of occurrence, the "trivial many" data are often pooled together as "miscellaneous" or "other," and the chart contains a cumulative percent line.

These characteristics make the Pareto chart more informative and useful compared to an ordinary bar graph. The Pareto chart helps us to visualize the items charted as "vital few" and "trivial many" using the famous 20th-century Italian economist Vilfredo Pareto's principle of 80:20. Credit has been given to Dr. Joseph Juran for first applying this principle in quality improvement.

In the final assembly inspection example shown in Figure 10.6, the data is presented as a Pareto diagram based on frequency of occurrence. While these

Defect code	Defect description	Occurrences
A	Scratches	15
B	Stains	17
C	Label smudge	12
D	Dent	14
E	Device nonfunctional	5
F	Broken LED	7
G	Missing screw	3

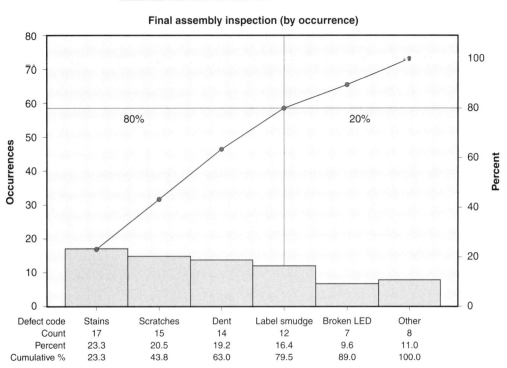

Defect code	Stains	Scratches	Dent	Label smudge	Broken LED	Other
Count	17	15	14	12	7	8
Percent	23.3	20.5	19.2	16.4	9.6	11.0
Cumulative %	23.3	43.8	63.0	79.5	89.0	100.0

Figure 10.6   Pareto chart of final assembly inspection defect codes.

data are important, one might want to put their resources into issues critical to the customer or issues that have more financial impact. So the data are assigned weights based on criticality and multiplied by occurrence, and a Pareto diagram is created based on the weighted score. The table in Figure 10.7 shows the repriori-tized defects based on criticality. Cost of repair or rework can also be used in place of weight, and the Pareto chart can be expressed in dollars.

One important point to remember before performing a Pareto analysis is to make sure that the data are not too specific, with few occurrences for each specific

Defect code	Defect description	Occurrences	Criticality	Weight	Weighted score
A	Scratches	15	Minor	10	150
B	Stains	17	Minor	10	170
C	Label smudge	12	Minor	10	120
D	Dent	14	Major	25	350
E	Device nonfunctional	5	Critical	100	500
F	Broken LED	7	Critical	100	700
G	Missing screw	3	Major	25	75

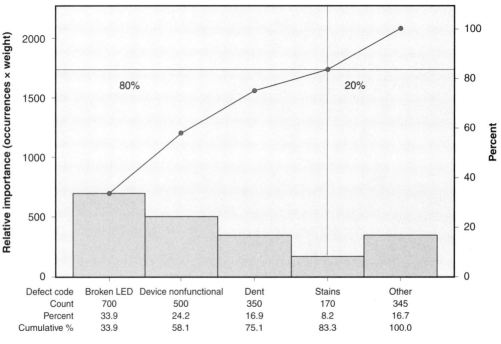

Final assembly inspection (weighted)

Defect code	Broken LED	Device nonfunctional	Dent	Stains	Other
Count	700	500	350	170	345
Percent	33.9	24.2	16.9	8.2	16.7
Cumulative %	33.9	58.1	75.1	83.3	100.0

Figure 10.7   Pareto chart of final assembly inspection defect codes (weighted).

item. This will result in a poor Pareto chart resulting in vital many and trivial few—the exact opposite of the intended purpose (Figure 10.9).

While defect data with specific locations or appearance are important, they may not serve the purpose "as is" in a Pareto diagram. You may have to understand the defect or data and move one level up (that is, generalizing as scratches or dent or nonfunctional device) to be able to best leverage Pareto's strength. This way, they point to systemic issues that require a root cause resolution. Data with specific locations can be better visualized with a *measles chart.*

Figure 10.8   Example of a measles chart (pictorial check sheet).

Measles charts are very useful where the product is large (for example, automobiles) and opportunities for defects are numerous. It is difficult to explain in words the type and location of defects, and a measles chart can also save time at the repair or rework station. We often see an example of a measles chart in the car rental contract form that we sign when we rent a car. It will typically have a picture of a car in front and side views for the rental office to circle preexisting scratches and damages (Figure 10.8).

Depending on the nature of the data and its intended purpose, appropriate quality tools can be selected. Once a team has decided to focus on the specific top items in the Pareto chart, then the team can drill down further using the specific data for those top items. This will help the team to focus on the problem and obviate trying to solve all issues at one time.

The table in Figure 10.9 shows an example of detailed defect data with specifics as to location and appearance. Figure 10.9 also shows a Pareto chart generated from this data that is spread out and *not useful* for analysis.

Relationship Diagram

The relationship diagram is used to display the degree of the relationship between variables, causes and effects, and so on. The degree is often expressed as strong (■), medium (O), and weak (Δ) or numerically, 9 for strong, 3 for medium, and 1 for weak. The total of rows and columns are added and prioritized based on the total score. This analysis is further strengthened by adding a "weights" column and/or row to the matrix. In this case, the overall weighted score is used for prioritization.

The relationships between causes and effects can be shown in a relational matrix as shown in Figure 10.10. In this example causes are listed on the left side of the matrix and various customer issues are placed along the top. For example,

Defect description	Occurrences	Defect description	Occurrences
Broken red LED	4	Label with edges smudge	3
Broken green LED	3	Label with fonts smudge	5
Device with no display	1	Stains on the cover	7
Device with erroneous reading	1	Stains on the display monitor	10
Device with error display	2	Scratches on the body	3
Device with fading display	1	Scratches on the display screen	7
Missing screw on lid	1	Scratches on the name plate	5
Missing screw on the stand	1	Dent on the casing	5
Missing screw on the handle	1	Dent on the front panel	7
Label with logo smudge	4	Dent on the name plate	2

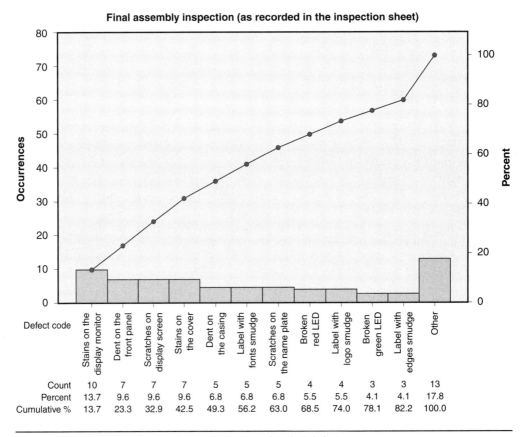

Figure 10.9   Example of a Pareto chart of a too-detailed defect summary.

Relationships Δ = weak O = moderate ⊙ = strong	Pizza not hot enough	Delivered late	Toppings not as per order	Wrong pizza delivered	Burnt crust
Traffic jam	O	⊙			
Oven heater error	O				⊙
Heat insulation quality	⊙				
Difficulty finding address	Δ	⊙			
Did not understand customer accent			Δ	Δ	
Clerical error during order receipt			⊙	⊙	
Order not clearly identified		Δ	⊙	⊙	
Mix-up on the delivery shelf		Δ	O	O	O

Figure 10.10   Relationship diagram.

cause "traffic jam" has a strong relationship to customer issue "delivered late." A team can use brainstorming and/or data collection techniques to determine the list on the left side and the relationship symbols shown in the matrix.

In the example in Figure 10.10, "traffic jam" is an unpredictable scenario that is beyond the caterer's control. However, the pizza caterer could invest in a better quality heat-insulated container, get the address correct, and travel in a path less prone to traffic incidents so that the pizza is still delivered hot.

By taking actions to identify pizza by customer information on the delivery shelf and reduce the clerical errors, the caterer can reduce customer issues like delivering wrong toppings and wrong pizza.

The relationship matrix can also be used to describe the connection between process inputs and desirable process outputs. Refer to the discussion of QFD, page 118, for a more elaborate example.

Chapter 11

B. Probability and Statistics

1. DRAWING VALID STATISTICAL CONCLUSIONS

> Distinguish between enumerative
> (descriptive) and analytical (inferential)
> studies, and distinguish between a
> population parameter and a sample statistic.
> (Apply)
>
> **Body of Knowledge III.B.1**

Does this sound familiar?

- Is process A better than process B? (Manufacturing organization)
- Can we guarantee our customers "15 minutes or free?" (Restaurant)
- Is same-day delivery feasible? (Package forwarding company)
- Does medicine X reduce cholesterol? (Healthcare)
- How many missiles are required to destroy enemy target? (Army)

In our everyday life, we come across many situations that demand decision making. Whether in the office or at home or in society, decisions made can impact the organizational bottom line, personal finances, and the economics of society. Decisions of such criticality can not be made just by "gut feeling." Comparing two scenarios merely by looking at the numbers may be better than gut feeling but still not good enough. The question is "Is the difference statistically significant?" Hence, statistics is used to draw valid conclusions.

In this area of study what we do is to draw representative samples from a homogenous population. By analyzing the samples we draw conclusions about the population. There are two types of studies used for drawing statistical conclusions, namely *descriptive* and *analytical*. (See Table 11.1.)

In a statistical study, the word "population" refers to the collection of all items or data under consideration. A descriptive study typically uses all the data from a population. Significant values from a population are referred to as population

Table 11.1 Descriptive versus analytical statistics.

Descriptive (or enumerative) statistics	Analytical (or inferential) statistics
This consists of a set of collecting, organizing, summarizing, and presenting the data	This consists of a set of making inferences, hypothesis testing, and making predictions
A descriptive study shows various properties of a set of data such as mean, median, mode, dispersion, shape, and so on	Uses data from a sample to make estimates or inferences about the population from which the sample was drawn
Graphical tools include histograms, pie charts, box plots, and others	Uses tools such as hypothesis testing and scatter diagrams to determine the relationships between variables and make predictions using regression equations

Table 11.2 Sample versus population notations.

	Sample	Population
Size	n	N
Mean	$\bar{x}$	μ
Standard deviation	s	σ

Part III.B.2

parameters. Examples of population parameters are *population mean* and *population standard deviation*. A sample is a subset of the population. Samples are selected randomly so that they represent the population from which they are drawn.

It is traditional to denote sample statistics using Latin letters and population parameters using Greek letters. An exception is made for the size of the set under consideration. The symbols shown in Table 11.2 are the most commonly used in textbooks.

The Greek letter μ is pronounced "mew." The Greek letter σ is pronounced "sigma." This is a lower-case sigma. The capital sigma, Σ, is used to designate summation in formulas.

2. CENTRAL LIMIT THEOREM AND SAMPLING DISTRIBUTION OF THE MEAN

> Define the central limit theorem and describe its significance in the application of inferential statistics for confidence intervals, control charts, etc. (Apply)
>
> **Body of Knowledge III.B.2**

Key Point: The central limit theorem (CLT) is an important principle used in statistical process control.

Central Limit Theorem

The central limit theorem is the foundation for several statistical procedures. In a nutshell, the distribution of averages tends to be normal, even when the distribution from which the average data are computed is from nonnormal distributions.

Mathematically, if a random variable X has a mean μ and variance σ^2, as the sample size n increases, the sample mean $\bar{x}$ approaches a normal distribution with mean μ and variance $\sigma_{\bar{x}}^2$:

$$\sigma_{\bar{x}}^2 = \frac{\sigma_x^2}{n} \qquad \text{(See number 2 below)}$$

$$\sigma_{\bar{x}} = \frac{\sigma_x}{\sqrt{n}}$$

The central limit theorem consists of three statements:

1. The mean of the sampling distribution of means is equal to the mean of the population from which the samples were drawn.

2. The variance of the sampling distribution of means is equal to the variance of the population from which the samples were drawn divided by the size of the samples.

3. If the original population is distributed normally (that is, it is bell shaped), the sampling distribution of means will also be normal. If the original population is not normally distributed, the sampling distribution of means will increasingly approximate a normal distribution as sample size increases (that is, when increasingly large samples are drawn). Weirder populations will require larger sample sizes for the sampling distribution of the mean to be nearly normal. Statisticians usually consider a sample size of 30 or more to be sufficiently large.[1] See Figure 11.1.

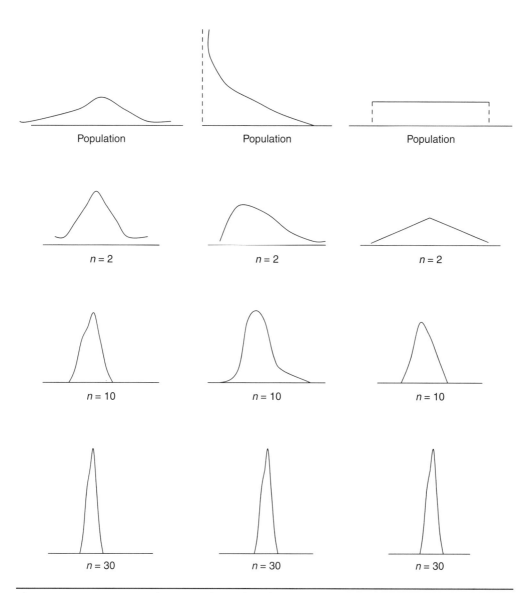

Figure 11.1   Various populations and sampling distributions of the mean for selected sample sizes.

Source: D. W. Benbow and T. M. Kubiak, *The Certified Six Sigma Black Belt Handbook* (Milwaukee: ASQ Quality Press, 2005): 58.

Part III.B.2

The *standard error of the mean* is expressed as:

$$\frac{\sigma_x}{\sqrt{n}}$$

It is used extensively to calculate the margin of error, which is used to calculate confidence intervals.

- The *sampling distribution of the mean* roughly follows a *normal* distribution

- 95 percent of the time, an individual sample mean lies within two (actually 1.96) standard deviations of the mean:

$$pr\left[\left(\bar{x} - 1.96\frac{\sigma}{\sqrt{n}}\right) \le \mu \le \left(\bar{x} + 1.96\frac{\sigma}{\sqrt{n}}\right)\right] = 0.95$$

Or, 95 percent of the time the true mean should lie within $\pm 1.96(\sigma/\sqrt{n})$ of the sample mean:

$$pr\left[\left(\bar{x} - z_\alpha\frac{\sigma}{\sqrt{n}}\right) \le \mu \le \left(\bar{x} + z_\alpha\frac{\sigma}{\sqrt{n}}\right)\right] = 1 - \alpha$$

where

$$\frac{\sigma}{\sqrt{n}}$$

is standard error and

$$z_\alpha\frac{\sigma}{\sqrt{n}}$$

is margin of error.

In the real world, not all processes are normally distributed. By applying the central limit theorem when taking measurement samples, the status of the process can be monitored by averaging the measurement values in subgroups, for example in SPC control charts. Since control charts like $\bar{X}$ and R charts and $\bar{X}$ and s charts are plotted with averages of the individual readings, the charts are robust to departures from normality.

Exercise Using the Central Limit Theorem. Historical standard deviation of a chemical filling process σ is 0.012 milligram. Estimate the sample standard deviation for a sample size of 16 fillings.

$$\sigma_{\bar{x}} = \frac{\sigma_x}{\sqrt{n}} = \frac{0.012}{\sqrt{16}} = 0.003 \text{ milligrams}$$

Calculate the 95 percent confidence interval for the mean if the process average is 10 milligrams.

$$= 10 \pm 1.96\left(\sigma / \sqrt{n}\right) = 10 \pm 1.96(0.003) = 10 \pm 0.0059$$
$$= 9.9941 \text{ to } 10.0059 \text{ milligrams}$$

3. BASIC PROBABILITY CONCEPTS

Describe and apply concepts such as
independence, mutually exclusive,
multiplication rules, etc. (Apply)

Body of Knowledge III.B.3

SUMMARY OF KEY PROBABILITY RULES

For events A and B:

Special addition rule: P(A or B) = P(A) + P(B)　　[Use only if A and B are mutually exclusive]

General addition rule: P(A or B) = P(A) + P(B) – P(A & B)　　[Always true]

Special multiplication rule: P(A & B) = P(A) × P(B)　　[Use only if A and B are independent]

General multiplication rule: P(A & B) = P(A) × P(B|A)　　[Always true]

Conditional probability: P(B|A) = P(A & B) ÷ P(A)

Mutually exclusive (or disjoint):

1. A and B are mutually exclusive if they can't occur simultaneously

2. A and B are mutually exclusive if P(A & B) = 0

3. A and B are mutually exclusive if P(A or B) = P(A) + P(B)

Independence:

1. A and B are independent events if the occurrence of one does not change the probability that the other occurs

2. A and B are independent events if P(B|A) = P(B)

3. A and B are independent events if P(A & B) = P(A) × P(B)

Part III.B.3

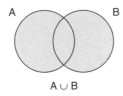 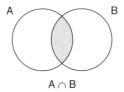

A ∪ B   A ∩ B

Figure 11.2   Venn diagram.

Probability is probably the word most often used when people expect something to happen based on data or historical knowledge or experience.

"It is probably going to rain today."

"The flight is probably going to be late."

Hence, probability is closely attached to an event. Saying "it is not going to rain today" is probability 0 while "It will rain today" with complete certainty is probability of 1. In real life we can provide a complete certainty to events only very rarely. Most of the time the probability of an event happening is between 0 and 1.

The sum of the probabilities of all possible outcomes of an event is 1.

The probability that a particular event will occur is a number between 0 and 1 inclusive. For example, if an urn containing 100 marbles has five red marbles, we would say the probability of randomly drawing a red marble is .05 or 5 percent. Symbolically this is written P (Red) = .05.

The word "random" implies that each marble has an equal chance of being drawn. If the urn had no red marbles, the probability would be 0 or zero percent. If the urn had all red marbles, the probability would be 1 or 100 percent.

Simple Events Probability

Probability of getting a head or tail in a fair coin = 1/2

Probability of getting 2 in a single toss of a die = 1/6

Compound Events Probability

Compound events are formed by two or more events.

Compound events can be better explained by the concept of the Venn diagram. See Figure 11.2.

Relations Between Events

Complementation Rule. The probability that event A will not occur is 1 − (the probability that A does occur). Stated symbolically, P (not A) = 1 − P(A). Some texts use other symbols for "not A" including −A, ~A, A′, and sometimes A with a bar over it.

EXAMPLE

If the probability of a car starting on a rainy day is 0.4, the complement of not starting would be 0.6. Pa = 0.4, (1 – Pa)= 0.6

Conditional Probability. Conditional probability is the probability of an event happening given that another event has happened. This concept is used extensively in reliability calculations. A formal definition for conditional probability is:

$$P(B|A) = P(A \& B) / P(A)$$

EXAMPLE

Probability of getting 4 from throwing a die is 1/6.

Probability of getting 6 from throwing a die is 1/6.

Probability of getting either 4 or 6 is 1/6 + 1/6 = 1/3.

Probability of getting both 4 and 6 in a single throw is 0 (because we can get either of those but not both simultaneously). This means the two events are mutually exclusive.

If the two events are not mutually exclusive:

$$P(A \cup B) = P(A) + P(B) - P(A \cap B)$$

If an organization has two injection molding machines each having a probability of working 0.8. What is the probability the organization will meet the weekly production?

$$P(A \cup B) = 0.8 + 0.8 - (0.8 \times 0.8) = 1.6 - 0.64 = 0.96$$

(This is like building a redundancy for improving the reliability.)
    Since both injection-molding machines can work simultaneously this situation is not mutually exclusive.
    If the two events are mutually exclusive, the additive law reduces to:

$$P(A \cup B) = P(A) + P(B)$$

Figure 11.3   Mutually exclusive events.

Part III.B.3

Suppose an urn contains three white marbles and two black marbles. The probability that the first marble drawn is black is:

$$2/(2 + 3) = 2/5$$

The probability that the second marble drawn is black (given that the first marble drawn is black) is:

$$1/(1 + 3) = 1/4$$

The probability that both marbles drawn are black is:

$$2/5 \times 1/4 = 2/20 = 1/10$$

(Without replacement.)

Mutually Exclusive Events

If occurrence of any one of the events excludes the occurrence of others, the events are mutually exclusive (see Figure 11.3). If two events A and B are mutually exclusive, then $P(A \cup B) = P(A) + P(B)$.

EXAMPLE:

The assembly of product requires an electronic board. This electronic board is supplied by 3 different suppliers. Probability of the board from Supplier A working on the product is 0.2, board from Supplier B is 0.3, board from Supplier C is 0.5. What is the probability that either board from B or C is working on the product?

$$P(B \cup C) = 0.3 + 0.5 = 0.8$$

The Multiplicative Law

If the events are dependent (no replacement):

EXAMPLE

A production lot of 50 units has 10 defective units. Three units were sampled at random from the production lot. What is the probability that all three are defective?

$$P(A \cap B) = 10/50 \times 9/49 \times 8/48 = 720/117{,}600 = 0.0061 \text{ or } 0.6\%$$

If events are independent (replacement):

EXAMPLE

The assembly of an electronic board has two major components. Probability of component A working is 0.7, component B is 0.8. What is the probability the assembly will work?

$$P(A \cap B) = 0.7 \times 0.8 = 0.56$$

(The probability of component A and B working to make the assembly work.)

Permutations and Combinations

Permutations. Permutation is an ordered arrangement of n distinct objects. The number of ways of ordering the arrangement of n objects taken r at a time is designated by $_nP_r$. Permutations are an important concept that we use in our everyday life.

EXAMPLE

One might think AB and BA are same. It matters when arranging people for seating. In an airplane, AB seating is not the same as BA. One has a window and the other the aisle! Maybe A is a right-hander and B is a left-hander. Seating AB may cause inconvenience as their elbows interfere, whereas BA is a convenient seating arrangement.

The counting rule:

$$_nP_r = n(n-1)(n-2)...(n-r+1) = {_nP_r} = \frac{n!}{(n-r)!}$$

Important factorials to remember during calculations (proof beyond the scope of this book):

$$0! = 1, {_nP_n} = n!, {_nP_0} = 1$$

$$n! = 1 \times 2 \times 3 \times ...n \quad \text{(! is pronounced "factorial")}$$

Note: Calculators have an upper limit to the value that can use the x! key. If a problem requires a higher factorial, use the statistical function in a spreadsheet program such as Excel.

How many words can be made by using the letters of the word "sigma" taken all at a time?

There are five different letters in the word sigma.

Number of permutations taking all the letters at a time = $_5P_5$

We know that $_nP_n = n! = 5! = 120$.

Combination. The number of distinct combinations of n distinct objects taken r at a time. This is denoted by $_nC_r$. Combinations are used when order is not significant. Example: AB and BA are the same and hence the result shows only AB. (Unlike permutation where the result will have both AB and BA.)

The counting rule:

Number of combinations of r objects from a collection of n objects =

$$_nC_r = \frac{n!}{r!(n-r)!}$$

Note: Another symbol for number of combinations is $\binom{n}{r}$

Important factorials to remember during calculations (proof beyond the scope of this book):

$$0! = 1, \; _nC_n = 1!, \; _nC_0 = 1$$

Let us consider an example where order arrangement is not a concern:

Selection of r people from n available people.

EXAMPLE

A local ASQ section with 10 volunteers wants to form a task force of three volunteers to send for proctor training to potentially become exam proctors. How many different three-person combinations could be formed?

The combinations formula will be used to calculate the number of combinations of three objects from a collection of seven objects.

$$_{10}C_3 = \frac{10!}{(10-3)!3!} = 120$$

Now with the 120 different combinations, the section chair can find out which combination of people are available on a given date.

Excel formula: =COMBIN(10,3)

Chapter 12

C. Collecting and Summarizing Data

1. TYPES OF DATA AND MEASUREMENT SCALES

> Identify and classify continuous (variables) and discrete (attributes) data. Describe and define nominal, ordinal, interval, and ratio measurement scales. (Analyze)
>
> **Body of Knowledge III.C.1**

Table 12.1 gives the description and definition of nominal, ordinal, interval, and ratio measurement scales with examples and applicable arithmetic and statistical operations.

Quantitative data are grouped into two types, *continuous* (also called *variables*) and *discrete* (also called *attributes*). Continuous data result from measurement on some continuous scale such as length, weight, temperature, and so on. These scales are called continuous because between any two values there are an infinite number of other values. For example, between 1.537 inches and 1.538 inches there are 1.5372, 1.5373, 1.53724, and so on.

Discrete data result from counting the occurrence of events. Examples might include the number of paint runs per batch of painted parts, the number of valves that leaked, or the number of bubbles in a square foot of floated glass.

There is another type of data called *locational* data. This is very useful to identify *where* the data are coming from. An example is paint defects in an automobile assembly line. It is not adequate if the data are collected as continuous or discrete. The rework technician needs to know where the defect is found in the massive surface area of the automobile. More details on location data displayed as a measles chart (Figure 10.8) are explained in Chapter 10.

Table 12.1 Measurement scales.

The measurement scales

Nominal	Ordinal	Interval	Ratio
The values of the scale have no 'numeric' meaning in the way that usually applies with numbers and no ordering scheme.	The intervals between adjacent scale values are indeterminate. *ex.* 1 = satisfied 2 = neutral 3 = dissatisfied	Intervals between adjacent scale values are equal with respect to the attribute being measured.	There is a rational zero point for the scale.
Example: Color-coded wires by quantity in an electrical cable. ✱ least informative	Example: Categorization of defects by criticality. Functional failures, performance degradation, cosmetic defects, and so on.	Example: The difference between 20°C and 40°C is the same as the difference between −10°C and −30°C.	Example: Ratios are equivalent; for example, the ratio of 10 to 5 is the same as the ratio of 64 to 32.

Applicable arithmetic and statistical operations for the measurement scales

Nominal	Ordinal	Interval	Ratio
Counting Mode Chi square	"Greater than" or "less than" operations Median Interquartile range Sign test	Addition and subtraction of scale values Arithmetic mean Standard deviation t-test, F test	Multiplication and division of scale values Geometric mean Coefficient of variation

For more details please refer to: http://en.wikipedia.org/wiki/Level_of_measurement

Effort should always be made to move from discrete to continuous measurements. There are two reasons for doing this:

- Control charts based on continuous data are more sensitive to process changes than those based on discrete data.

- When designed experiments are used for process improvement, changes in continuous data may be observed even though the discrete measurement hasn't changed.

2. DATA COLLECTION METHODS

> Define and apply methods for collecting data
> such as check sheets, coded data, etc. (Apply)
>
> **Body of Knowledge III.C.2**

Data collection is performed in an organization for various reasons:

• Legal, regulatory, or statutory requirements

• Analysis, improvement, and knowledge management

• Contractual requirements of customers

Irrespective of reasons, data collection can be very expensive if the data collection is not planned and effectively implemented. Many organizations tend to collect more data than required. Answering some basic questions before actually starting to collect the data such as what, why, where, when, who, and how (5W1H), can help make planning the data collection more effective. Where possible, real-time data acquisition from equipment is more effective and reduces human errors and data transfer errors.

Where manual data entry is involved, it is more efficient to use data coding to avoid repetitive recording of numbers and errors due to fatigue. Decoding may be applied depending on the analysis to be performed.

There are several methods for collecting data:

• Surveys

• Face-to-face interviews

• Focus groups

• Mystery shopping

• Customer feedback

• Automatic data capture

• Manual data capture

Data collection methods that are one-on-one like focus groups and face-to-face interviews have higher integrity of data and opportunity to clarify with the respondents, while data collection methods like surveys have low response rates (approximately 10 to 15 percent), and improperly constructed surveys can result in misleading responses.

Customer feedback after product failure or service issue is reactive. Hence, organizations should strive to gather as much up-front information as possible before designing the product or service. Automatic real-time data capture from equipment can eliminate the errors involved in manual data entry.

3. TECHNIQUES FOR ASSURING DATA ACCURACY AND INTEGRITY

Define and apply techniques such as random sampling, stratified sampling, sample homogeneity, etc. (Apply)

Body of Knowledge III.C.3

Even sophisticated data collection and analysis techniques can be defeated if the data are entered with errors. Common causes of errors include:

- Units of measure not defined (for example, feet or meters?)
- Closeness of handwritten characters/legibility (for example, 2 or Z?)
- Inadequate measurement system resolution/discrimination
- Rounding off measurements and losing precision
- Emotional bias resulting in distortion of data
- Inadequate use of validation techniques—using guesswork or personal bias
- Multiple points of data entry—opportunity for inconsistency and errors
- Poor instructions or training causing erroneous data entry
- Ambiguous terminology
- Clerical or typographical errors

To minimize error:

- Have a carefully constructed data collection plan
- Maintain a calibration schedule for data collection equipment
- Conduct repeatability and reproducibility (R & R) studies on measurement system
- Record appropriate auxiliary information regarding units, time of collection, conditions, measurement equipment used, name of data recorder, and so on
- Use appropriate statistical tests to remove outliers
- If data are transmitted or stored digitally, use an appropriate redundant error correction system
- Provide clear and complete instruction and training

Types of Sampling

Random Sampling. Every sample randomly picked from the lot has equal probability of getting picked. If effectively administered, sampling can save money for the organization. The lot being sampled has to be homogeneous for random sampling.

Sequential Sampling. Sequential sampling is used in destructive testing and reliability testing applications where higher cost is involved in testing the unit. The samples are tested one by one sequentially until the desired results are reached.

Stratified Sampling. When there is a mixture of parts from different machines, different streams, different raw material lots, or different process settings, there is no homogeneity of the lot. Hence, random sampling will not yield the right results. It will be more effective to stratify the lot based on the criteria (by machine, stream, lot, or settings) and pick random samples from the stratified group.

4. DESCRIPTIVE STATISTICS

Define, compute, and interpret measures
of dispersion and central tendency,
and construct and interpret frequency
distributions and cumulative
frequency distributions. (Analyze)

Body of Knowledge III.C.4

Two principal types of statistical studies are *descriptive* and *inferential.* Inferential studies analyze data from a sample to infer properties of the population from which the sample was drawn. The purpose of descriptive statistics is to present data in a way that will facilitate understanding.

The following data represent a sample of critical dimensions of a chemical deposition operation. What conclusions can be reached by looking at the data set?

5.551, 5.361, 5.392, 5.479, 5.456, 5.542, 5.423, 5.476,
5.298, 5.499, 5.312, 5.319, 5.317, 5.314, 5.382

The charts in Figure 12.1 reveal information about the sample data that was not obvious from the data list, such as:

- The *spread* of the sample

- An indication of the *shape* of the sample

- *Center* of the sample

- Fitting of normal distribution of the sample (explained later in this chapter)

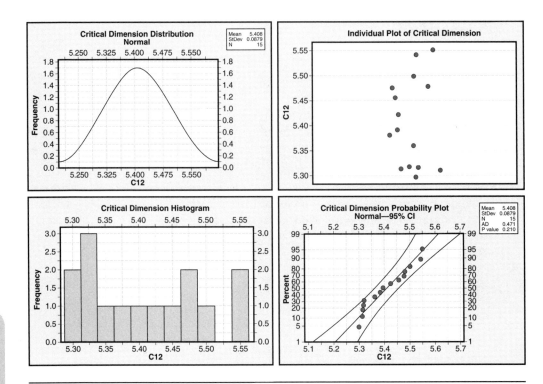

Figure 12.1   Example of a data set as illustrated by a frequency distribution, individual plot, histogram, and probability plot.

The first three attributes, spread, shape, and center, are key to understanding the data and the process that generated them.

The *spread* of the sample is also referred to as *dispersion* or *variation* and is usually quantified with either the sample range (defined as the highest value minus the lowest value) or the sample standard deviation. The sample standard deviation is the more sophisticated metric and is defined as

$$s = \sqrt{\frac{\Sigma\left(x - \overline{x}\right)^2}{n - 1}}$$

where

   $\overline{x}$ = the sample mean or average

   n = sample size

This formula produces an estimate of the standard deviation of the population from which the sample was drawn. If data for the entire population are used (rare in practical applications), the population standard deviation is defined as

$$\sigma = \sqrt{\frac{\Sigma\left(x - \mu\right)^2}{N}}$$

where

μ = the population mean or average

N = population size

Due to the complexity of these formulas, one should use a calculator with standard deviation capabilities.

The *shape* of the sample refers to a smooth curve that serves as a sort of umbrella approximately covering the tops of the bars in the histogram. In this case, it appears that the sample came from a normally distributed population. Other descriptors of shape include *kurtosis, symmetry,* and *skewness.* For further discussion of shape see Chapter 13.

The *center* of the sample may be quantified in three ways:

- The *mean,* statistical jargon for the more common word "average" (central tendency)

- The *median,* which is defined as the value that is in the middle of a sorted list

- The *mode,* which is the value that appears most frequently in the sample

In the example in Figure 12.1:

- The mean = (sum of the values) ÷ (number of values) = $\Sigma x / n$ = 81.121/15 = 5.408

- The median of the 15 values would be the eighth value when the sample is sorted in ascending order, in this case 5.392. If there are an even number of values, the median is obtained by averaging the two middle values.

Of these three measures, the mean is the most useful in quality engineering applications. The sample mean is often denoted as an x with a bar above it and pronounced "x-bar."

SUMMARY OF DESCRIPTIVE MEASURES		
Name	Symbol	Formula/Description
Measures of central tendency		
Mean	$\bar{x}$	$\dfrac{\Sigma x}{n}$
Median	$\tilde{x}$	Middle number in sorted list
Mode		Most frequent number
Measures of dispersion		
Range	R	High value–low value
Sample standard deviation	s	$\sqrt{\dfrac{\Sigma(x-\bar{x})^2}{n-1}}$

x	Frequency	Cumulative frequency
.120	1	1
.121	3	4
.122	4	8
.123	7	15
.124	4	19
.125	4	23
.126	3	26
.127	1	27

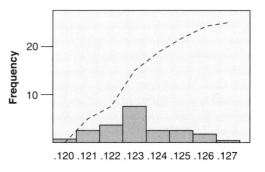

Figure 12.2 Cumulative frequency distribution in table and graph form.

The population standard deviation σ uses the same formula as sample standard deviation with a denominator n.

Cumulative Frequency Distribution

If a column showing totals of the frequencies to that point is added to the frequency distribution, the result is called a *cumulative frequency distribution*. An example is shown in Figure 12.2.

5. GRAPHICAL METHODS

> Depict relationships by constructing, applying, and interpreting diagrams and charts such as stem-and-leaf plots, box-and-whisker plots, run charts, scatter diagrams, Pareto charts, etc. Depict distributions by constructing, applying, and interpreting diagrams such as histograms, normal probability plots, etc. (Create)
>
> **Body of Knowledge III.C.5**

Table 12.2 provides an overview of the graphical methods discussed in this section. The following paragraphs provide more information about those not already discussed.

Table 12.2 Comparison of various graphical methods.

Name	Purpose	Application	Interpretation	Ease of use
Tally	Provides a quick tally of total quantity and by class interval. Provides visual idea of the distribution shape.	Used to count defect quantity by type, class, and/or category	Tally mark concentration and spread roughly indicate distribution shape. Tally marks of five are crossed out as a group for easy counting. Isolated groups of tally marks indicate uneven distribution.	Very easy to create and interpret
Frequency distribution	Provides a pictorial view of numerical data about location and spread	Especially useful if tally column cells have a large number of marks	Concentration of data is seen as a peak, and spread of the data is demonstrated by the width of the curve. Thinner distribution indicates lesser variation. Distribution can be unimodal (with one peak), bimodal (two peaks), or multimodal (multiple peaks) indicating a mixture of populations. Distribution with no peak and flat curve indicates rectangular distribution.	Not so easy to create but easier to interpret
Stem-and-leaf plot	Provides numerical data information about the contents of the cells in a frequency distribution	Useful to quickly identify any repetitive data within the class interval	If data values within cells are not fairly evenly distributed, measurement errors or other anomalous conditions may be present	Easy to create but difficult to interpret
Box-and-whisker plot	Provides a pictorial view of minimum, maximum, median, and interquartile range in one graph.	Provides more information than distribution plot but easier to interpret. Outliers are easily identified on the graph.	If the location of the center line of box is right in the middle, the data may be normally distributed. If moved to one of the sides, may be skewed. The data points outside the whiskers indicate outliers. Unequal whiskers indicate skewness of the distribution.	Easy to create and interpret

Continued

Part III.C.5

Table 12.2 Comparison of various graphical methods. *(Continued)*

Name	Purpose	Application	Interpretation	Ease of use
Scatter diagram	Detects possible correlation or association between two variables, or cause and effect	Used for root cause analysis, estimation of correlation coefficient, making prediction using a regression line fitted to the data	To estimate correlation, the relationship has to be linear. Nonlinear relationship may also exist between variables. If the plotted data flow upward left to right, the relationship is positively correlated. If the plotted data flow downward from left to right, the relationship is negatively correlated. If data are spread about the center with no inclination to right or left, there may not be any correlation.	Easy to create and interpret
Run chart	Provides a visual indicator of any nonrandom patterns	Used when real-time feedback is required for variables data	Patterns like cluster, mixture, trend, and oscillation are spotted based on the number of runs above and below the mean or median. P value identifies the statistical significance of a nonrandom pattern. P value less than 0.05 identifies a stronger significance.	Easy to create and interpret

Stem-and-Leaf Plot

A stem-and-leaf plot is constructed much like a tally column except that the last digit of the data value is recorded instead of the tally mark. This plot is often used when the data are grouped. Consider the following example:

These are the power values in milliwatts collected from a transmission product at a given frequency:

10.3, 11.4, 10.9, 9.7, 10.4, 10.6, 10.0, 10.8, 11.1, 11.9, 10.9, 10.8, 11.7, 12.3, 10.6, 12.2, 11.6, 11.2, 10.7, 11.4

The normal histogram would look like the first chart in Figure 12.3.

The stem-and-leaf plot on the right conveys more information than a tally column or the associated histogram would. Note that the ordered stem-and-leaf sorts the data and permits easy determination of the median.

The display has three columns:

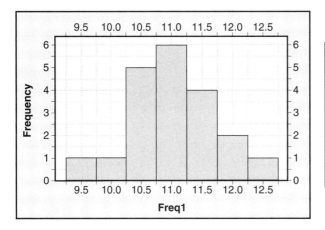

Figure 12.3   Histogram and stem-and-leaf plot comparison.

1. The leaves (right). Each value in the leaf column represents a digit from one observation. The "leaf unit" (declared above the plot) specifies which digit is used. In the example, the leaf unit is 0.1. Thus, the leaf value for an observation of 7 is 7 while the leaf value for an observation of 10 is 0.

2. The stem (middle). The stem value represents the digit immediately to the left of the leaf digit. In the example, the stem value of 10 indicates that the leaves in that row are from observations with values greater than or equal to 10. (Example: 10.0, 10.3, 10.4.)

3. Counts (left). If the median value for the sample is included in a row, the count for that row is enclosed in parentheses. The values for rows above and below the median are cumulative. The count for a row above the median represents the total count for that row and the rows above it. The value for a row below the median represents the total count for that row and the rows below it.

In the example, the median for the sample is 10.9, so the count for the third row is enclosed in parentheses. The count for the second row represents the total number of observations in the first two rows. Similarly the fourth row provides the count of the fourth, fifth, and sixth rows.[1]

Box Plots

The box plot (also called a box-and-whisker plot), developed by Professor John Tukey of Princeton University, uses the high and low values of the data as well as the quartiles.

The quartiles of a set of data divide the sorted data values into four approximately equal subsets. The quartiles are denoted Q_1, Q_2, and Q_3. Q_2 is the median. Q_1 is the median of the set of values at or below Q_2. Q_3 is the median of the set of values at or above Q_2. This is illustrated in Figure 12.4.

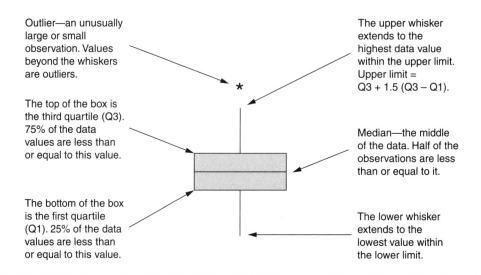

Outlier—an unusually large or small observation. Values beyond the whiskers are outliers.

The top of the box is the third quartile (Q3). 75% of the data values are less than or equal to this value.

The bottom of the box is the first quartile (Q1). 25% of the data values are less than or equal to this value.

The upper whisker extends to the highest data value within the upper limit. Upper limit = Q3 + 1.5 (Q3 − Q1).

Median—the middle of the data. Half of the observations are less than or equal to it.

The lower whisker extends to the lowest value within the lower limit.

Figure 12.4 Box plot.
Source: Copyright Minitab Inc.

EXAMPLE

Let us work with some bond strength data:

8.250, 8.085, 8.795, 9.565, 11.880, 9.180, 9.950, 9.630, 8.150

The data after sorting:

8.085, 8.150, 8. 250, 8.795, 9.180, 9.565, 9.630, 9.950, 11.880

Low value is 8.085, high value is 11.88, Q_1 = 8.20, Q_2 = 9.18, and Q_3, = 9.79. (Note that quartiles need not be values in the data set itself.) The resulting plot is shown in Figure 12.5. Figure 12.6 shows how the shape of the dot plot is reflected in the box plot.

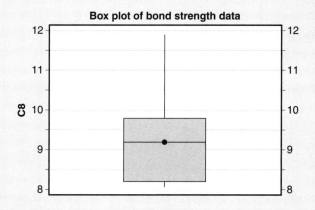

Box plot of bond strength data

Figure 12.5 Example box plot.

Continued

Continued

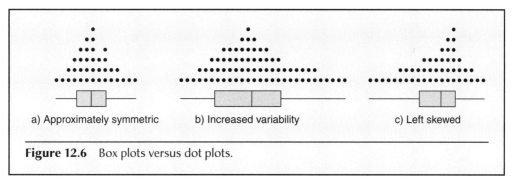

a) Approximately symmetric   b) Increased variability   c) Left skewed

Figure 12.6   Box plots versus dot plots.

Box plots can be used to minc information from a database. Box plots can be used to compare two or more populations visually and see the shift in median and variation.

EXAMPLE

An experiment was conducted in an assembly process with three different process settings. The Six Sigma Green Belt wants to know visually if there is any variation between processes. (More appropriate statistical methods like ANOVA are discussed elsewhere in this book for this application.)

Partial data from the experiment are shown in Table 12.3.

Table 12.3   Example yield data of three periods.

Yield	Period	Yield	Period	Yield	Period
87.0%	1	57.1%	2	77.1%	3
84.4%	1	62.5%	2	74.2%	3
76.9%	1	60.0%	2	62.3%	3
90.0%	1	72.3%	2	66.7%	3
84.4%	1	42.9%	2	80.0%	3
86.2%	1	69.1%	2	71.4%	3
89.6%	1	59.5%	2	55.1%	3
94.2%	1	71.3%	2	36.2%	3
95.6%	1	79.5%	2	94.3%	3
85.2%	1	43.8%	2	71.4%	3
89.7%	1	94.7%	2	67.1%	3
100.0%	1	66.0%	2	91.4%	3
89.1%	1	40.0%	2	71.4%	3
96.9%	1	67.8%	2	61.4%	3
93.6%	1	65.0%	2	75.4%	3

Continued

Part III.C.5

Continued

The resultant data and box plots are shown in Figure 12.7.

The period can be further divided into major process settings like gas flow or temperature between the three periods and further analyzed to get even greater insight. The box plots in Figure 12.7 show that the largest variation is in period 2. The Green Belt would probe further to see what may have caused the largest variation in the second setting using more appropriate root cause analysis tools.

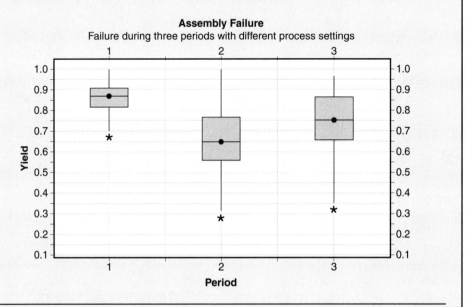

Figure 12.7 Box plot by period.

The Run Chart

The run chart is used to identify patterns in process data. There are also related statistical tests that can be performed to detect any nonrandom behavior. All of the individual observations are plotted in time sequence and a horizontal reference line is drawn at the median. Typically, a run chart is used when the subgroup size is one. When the subgroup size is greater than one, the subgroup means or medians are calculated and connected with a line, similarly to control charts.

Run chart tests can detect trends, oscillation, mixtures, and clustering. These are nonrandom patterns and suggest that the variation observed can be attributed to special causes. Common cause variation is variation that is inherent in the process. A process is in control when only common causes are present.

Lack of steadiness in a process can cause oscillation. In the example shown in Figure 12.8, the P value for oscillation is 0.78, indicating that it is not significant. A trend can be either upward or downward due to tool wear, loosening of fixture, gradual change in temperature setting, and so on. Since the P value for trends is 0.21 in this example, we can conclude that it is not very significant. (Although a

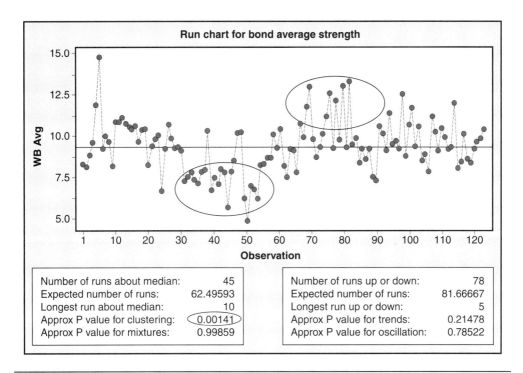

Figure 12.8   Run chart analysis (using statistical software).

visual trending can be seen in two regions.) When there is a mix-up between parts from two different machines, two different operators, or two lots of materials, the process points tend to appear on either side of the chart with nothing closer to the centerline. We don't see that in this example as the P value is 0.998 (almost so high that we can rule out this possibility). Now we have a problem with clustering, which is highly significant and may be due to measurement problems, or lot-to-lot or setup variability. Carefully reviewing the measurement system analysis reports and procedure for setting up the machine, and verifying whether the operator is trained for machine-setting, and so on, can reveal some insight into clustering.

Key Point: The common run chart is an extremely powerful tool for showing how stable a process is behaving. This assumes, of course, that you want to see process behavior. Otherwise, use a bar graph.

Scatter Diagrams

The scatter diagram is a powerful visual tool used to display relationship or association between two variables, cause and effect, and so on. While plotting the scatter diagram, the independent variable corresponds to the *x* axis or horizontal axis, with the dependent variable on the *y* axis or vertical axis. The plot pattern identifies whether there is any positive or negative correlation, or no correlation. There is also the possibility for a nonlinear relationship between the variables.

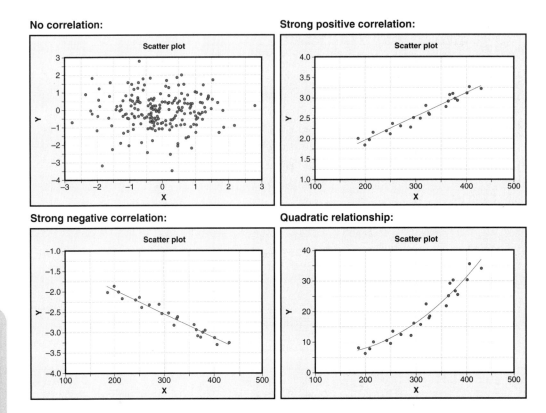

Figure 12.9 Scatter diagrams.

Figure 12.9 shows different types of relationships between two variables or between causes and effects. A scatter diagram simulation Flash page can be seen at http://noppa5.pc.helsinki.fi/koe/flash/corr/ch16.html.

EXAMPLE

Let us take an example from an injection-molding process. The following potential causes have been suggested using engineering judgment by a cross-functional team during a brainstorming session.

- Mold compression pressure

- Coolant temperature

- Mold cooling time

- Mold hold time

The team is trying to identify the relationship of these variables to the quality characteristic "part surface finish." The data are shown in Table 12.4.

Continued

Continued

Four scatter diagrams have been plotted in Figure 12.10. In each plot, "surface finish" is on the vertical axis. The first plot shows mold pressure versus surface finish. On each diagram, one point is plotted for each batch.

Table 12.4   Mold process data.

Batch no.	Mold compression pressure	Coolant temperature	Mold cooling time	Mold hold time	Part surface finish
1	242	112.75	15.95	0.792	40.70
2	220	110.88	17.60	1.001	33.00
3	451	112.86	16.50	0.99	44.00
4	385	111.65	17.82	0.748	35.20
5	539	110.88	18.48	0.935	29.70
6	396	111.54	16.28	0.836	38.50
7	407	112.75	15.73	1.034	47.30
8	363	109.78	18.15	0.781	25.30
9	308	110.88	16.50	0.715	35.20
10	440	111.32	18.26	1.056	33.00

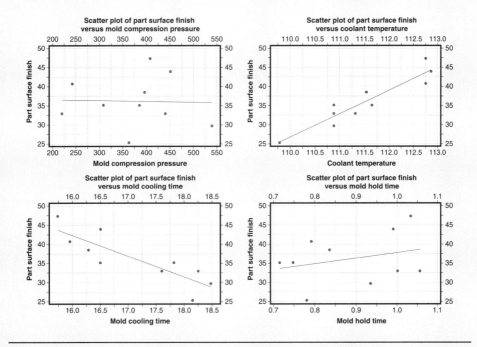

Figure 12.10   Examples of scatter diagrams (variables versus effects).

Continued

Continued

A best-fit line is drawn to cover the plotted points across the axes. In the manual approach, practitioners use an "eyeball" estimation to draw a line approximately in the middle of the plotted points covering end to end. Statistical software does a more thorough job in fitting a line. If the points are closer to each other, the fitted line identifies a lesser variation in the relationship estimation. The relationship between the two variables or causes and effects can be mathematically expressed and represented by a letter "r," called the *correlation coefficient* or *Pearson correlation*. The value of r is always between -1 and $+1$ inclusive. This may be stated symbolically as $-1 \le r \le +1$.

$$r = \frac{\Sigma xy - \dfrac{\Sigma x \Sigma y}{N}}{\sqrt{\left(\Sigma x^2 - \dfrac{(\Sigma x)^2}{N}\right)\left(\Sigma y^2 - \dfrac{(\Sigma y)^2}{N}\right)}}$$

	Mold compression	Coolant temperature	Mold cooling time	Mold hold time
Coolant temperature	0.028 0.940			
Mold cooling time	0.336 0.342	−0.712 0.021		
Mold hold time	0.328 0.355	0.292 0.412	0.082 0.821	
Part surface finish	−0.033 0.927	0.935 0.000	−0.855 0.002	0.281 0.432

Pearson correlation

P value

Figure 12.11 Correlation between variables (using statistical software).

To be able to calculate the correlation coefficient, a linear relationship is required. This can be visually verified without any sophisticated software. For example, suppose a relationship is suspected between exercise time in minutes/day and weight loss in pounds. To check that relationship, four readings are taken from a weight loss center's data, although in an actual application much more data would be desirable to reduce the error in estimation.

Exercise time in minutes/day	30	45	60	75
Weight loss in pounds	1	2	4	4.5

The first step is to plot the data as shown Figure 12.12 to see if it seems reasonable to approximate it with a straight line.

Although a straight line can't be drawn through these four points, the trend looks linear. The next step would be to calculate the coefficient of linear correlation.

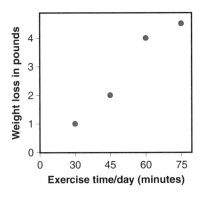

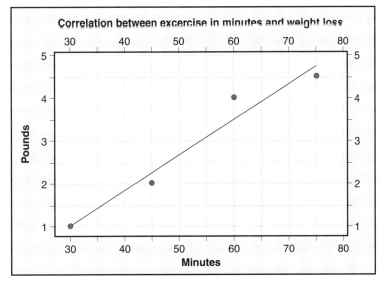

Pearson correlation of pounds and minutes = 0.977
P value = 0.023

Figure 12.12   Example scatter plots—exercise versus weight loss.

This can be done using the statistical functions in a spreadsheet or the following formula:

$$r = \frac{S_{xy}}{\sqrt{S_{xx}S_{yy}}}$$

where

n = number of points

$S_{xx} = \Sigma x^2 - (\Sigma x)^2 / n$

$S_{xy} = \Sigma xy - \Sigma x \Sigma y / n$

$S_{yy} = \Sigma y^2 - (\Sigma y)^2 / n$

In the above example, using x for minutes and y for pounds:

	x	y	x^2	xy	y^2
	30	1	900	30	1
	45	2	2,025	90	4
	60	4	3,600	240	16
	75	4.5	5,625	337.5	20.25
Σ	210	11.5	12,150	697.5	41.25

$S_{xx} = 12{,}150 - 210^2/4 = 1125$

$S_{xy} = 697.5 - 210 \times 11.5/4 = 93.75$

$S_{yy} = 41.25 - 11.5^2/4 = 8.1875$

So

$$r = \frac{93.75}{\sqrt{(1125)(8.1875)}} \approx 0.9768$$

The value of r will always satisfy the inequality $-1 \leq r \leq 1$.

When r is positive, the scatter diagram displays a positive slope and when r is negative it displays a negative slope as per the figures displayed earlier. The closer r is to 1 or -1, the stronger the association between the two variables and the higher the likelihood that the variables are related. A key issue here is the distinction between association and causality. When engineering judgment is used to select the variables, relationships between variables can reveal opportunities for improvement. Similarly, scatter diagrams also help as a root cause analysis tool.

The reason engineering judgment is required is because mathematical relationships can be identified even between irrelevant variables. Example: a relationship could exist between two unrelated variables like price of gold and infant mortality rate from 1930 to 2000. We should not be making the conclusion that as gold prices increase over the years, infant mortality is decreasing. This can misguide rather than help with root cause identification. This is an example of correlation that does not imply causation. Hence, engineering judgment should be solicited before exploring relationships.

The fact that there is a strong association or correlation between exercise time and weight loss in that example might lead one to believe that weight loss could be controlled by increasing or decreasing exercise time. This is not necessarily always true. Many variable pairs have a strong association with no causal relationship.

Another related value is the coefficient of determination denoted by r^2 or R. It is defined as the square of the correlation coefficient, as the notation implies. The coefficient of determination is a measure to indicate the regression line fitting the data. In other words, r^2 explains how much of the variability in the y's can be explained by the fact that they are related to x.

Normal Probability Plots

Normal probability plots are constructed to test whether random data come from a normal probability distribution. Several statistical analyses have a base assumption of normality. Hence it is important to test the normality before proceeding with further analysis. Normal probability plots can be constructed either manually or by statistical software. Software packages are a more efficient and accurate way of generating probability plots. Normal probability graph paper is designed so that a random sample from a normally distributed population will form an approximately straight line (using the manual construction).

There are several tests to check normality of random data. To name a few:

- The Anderson-Darling test for normality, an ECDF (empirical cumulative distribution function)–based test

- The Ryan-Joiner test, a correlation–based test

- The Shapiro-Wilk test, similar to the Ryan-Joiner test

- The Kolmogorov-Smirnov test for normality, also an ECDF-based test

Of these tests, Anderson-Darling is most widely used by statistical software.

EXAMPLE

Following is the data for bond strength tested on an assembly. Does it appear that the following randomly selected measurements came from a normal population?

8.250, 8.085, 8.795, 9.565, 11.880, 9.180, 9.950, 9.630, 8.150, 10.800,
10.800, 11.080, 10.730, 10.520, 10.380, 10.535, 9.600, 10.340, 10.410

The analysis shown in Figure 12.13 performed using Minitab also tests the data using the Anderson-Darling formula. Notice the term "AD" in the graphic output. When the Anderson-Darling values are smaller, the distribution fits the data better. This is also reflected in the higher P value. As the P value is greater than 0.05 (alpha risk), we can conclude that these data come from a normal distribution.

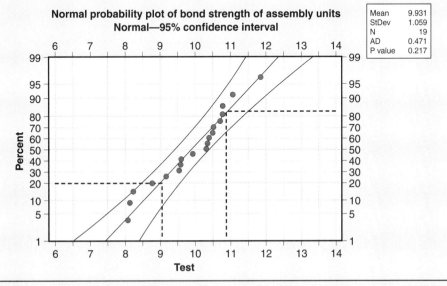

Figure 12.13   Normal probability plot.

Continued

Continued

Assuming that the specification (or tolerance) for the bond strength is 9 to 11 as indicated by the vertical dashed lines, the horizontal dashed lines show that about 20 percent of the parts will be below the lower specification limit and about 17 percent will be above the upper specification limit (Figure 12.13).

Weibull Plots

The Weibull distribution has the general form

$$P(x) = \alpha\beta(x - \gamma)^{\beta-1}e^{-\alpha(x-\gamma)^\beta}$$

where

α = scale parameter

β = shape parameter

γ = location parameter

The Weibull function is mainly used for reliability data when the underlying distribution is unknown. Weibull probability paper can be used to estimate the shape parameter β and mean time between failures (MTBF) or failure rate. Weibull plots can be generated manually as well as by using computerized software packages. Software packages are a more efficient and accurate way of generating Weibull plots. There is relevance between all these parameters and the lifecycle of a product.

EXAMPLE:

Fifteen units were tested for environmental stress and the number of hours the units managed to remain in operation under testing was collected from a precision timer. Estimate the value of the shape parameter β, MTBF, and the reliability at 3.9 hours. (See Figure 12.14.)

Fail duration 4.011, 3.646, 5.226, 4.740, 4.739, 5.833, 4.861, 4.618, 4.012, 3.646, 4.497, 3.646, 4.49, 3.281, 3.889

In this example we need to find β (shape parameters) to know if these units are failing at a particular period of the lifecycle such as infant mortality, constant failure, or wearout failure. Secondly, MTBF is required from the problem. For a normal distribution, the mean is the 50th percentile, whereas for a Weibull distribution, the mean is at the 63.2 percentile. The problem also requires the reliability at 3.9 hours.

The data is input into Minitab statistical software, and the Weibull distribution is chosen to perform this analysis. Several commercially available software packages can perform this function.

The software generates the Weibull plot on probability paper. The P value is > 0.25 and hence there is higher probability that the data come from a Weibull distribution.

Continued

Continued

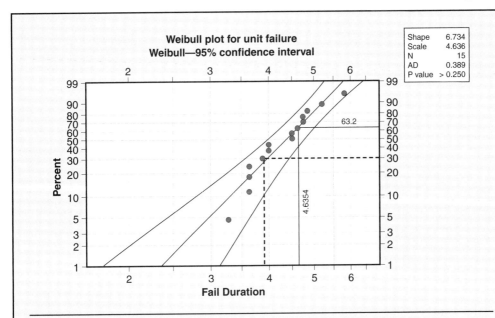

Figure 12.14   Example of Weibull plot.

The software also creates a 95 percent confidence interval for the data analyzed. This is useful for creating an interval estimate at a desired point.

The vertical axis on most Weibull paper is labeled "percent failure." Since MTBF is located at 36.8 percent on a reliability scale, it is located at 63.2 percent on a failure scale. The horizontal coordinate of the point where the 63.2 percent line crosses the best-fit line is the estimate for MTBF. Interpolation on this curve provides estimates for other values. From the above plot, by finding the point of intersection for 63.2 percent, we can find the MTBF as 4.635 hours.

The β (shape) value is 6.734. We can conclude that the unit is failing at wearout period.

A vertical line drawn through the 3.9-hour point on the horizontal axis crosses the fitted line at about 30 percent on the percent failure scale so the estimate for reliability at 3.9 hours is R(3.9) ≈ 0.70.

Chapter 13

D. Probability Distributions

> Describe and interpret normal, binomial, and Poisson, chi square, Student's t, and F distributions. (Apply)
>
> **Body of Knowledge III.D**

Formulas for some of the probability distributions are shown in Table 13.1.

BINOMIAL

The "bi-" prefix indicates that a binomial distribution should be applied in situations where each part has just two states, typically:

- Good or bad
- Accept or reject

Table 13.1 Formula, mean, and variance of certain distributions.

Name	Formula	Mean	Variance
Normal	$P(x) = \dfrac{e^{-\frac{(x-\mu)^2}{2\sigma^2}}}{\sigma\sqrt{2\pi}}$	μ	σ^2
Exponential	$P(x) = \lambda e^{-\lambda x}$	$\dfrac{1}{\lambda}$	$\dfrac{1}{\lambda^2}$
Binomial	$P(x) = \dfrac{n!}{x!(n-x)!} p^x (1-p)^{n-x}$	np	$np(1-p)$
Poisson	$P(x) = \dfrac{e^{-\lambda}\lambda^x}{x!}$	λ	λ
Hypergeometric	$P(x) = \dfrac{{}_dC_x \left[{}_{(N-d)}C_{(n-x)} \right]}{{}_NC_x}$	$\dfrac{nd}{N}$	$\dfrac{nd(N-d)(N-n)}{N^3 - N^2}$

* mean = variance for Poisson

$\sigma = \sqrt{variance}$

- Conformance or nonconformance
- Success or failure

The binomial distribution (Figure 13.1) is used to model discrete data. Examples of binomial data that are frequently used in everyday life are:

- The number of defectives in a manufacturing lot
- The number of defective quotes sent by an insurance company
- The number of wrong patient prescriptions issued by a healthcare professional
- The number of goods shipped to a wrong address by a forwarding company

The binomial distribution has some conditions. It is applicable when the population denoted by N is greater than 50. In other words, for smaller lots, binomial modeling will not be accurate.

Another important condition is the ratio of the sample n to population N. The binomial model best applies when $n < 0.1N$ (that is, sample size is less than 10 percent of the population).

In one type of problem that is frequently encountered, the Six Sigma Green Belt needs to determine the probability of obtaining a certain number of defectives in a sample of known size from a population with known percent defective. The symbols are: n = sample size, x = number of defectives, p = defective rate in the population.

The binomial formula is:

$$P(x) = \frac{n!}{x!(n-x)!} p^x (1-p)^{n-x}$$

As discussed in Chapter 11, $x!$ is pronounced "x factorial" and is defined as $x(x-1)(x-2) \ldots (1)$. Most scientific calculators have a factorial key.

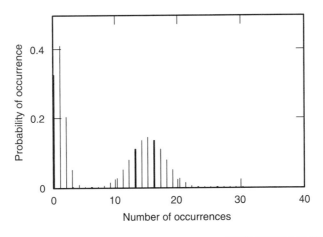

Figure 13.1   Binomial distribution.

Part III.D

EXAMPLE

A sample of size five is randomly selected from a batch with 10 percent defective. Find the probability that the sample has exactly one defective. Substitute $n = 5$, $x = 1$, $p = .10$ into the above formula:

$$P(1) = [5!/(1!(5-1)!)](.10)^1(.9)^{5-1} = [120/(1\times24)](.10)(.6561) \approx .328$$

This is the probability that the sample contains exactly one defective.

The same can be calculated using a simple Excel formula (see Figure 13.2):

$$=BINOMDIST(1,5,0.1,FALSE)$$

We can also use several online Java interactive calculators. An example of a binomial calculator can be found at http://www.stat.tamu.edu/~west/applets/binomialdemo.html.

Teaser: Try the following ASQ exam example using the calculator above:

An ASQ Six Sigma Green Belt exam has 100 questions and four choices per question. Assuming the exam requires 80 right answers, what is the probability of a student passing the exam if he/she randomly chose from the four choices for all

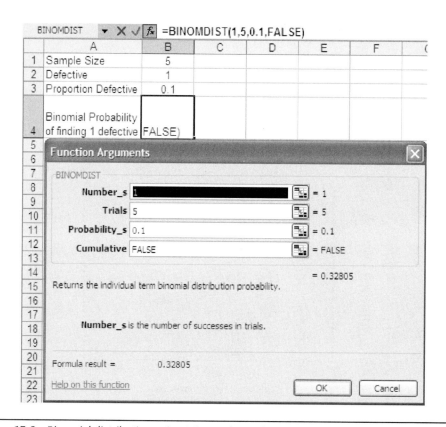

Figure 13.2   Binomial distribution using Microsoft Excel.

100 questions (let us believe that this student doesn't have an iota of a clue about any question—no knowledge bias). Also find out up to how many questions on which the student may get lucky with maximum binomial probability.

As per Table 13.1, the mean and variance can also be calculated for the binomial distribution.

EXAMPLE

If we take an unbiased coin and toss 60 times, what is the average and standard deviation of the number of tails?

Unbiased coin: Having equal probability to be heads or tails.

$$p = (1/2) \text{ or } 0.5$$

$$n = 60$$

$$\mu = np, \; \mu = (60 \times 0.5) = 30 \text{ tails}$$

$$\sigma = \sqrt{np(1-p)}, \; \sigma = (30(1-0.5))^{1/2} = 3.872$$

NORMAL APPROXIMATIONS OF THE BINOMIAL

For large values of n, the distributions of the count X and the sample proportion p are approximately normal. This is understood from the central limit theorem. The normal approximation is not accurate for small values of n; a good rule of thumb is to use the normal approximation only if $np \geq 10$ and $np(1 - p) \geq 10$.

POISSON DISTRIBUTION

The Poisson is also a discrete probability distribution (Figure 13.3). Examples of Poisson data that are frequently used in everyday life are:

- The number of defects in an assembly unit (also known as defects per unit [DPU])

- The number of defects on a painted surface

- The number of errors per quote by an insurance company

- Number of bugs in software code

Defects per unit is the basis for the other metrics like defects per opportunity (DPO), defects per million opportunities (DPMO), and related Six Sigma metrics.

The formula for Poisson probability is

$$P(x) = \frac{e^{-\lambda} \lambda^x}{x!}$$

where

$$\lambda > 0$$

$$x = 0, 1, 2, \ldots$$

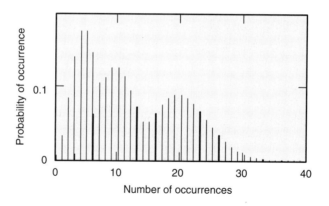

Figure 13.3   Poisson distribution.

EXAMPLE

The number of defects on an assembly unit has a Poisson distribution with $\lambda = 5$. Find the probability that the second unit produces fewer than two defects.

The probability that the second unit has fewer than two defects is the sum of the probability of zero defects and the probability of one defect.

$$P\big(x < 2\big) = P\big(x = 0\big) + P\big(x = 1\big)$$

$$P\big(x = 0\big) = \frac{e^{-5}5^0}{0!} \approx 0.006$$

$$P\big(x = 1\big) = \frac{e^{-5}5^1}{1!} \approx 0.034$$

$$P\big(x < 2\big) = 0.04$$

The Poisson distribution also has a mean and standard deviation. An interesting fact is that the mean and variance of a Poisson distribution are the same! (λ)

EXAMPLE

A mechanical assembly process has a historical defective rate of 10 percent. What is the probability that a lot of 50 units will contain exactly five defectives?

$n = 50$

Proportion defective $p = 10\%$, that is, 0.1

$\lambda = np = 50 \times 0.1 = 5$

$x = 5$ defectives as per the problem

Continued

Continued

$$P(x) = \frac{e^{-\lambda} \lambda^x}{x!}$$

$$P(x = 5) = \frac{e^{-5} 5^5}{5!} \approx 0.175, \sim 18\%$$

The same can be calculated using a simple Excel formula (see Figure 13.4):

$$=POISSON(B2,B4,FALSE)$$

Additional exercises:

a. Try calculating the Poisson probability for defectives = 0, 1, 2, 3, 4

b. Try calculating the Poisson probability for historical defective rates of two percent, five percent, and seven percent

c. Now try creating the matrix of Poisson probability for the historical defective rate in (b) and defectives 0 to 5 in (a).

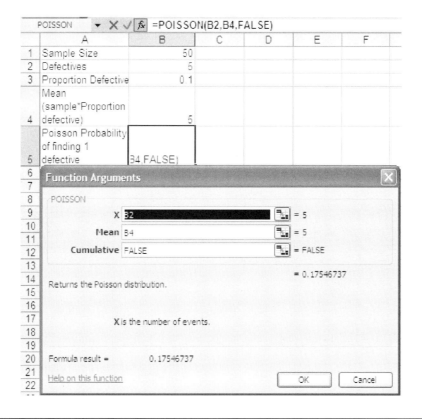

Figure 13.4 Poisson distribution using Microsoft Excel.

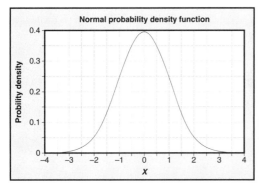
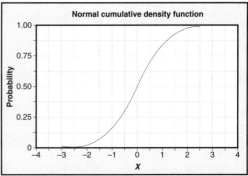

Figure 13.5 Normal probability density function and cumulative density function.
Source: http://www.itl.nist.gov/div898/handbook/eda/section3/eda3661.htm.

NORMAL DISTRIBUTIONS

The normal distribution is the one most frequently used by various professionals.

This is a continuous distribution used for variable data like measurement of length, mass, time, and so on. Several statistical analyses make an assumption that the data are following a normal distribution. According to the central limit theorem, the averages of measurements of individual data follow a normal distribution even if the individual data are from a different distribution. Since the distribution is in the shape of a bell, it is often referred to as a *bell curve*.

Mathematically, the formula for the normal distribution probability density function is:

$$P(x) = \frac{e^{-\frac{(x-\mu)^2}{2\sigma^2}}}{\sigma\sqrt{2\pi}}$$

See Figure 13.5.

The area under the curve between any two points, expressed in standard deviation units (Z scores) can be determined from the statistical tables shown in Appendix E. The standard normal distribution has mean = 0 and standard deviation = 1.

EXAMPLE

Find the area under the standard normal curve between +1.50 standard deviations and +2.50 standard deviations.

Solution: Refer to Figure 13.6. Find the area to the right of 1.50 and subtract the area to the right of 2.50:

Continued

Continued

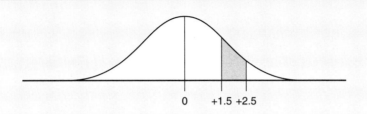

Figure 13.6   Normal curve example.

Using the standard normal tables, the area to the right of 1.50 = 0.0668 and

the area to the right of 2.50 = 0.0062

subtracting: 0.0606

Using Minitab and Excel, the analysis results are:

Cumulative Distribution Function

Normal with mean = 0 and standard deviation = 1

$xP(X \leq x)$

2.5   0.993790

Excel function =NORMDIST(2.5,0,1,TRUE)

Cumulative Distribution Function

Normal with mean = 0 and standard deviation = 1

$xP(X \leq x)$

1.5   0.933193

Excel function =NORMDIST(1.5,0,1,TRUE)

Therefore the area under the curve between the two values is 0.0606. The total area under the standard normal curve is 1 so the area under the curve between the two vertical lines is 6.06 percent of the area under the curve. Hence, we can mathematically calculate the area between any two Z scores of interest. This is a very important concept as this calculation is used for process capability measurement. In this example, the Z score is provided directly. Let us explore a real-life example where we have to compute the Z score and find out the area under the curve.

EXAMPLE

A pizza restaurant's order processing time is normally distributed. A random sample has mean 30 minutes and standard deviation five minutes. Estimate the percent of the orders that are between 35 and 20 minutes.

Continued

Continued

> *Solution:* Find the Z score for 20 and 35. The Z score is the number of standard deviations that the measurement is from the mean and is calculated by the formula $Z = (x - \mu)/\sigma$.
>
> $$Z(20) = (20 - 30)/5 = -2.00$$
>
> $$Z(35) = (35 - 30)/5 = 1$$
>
> $$\text{Area to the right of } -2.00 = 0.97724$$
>
> $$\text{Area to the right of } +1.00 = \underline{0.15865}$$
>
> $$\text{Subtracting: } 0.8186$$
>
> Approximately 82 percent of the orders are processed between 35 minutes and 20 minutes. Put another way, the probability that a randomly selected order will have a processing time between 35 minutes and 20 minutes is approximately 0.82.

Extended exercise:

If the pizza restaurant promises their customers "35-minute delivery or free" and average order cost is $30, estimate the total cost of free food the restaurant has to give away with the current process variation.

Distributions like chi-square (χ^2), *t*, and F are used for decision–making using hypothesis testing.

CHI-SQUARE DISTRIBUTION

If *w*, *x*, *y*, and *z* are random variables with standard normal distributions, then the random variable defined as $f = w^2 + x^2 + y^2 + z^2$ has a chi-square distribution. The chi-square (χ^2) distribution is obtained from the values of the ratio of the sample variance and population variance multiplied by the degrees of freedom. This occurs when the population is normally distributed with population variance σ^2. The most common application of the chi-square distribution is testing proportions. As the degrees of freedom increase, the chi-square distribution approaches a normal distribution. See Figure 13.7.

Properties of the chi-square distribution:

- Chi-square is nonnegative. (It is the ratio of two nonnegative values, therefore must be nonnegative itself).

- Chi-square is nonsymmetric.

- There are many different chi-square distributions, one for each degree of freedom.

- The degrees of freedom when working with a single population variance is $n - 1$.[1]

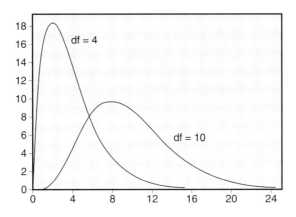

Figure 13.7   Chi-square distribution example.

EXERCISE

Find the critical value for one percent of the area under the chi-square probability density for a random variable that has five degrees of freedom.

From the chi-square table (included on this book's CD-ROM), df = 5 and $\chi^2_{0.01}$ is 15.09.

---

t DISTRIBUTION

If x is a random variable with a standard normal distribution and y is a random variable with a χ^2 distribution, then the random variable defined as

$$t = \frac{x}{\sqrt{\dfrac{y}{k}}}$$

is the t distribution with k degrees of freedom where

k = the degrees of freedom for the χ^2 variable

Notice that as $k \to \infty$, t approaches the normal distribution. This distribution is used in hypothesis tests as illustrated in Chapter 17.

Following are the important properties of Student's t distribution:

1. Student's t distribution is different for different sample sizes.

2. Student's t distribution is generally bell-shaped, but with smaller sample sizes shows increased variability (flatter). In other words, the distribution is less peaked than a normal distribution and with thicker tails. As the sample size increases, the distribution approaches a normal distribution. For $n > 30$, the differences are negligible.

3. The mean is zero (much like the standard normal distribution).

4. The distribution is symmetrical about the mean.

5. The variance is greater than one, but approaches one from above as the sample size increases ($\sigma^2 = 1$ for the standard normal distribution).

6. The population standard deviation is unknown.

7. The population is essentially normal (unimodal and basically symmetric).[2]

EXAMPLE

Twelve randomly selected chemical packs were measured before mixing with the raw material. The weights in grams of chemicals supplied by a vendor to an organization are as follows:

$$7.3, 7.9, 7.1, 7.3, 7.4, 7.3, 7.0, 7.3, 7.7, 7.3, 7.1, 7.8$$

The weight on the pack says 7.5 grams.

What is the probability that the weight of the rest of the packs in storage is greater than 7.5?

Solution:

The mean of the 12 packs is 7.375

The sample standard deviation of the 12 packs is 0.2832

To find the area under the curve:

$$t = \frac{\bar{x} - \mu}{s / \sqrt{n}}$$

Minitab analysis:

Test of $\mu = 7.5$ versus > 7.5

Variable	N	Mean	StDev	SE Mean	95% Lower Bound	T	P
Weight	12	7.37500	0.28324	0.08177	7.22816	−1.53	0.923

Approximately 7.8 percent of the packs could be greater than 7.5.

F DISTRIBUTION

The F distribution is the ratio of two chi-square distributions with degrees of freedom v_1 and v_2, respectively, where each chi-square has first been divided by its degrees of freedom. The F distribution is commonly used for analysis of variance (ANOVA), to test whether the variances of two or more populations are equal. This distribution is used in hypothesis tests.

$$f(x) = \frac{\Gamma\left(\dfrac{v_1 + v_2}{2}\right)\left(\dfrac{v_1}{v_2}\right)^{\frac{v_1}{2}} x^{\frac{v_1}{2} - 1}}{\Gamma\left(\dfrac{v_1}{2}\right)\Gamma\left(\dfrac{v_2}{2}\right)\left(1 + \dfrac{v_1 x}{v_2}\right)^{\frac{v_1 + v_2}{2}}}$$

where v_1 and v_2 are the shape parameters and Γ is the gamma function. The formula for the gamma function is

$$\Gamma(\alpha) = \int_0^\infty t^{\alpha - 1} e^{-t} dt$$

The F probability density function for four different values of the shape parameters is shown in Figure 13.8.

EXERCISE

Find the F ratio given that $F_{0.05}$ with degrees of freedom (v_1) 4 and (v_2) 6 is 4.53. Find $F_{0.95}$ with degrees of freedom (v_1) 6 and (v_2) 4.

$$F_{0.95, 6, 4} = 1/F_{0.05, 4, 6} = 1/4.53 = 0.22$$

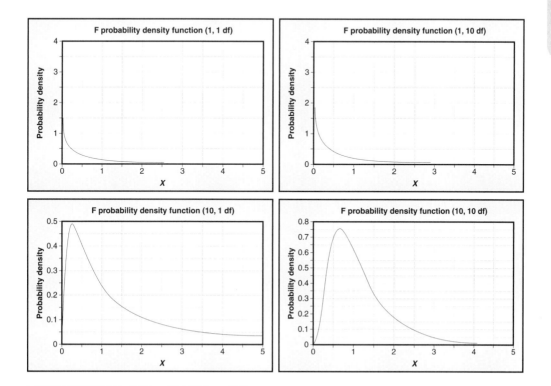

Figure 13.8   F distribution with varying degrees of freedom.

Chapter 14

E. Measurement System Analysis

> Calculate, analyze, and interpret
> measurement system capability using
> repeatability and reproducibility (GR&R),
> measurement correlation, bias, linearity,
> percent agreement, and precision/tolerance
> (P/T). (Evaluate)
>
> **Body of Knowledge III.E**

Measurement system analysis (MSA) is an area of statistical study that explores the variation in measurement data due to:

- *Calibration.* Drift in average measurements of an absolute value.

- *Stability.* Drift in absolute value over time.

- *Repeatability.* Variation in measuring equipment when measured by one appraiser in the same setting at the same time.

- *Reproducibility.* Variation in measurement when measured by two or more appraisers multiple times.

- *Linearity.* Accuracy of measurement at various measurement points of measuring range in the equipment.

- *Bias.* Bias (difference between absolute value and true value) with respect to a standard master at various measurement points of the measuring range.

Until the early 1990s MSA was used extensively in measurement laboratories and less known to the industrial world. After the inception of the QS-9000 (now ISO/ TS 16949) standard in the automobile industry, the importance of MSA has been well understood by other sectors as well.

An important issue for the practitioner here is that in the quest to reduce variation, the measurement system should be one of the first things analyzed for two reasons:

- All data from the process is, in effect, filtered through the measurement system

- It often represents the most cost-effective way to reduce variation

Even statistical process control experts started to rewrite their SPC flow with conducting an MSA study as a starting step. MSA is actually that important. It is not uncommon for measurement systems to have an error of 40 to 50 percent of the process specification.

Repeatability is the equipment measurement variation expressed as standard deviation. Measurements are taken from the same equipment by one appraiser over a short period of time. See Figure 14.1.

Reproducibility is the appraiser measurement variation expressed as standard deviation. Measurements are taken from the same equipment by more than one appraiser. See Figure 14.2.

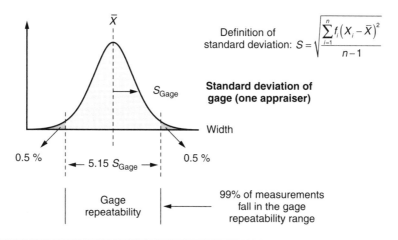

Definition of standard deviation: $S = \sqrt{\dfrac{\sum_{i=1}^{n} f_i\left(X_i - \bar{X}\right)^2}{n-1}}$

Figure 14.1   Gage repeatability.

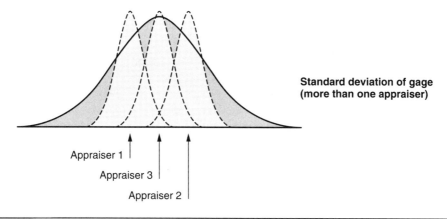

Standard deviation of gage (more than one appraiser)

Figure 14.2   Gage reproducibility.

The repeatability portion of the measurement variation is attributed to the inherent variation of the measurement equipment. Factors that influence this portion of variation include the design of the measurement system itself. In the case of reproducibility, the influential factors are the setting of the work piece (any special loading and unloading), operator training, skill, and knowledge, consistency in measurement, and so on.

Steps for conducting a GR&R study:

1. Plan the study in detail by communicating to the line supervisor, making sure the equipment and appraisers are available for study, equipment is calibrated and in good working condition, the samples are in good condition, and so on. Some studies can take a very long time to complete all the trials due to the measurement duration of a specific characteristic. Make sure that the appraisers are aware of the measurement criteria and inspection method and are trained to perform this measurement. These should be the appraisers who perform these measurements in the process on a regular basis. Time is money. Think of everything that can go wrong and plan for contingencies during the study.

2. The first step is to select and identify samples for the GR&R study. It is important to handpick the samples covering the spread rather than picking random samples from the production bin. It is also recommended that the experimenter identify the samples in a location that is not obviously visible to the appraisers. It is also recommended that the experimenter be present during the R&R study.

3. The next step is to create a table for experimentation purposes with randomized samples between trials and appraisers. The table shown in Figure 14.3 is just for collecting the data in a randomized manner.

4. Appraisers are called one after the other as per the randomized table and requested to perform measurements. This includes multiple trials by every appraiser. It is important that each appraiser complete the study by measuring all samples for every trial. The calculations assume a complete study. An incomplete study can cause imbalances in data and most statistical software will indicate an error message.

5. The complete study is entered from the randomized data collection sheet into the calculation tabular sheet. This sheet is arranged in the sample number sequence. The experimenter may also directly collect the data on the tabular calculation sheet. However, care should be taken not to mistakenly fill in the wrong worksheet cells.

6. Calculations: Calculate the values for row 16 by averaging the values in rows 4, 9, and 14. Calculate the values in the far right-hand column of rows 4, 5, 9, 10, 14, and 15 by averaging the 10 values in their respective rows. Calculate the two entries in the right-hand column of row 16 by finding the average and ranges of the 10 values in that row. Substitute from the right-hand columns of rows 5, 10, and 15 into the formula in row 17 to calculate $\bar{\bar{R}}$. For clarity the formula is repeated here:

Gage Repeatability and Reproducibility Data Collection Sheet

	Appraiser/ trial #	Part										Average
		1	2	3	4	5	6	7	8	9	10	
1	A 1											
2	2											
3	3											
4	Average											
5	Range											
6	B 1											
7	2											
8	3											
9	Average											
10	Range											
11	C 1											
12	2											
13	3											
14	Average											
15	Range											
16	Part average											
17	$([\bar{R}_a = \quad] + [\bar{R}_b = \quad]) + [\bar{R}_c = \quad]) / [$# of appraisers $= \quad] =$										$\bar{\bar{R}} =$	
18	$\bar{X}_{DIFF} = [Max\ \bar{X} = \quad] - [Min\ \bar{X} = \quad] =$										$\bar{X}_{DIFF} =$	
19	$^*UCL_R = [\bar{\bar{R}} = \quad] \times [D_4 = \quad] =$											

$^*D_4 = 3.27$ for two trials and 2.58 for three trials. UCL_R represents the limit of individual R's. Circle those that are beyond this limit. Identify the cause and correct. Repeat these readings using the same appraiser and unit as originally used or discard values and re-average and recompute $\bar{\bar{R}}$ and the limiting value from the remaining observations.

Figure 14.3   Gage R&R data collection sheet.
Used with permission of the Automotive Industry Action Group (AIAG).

$$\bar{\bar{R}} = \frac{\bar{R}_a + \bar{R}_b + \bar{R}_c}{k}$$

where k = number of appraisers. Record this value in the right-hand column of row 17.

Let max $\bar{X}$ = the largest of $\bar{X}_a$, $\bar{X}_b$, and $\bar{X}_c$

Let min $\bar{X}$ = the smallest of $\bar{X}_a$, $\bar{X}_b$, and $\bar{X}_c$

Calculate $\bar{X}_{\text{DIFF}}$ = max $\bar{X}$ – min $\bar{X}$ and place the value in the right-hand column of line 18.

Calculate the upper control limit for the R values using the formula shown in line 19. The $\bar{\bar{R}}$ value is from the right-hand column of row 17 and the D_4 value is 2.58 if each part was measured three times as outlined above. If, instead, each part was measured only twice, the D_4 value is 3.27.

Note the instructions at the bottom of the form. They indicate that each of the 10 R values in row 5 should be compared to the UCL_R value calculated in row 19. Any R value that exceeds UCL_R should be circled. Repeat this for the R values in rows 10 and 15. The circled R values are significantly different from the others and the cause of this difference should be identified and corrected. Once this has been done, the appropriate parts can be remeasured using the same appraiser, equipment, and so on, as the original measurements. All impacted values must be recomputed.

Recall that repeatability is the variation in measurements that occurs when the same measuring system, including equipment, material, appraiser, and so on, are used. Repeatability, then, is reflected in the R values as recorded in rows 5, 9, and 15 and summarized in row 17. Repeatability is often referred to as equipment variation but the individual R averages may indicate differences between appraisers. In the example in Figure 14.4, R_a is somewhat smaller than R_b or R_c. This indicates that appraiser A may have done better at getting the same answer on repeated measurements of the same part than the other two appraisers. Further analysis may be required to investigate why a certain appraiser has wider variation than others.

Reproducibility is the variation that occurs between the overall average measurements for the three appraisers. It is reflected by the $\bar{X}$ values in rows 4, 9, and 14 and summarized in the value of $\bar{X}_{\text{DIFF}}$ in row 18. If, for instance, $\bar{X}_a$ and $\bar{X}_b$ had been quite close and $\bar{X}_c$ were significantly different, it would appear that appraiser C measurements have some sort of bias. Again, further investigation can be very productive.

The next step in the study is to complete the Gage Repeatability and Reproducibility Report as shown in Figure 14.5. A completed report based on the data from Figure 14.4 is shown in Figure 14.6. The quantity labeled EV for *equipment variation* is an estimate of the standard deviation of the variation due to repeatability. It is sometimes denoted σ_E or σ_{rpt}. The quantity labeled AV for *appraiser variation* is an estimate of the standard deviation of the variation due to reproducibility and is sometimes denoted σ_A or σ_{rpd}. The quantity labeled GRR is an estimate of the standard deviation of the variation due to the measurement system and is sometimes denoted σ_M. The quantity labeled PV is an estimate of the standard deviation of the part-to-part variation and is sometimes denoted σ_P. The quantity

Gage Repeatability and Reproducibility Data Collection Sheet											
Appraiser/ trial #	Part										
	1	2	3	4	5	6	7	8	9	10	Average
1 — A 1	0.29	−0.56	1.34	0.47	−0.80	0.02	0.59	−0.31	2.26	−1.36	0.194
2 — 2	0.41	−0.68	1.17	0.50	−0.92	−0.11	0.75	−0.20	1.99	−1.25	0.166
3 — 3	0.64	−0.58	1.27	0.64	−0.84	−0.21	0.66	−0.17	2.01	−1.31	0.211
4 — Average	0.447	−0.607	1.260	0.537	−0.853	−0.100	0.667	−0.227	2.087	−1.307	$\bar{X}_a = 0.1903$
5 — Range	0.35	0.12	0.17	0.17	0.12	0.23	0.16	0.14	0.27	0.11	$\bar{R}_a = 0.184$
6 — B 1	0.08	−0.47	1.19	0.01	−0.56	−0.20	0.47	−0.63	1.80	−1.68	0.001
7 — ?	0.06	1.00	0.94	1.03	−1.20	0.22	0.55	0.08	2.12	−1.62	0.115
8 — 3	0.07	−0.68	1.34	0.20	−1.28	0.06	0.83	−0.34	2.19	−1.50	0.089
9 — Average	0.133	−0.790	1.157	0.413	−1.013	0.027	0.617	−0.297	2.037	−1.600	$\bar{X}_b = 0.068$
10 — Range	0.18	0.75	0.40	1.02	0.72	0.42	0.36	0.71	0.39	0.18	$\bar{R}_b = 0.513$
11 — C 1	0.04	−1.38	0.88	0.14	−1.46	−0.29	0.02	−0.46	1.77	−1.49	−0.223
12 — 2	−0.11	−1.13	1.09	0.20	−1.07	−0.67	0.01	−0.56	1.45	−1.77	−0.256
13 — 3	−0.15	−0.96	0.67	0.11	−1.45	−0.49	0.21	−0.49	1.87	−2.16	−0.284
14 — Average	0.073	−1.157	0.880	0.150	−1.327	−0.483	0.080	−0.503	1.697	−1.807	$\bar{X}_c = -0.2543$
15 — Range	0.19	0.42	0.42	0.09	0.39	0.38	0.20	0.10	0.42	0.67	$\bar{R}_c = 0.328$
16 — Part average	0.169	−0.851	1.099	0.367	−1.064	−0.186	0.454	−0.342	1.940	−1.571	$\bar{\bar{X}} = 0.0015$ $\bar{R}_p = 3.511$
17 — $([\bar{R}_a = 0.184] + [\bar{R}_b = 0.513]) + [\bar{R}_c = 0.328]) / [\text{\# of appraisers} = 3] =$											$\bar{\bar{R}} = \mathbf{0.3417}$
18 — $\bar{X}_{DIFF} = [Max\ \bar{X} = 0.1903] - [Min\ \bar{X} = -0.2543] =$											$\bar{X}_{DIFF} = \mathbf{0.4446}$
19 — $^*UCL_R = [\bar{\bar{R}} = 0.3417] \times [D_4 = 2.58] = 0.8816$											

$^*D_4 = 3.27$ for two trials and 2.58 for three trials. UCL_R represents the limit of individual R's. Circle those that are beyond this limit. Identify the cause and correct. Repeat these readings using the same appraiser and unit as originally used or discard values and re-average and recompute $\bar{R}$ and the limiting value from the remaining observations.

Figure 14.4   Gage R&R data collection sheet with data entered and calculations completed.
Used with permission of the Automotive Industry Action Group (AIAG).

labeled TV is an estimate of the standard deviation of the total in the study and is sometimes denoted σ_T. The right-hand column in Figure 14.6 shows for each type of variation the percent of total variation it consumes. Sometimes the right-hand column is based on the tolerance for the dimension.

Part III.E

Gage Repeatability and Reproducibility Report		
Part no. & name:	Gage name:	Date:
Characteristics:	Gage no.:	Performed by:
Specifications:	Gage type:	
From data sheet: $\bar{\bar{R}} =$	$\bar{X}_{DIFF} =$	$R_p =$

Measurement Unit Analysis			% Total Variation

Repeatability—Equipment Variation (EV)

$EV = \bar{\bar{R}} \times K_1$

$= \_\_\_\_ \times \_\_\_\_$

$= \_\_\_\_$

Trials	K_1
2	0.8862
3	0.5908

% EV = 100[EV / TV]
= 100[____ / ____]
= ____%

Reproducibility—Appraiser Variation (AV)

$AV = \sqrt{(\bar{X}_{DIFF} \times K_2)^2 - (EV^2 / (nr))}$

$\sqrt{(\_\_\_ \times \_\_\_)^2 - (\_\_\_^2 / (\_\_ \times \_\_))}$

$= \_\_\_\_$

$n = parts \quad r = trials$

Appraisers	2	3
K_2	0.7071	0.5231

% AV = 100[AV / TV]
= 100[____ / ____]
= ____%

Repeatability & Reproducibility (GRR)

$GRR = \sqrt{EV^2 + AV^2}$

$= \sqrt{\_\_\_^2 + \_\_\_^2}$

$= \_\_\_\_$

Parts	K_3
2	0.7071
3	0.5231
4	0.4467
5	0.4030
6	0.3742
7	0.3534
8	0.3375
9	0.3249
10	0.3146

% GRR = 100[GRR / TV]
= 100[____ / ____]
= ____%

Part Variation (PV)

$PV = R_p \times K_3$

$= \_\_\_\_ \times \_\_\_\_$

$= \_\_\_\_$

% PV = 100[PV/ TV]
= 100[____ / ____]
= ____%

Total Variation (TV)

$TV = \sqrt{GRR^2 + PV^2}$

$= \sqrt{\_\_\_^2 + \_\_\_^2}$

$= \_\_\_\_$

ndc = 1.41 (PV / GRR)
= 1.41 (___ / ___)
= ____

Figure 14.5 Gage Repeatability and Reproducibility Report.
Used with permission of the Automotive Industry Action Group (AIAG).

Gage Repeatability and Reproducibility Report		
Part no. & name: Characteristics: Specifications:	Gage name: Gage no.: Gage type:	Date: Performed by:
From data sheet: $\bar{\bar{R}} = 0.3417$	$\bar{X}_{DIFF} = 0.4446$	$R_p = 3.511$

Measurement Unit Analysis				% Total Variation	
Repeatability—Equipment Variation (EV)					
$EV = \bar{\bar{R}} \times K_1$		Trials	K_1	% EV	$= 100[EV / TV]$
$= 0.3417 \times 0.5908$		2	0.8862		$= 100[0.20188 / 1.14610]$
$= 0.20188$		3	0.5908		$= 17.62\%$
Reproducibility—Appraiser Variation (AV)					
$AV = \sqrt{(\bar{X}_{DIFF} \times K_2)^2 - (EV^2 / (nr))}$				% AV	$= 100[AV / TV]$
$\sqrt{(0.4446 \times 0.5231)^2 - (0.20188^2 / (10 \times 3))}$					$= 100[0.22963 / 1.14610]$
$= 0.22963$	Appraisers	2	3		$= 20.04\%$
n = parts r = trials	K_2	0.7071	0.5231		
Repeatability & Reproducibility (GRR)					
$GRR = \sqrt{EV^2 + AV^2}$				% GRR	$= 100[GRR / TV]$
$= \sqrt{0.20188^2 + 0.22963^2}$		Parts	K_3		$= 100[0.30575 / 1.14610]$
$= 0.30575$		2	0.7071		$= 26.68\%$
Part Variation (PV)		3	0.5231		
$PV = R_p \times K_3$		4	0.4467	% PV	$= 100[PV / TV]$
$= 3.511 \times 0.3146$		5	0.4030		$= 100[1.10456 / 1.14610]$
$= 1.10456$		6	0.3742		$= 96.38\%$
Total Variation (TV)		7	0.3534		
$TV = \sqrt{GRR^2 + PV^2}$		8	0.3375	ndc	$= 1.41 \ (PV / GRR)$
$= \sqrt{0.30575^2 + 1.10456^2}$		9	0.3249		$= 1.41 \ (1.10456 / 0.30575)$
$= 1.14610$		10	0.3146		$= 5.094 = 5$

Figure 14.6   Gage Repeatability and Reproducibility Report with calculations.
Used with permission of the Automotive Industry Action Group (AIAG).

Part III.E

Precision to tolerance ratio (P/T): In this case the value of the divisor TV is replaced by one sixth of the tolerance, that is (tolerance) ÷ 6. Most authorities agree that in this situation the %GRR is defined as:

$$(100 \text{ GRR}) \div (\text{tolerance}/6)$$

Six is used to cover 99.73 percent of variation. Some practitioners also use 5.15 to cover 99 pecent of the variation. For information on the theory and constants used in this form see *MSA Reference Manual,* Third Edition.

There are also many inexpensive Excel-based macro applications available as off-the-shelf software. Figure 14.7 shows the same data analyzed using Minitab statistical software.

Notice that there are several points outside the control limits in the sample mean chart. This is the way it is supposed to be as we intentionally picked the samples to cover the spread of the process specification. On the other hand, the points in the sample range charts should be within the control limits. We notice that the fourth measurement point of appraiser B is outside the control limits. Investigate to verify whether this is a recording error or due to any special causes.

The other charts visually indicate the spread of measurement points and any noticeable outliers, analyzed by sample and by appraiser. If a sample had issues with retaining certain measurements during the study period, this will probably show up in the chart (by sample). Also, if an appraiser is consistently measuring higher or lower than the others, it will be noticeable in the chart (by appraiser). In our example, appraiser C is consistently measuring lower. This is also visible in the appraiser * sample interaction graph.

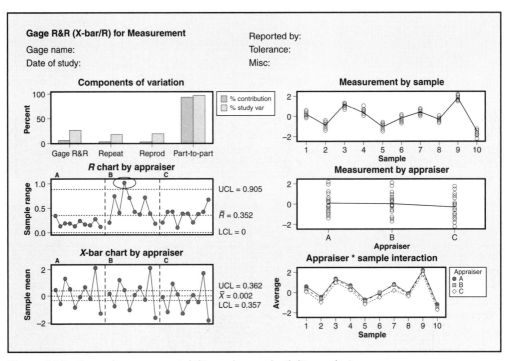

Figure 14.7   Example gage repeatability and reproducibility analysis.

Gage R&R study—XBar/R method

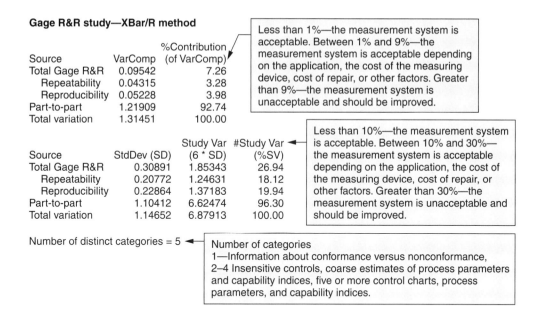

Source	VarComp	%Contribution (of VarComp)
Total Gage R&R	0.09542	7.26
Repeatability	0.04315	3.28
Reproducibility	0.05228	3.98
Part-to-part	1.21909	92.74
Total variation	1.31451	100.00

> Less than 1%—the measurement system is acceptable. Between 1% and 9%—the measurement system is acceptable depending on the application, the cost of the measuring device, cost of repair, or other factors. Greater than 9%—the measurement system is unacceptable and should be improved.

Source	StdDev (SD)	Study Var (6 * SD)	#Study Var (%SV)
Total Gage R&R	0.30891	1.85343	26.94
Repeatability	0.20772	1.24631	18.12
Reproducibility	0.22864	1.37183	19.94
Part-to-part	1.10412	6.62474	96.30
Total variation	1.14652	6.87913	100.00

> Less than 10%—the measurement system is acceptable. Between 10% and 30%—the measurement system is acceptable depending on the application, the cost of the measuring device, cost of repair, or other factors. Greater than 30%—the measurement system is unacceptable and should be improved.

Number of distinct categories = 5

> Number of categories
> 1—Information about conformance versus nonconformance,
> 2–4 Insensitive controls, coarse estimates of process parameters and capability indices, five or more control charts, process parameters, and capability indices.

Figure 14.8   GR&R report using statistical software.

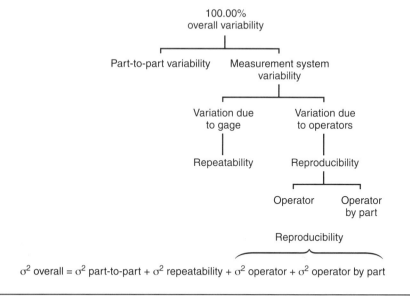

$$\sigma^2 \text{ overall} = \sigma^2 \text{ part-to-part} + \sigma^2 \text{ repeatability} + \sigma^2 \text{ operator} + \sigma^2 \text{ operator by part}$$

Figure 14.9   Sources of measurement variation.

Sources of measurement variation are shown in Figure 14.9.

Number of distinct categories: Measurement system discrimination is the ability to detect changes in the measured characteristic. If a measurement system's discrimination is inadequate, it may not be possible to accurately measure process variation or quantify characteristic values (such as the mean) of individual parts.[1]

There are minor differences between the manual method and Minitab software due to rounding errors. The Minitab analysis is more accurate.

Effect of R&R on capability: As mentioned earlier, the measurement system plays a major role in process capability (C_p) assessment. The higher the gage R&R, the higher the error in C_p assessment. This increases even more as the capability increases. Example: With an observed C_p of 1 and a GR&R of 50 percent, the actual C_p is 1.23. By bringing the GR&R to 10 percent, the actual C_p is more reflective of the actual process, that is, 1.01. See Figure 14.10. More details on this table, formula, and graphs are available in *Concepts of R&R Studies* by Larry B. Barrentine.

Following are some common errors made while performing GR&R:

1. *In process control situations, not selecting samples covering the tolerance spread.* In fact, it is recommended to even pick samples outside the specification limits. It is a common tendency for experimenters to pick some random samples from the process to study GR&R. See AIAG Reference notes on page 204 for rationale.

2. *Not randomizing the samples during measurement.* Randomizing the experiment takes some effort and care from the experimenter but it is really worth it. Not randomizing the R&R study will probably introduce knowledge bias in the repetitive measurement trials.

3. *Using untrained appraisers or process-unrelated employees in the experiment because there are not enough appraisers to conduct the studies.* This will result in inflated reproducibility errors. Using engineers instead of the appraisers will also impact the results.

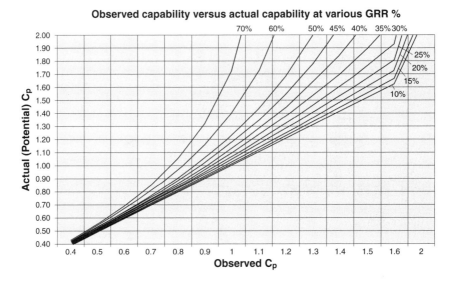

Figure 14.10 Observed versus actual capability.

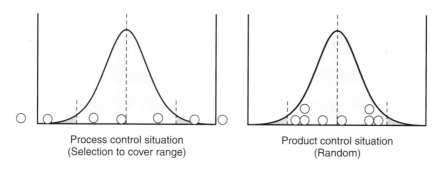

Process control situation
(Selection to cover range)

Product control situation
(Random)

Figure 14.11   GR&R sample selection.

4. *Altering the samples during the study.* This includes accidental dropping of the samples.

5. *Experimenter not present during the R&R study.* (Assigning to the appraisers directly and/or trying to study from a remote location.) R&R studies are expensive as they involve resources like equipment and labor. Any mistakes performed during the study can invalidate the results and require starting all over. There are cases where the measurement is automated and duration long enough that the experimenter need not stay. However, it is important to be present during the human interaction portion of the measurement, that is, loading, setting, aligning, unloading, and so on.

6. *Publishing the results with appraisers' names.* It is important for the experimenters to know who has introduced more variation and analyze the root causes, assign additional training, and so on. It is not required to release the analysis with actual appraiser names for general viewing. This can create unhealthy comparisons between appraisers or make some appraisers uneasy. This may result in not cooperating for future studies. It is recommended to present the results as appraiser A, B, C, and so on.

7. *Assuming that the GR&R results are valid forever.* GR&R results have to be periodically validated just as we do gage calibration at a regular frequency. Over a period of time, the measurement methods change, the appraisers change, settings change. Equipment that uses software/firmware (embedded software) may also change.

8. *Assuming that GR&R performed on a specific piece of equipment is the same as for all other equipment of that kind* (sometimes referred to as a 'family of gages'). This may not be true. Equipment #1 may be used by a set of appraisers from three shifts and equipment #2 used by a different set of appraisers. One piece of equipment may be used under controlled environmental conditions and others used under rugged conditions

on the shop floor. They may be the same type of equipment but from different manufacturers or used in very different ways or settings.

Linearity and Bias: Having discussed equipment variation and appraiser variation, we still have some unanswered questions. What if the equipment is accurate at one point of measurement and not at other points of measurement across the measurement range? We need to perform a linearity study to answer this question. Also, we would like to know how biased the measuring equipment is compared to a "master." Let us review using a Minitab analysis: appraiser A measurements from the previous example were taken and compared with process variation to estimate percent linearity and compared with a master value of measurement at the point where the measurement was made in the measuring range. See Table 14.1

Figure 14.12 shows the Minitab analysis of this data. Our first important observation is: the R-Sq value is 0.0%. This shows a nonlinearity issue with the measuring equipment.

Possible causes of nonlinearity include: instrument not calibrated properly at both the high and low end of the operating range, error in one or more of the master part measurements, worn instrument, and characteristics of the instrument design.[2]

Percent linearity is smaller; however, due to the nonlinearity issue, the percent linearity is not valid.

In the same graph, we see that the average percent bias gives a P value of zero, indicating a higher significance of bias issues with the instrument. The report also provides a breakdown of percent bias at the measurement points covered during the study.

The experimenter is advised to look into nonlinearity issues and also to try conducting the study on a broader range of measurements of the equipment to reassess the linearity.

Measurement correlation: Measurement correlation is used when measurements are taken simultaneously with multiple measurement devices of the same type for parts coming from multiple streams of manufacturing. Creating scatter diagrams and estimating the correlation coefficient between measurement systems can provide insight into whether the multiple measuring devices are contributing to a special cause. A more sophisticated approach would be to conduct an experiment with multiple appraisers, multiple measuring devices, and samples and trials fully randomized, and analyzing for "components of variance." If the variance between measuring equipment shows a significant P value, then this is an area for the experimenter to investigate.

Percent agreement: An R&R study can also be extended to attribute characteristics like go/no-go results. In the transactional process (service) industries, data may not always be continuous. Results may be expressed as yes/no, OK/not OK, accept/reject, with rating scales from 1 to 5, and so on. In such cases, an attribute agreement study is used to assess the variation. In many cases this is purely human variation in judgment and/or evaluation. In some cases it is purely machine variation, for example, automatic measurement gauging where parts are automatically screened as good or bad by the machine.

Table 14.1 Measurement test data for linearity and bias.

Sample	Appraiser	Trial	Measurement	Master
1	A	1	0.29	0.4
1	A	2	0.41	0.4
1	A	3	0.64	0.4
2	A	1	−0.56	0.6
2	A	2	−0.68	0.6
2	A	3	−0.58	0.6
3	A	1	1.34	1.2
3	A	2	1.17	1.2
3	A	3	1.27	1.2
4	A	1	0.47	0.5
4	A	2	0.5	0.5
4	A	3	0.64	0.5
5	A	1	−0.8	−0.85
5	A	2	−0.92	−0.85
5	A	3	−0.84	−0.85
6	A	1	0.02	−0.1
6	A	2	−0.11	−0.1
6	A	3	−0.21	−0.1
7	A	1	0.59	0.7
7	A	2	0.75	0.7
7	A	3	0.66	0.7
8	A	1	−0.31	−0.2
8	A	2	−0.2	−0.2
8	A	3	−0.17	−0.2
9	A	1	2.26	2
9	A	2	1.99	2
9	A	3	2.01	2
10	A	1	−1.36	−1.2
10	A	2	−1.25	−1.2
10	A	3	−1.31	−1.2

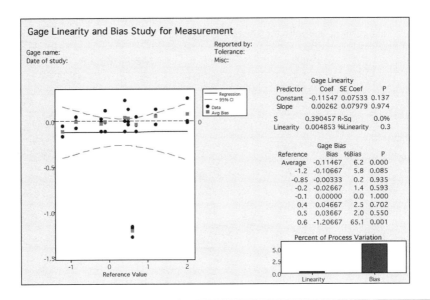

Figure 14.12   Linearity and bias analysis using statistical software.

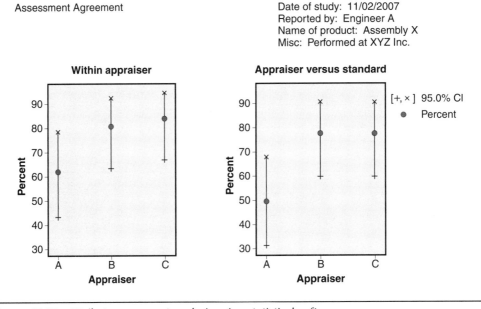

Figure 14.13   Attribute agreement analysis using statistical software.

A study was conducted with three appraisers inspecting 32 samples in a visual inspection criteria assessment of a polished glass surface. The appraisers inspected the surface and using the criteria made judgment of pass or fail. Following are the results and analysis (see Figure 14.13).

Assessment agreement:

Appraiser	# inspected	# matched	Percent (%)	95.0% CI
A	32	20	62.5	(43.7, 78.9)
B	32	26	81.3	(63.6, 92.8)
C	32	27	84.4	(67.2, 94.7)

Number matched: appraiser agrees with him/herself across trials.

"Within appraiser" shows the inconsistencies within an appraiser. Sometimes the appraiser may judge the same sample as "pass" and another time as "fail." These inconsistencies are not uncommon when human judgment is used. Inconsistencies may be caused due to not understanding the criteria properly, human mood swings, ergonomics of the inspection area, fatigue, and many other reasons.

The same results are matched with the "master results" from a senior appraiser or the process expert. Let us call that a standard.

Assessment agreement:

Appraiser	# inspected	# matched	Percent (%)	95.0% CI
A	32	16	50.0	(31.9, 68.1)
B	32	25	78.1	(60.0, 90.7)
C	32	25	78.1	(60.0, 90.7)

Number matched: appraiser's assessment across trials agrees with standard.

Appraisers B and C have higher percent matching to standard be it accept or reject.

Assessment disagreement:

Appraiser	# R/A	Percent (%)	# A/R	Percent (%)	# Mixed	Percent (%)
A	3	11.5	1	16.7	12	37.5
B	0	0.0	1	16.7	6	18.8
C	0	0.0	2	33.3	5	15.6

Number R/A: assessments across trials = R/standard = A.
Number A/R: assessments across trials = A/standard = R.
Number mixed: assessments across trials are not identical.

Here, appraiser A is rejecting 11.5 percent of good parts whereas appraisers B and C are not rejecting any good parts. Appraisers A and B are accepting 16.7 percent of bad parts whereas appraiser C is accepting 33.3 percent of bad parts. This is not good either as the customer may get bad parts. Since appraiser C is more consistent in judgment, it is easier to train appraiser C to reduce the risk of accepting bad parts.

More advanced statistics are available for this type of attribute study involving ranking scores. Examples of this application where objectivity is added to subjective measures:

- Tasting tea, coffee, and wine and assigning a score for taste attributes
- Examiners correcting a paper and assigning a score
- Fabrics or polished surfaces where the score is assigned by feeling the surface

Practical challenges in GR&R studies:

1. Management commitment to conduct the study on a periodic basis and monitoring the GR&R percent for critical parameters. Since there is a lot of resource commitment in this type of study, management buy-in is required for sustainability.

2. GR&R can be challenging as all applications are not as straightforward as textbook examples. Some of the challenges that the author has experienced:

   a. One-sided specification

   b. Skewed distribution

   c. Fully automated equipment with no or minimal appraiser interaction

   d. Destructive testing

   e. New product introduction where only a few units are available

   f. Multiple station comparison

   g. Equipment that requires resetting or calibration after every measurement

   h. Incomplete GR&R data (units shipped during the study due to urgency)

This is an area of study that is developing new ideas. There are several technical papers that discuss GR&R for destructive testing using nested design. Green Belts and Black Belts are encouraged to expand their knowledge by understanding the new concepts for various challenging applications of GR&R.

AIAG Reference. For product control situations where the measurement result and decision criteria determine "conformance or nonconformance to the feature specification" (that is, 100 percent inspection or sampling), samples (or standards) must be selected, but need not cover the entire process range. The assessment of the measurement system is based on the feature tolerance (that is, percent GR&R to tolerance).

For process control situations where the measurement result and decision criteria determine "process stability, direction, and compliance with the natural process variation" (that is, SPC, process monitoring, capability, and process improvement), the availability of samples over the entire operating range becomes very important. An independent estimate of process variation (process capability study) is recommended when assessing the adequacy of the measurement system for process control (that is, percent GR&R to process variation).[3]

When an independent estimate of process variation is not available, *or* to determine process direction and continued suitability of the measurement system for process control, *the sample parts must be selected from the process and represent the entire production operating range.* The variation in sample parts (PV) selected for MSA study is used to calculate the total variation (TV) of the study. The TV index (that is, percent GR&R to TV) is an indicator of process direction and continued suitability of the measurement system for process control. If the sample parts *do not* represent the production process, TV must be ignored in the assessment. Ignoring TV does not affect assessments using tolerance (product control) or an independent estimate of process variation (process control).

Key Point: The underlying reason to conduct ongoing measurement system analysis of your measurement equipment is to understand the uncertainty of the measurement system. That is, what exactly are you really measuring?

Part III.E

Chapter 15

F. Process Capability and Performance

1. PROCESS CAPABILITY STUDIES

Identify, describe, and apply the elements of designing and conducting process capability studies, including identifying characteristics, identifying specifications and tolerances, developing sampling plans, and verifying stability and normality. (Evaluate)

Body of Knowledge III.F.1

Process capability is the ability of the process to meet the expected specifications. Every process has variation due to common causes and special causes, both internal and external to the process.

Examples of common causes include interaction between process steps caused by the way the processes are sequenced, manufacturing equipment design, natural variation in incoming material supply, measuring equipment design, and so on. Special cause examples include significant changes in incoming material quality, operators with varying skill levels, changes to process settings, environmental variations, and so on.

The random process variations caused by common causes influence the ability of the process to meet the expected specifications (process capability). Assignable (special) causes are investigated and removed before estimating the process capability.

In practice, people familiar with the process are usually able to identify the few characteristics that merit a full capability study. These are the characteristics that past experience has shown to be difficult to hold to specification. In some industries, the customers themselves identify critical characteristics that need to be monitored by SPC.

But, best practice is to perform a comprehensive process FMEA, identify the parameters or characteristics that require statistical process control, and create a control plan with detailed SPC planning. The reason is that implementing SPC and measuring process capability costs money to the organization. Hence, selection of appropriate process parameters and characteristics is important. More details on FMEA and control plans can be found in Chapter 9.

Specifications and tolerances are obtained from engineering drawings and customer contracts.

Sometimes they are also publicly announced as guarantees to customers. Have you seen advertisements guaranteeing the following?

- Expediters: next-day delivery

- Restaurants: (Wait time) 15 minutes or free

- Even rental apartments: emergency maintenance resolution in 24 hours or one-day rental free

All the above are examples of specifications and tolerances. Unlike manufacturing, these are areas where customers do not explicitly state their expectations. Service providers study the market and customer expectations through surveys and informal interviews and identify specifications and tolerances themselves to be competitive in the market.

Steps for Process Capability Studies

Measurement system verification: The first step in conducting a process capability study is to perform measurement system analysis. Measurement system variation can mislead the process capability assessment and process stability monitoring. As discussed in the previous chapter, Larry Barrentine, in his book *Concepts for R&R Studies*, presents a graph that shows the relationship between actual process capability and observed process capability for various measurement system error percentages. Once the MSA is performed and sources of variation are identified and removed, the percentage of measurement variation reduces to a small proportion of overall process variation and process tolerance. Now we can proceed to performing the process capability studies.

The next step is to identify appropriate rational subgrouping of samples for control chart plotting. Subgroup size can be anywhere between two and 10. However, subgroups greater than five are uncommon. A typical SPC chart has five consecutive samples taken at equal intervals from a process and average/range plotted to observe the stability of the process. Care has to be taken that within-subgroup variation is smaller than between-subgroup variation. For low-volume processes, individual charts are plotted to monitor the stability where the subgroup size is one. Average standard deviation charts are used when the subgroup size is greater than 10. This is a more powerful chart for detecting shifts in processes but can be costly for data collection. An individual chart with subgroup size one is on the other hand less sensitive to detecting shifts. An average range chart provides an economic balance between the cost of running SPC and information that can be usefully derived.

Stability is a fairly sophisticated statistical concept, equivalent to the absence of special causes of variation. After 20 subgroups of points have been plotted, if the chart shows that no special causes are present, the process is considered to be stable. Although authorities disagree on the number of points needed, 20 or 30 points commonly are used. More points are plotted for higher confidence in the stability conclusion.

Control chart monitoring is not impacted even if the distribution of the data is nonnormal. However, to measure the process capability, normality is required for continuous data.

To do this, construct a histogram using the original readings (not the averages) from the control chart. If the histogram looks normal, with most points grouped around a single peak and fairly symmetric tails on each side, it is assumed that the data constitutes a sample drawn from an approximately normal population. Again, the more data used, the greater the confidence one can have in this conclusion. All commercially sold statistical software can construct a probability plot with confidence intervals and test for normality.

If the process data are not normally distributed, techniques like the Box-Cox transformation and Johnson transformations are used for nonnormal to normal data transformations. If the data are normally distributed, the next step is to use a normal distribution table to estimate process capability. The most common method is to use the data from a control chart to estimate μ and σ.

The overall objective of the process capability study is to monitor whether a process is in statistical control and the process is capable of meeting specifications. If the process is capable, we move on to review other characteristics. If not, we take action to improve the capability. Given that the process is stable, the first obvious step is to try to center the process and review the percent nonconformance outside the specification limits. If the process variation is smaller than the specifications, this can reduce the number of nonconformances. The next important action is to reduce the variation. This is the crux of Six Sigma methodology and the major payback on effort. Sometimes for economic reasons it is unfortunately required to off-center the process distribution in a direction that creates rework and salvage rather than scrapping of parts. This is a containment action until engineering figures out a means for reducing the variation. Another possibility is to revisit the specification limits from the customer and engineering standpoint. Surprisingly, it is not uncommon to see specifications that are set unrealistically tight by designers without reviewing the capability of the process and limitations of technology.

Sampling with Respect to Statistical Process Control

Random sampling is particularly useful if we have a batch process like oven baking, spray painting, heat treatment, group therapy, and so on. If in the earlier experiments it is proven that the part selected at random from a batch is representative of the group, we can pick random samples, average the measurements of the samples, and plot them as one data point of a subgroup. Note that the measurements made within a batch are *not* a subgroup. Batch-to-batch variation can be represented as an average moving range. Within-batch variation can be represented with a range or standard deviation chart.

Systematic sampling can be used when performing individual moving range SPC monitoring by sampling every *n*th part. This is typically applied when parts are coming out of a conveyor line. In a transactional process situation such as a

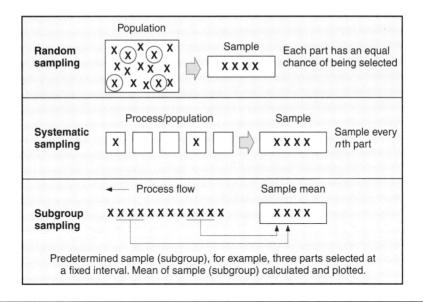

Figure 15.1   Types of sampling for SPC data collection.

banking mortgage transaction, sampling every nth customer might be used to assess service quality.

The subgroup approach of sampling is the typical approach used for plotting $\overline{X}$ and R charts or $\overline{X}$ and s charts. An important factor to keep in mind is that the within-subgroup variation should contain only chance causes. This is the reason that consecutive parts are sampled in the $\overline{X}$ chart approach. The subgroup intervals should be carefully planned to capture special causes, if any. See Figure 15.1 for a summary of these types of sampling.

2. PROCESS PERFORMANCE VS. SPECIFICATION

Distinguish between natural process limits and specification limits, and calculate process performance metrics such as percent defective. (Evaluate)

Body of Knowledge III.F.2

Natural process limits are calculated from process variation. This is done after removal of all special causes and the process has achieved statistical stability. Specifications, on the other hand, are expectations from the engineering or customer point of view. When the process variation is significantly lower than the

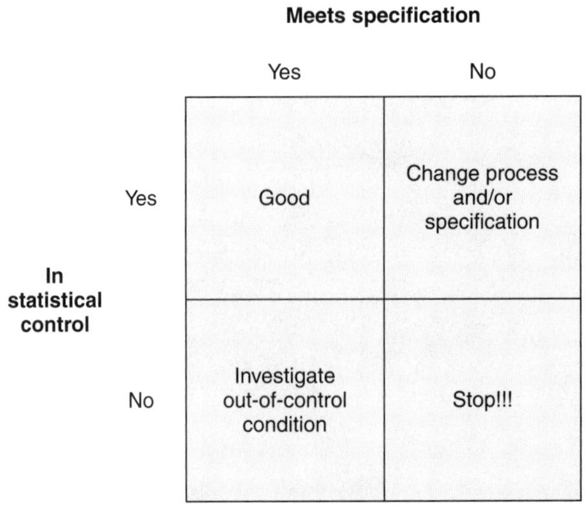

Meets specification

		Yes	No
In statistical control	Yes	Good	Change process and/or specification
	No	Investigate out-of-control condition	Stop!!!

Figure 15.2   Control limit versus specification limit grid.

width of the specification (upper limit–lower limit), then we call the process a capable process.

The matrix in Figure 15.2 explains in brief the type of action a Green Belt should take in a process based on one of the four given scenarios.

EXAMPLE

First quadrant. If the process is in a state of statistical control (within natural process control limits and follows other applicable rules) and meets specification, the situation is "good."

Third quadrant. If the process is not in a state of statistical control (within natural process control limits and follows other applicable rules) and does not meet specification, the Green Belt should stop the process and immediately investigate.

Engineers often get confused between natural process limits and specification limits. Many who are in the fourth quadrant scenario may even argue that they need not worry as they are producing products that meets specification. They may be hesitant to invest any time in investigating out-of-control conditions. It is important that Green Belts explain to those engineers that out-of-control situations cause lack of predictability in the process. Once a process is unpredictable, the process may go out of spec at any time.

The chart in Figure 15.3 identifies the natural process limits. As you can see, the square points are those subgroups that have assignable causes. The numbers adjacent to the square points are the rule numbers being violated. Modern statistical software has made this analysis very easy. However, the interpretation of the chart and taking appropriate action to remove the assignable causes are still human endeavors. Six Sigma Green Belts are expected to review those out-of-control violations, assign special causes, and recalculate the control limits before firming up the limits for implementation. Chapter 21 will cover this topic more extensively.

Test Results for $\bar{X}$ Chart of Length

Test 1. One point more than 3.00 standard deviations from centerline (see Figure 15.3). Test failed at point: 12

Test 4. 14 points in a row alternating up and down. Test failed at points: 54, 55, 56, 57

Test 5. Two out of three points more than two standard deviations from centerline (on one side of centerline). Test failed at points: 24, 45

Test Results for R Chart of Length

Test 1. One point more than 3.00 standard deviations from centerline (see Figure 15.3). Test failed at point: 8

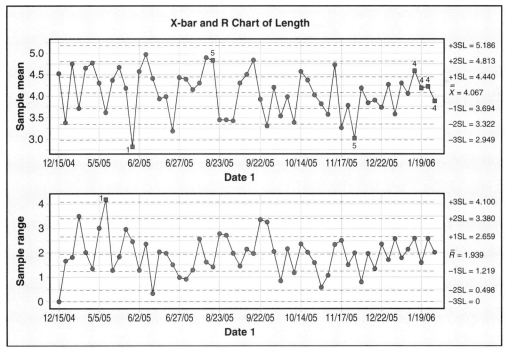

Figure 15.3   Example of $\bar{X}$ and R control chart.

EXAMPLE

A product after packing is specified to weigh between 1.00 to 1.10 lbs. Data collected from shipping over a period of 30 days indicates that the distribution is normally distributed and the associated control chart is stable. The control chart used a subgroup sample size of four every two hours. The control chart calculations show that the grand process average is 1.065 lbs. and the average range is 0.05. A Green Belt is assigned to estimate the percent of product that could have been shipped underweight and overweight.

Solution: The point estimate for μ is 1.065 lbs. The point estimate for process standard deviation is given by the formula

$$\hat{\sigma} = \frac{\bar{R}}{d_2} = \frac{0.05}{2.059} \approx 0.024 \text{ lbs.}$$

(The value of statistical constant d_2 for a subgroup of size four is 2.059.)

The distance from the upper specification limit to the process average is 1.10 − 1.065 = 0.035. Dividing this by the standard deviation gives 0.035/.024 = 1.46, which may be thought of as the number of standard deviations between the process average and the upper specification limit. It is customary to label this quantity Z_U. The formula for Z_U would then be

$$Z_U = \frac{\text{USL} - \bar{\bar{X}}}{\hat{\sigma}}$$

where

USL = upper specification limit

$\bar{\bar{X}}$ = the process average

Similarly, Z_L, the number of standard deviations between the process average and the lower specification limit, is given by the formula

$$Z_L = \frac{\bar{\bar{X}} - \text{LSL}}{\hat{\sigma}}$$

where

LSL = lower specification limit

$\bar{\bar{X}}$ = the process average

In this example, the value of Z_L is about 2.70. The area beyond each of these Z values can be found using the areas under standard normal curve table on the CD-ROM. These areas correspond to the proportion of production that falls outside specifications. From the table, the area beyond 1.46 standard deviations is 0.0721 and the area beyond 2.70 standard deviations is 0.0035. The capability analysis indicates that approximately 7.21 percent of shipped packages could have been shipped overweight and approximately 0.35 percent of shipped packages could have been shipped underweight.

The traditional definition of natural process limits is ±3σ. In the previous example, the natural process limits are 1.065 ± 3(0.024) or approximately 0.993 to 1.137. The fact that the natural process limits are outside the specification limits of 1.00–1.10 indicates that the process is not capable of meeting the specification.

3. PROCESS CAPABILITY INDICES

> Define, select, and calculate C_p and C_{pk}, and assess process capability. (Evaluate)
>
> **Body of Knowledge III.F.3**

Various capability indices have been developed in an attempt to quantify process capability in a single number. Three of the most common indices are C_{pk}, C_p, and C_r. These are defined and illustrated in the following paragraphs.

$$C_{pk} = \frac{\text{Min}(Z_U, Z_L)}{3}$$

where min (Z_U, Z_L) is defined as the value of the smallest Z value.

In the previous example $C_{pk} = 1.46 \div 3 = 0.49$. The "min" in the formula for C_{pk} means that this index looks at the nearest specification limit.

Historically, a C_{pk} value of one or larger was considered "capable." This would be equivalent to stating that the natural process limits lie inside the specification limits. More recently, quality requirements have become more stringent and many customers require C_{pk} values of 1.33, 1.66, or 2.00. Notice that this is the equivalent of requiring ±4σ, ±5σ, and ±6σ to be inside the specification. It is the move toward $C_{pk} = 2$ or ±6σ that inspired the Six Sigma terminology. Most authors currently define a 6σ process as one with σ ≤ 1/12 (specification) and with the process average not drifting more than 1.5σ over time. Therefore the percent violating each specification limit is based on values from the Z table corresponding to 4.5σ.

$$C_p = \frac{\text{Tolerance zone}}{6\sigma}$$

In the previous example, $C_p = 0.1 \div 0.144 \approx 0.69$. The formula for C_p doesn't take into consideration whether the process is centered in the specification. In fact, it shows how good C_{pk} could be if the process were centered.

C_r is the inverse of C_p. C_r expressed as a percent (by multiplying by 100) shows the percent of specification used up by the process variation.

$$C_r = 1/C_p$$

In the previous example, $C_r \approx 1.45$. (145 percent of the specification is consumed by the process variation.) Lower C_r values are better.

Part III.F.3

Process Capability

There are typically two calculations done to identify how capable a process is. This is done so that we can determine if the possibility of improvement exists for the process in question. These two calculations are called C_p (capability index) and C_{pk} (process performance).

Assuming the processes are centered, Figure 15.4 is the illustration of four processes with different process capability (C_p).

Some examples of common values seen on the shop floor include:

1. $C_p = 2$ and $C_{pk} = 1.5$ are the values given when a process has achieved six sigma quality.

2. C_p, $C_{pk} \geq 1.33$ shows that the process is capable.

3. A C_p, C_{pk} value of 1.0 means that the process barely meets the specification. This will produce 0.27 percent defective units.

4. A C_p, C_{pk} value less than 1.0 means that the process is producing units outside engineering specifications.

5. Abnormally high C_p, C_{pk} (> 3) shows either that the specification is loose or identifies an opportunity to move to a less expensive process. (Often people do nothing fearing that they may worsen the situation.)

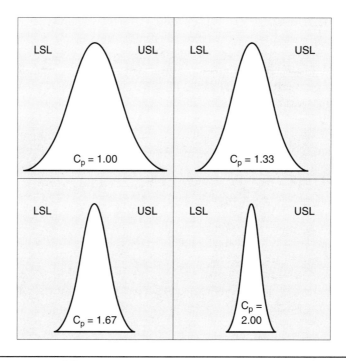

Figure 15.4 Process capability scenarios.

Some common interpretations of C_p and C_{pk}:

1. In both C_p and C_{pk}, the higher the value, the better.

2. The C_p value does not change as the process is being centered to target unless something in the process changes.

3. The C_p and C_{pk} values will be equal if the process is perfectly centered.

4. C_{pk} is always equal to or smaller than C_p.

5. If the C_{pk} value becomes a negative number, then the process average is outside one of the engineering specifications.

6. In a process with one-sided specification, either C_p upper limit or C_p lower limit is calculated.

7. Higher C_{pk} observed from a small sample may not be of much use as the confidence interval for C_{pk} will be very wide.

4. PROCESS PERFORMANCE INDICES

Define, select, and calculate P_p, P_{pk}, C_{pm}, and assess process performance. (Evaluate)

Body of Knowledge III.F.4

Performance indices provide a picture of current process operation and can be used for comparison and prioritization of improvement efforts. Three such indices are P_{pk}, P_p, and C_{pm}, which require stability of the process as well. The formulas for P_{pk} and P_p are equivalent to the corresponding capability indices except that sample standard deviation is used instead of σ. The formulas are:

$$P_{pk} = \min\left(\frac{USL - \bar{\bar{X}}}{3s}, \frac{X - LSL}{3s}\right)$$

where s is the sample standard deviation

$$s = \sqrt{\frac{1}{N-1}\sum_{i=1}^{N}(x_i - \bar{x})^2}$$

$$P_p = \frac{\text{Tolerance zone}}{6s}$$

where s is the sample standard deviation

EXAMPLE

A manufacturing assembly line that ships built devices on a weekly basis performs random sampling of the devices' critical parameters. The quality engineer uses this data to measure performance indices for those critical parameters. Since the data also include long-term variations and shifts, the engineer should not use the metrics C_p and C_{pk}. Measures like C_p and C_{pk} are used when process stability is monitored through SPC and the standard deviation is derived from the mean range. The engineer measures a sample standard deviation of 0.004 and a mean of 10.014

The specification limits for this critical parameter are 9.99 to 10.03.

$$s = \sqrt{\frac{1}{N-1}\sum_{i=1}^{N}(x_i - \bar{x})^2}$$

$$s = 0.004$$

$$P_p = \frac{\text{Tolerance}}{6s} = \frac{0.04}{6(0.004)} = \frac{0.04}{0.024} = 1.667$$

$$P_{pk} = \text{Min}\left(\frac{\text{USL} - \bar{\bar{X}}}{3s}, \frac{\bar{\bar{X}} - \text{LSL}}{3s}\right) = \text{Min}\left(\frac{10.03 - 10.014}{3(0.004)}, \frac{10.014 - 9.99}{3(0.004)}\right)$$

$$P_{pk} = \text{Min}\left(\frac{0.016}{0.012}, \frac{0.024}{0.012}\right) = \text{Min}(1.33, 2.00) = 1.33$$

The engineer now compares the contractual requirement from the customer on P_p and P_{pk} with the measured values of P_p of 1.667 and P_{pk} of 1.33.

The Automotive Industry Action Group (AIAG) and the American National Standards Institute (ANSI) recommend the use of P_p and P_{pk} when the process is not in control. This is a somewhat controversial position because an out-of-control process is by definition unpredictable. Montgomery[1] states that, "The process performance indices P_p and P_{pk} are actually more than a step backwards. They are a waste of engineering and management effort—they tell you nothing."

Figure 15.5 shows an example of P_p, P_{pk}, and C_{pm} analysis of a vendor-supplied product feature using Minitab statistical software.

$$C_{pm} = \frac{\text{Tolerance}}{6s}$$

where

$$s = \sqrt{\sum_{i=1}^{n}\frac{(x_i - T)^2}{n-1}}$$

and

T = specification target

x_i = sample reading

n = number of sample readings

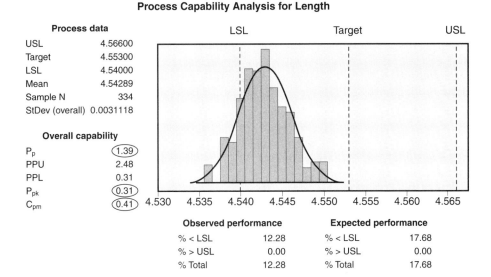

Figure 15.5   Process performance indices P_p, P_{pk}, and C_{pm}.

Undoubtedly C_p, C_{pk} is a better measure as it reflects capability derived from common cause variation. P_p, P_{pk} can be applied to data collected from incoming inspection material to obtain an indication of process capability at the supplier end where the SPC data are not available. Given that the process data may contain special causes as well, as long as the data follows normal distribution, P_p, P_{pk} can provide some idea about processes. It is unlikely that all suppliers have SPC implementation in place. It is also unlikely that SPC-implemented suppliers will be willing to share their process data in time sequence with their customers. Hence, P_p, P_{pk} can serve as an indicator for these situations.

C_{pm} is a useful measure where the process has a target value rather than a conventional nominal value, which is typically the midpoint of specifications. An example would be tolerances for shafts/holes where specific mechanical fit is involved, for example, clearance fit, interference fit, and transition fit.

5. SHORT-TERM VS. LONG-TERM CAPABILITY

> Describe the assumptions and conventions that are appropriate when only short-term data are collected and when only attributes data are available. Describe the changes in relationships that occur when long-term data are used, and interpret the relationship between long- and short-term capability as it relates to a 1.5 sigma shift.
> (Evaluate)
>
> **Body of Knowledge III.F.5**

Short-term capability is calculated from the data collected from a stable process monitored for a short time of approximately 20 to 30 subgroups. For such a short interval, the variability is often relatively small due to a focus on specific equipment, a set of trained operators, homogeneous material, the same measuring equipment, and so on. The process capability (C_p, C_{pk}) calculated with this data uses the sigma value computed from the average process range. For long-term capability, the sample measurements may include different streams of machines, multiple spindles, cavities, operators, and measuring equipment, and even external factors like temperature and humidity may be different. Hence, the variation is generally wider than with short-term capability. This process capability calculation (P_p, P_{pk}) is performed using the sample standard deviation of the values. The assumption in both cases is that the data come from a normal distribution. There are process parameters that do not necessarily follow the normal distribution. Examples include: flatness, wait time, and so on. Transformation techniques are used to normalize the data before analyzing for process capability.

The AIAG manual advises that P_p, P_{pk} should be used in combination with C_p, C_{pk} for comparison and prioritization of improvement efforts.

We discussed increase in variation for a process over the long term. It is also important to note that the mean also shifts over the long term. The concept of 1.5 sigma shift advocated by the late Bill Smith, a reliability engineer from Motorola, has been explained earlier in this book. In the context of short- and long-term variation, Figure 15.6 shows how the mean from short-term variation can shift over time.

The dynamic variation of a process with respect to time is explained further in Figure 15.7. The long-term capability of the process is due to changes to the mean and variation over time.

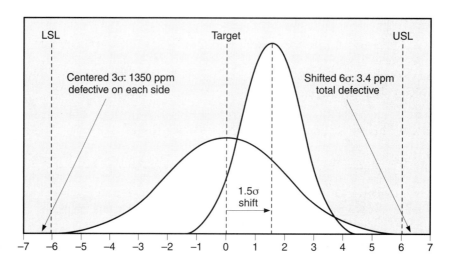

Figure 15.6   Process performance 1.5 sigma shift.

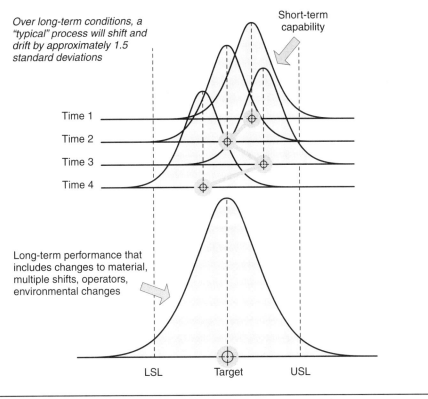

Over long-term conditions, a "typical" process will shift and drift by approximately 1.5 standard deviations

Short-term capability

Time 1

Time 2

Time 3

Time 4

Long-term performance that includes changes to material, multiple shifts, operators, environmental changes

LSL   Target   USL

Figure 15.7   Short–term versus long–term performance with 1.5 sigma shift.

6. PROCESS CAPABILITY FOR ATTRIBUTES DATA

> Compute the sigma level for a process and describe its relationship to P_{pk}. (Apply)
>
> **Body of Knowledge III.F.6**

So far we have dealt with computing process capability for variable data (continuous data). In the case of attribute data (discrete data), the process capability is simply the average of proportion defective. This is called binomial process capability. Using the normal approximation of binomial data, the average proportion defective is converted to process sigma Z.

Let us review an example of binomial data. Samples were taken at regular intervals and the process has not been intentionally modified during the data collection period. See Figures 15.8 and 15.9.

Sample no.	Defective	Sample size	Proportion defective
1	3	117	0.025641
2	4	95	0.042105
3	6	161	0.037267
4	4	87	0.045977
5	5	133	0.037594
6	6	157	0.038217
7	2	79	0.025317
8	7	180	0.038889
9	3	120	0.025000
10	4	111	0.036036
	44	**1240**	**0.035483**

Inferences:

a. The process is stable with an average of 3.55% defectives. (See P chart.)

b. The proportion defective does not seem to change with increase in sample size. (See rate of defectives.)

c. The defective rate is starting to settle at 3.5%. This should be monitored for a few more samples. (See cumulative percent defective.)

d. There are three samples that have lower percent defective than the rest of the samples. This, however, reflects as a natural process variation in P chart. (Distribution of percent defective.)

The variation in control limits in P charts is due to change in sample sizes.

Figure 15.8 Proportion defective summary.

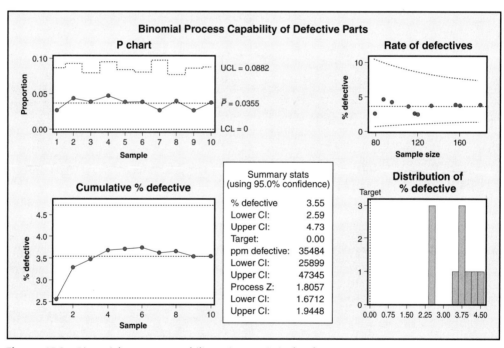

Figure 15.9 Binomial process capability using statistical software.

Percent defective: The percentage of parts sampled during final inspection that are defective

Percent defective = (100 × Average P) = (100 × 0.035484) = 3.55% (rounded to two places)

Parts per million defective: The expected number of defective parts out of one million parts

Parts per million defective = 1,000,000 × Average P = 1,000,000 × 0.035484 = 35,484

Process Z: Process Z is a capability index. The larger the process Z is, the better the process is performing.

Process Z is computed from the average P by finding the value from a standard normal (0, 1) distribution such that the area to the right of the value is the average P. So an average P of .5 corresponds to a Z of zero. An average P of 0.1 corresponds to a Z of 1.28 and so on.

$$\text{Process } Z = -1\phi^{-1}(\text{Average P})$$

In our example, an average of 0.035484 corresponds to

$$Z = -1\phi^{-1}(0.035484) = 1.80568$$

This can also be solved using Excel formula NORMSINV(0.035484)

ϕ^{-1} is the inverse cumulative density function (cdf) of a standard normal distribution.

Confidence intervals of capability indices are calculated using chi-square distribution. This calculation is beyond the scope of the Green Belt Body of Knowledge. Most off-the-shelf (OTS) statistical software like Minitab can perform this analysis.[1]

Mean DPU: defects per unit of measurement in the sample. See Figure 15.10.

$$D_{total}/N_{total}$$

where D_{total} is the sum of all defectives and N is the total number of samples.

Sample no.	Defects	Sample size	DPU
1	5	117	0.042735
2	7	95	0.073684
3	10	161	0.062112
4	8	87	0.091954
5	12	133	0.090226
6	9	157	0.057325
7	5	79	0.063291
8	9	180	0.050000
9	5	120	0.041667
10	7	111	0.063063
	77	1240	0.062096

Figure 15.10   Defect per unit (DPU) summary.

Minimum DPU: The minimum defects per unit of measurement among all samples.

Maximum DPU: The maximum defects per unit of measurement among all samples.

Process sigma can be calculated using inverse CDF of the DPU.

Process sigma = NORMSINV(1–((Total defects)/(Total opportunities)))

From our example, process sigma = NORMSINV(1–((77)/(1240))) = 1.537

The relationship between process capability and sigma level (with long-term shift) is tabulated in Table 15.1.

$$Z_{min}/3 = C_{pk}$$

Key Point: When talking about capability, some references talk about short-term and long-term capability. Others add either prototype or surrogate capability. A good rule to follow is: any time the data are normal but not stable, use P_p and P_{pk}. If the data are normal and stable, then use C_p and C_{pk}.

Table 15.1 Sigma conversion table.

Defects per million opportunities	Sigma level (with 1.5 sigma shift)	Cpk (Sigma level/3) with 1.5 sigma shift
933,200	0.000	0.000
500,000	1.500	0.500
66,800	3.000	1.000
6,200	4.000	1.333
230	5.000	1.667
3	6.000	2.000

For a more comprehensive table please refer to http://www.moresteam.com/toolbox/t414.cfm.

Part IV
Six Sigma—*Analyze*

Chapter 16   A. Exploratory Data Analysis
Chapter 17   B. Hypothesis Testing

OVERVIEW

In the *analyze* phase, statistical methods and tools are used to isolate key pieces of information that are critical to explaining defective products. In this phase, practical business problems are analyzed using statistical tools. Data are collected to determine the relationships between the variable factors in the process and to determine the direction of improvements. This phase determines how well or how poor the process is currently performing, and identifies possible root causes of variation in quality. The data analyzed can reveal the basic nature and behavior of the process, and show how capable and stable the process is over an extended period of time. For example, is the problem sporadic or persistent? Or is the problem technology- or process-related?

This section covers exploratory data analysis, which includes multivariate studies to differentiate positional, cyclical, and temporal variation, and simple linear correlation and regression to determine the statistical significance (p value) and difference between correlation and causation. Part IV also offers an introduction to hypothesis testing, tests for means, variances, and proportions, paired-comparison parametric hypothesis tests, analysis of variance (ANOVA), and chi-square testing to determine statistical significance.

Chapter 16
A. Exploratory Data Analysis

1. MULTI-VARI STUDIES

> Create and interpret multi-vari studies to interpret the difference between positional, cyclical, and temporal variation; apply sampling plans to investigate the largest sources of variation. (Create)
>
> **Body of Knowledge IV.A.1**

The multi-vari chart is a useful tool for analyzing the three types of variation: cyclical, temporal, and positional variation (see Table 16.1). It also helps to minimize variation by identifying areas in which to look for excessive variation and less excessive variation.

Multi-vari studies are the perfect tool for investigating the stability or consistency of a process. They help to determine where the variability is coming from within a process.

Often, positional variation is called within-part variation and refers to variation of a characteristic on the same product. Cyclical variation is also called part-to-part or lot-to-lot variation. Temporal variation, also called shift-to-shift variation, occurs as change over time.

Figure 16.1 illustrates a multi-vari line chart. The chart consists of a series of vertical lines, or other appropriate schematics, along a time scale. The length of each line or schematic shape represents the range of values found in each sample set. Figures 16.2 through 16.4 illustrate excessive variability, less variability, and a variability shift over time, respectively.

Table 16.1   Areas of variation.

	Product/process under consideration	
Areas of variation	**Piece**	**Batch/lot**
Positional	Within-part	Within-batch/within-lot
Cyclical	Part-to-part	Batch-to-batch/lot-to-lot
Temporal	Over time (shift-to-shift)	Over time (shift-to-shift)

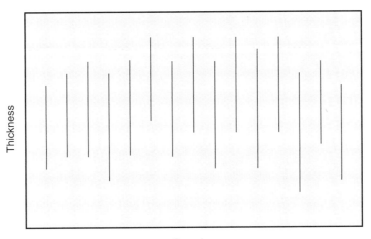

Figure 16.1   Variation within samples.

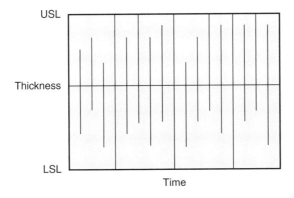

Figure 16.2   Excessive variability (part is tapered).

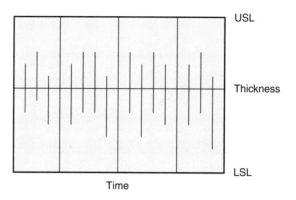

Figure 16.3   Less variability (center is thicker).

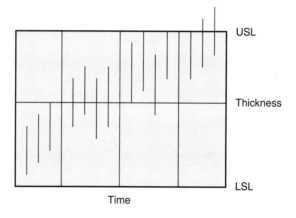

Figure 16.4   Variability shift over time (part is getting larger).

Procedure for Multi-Vari Sampling Plan

1. Select the process and the characteristics to be investigated

2. Select the sample size and time frequency

3. Record the time and values from each sample set in a table format

4. Plot a graph with time along the horizontal scale and the measured values on the vertical scale

5. Connect the observed values with lines

6. Observe and analyze chart for variation within the sample, sample-to-sample, and over time

7. Conduct additional studies to concentrate on the area(s) of apparent maximum variation

8. Make process improvements and repeat multi-vari study to confirm the results

EXAMPLE

A stainless steel casting is used as an example for this study. This part has a tight tolerance on its machined inner diameter (ID) as a piston moves inside it that must make a good seal. The part is a closed-end cylinder as illustrated in Figure 16.5. The pistons leak as a result of a poor seal. For machinists, this is considered a difficult design, since the walls are very thin, the depth is great, and the dead end adds to the problems. This issue had been around for quite some time and various team members had ideas they'd like to try. One of the engineers suggested that the lathe chucks are clamping too tightly and squeezing the part out of round. Another would like to change the tooling, and so on. Many of the ideas have been tried in the past with little improvement.

To solve this problem, a multi-vari study with a data collection scheme that will capture the various types of variation is initiated. The data are displayed on graphs that will aid in identifying the type of variation that is greatest. To cover the within-part variation, the IDs are measured at the top, middle, and bottom as indicated by the section lines T, M, and B in Figure 16.6a. Additional within-part variation is measured by checking for out-of-round conditions. To detect this out-of-round variation, the ID is measured at three different angles, 12 o'clock, two o'clock, and four o'clock, with 12 o'clock on the top as shown in Figure 16.6b.

The 12 o'clock measurement is the diameter from 12 o'clock to six o'clock.

The two o'clock measurement is the diameter from two o'clock to eight o'clock.

The four o'clock measurement is the diameter from four o'clock to 10 o'clock.

To capture the variation over time, five pieces are selected at approximately equal time intervals during a shift. All measurements are obtained with a dial bore gage and recorded on the data sheet shown in Figure 16.7.

The measurement results from five parts from one shift are shown in Table 16.2. What can be learned by looking at these numbers? The answer is "very little." Plotting the numbers on a graph as shown in Figure 16.8 does reveal an interesting pattern.

A visual study of Figure 16.8 may help determine what type of variation is most dominant—is it out-of-round, top-to-bottom or part-to-part? This may be analyzed by drawing a different type of line for each type of variation as shown in Figure 16.9.

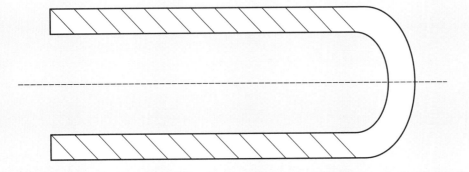

Figure 16.5   Stainless steel casting with critical inner diameter.

Continued

Part IV.A.1

Continued

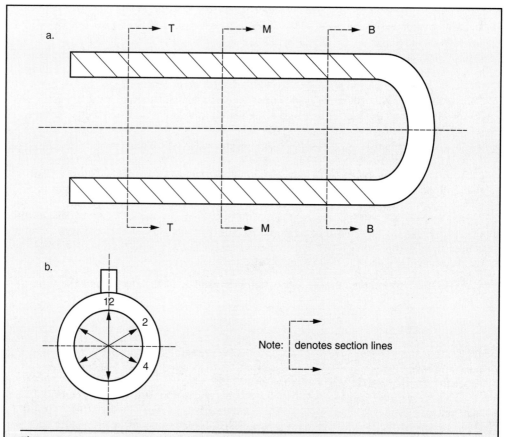

Figure 16.6   Sectional views of stainless steel casting.

Angle	Section T-T	Section M-M	Section B-B
12 o'clock			
Two o'clock			
Four o'clock			

Figure 16.7   Data collection sheet.

This figure illustrates that the most significant variation is caused by part-to-part differences. The team brainstormed on possible causes for part-to-part variation. People with ideas on how to reduce other variation, such as out-of-round, were asked to hold those ideas until later because they wouldn't reduce the large part-to-part variation. It

Continued

Continued

Table 16.2   Measurement data from five parts produced during one shift.

Part #1			Part # 2			Part # 3			Part # 4			Part # 5		
T	M	B	T	M	B	T	M	B	T	M	B	T	M	B
.998	.992	.996	.984	.982	.981	.998	.998	.997	.986	.987	.986	.975	.980	.976
.994	.996	.994	.982	.980	.982	.999	.998	.997	.985	.986	.986	.976	.976	.974
.996	.994	.995	.984	.983	.980	.996	.996	.996	.984	.985	.984	.978	.980	.974

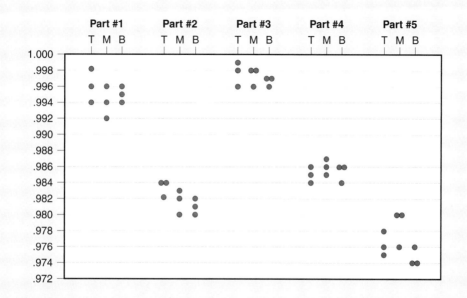

Figure 16.8   Graph of data from Table 16.2.

was finally hypothesized that the part-to-part variation was caused by the casting process and a new foundry that could do precision casting instead of investment casting was sourced.

The new batch of precision-cast parts arrived and again five parts were selected from a shift. The machined parts were measured and the results are shown in Table 16.3. Note that a more discriminating measurement system was used for these castings and the scale for the graph was also changed.

Since Table 16.3 does not provide much information, the data were graphed as shown in Figure 16.10. Does it appear that the part-to-part variation has been reduced? Assuming that the part-to-part variation remains relatively small, which type of variation is now the most dominant? Figure 16.10 suggests that the out-of-round variation is now dominant.

Continued

Part IV.A.1

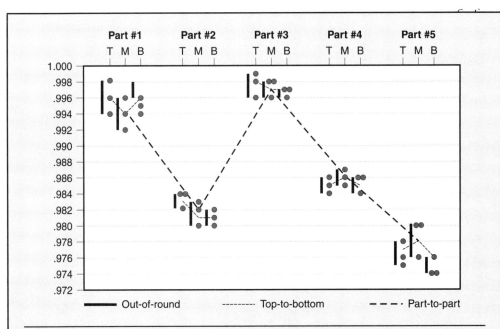

Figure 16.9 Part-to-part variation (graph of data from Table 16.2).

Table 16.3 Data from five parts produced during one shift using precision castings.

Part #1			Part # 2			Part # 3			Part # 4			Part # 5		
T	M	B	T	M	B	T	M	B	T	M	B	T	M	B
.985	.984	.980	.981	.985	.983	.982	.982	.982	.984	.984	.983	.981	.981	.984
.982	.981	.982	.985	.982	.981	.985	.984	.984	.981	.982	.982	.984	.982	.981
.985	.983	.983	.983	.981	.984	.982	.983	.982	.982	.981	.981	.983	.983	.982

The team now began to discuss possible causes for the out-of-round variation. At this point some team members returned to the theory that chuck pressure was causing the part to be squeezed into an out-of-round contour and a round hole was then machined so that when the chuck pressure was released the part snapped back to a round contour, which left an out-of-round hole. They suggested a better pressure regulator for the air line feeding the pneumatic chuck. But one observer, focusing on the top of the hole where the out-of-round should be most prominent, noticed that sometimes the 12 o'clock dimension is longest as in part #4 and sometimes another dimension is longer (see the numbers in Table 16.3). Since the parts are always chucked with the same orientation, the chuck pressure could not be the cause. The team wondered if there might be a pattern relating the various orientations and the diameters so they placed orientation numbers by each dot as shown in Figure 16.11 and tried to find

Continued

Continued

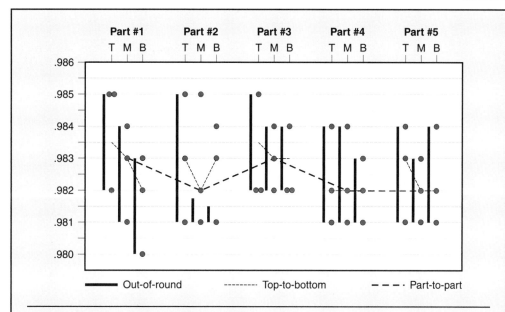

Figure 16.10   Graph of data from Table 16.3.

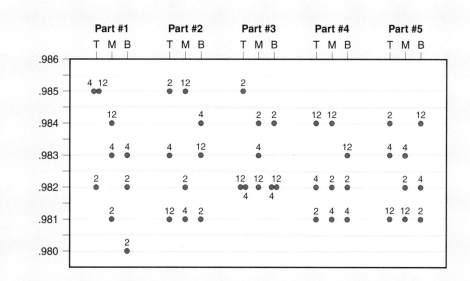

Figure 16.11   Graph of data from Table 16.3 with orientation measurement numbers.

a pattern. Unfortunately, no pattern was discovered and the relationship seemed to be random.

So the issue now is, why is there a random difference in diameters and what is causing it? At this point a second-shift operator mentioned the fact that after the ID

Continued

Part IV.A.1

Continued

is cut, a burnishing tool is passed across the surface. He suggested that the machining chips could cause this diameter difference as these chips may be burnished into the surface. He also suggested that the parts be removed from the chuck and pressure-washed before the burnish operation. Some team members objected that this had been tried a year ago with no noticeable improvement. Others pointed out, however, that at that time the large part-to-part variation would have masked any reduction in the minor variation now being seen. The team agreed that the pressure-wash should be tried again. The measurements that resulted are shown in Table 16.4.

Plotting these data shows that the out-of-round variation has been noticeably reduced. One of the team members noticed a remaining pattern of variation present and suggested a tooling change, which resulted in reducing variation even further.

Table 16.4 Data from five parts after pressure-washing.

Part #1			Part #2			Part #3			Part #4			Part #5		
T	M	B	T	M	B	T	M	B	T	M	B	T	M	B
.9825	.9825	.9815	.9830	.9830	.9815	.9830	.9820	.9820	.9820	.9825	.9820	.9835	.9830	.9820
.9835	.9851	.9825	.9840	.9830	.9825	.9845	.9820	.9830	.9830	.9825	.9825	.9845	.9830	.9825
.9820	.9820	.9820	.9832	.9820	.9820	.9825	.9812	.9820	.9820	.9820	.9820	.9835	.9830	.9820

2. SIMPLE LINEAR CORRELATION AND REGRESSION

> Interpret the correlation coefficient and determine its statistical significance (*p*-value); recognize the difference between correlation and causation. Interpret the linear regression equation and determine its statistical significance (*p*-value). Use regression models for estimation and prediction. (Evaluate)
>
> **Body of Knowledge IV.A.2**

Correlation

Correlation is finding a relationship between two or more sets of data. It measures the strength and direction of the relationship between variables. In order to find a correlation one needs an independent variable (x) that causes an observed variation, which is considered the dependent variable (y). Table 16.5 lists a few examples of independent and dependent variable pairs.

Table 16.5 Examples of dependent and independent variables.

Independent variable (x)	Dependent variable (y)
Hours studied	Exam grade
Hours of exercise	Weight loss
Level of advertising	Volume of sales

Correlation versus Causation

A cause that produces an effect, or that which gives rise to any action, phenomenon, or condition, is termed causation. For example, "if a change in X produces a change in Y, the X is said to be a cause of Y." One may also observe, however, that there is a W that caused X, a V that caused W, a U that caused V, and so on. Every cause is itself the result of some prior cause or causes. There is no such thing as an absolute cause for an event, the identification of which satisfies and completes all inquiry. The alphabetic example just given implies a "causal chain."

Two variables may be found to be causally associated, depending on how the study was conducted. If two variables are found to be either associated or correlated, that doesn't mean that a cause-and-effect relationship exists between the two variables. This has to be proved by a well-designed experiment or several different observational studies to show that an association or correlation crosses over into a cause-and-effect relationship.

A scatter plot provides a complete picture of the relationship between two variables. Figure 16.12 illustrates the four different types of correlation that exist in scatter plots. The convention is to place the x variable on the horizontal axis and the y variable on the vertical axis.

Caution: Be careful when deciding which variable is independent and which is dependent. Examine the relationship from both directions to see which one makes the most sense. The use of a wrong choice may lead to meaningless results.

Correlation Coefficient

The correlation coefficient, r, provides both the strength and direction of the relationship between the independent and dependent variables. Values of r range between –1.0 and +1.0. When r is positive, the relationship between x and y is positive (Figure 16.12a) and when r is negative, the relationship is negative (Figure 16.12b). A correlation coefficient close to zero is evidence that there is no relationship between x and y (Figures 16.12c and 16.12d).

The strength of the relationship between x and y is measured by how close the correlation coefficient is to +1.0 or –1.0 (Figures 16.12a and 16.12b).

We can calculate the correlation coefficient using the following formula:

$$r = \frac{1}{n-1}\sum \frac{(x-\bar{x})(y-\bar{y})}{S_x S_y}$$

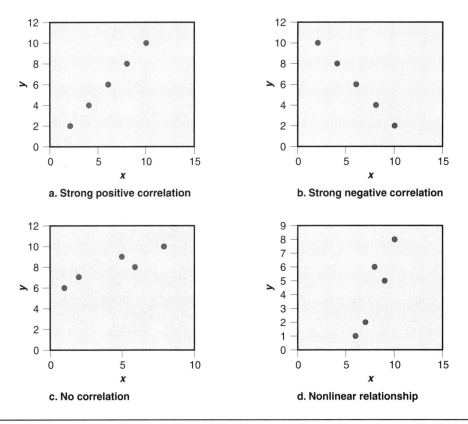

Figure 16.12 The four types of correlation in scatter plots.

Procedure for Calculating the Correlation Coefficient

1. Calculate the mean for all x values ($\bar{x}$) and the mean for all y values ($\bar{y}$)

2. Calculate the standard deviation of all x values (S_x) and the standard deviation for y values (S_y)

3. Calculate $(x - \bar{x})$ and $(y - \bar{y})$ for each pair (x, y) and then multiply these differences together

4. Get the sum by adding all these products together

5. Divide the sum by $S_x \times S_y$

6. Divide the results of step 5 by $n - 1$, where n is the number of (x, y) pairs

---

EXAMPLE

Let us say that the x values are 3, 3, and 6, and the y values are 2, 3, and 4, and the data sets are (3,2), (3,3), and (6,4). The correlation coefficient is given by

x values	y values	$(x - \bar{x})(y - \bar{y})$
3	2	1
3	3	0
6	4	2
$\bar{x} = 4$	$\bar{y} = 3$	$\Sigma(x - \bar{x})(y - \bar{y}) = 3$

$$S_x = 1.73, \; S_y = 1.00$$

$$r = \frac{1}{n-1} \Sigma \frac{(x-\bar{x})(y-\bar{y})}{S_x S_y} = \frac{1}{3-1} \times \frac{3}{(1.73)(1)} = 0.867$$

The Strength of the Relationship

The graph in Figure 16.12a shows an example of positive linear correlation; as x increases, y also tends to increase in a linear (straight line) fashion.

The graph in Figure 16.12b shows an example of negative linear correlation; as x increases, y tends to decrease linearly.

The graph in Figure 16.12c shows an example of no correlation between x and y. This set of variables appears to have no impact on each other.

The graph in Figure 16.12.d shows an example of a nonlinear relationship between variables.

Figure 16.12a illustrates a perfect positive correlation (positive slope) between x and y with $r = +1.0$. Figure 16.12b shows a perfect negative correlation (negative slope) between x and y with $r = -1.0$. Figures 16.12c and 16.12d are examples of weaker relationships between the independent and dependent variables.

$$r = \frac{n\sum xy - \left(\sum x\right)\left(\sum y\right)}{\sqrt{n\left(\left(\sum x^2\right) - \left(\sum x\right)^2\right)} \times \sqrt{n\left(\left(\sum y^2\right) - \left(\sum y\right)^2\right)}}$$

EXAMPLE

Let's investigate the relationship between exercise time and weight loss for an individual. Table 16.6 shows sample data from six candidates who were randomly chosen.

Using these values, with $n = 6$, the number of ordered pairs, we have:

$$r = \frac{6(217)-(38)(24)}{\sqrt{\left[6(372)-(38)^2\right]\left[6(130)-(24)^2\right]}}$$

$$r = \frac{390}{\sqrt{(788)(204)}} = 0.972$$

Thus, one can see that there is a strong positive correlation between hours of exercise and weight lost.

Caution: Be careful when distinguishing between Σx^2 and $(\Sigma x)^2$. With Σx^2, we first square each value of x and then add each squared term. With $(\Sigma x)^2$, we first add each value of x, and then square this total. The two results are very different.

Table 16.6 Data table for correlation calculation.

Hours of exercise in a week (x)	Weight reduction in lbs. (y)	xy	x^2	y^2
3	2	6	9	4
5	4	20	25	16
10	6	60	100	36
15	8	120	225	64
2	1	2	4	1
3	3	9	9	9
$\Sigma x = 38$	$\Sigma y = 24$	$\Sigma xy = 217$	$\Sigma x^2 = 372$	$\Sigma y^2 = 130$

Inferences in Correlation/Testing the Significance of the Correlation Coefficient

The letter r denotes the sample correlation coefficient. It is conventional to use the Greek letter ρ, (small case rho) to denote the population correlation coefficient. A confidence interval for ρ can be obtained from the sample r statistic using

$$r \pm t_{\alpha/2}\sqrt{\frac{1-r^2}{n-2}}$$

where $1 - \alpha$ = confidence level and df = $n - 1$

Procedure for Testing the Significance of the Correlation Coefficient

1. Conditions for using this test are: population regression equation $y = \beta_0 + \beta_1 x$; for a given value of x the mean of the response variable y is $\beta_0 + \beta_1 x$; for a given value of x the distribution of y-values is normal and independent; distributions of y-values have equal standard deviations.

2. Decide the significance level α.

3. H_o: $\rho = 0$; H_1 could be any of these: $\rho \neq 0$, $\rho < 0$, or $\rho > 0$ for a two-tail, left-tail, or right-tail test respectively.

4. Critical values are obtained from the t-table (Appendix K) using $n - 1$ degrees of freedom: $\pm t_{\alpha/2}$ for the two-tail test, $-t_\alpha$ for the left-tail test and t_α for the right-tail test.

5. The test statistic is given by the formula

$$t = \frac{r}{\sqrt{\dfrac{1-r^2}{n-2}}}$$

6. Reject the null hypothesis if the test statistic $-t_{\alpha/2}$ is $<$ or $t_{\alpha/2}$ is $>$ for the two-tail test or $-t_\alpha$ is $<$ for the left-tail test or t_α is $>$ for the right-tail test. If not, do not reject the null hypothesis.

7. State the conclusion in terms of the problem context.

EXAMPLE

Using the above weight loss example, the calculated t-statistic becomes:

$$t = \frac{r}{\sqrt{\dfrac{1-r^2}{n-2}}} = \frac{0.972}{\sqrt{\dfrac{1-(0.972)^2}{6-2}}}$$

$$t = \frac{0.972}{\sqrt{\dfrac{.0552}{4}}} = 8.273$$

The critical t-statistic is based on df $= n - 2$. We chose $\alpha = 0.05$, $t_c = 2.132$ (from t-table) for a one-tail test. Because $t > t_c$, we reject H_0 and conclude that there is indeed a positive correlation between hours of exercise and weight loss.

Part IV.A.2

Using Excel to Calculate Correlation Coefficients

One can use Excel to calculate correlation coefficients. One has to use the CORREL function, which has the following characteristics:

$$CORREL(array1, array2)$$

where

array1 = the range of data for the first variable

array2 = the range of data for the second variable

Figure 16.13 shows the CORREL function being used to calculate the correlation coefficient for the weight loss example. Cell C8 contains the Excel formula =CORREL(A2:A7,B2:B7) with the result being 0.972717.

Simple Regression

Simple regression is used to describe a straight line that best fits a series of ordered pairs (x,y). An equation for a straight line, known as a linear equation, takes the form:

$$\hat{y} = a + bx$$

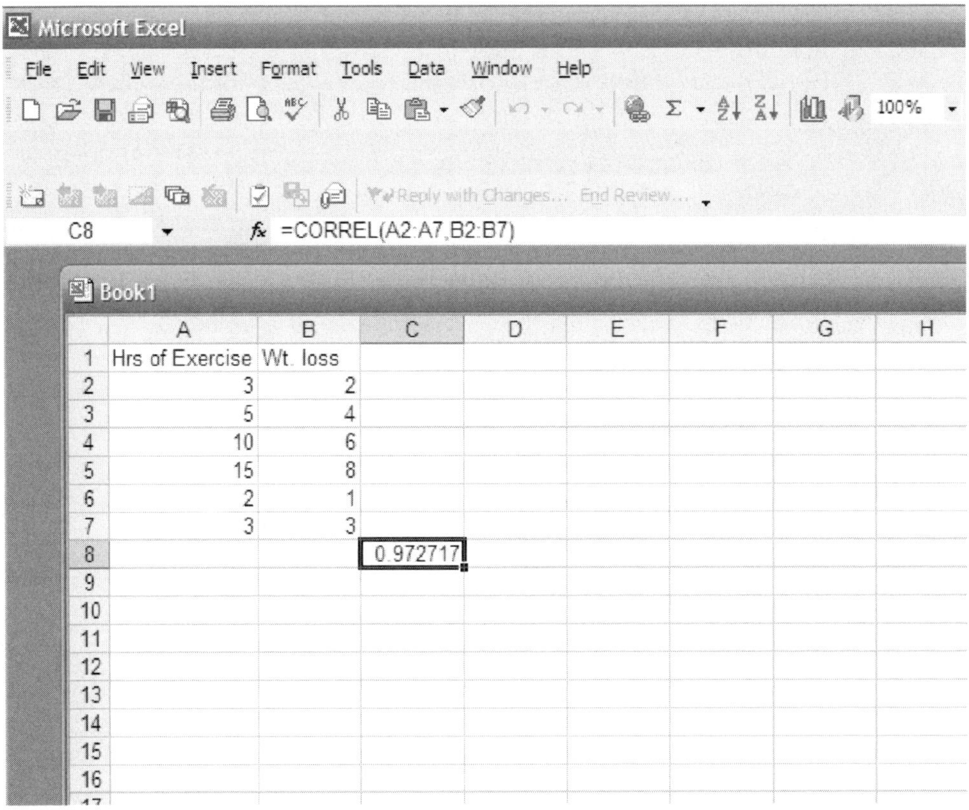

Figure 16.13   CORREL function in Excel.

where

$\hat{y}$ = the predicted value of y, given a value of x

x = the independent variable

a = the y-intercept for the straight line

b = the slope of the straight line

The Least Squares Method

This is a mathematical procedure to identify the linear equation that best fits a set of ordered pairs by finding values for a, the y-intercept, and b, the slope. The goal of the least squares method is to minimize the total squared error between the values of y and $\hat{y}$.

If we denote the predicted value of y obtained from the fitted line as $\hat{y}$, the prediction equation is:

$$\hat{y} = \hat{a} + \hat{b}x$$

where

$\hat{a}$ and $\hat{b}$ represent estimates of true a and b.

Since we need to choose the best-fitting line, we need to define what we mean by "best."

For the purpose of getting the best-fitting criteria, the principle of least squares is employed, that is, one has to choose the best-fitting line, the line that minimizes the sum of squares of the deviations of the observed values of y from those predicted.

Procedure for Least Squares Method

1. Calculate xy, x^2, and y^2 values and enter them in a table

2. Calculate the sums for x, y, xy, x^2, y^2, and $\bar{x}$ and $\bar{y}$

3. Find the linear equation that best fits the data by determining the value for a, the y-intercept, and b, the slope, using the following equations:

$$b = \frac{n\sum xy - (\sum x)(\sum y)}{n\sum x^2 - (\sum x)^2}$$

$$a = \bar{y} - b\bar{x}$$

where

$\bar{x}$ = the average value of x, the dependent variable

$\bar{y}$ = the average value of y, the independent variable

EXAMPLE

Obtain the least squares prediction for the table containing the month and number of complaints received in a manufacturing facility. The data are shown in Table 16.7.

$$b = \frac{n\sum x_i y_i - \left(\sum x_i\right)\left(\sum y_i\right)}{n\sum x_i^2 - \left(\sum x_i\right)^2} = \frac{8(353) - (36)(73)}{8(204) - (36)^2} = 0.5833$$

$$a = \bar{y} - b\bar{x} = 9.125 - 0.5833(4.5) = 6.50015$$

The regression line would be $\hat{y} = 6.50015 + 0.5833x$.

Because the slope of this equation is positive 0.5833, there is evidence that the number of complaints increases over time at an average rate of one per month. If someone wants to predict how many complaints there will be in another six months at this rate, the equation would be

$$\hat{y} = 6.50015 + 0.5833(14) = 14.666 \approx 14 \text{ complaints}$$

Table 16.7   Least squares example.

Month, x_i	Complaints, y_i	x_i^2	$x_i y_i$	y_i^2
1	8	1	8	64
2	6	4	12	36
3	10	9	30	100
4	6	16	24	36
5	10	25	50	100
6	13	36	78	169
7	9	49	63	81
8	11	64	88	121
$\Sigma x_i = 36$	$\Sigma y_i = 73$	$\Sigma x_i^2 = 204$	$\Sigma x_i y_i = 353$	$\Sigma y_i^2 = 707$
$\bar{x} = 4.5$	$\bar{y} = 9.125$			

Confidence Interval for the Regression Line

In order to calculate the accuracy for y versus x, we need to determine the standard error of estimate s_e, which is given by

$$s_e = \sqrt{\frac{\sum y^2 - a\sum y - b\sum xy}{n-2}}$$

The standard error of the estimate measures the amount of dispersion of the observed data around the regression line. The standard error of the estimate is relatively low if the data points are very close to the line and vice versa.

The confidence interval around the mean of y given a specific value of x is given by

$$CI = \hat{y} \pm t_c s_e \sqrt{\frac{1}{n} + \frac{(x - \bar{x})^2}{(\sum x^2) - \frac{(\sum x)^2}{n}}}$$

where

t_c = critical t-statistic from Student's t-distribution

s_e = standard error of the mean

n = number of ordered pairs

Procedure for Confidence Interval

1. Test for the slope of the regression line

2. Set conditions: if β is the slope of the true population, then the hypothesis would be

$$H_0: \beta = 0, \ H_1: \beta \neq 0$$

3. Decide on α significance level

4. Calculate the standard error of slope, s_b, using

$$s_b = \frac{s_e}{\sqrt{\sum x^2 - n\bar{x}^2}}$$

where s_e is the standard error of the estimate

5. Test for the hypothesis using

$$t = \frac{b - \beta_{H0}}{s_b}$$

where β_{H0} is the value of the population slope according to the null hypothesis

6. Find the critical t-statistic value from Student's t-distribution with $n - 2$ degrees of freedom

7. If $t > t_c$, reject the null hypothesis

Part IV.A.2

Part IV.A.2

EXAMPLE

Use the data from Table 16.7 to calculate confidence interval:

$$s_e = \sqrt{\frac{\sum y^2 - a\sum y - b\sum xy}{n-2}}$$

$$s_e = \sqrt{\frac{(707) - 6.50015(73) - 0.5833(353)}{6}} = 2.105$$

For month 8, there are 11 complaints; the regression line would have been

$$\hat{y} = 6.50015 + 0.5833(8) = 11.1666$$

For a 95 percent confidence level and using the critical *t*-statistic from the table:

$$CI = \hat{y} \pm t_c s_e \sqrt{\frac{1}{n} + \frac{(x - \bar{x})^2}{(\sum x^2) - \frac{(\sum x)^2}{n}}}$$

$$CI = 11.1666 \pm (2.447)(2.105) \sqrt{\frac{1}{8} + \frac{(8 - 4.5)^2}{(204) - \frac{(36)^2}{8}}}$$

$$CI = 14.49 \text{ and } 7.84$$

Our 95 percent confidence interval for the number of items in the table in month 8 is between 7.84 and 14.49 complaints.

Now let us calculate the slope of the regression line:

$$s_b = \frac{s_e}{\sqrt{\sum x^2 - n\bar{x}^2}}$$

$$s_b = \frac{2.105}{\sqrt{204 - 8(4.5)^2}} = 0.325$$

$$t = \frac{b - \beta_{H0}}{s_b} = \frac{0.5833 - 0}{0.325} = 1.7948$$

The critical *t*-statistic is taken from Student's *t*-distribution with $n - 2 = 6$ degrees of freedom. With a two-tail test and $\alpha = 0.05$, $t_c = 2.447$ as per the *t*-table. Because $t < t_c$, we can not reject the null hypothesis and must conclude that there is no relationship between the month and the number of complaints.

Multiple Linear Regression

Multiple linear regression is an extension of the methodology for linear regression to more than one independent variable. By including more than one independent variable, a higher proportion of the variation in *y* may be explained.

The general form for the equation is

$$y = b_0 + b_1x_1 + b_2x_2 + b_3x_3 + \ldots + b_kx_k$$

where

the b_i's are the coefficients and the x_i's are the variables.

Statistical software is usually employed to find the values of the b_i's.

Inferences in Regression

Usually, the sample data are used to calculate the coefficients b_is. One has to find out the closeness of the calculated b-values to the actual coefficient values for the population. For this purpose, we will refer to the values obtained from the sample data as b_i's and the coefficients for the population as β_i's. The b_i's are approximations for the β_i's. The accuracy of the approximation depends on sampling error. This discussion is restricted to simple linear regression that involves just one independent variable. It is assumed that the means of these distributions lie in a straight line whose equation is $y = \beta_0 + \beta_1 x$ and that the distributions are normal with equal standard deviations σ as indicated in Figure 16.14.

Under these assumptions a confidence interval for β_i can be calculated using the following formula: (confidence intervals are discussed in detail in Chapter 17).

$$b_i \pm \frac{t_{\alpha/2} s_e}{\sqrt{s_{xx}}}$$

where

$$s_e = \sqrt{\frac{\sum y^2 - a\sum y - b\sum xy}{n-2}}$$

$s_{xx} = \Sigma x^2 - (\Sigma x)^2/n$

$1 - \alpha$ = confidence level

$df = n - 2$

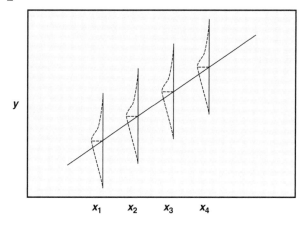

Figure 16.14 A schematic showing variation in y as a function of x.

To review, then, just like a sample mean is used to estimate a population mean, the values of b_0 and b_i are used to estimate the population values β_0 and β_i.

The formula for the best-fitting line (or regression line) is $y = mx + b$, where m is the slope of the line and b is the y-intercept. In other words, the best-fitting line does find the line that best fits the sample data, and if the sample is randomly chosen, that line should be close to the line that best fits the population data. The following hypothesis test can be applied to determine whether the independent variable x is useful as a predictor for the dependent variable y.

Procedure for Testing Simple Regression

1. Set conditions for this test:

   - Population regression equation $y = mx + b$

   - For a given specific value of x, the distribution of y-values is normal and independent and has equal standard deviations

2. H_0: $\beta_i = 0$ (that is, the equation is not useful as a predictor of values of y).

   H_1: $\beta_i \neq 0$ (that is, the equation is useful as a predictor of values of y).

3. Decide on a value of α.

4. Find the critical values $\pm t_{\alpha/2}$ from a t-table using $n - 2$ degrees of freedom.

5. Calculate the value of the test statistic t.

$$t = \frac{b_i}{s_e / \sqrt{s_{xx}}}$$

6. If the test statistic is beyond one of the critical values (that is, greater than $t_{\alpha/2}$ or less than $-t_{\alpha/2}$) reject the null hypothesis; otherwise, do not reject.

7. State the result in terms of the problem.

EXAMPLE

Test the hypothesis for the temperature–viscosity variation as shown below.

Temperature °C	10	15	20	15
Viscosity, C_p	2	3	5	4

1. Assume that the conditions are met.

2. H_0: $\beta_i = 0$ (that is, the equation is not useful as a predictor of values of viscosity).

   H_1: $\beta_i \neq 0$ (that is, the equation is useful as a predictor of values of viscosity).

Continued

Continued

3. Let $\alpha = .05$.

4. The critical values from the *t*-table are 4.303 and −4.303.

5. $t = .3/(.5/\sqrt{50}) = .3/.071 = 4.24$

6. Do not reject H_0.

7. At the .05 significance level, the data do not provide support for the conclusion that temperature is useful as a predictor of viscosity.

Using Excel for Simple Regression

1. Let us use the above example and sort the data into columns A and B in a blank Microsoft Excel spreadsheet.

2. Go to the Tools menu and select Data Analysis.

3. From the Data Analysis dialog box, select Regression as shown in Figure 16.15 and click OK.

4. Set up the regression dialog box as shown in Figure 16.16; enter input *x* and *y* range.

5. Click OK, which brings up the results shown in Figure 16.17.

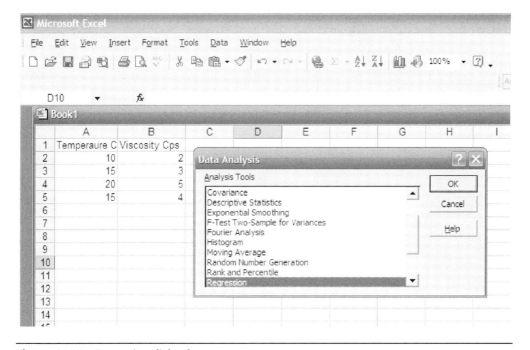

Figure 16.15   Regression dialog box.

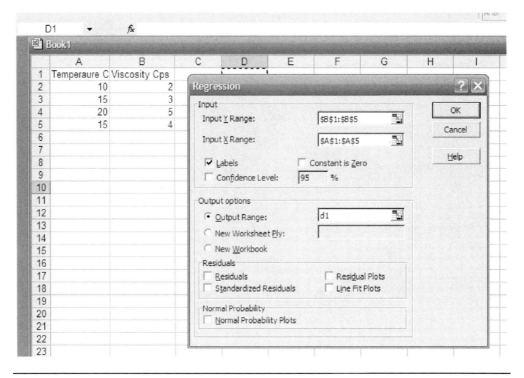

Figure 16.16   Regression data analysis.

These results are consistent with calculations. Since the *p*-value for the independent variable (temperature) is shown as 0.0513, which is greater than $\alpha = 0.05$, we can not reject the null hypothesis and must conclude that a relationship between the variables does not exist.

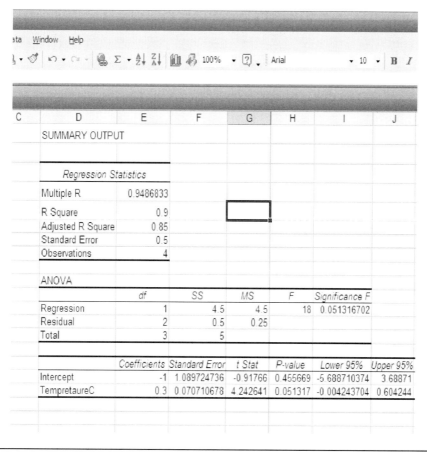

Figure 16.17 Simple regression results.

Chapter 17

B. Hypothesis Testing

1. BASICS

> Define and distinguish between statistical
> and practical significance and apply tests for
> significance level, power, type I and type II
> errors. Determine appropriate sample size
> for various tests. (Apply).
>
> **Body of Knowledge IV.B.1**

The Null and Alternative Hypotheses

A hypothesis is an assumption about a population parameter, for example:

The average adult drinks 1.7 cups of coffee per day

No more than two percent of our products that we sell to customers
are defective

The above statements about a population may or may not be true. The purpose
of hypothesis testing is to make a statistical conclusion about accepting or not
accepting such statements.

All hypothesis tests have both a null hypothesis and an alternative hypothesis. A null hypothesis, denoted by H_0, represents the status quo and involves
stating the belief that the mean of the population is $\geq$, $=$, or $\leq$ a specific value. The
null hypothesis is believed to be true unless there is overwhelming evidence to
the contrary. It is similar to a court trial. The hypothesis is that the defendant is
not guilty until proven guilty. However, the term "innocent" does not apply to a
null hypothesis. A null hypothesis can only be rejected or fail to be rejected; it can
not be accepted because of a lack of evidence to reject it. If the means of two populations are different, the null hypothesis of equality can be rejected if enough
data are collected. When rejecting the null hypothesis, the alternative hypothesis
must be considered. For example, the average weight of a component length is six
grams. The null hypothesis would be stated as:

$$H_0: \mu = 6.0, \; H_0: \mu \leq 6.0, \; H_0: \mu \geq 6.0$$

The alternative hypothesis, denoted by H_1, represents the opposite of the null hypothesis and holds true if the null hypothesis is found to be false. The alternative hypothesis always states that the mean of the population is $<$, $\neq$, or $>$ a specific value. The alternative hypothesis would be stated as

$$H_1: \mu \neq 6.0, \; H_1: \mu < 6.0, \; H_1: \mu > 6.0$$

In order to test a null hypothesis, a calculation must be made from sample information. This calculated value is called a *test statistic* and is compared to an appropriate critical value. A decision can then be made to reject or not reject the null hypothesis. The critical value is obtained from the t distribution table in Appendix K against a chosen level of significance. The typical levels of significance are 1 percent, 5 percent, and 10 percent (both tails).

Types of Errors

There are two types of errors possible when formulating a conclusion regarding a population based on observations from a small sample.

Type I error: This type of error results when the null hypothesis is rejected when it is actually true. For example, incoming products are good but were labeled defective. This type of error is also called α (alpha) and referred to as the producer's risk (for sampling).

Type II error: This type of error results when the null hypothesis is not rejected when it actually should have been rejected. For example, incoming products are defective, but labeled good. This type of error is also called β (beta) and referred to as the consumer's risk (for sampling).

The types of errors are shown in Table 17.1.

One-Tail Test

Any type of test on a hypothesis comes with a risk associated with it, and it is generally associated with the α risk (Type I error, which rejects the null hypothesis when it is true). The level of this α risk determines the level of confidence $(1 - \alpha)$ that we have in the conclusion. This risk factor is used to determine the critical value of the test statistic, which is compared to a calculated value.

If a null hypothesis is established to test whether a sample value is smaller or larger than a population value, then the entire α risk is placed on one end of a distribution curve. This constitutes a one-tail test (Figure 17.1).

$$H_0: \text{level} \geq 20\%, \; H_1: \text{level} < 20\%$$

Table 17.1 Error matrix.

	False	True
Reject H_0	$p = 1 - \beta$, correct outcome	$p = \alpha$, Type I error
Do not reject H_0	$p = \beta$, Type II error	$p = 1 - \alpha$, correct outcome

Note: $p = 1 - \beta$ is also called power. Higher power is better in a hypothesis test.

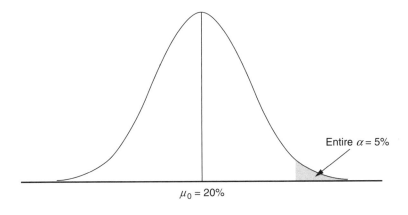

Entire $\alpha = 5\%$

$\mu_0 = 20\%$

Figure 17.1   One-tail test.

EXAMPLE

If a company invents a golf ball that it claims will increase the driving distance off the tee by more than 20 yards, the hypothesis would be set up as follows:

$$H_0: \mu \leq 20, \; H_1: \mu > 20$$

In Figure 17.1, there is only one rejection region, which is the shaded region on the distribution. We follow the same procedure outlined below for the two-tail test and plot the sample mean, which represents the average increase in distance from the tee with the new golf ball. Two possible scenarios exist:

- If the mean sample falls within the white region, we do not reject H_0. That is, we do not have enough evidence to support H_1, the alternative hypothesis, which states that the new golf ball will increase distance off the tee by more than 20 yards.

- If the sample mean falls in the rejection region, we reject H_0. That is, we have enough evidence to support H_1, which confirms the claim that the new golf ball will increase distance off the tee by more than 20 yards.

Note: For a one-tail hypothesis test, the rejection region will always be consistent with the direction of the inequality for H_1. For $H_1: \mu > 20$, the rejection region will be in the right tail of the sampling distribution. For $H_1: \mu < 20$, the rejection region will be in the left tail.

Two-Tail Test

If a null hypothesis is established to test whether a population shift has occurred in either direction, then a two-tail test is required. In other words, a two-tail hypothesis test is used whenever the alternative hypothesis is expressed as $\neq$. The allowable α error is generally divided into two equal parts (see Figure 17.2).

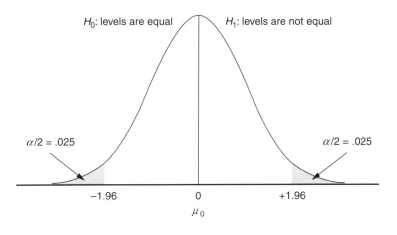

Figure 17.2   Two-tail test.

For example:

- An economist must determine if unemployment levels have changed significantly over the past year.

- A study is made to determine if the salary levels of company A differ significantly from those of company B.

Required Sample Size

So far it has been assumed that the sample size n for hypothesis testing has been given and that the critical value of the test statistic will be determined based on the α error that can be tolerated. The ideal procedure, however, is to determine the α and β error desired and then to calculate the sample size necessary to obtain the desired decision confidence.

The sample size n needed for hypothesis testing depends on:

- The desired Type I (α) and Type II (β) risk

- The minimum value to be detected between the population means ($\mu - \mu_0$)

- The variation in the characteristic being measured (s or σ)

Variable data sample size, only using α, is illustrated by the following example.

EXAMPLE

Let us say we want to determine whether an operational adjustment in a shipyard will alter the process hourly mean by as much as 10 metric tons per hour. What is the minimum sample size that at the 95 percent confidence level ($Z = 1.96$) would confirm the

---

Continued

Continued

significance of a mean shift greater than eight tons per hour? Historically, the standard deviation of the hourly output is 35 tons. The general sample size equation for variable data is

$$n = \frac{Z^2\sigma^2}{E^2} = \frac{(1.96)^2(35)^2}{10^2} = 470.59$$

Get 470 hourly yield values and determine the hourly average. If this mean deviates by more than eight tons from the previous hourly average, a significant change at the 95 percent confidence level has occurred. If the sample mean deviates by less than eight tons per hour, the observable mean shift can be explained by chance cause.

2. TESTS FOR MEANS, VARIANCES, AND PROPORTIONS

Define, compare, and contrast statistical and practical significance. (Apply)

Body of Knowledge IV.B.2

Confidence Intervals for the Mean

Continuous data—large samples: For this type of data one uses the normal distribution to calculate the confidence interval for the mean:

$$\bar{X} \pm Z_{\alpha/2}\frac{\sigma}{\sqrt{n}}$$

where

$\bar{X}$ = sample average

σ = population standard deviation

n = sample size

$Z_{\alpha/2}$ = normal distribution value for a desired confidence level

Procedure for Calculating Confidence Intervals for the Mean

1. Find the confidence level from the table for normal distribution (see Appendix E) and determine the appropriate Z-value

2. Calculate the sample mean $\bar{X}$, sample standard deviation σ, and sample size n

3. Calculate margin of error by multiplying Z times σ and divide by the square root of n

4. Calculate $\bar{X}$ plus or minus the margin of error to obtain confidence intervals

---

EXAMPLE

We will use the home shopping channel population as an example. Let's say from a sample of 32 customers, the average order is $78.25, and the population standard deviation is $37.50. (This represents the variation among orders within the population.) We can calculate the 95 percent confidence interval for the population mean as follows:

$$\mu = 78.25 \pm 1.96 \frac{(37.50)}{\sqrt{32}} = 78.25 \pm 13.00$$

$$91.25 \geq \mu \geq 65.25$$

Continuous data—small samples: For this type, where a small sample is used (< 30) then the t distribution must be used:

$$\bar{X} \pm t_{\alpha/2} \frac{s}{\sqrt{n}}$$

where:

$\bar{X}$ = sample average

s = sample standard deviation

n = sample size

$t_{\alpha/2}$ = t distribution value (Appendix K) for a desired confidence level with $(n-1)$ degrees of freedom

---

EXAMPLE

Let us say for the previous example the sample size is 25:

$$\mu = 78.25 \pm 2.064 \frac{(37.50)}{\sqrt{25}} = 78.25 \pm 15.48$$

$$93.73 \geq \mu \geq 62.77$$

Confidence Intervals for Variation

Confidence intervals for the mean are symmetrical about the average. This is not true for the variance, since it is based on the chi-square distribution, for which the formula is:

$$\frac{(n-1)s^2}{x^2_{\alpha/2},\, n-1} \le \sigma^2 \le \frac{(n-1)s^2}{x^2_{1-\alpha/2},\, n-1}$$

where:

n = sample size

s^2 = point estimate of variation

$x^2_{\alpha/2}$ and $x^2_{1-\alpha/2}$ are the table values for $(n-1)$ degrees of freedom

Procedure for Calculating the Confidence Intervals for Variation

1. Find the critical chi-square value from the chi-square distribution table (Appendix H) for $n-1$ degrees of freedom

2. Use the above formula and calculate the confidence interval for variance

3. Report the results

EXAMPLE

The sample variance for a set of 35 samples was found to be 46. Calculate the 90 percent confidence interval for the variance:

$$\frac{(34 \times 46)}{48.60} \le \sigma^2 \le \frac{(34 \times 46)}{21.66}$$

$$32.18 \le \sigma^2 \le 72.21$$

Confidence Intervals for Proportion

For large sample sizes with $n(p)$ and $n(1-p) \ge 4$ or 5, the normal distribution can be used to calculate a confidence interval for proportion. The following formula is used:

$$p \pm Z_{\alpha/2} \sqrt{\frac{p(1-p)}{n}}$$

where

p = population proportion estimate

$Z_{\alpha/2}$ = appropriate confidence level from a Z-table

n = sample size

Procedure for Calculating the Confidence Intervals for Proportion

1. Determine the confidence level and find the appropriate Z value in the Z-Table (Appendix E)

2. Find the sample proportion p by taking the number of people in the sample having the characteristic of interest divided by sample size n

3. Multiply p by $(1 - p)$ and then divide that amount by n

4. Take the square root of the result from step 3

5. Multiply your answer by Z (margin of error)

6. Take p plus or minus the margin of error to obtain the confidence interval

---

EXAMPLE

Let us say we want to estimate the proportion of female home shopping channel customers. Out of a sample of 175 random customers pulled, 110 were females. Calculate the 90 percent confidence interval for the proportion:

$$0.629 \pm 1.645 \sqrt{\frac{(0.629 \times 0.371)}{175}} = 0.629 \pm 0.0600$$

$$0.689 \geq p \geq 0.569$$

Other confidence interval formulas exist for percent nonconforming, Poisson distribution data, and very small sample size data.

Hypothesis Tests for Means

Z Test. If the null hypothesis is denoted by H_0 and the alternative hypothesis is denoted by H_1, the test statistic is given by

$$Z = \frac{\overline{X} - \mu_0}{\sigma_{\bar{x}}} = \frac{X - \mu_0}{\dfrac{\sigma_x}{\sqrt{n}}}$$

where

$\overline{X}$ = sample average

n = number of samples

σ_x = standard deviation of means

If the population follows a normal distribution, and the population standard deviation σ_x is known, then the hypothesis tests for comparing a population mean μ with a fixed value μ_0 are given by the following:

$$H_0: \mu = \mu_0, \; H_0: \mu \leq \mu_0, \; H_0: \mu \geq \mu_0$$

$$H_1: \mu \neq \mu_0, \; H_1: \mu > \mu_0, \; H_1: \mu < \mu_0$$

If $n > 30$, the standard deviation s is often used as an estimate of the population standard deviation σ_x. The test statistic Z is compared with a critical value Z_α or $Z_{\alpha/2}$, which is based on a significance level α for a one-tail test or $\alpha/2$ for a two-tail test. If the H_1 sign is $\neq$, it is a two-tail test. If the H_1 sign is $<$, it is a left one-tail test, if the H_1 sign is $>$, it is a right one-tail test.

Procedure for Testing the Mean

1. Set conditions:

   a. Normal population or large sample ($n \geq 30$)

   b. σ known

2. $H_0: \mu = \mu_0, \; H_1: \mu \neq \mu_0$, or $\mu < \mu_0$ or $\mu > \mu$

   It has a two-tail test when H_1 has a $\neq$ sign, left-tail test when H_1 has the $<$ sign, and a right-tail test when H_1 has the $>$ sign.

3. Determine the α value.

4. Determine the critical values:

   a. For a two-tail test, use a Z-table to find the value that has an area of $\alpha/2$ to its right. This value and its negative are the two critical values. The reject region is the area to the right of the positive value and the area to the left of the negative value.

   b. For a left-tail test, use a Z-table to find the value that has an area of α to its right. The negative of this value is the critical value. The reject region is the area to the left of the negative value.

   c. For a right-tail test, use a Z-table to find the value that has an area of α to its right. This value is the critical value. The reject region is the area to the right of the positive value.

5. Calculate the test statistic

$$Z = (\bar{x} - \mu_0) \frac{\sqrt{n}}{\sigma}$$

6. If the test statistic is in the reject region, reject H_0. Otherwise, do not reject H_0.

7. State the conclusion in terms of the problem.

EXAMPLE

A vendor claims that the average weight of a shipment of parts is 1.84. The customer randomly chooses 64 parts and finds that the sample has an average of 1.88. Suppose that the standard deviation of the population is known to be 0.03. Should the customer reject the lot? Assume that the customer wants to be 95 percent confident that the supplier's claim is incorrect before he or she rejects.

1. Conditions (a) and (b) are met.

2. H_0: $\mu = 1.84$, H_1: $\mu \neq 1.84$; this is a two-tail test.

3. From the problem statement, $\alpha = .05$.

4. Critical values are the Z-value that has .025 to its right and the negative of this value. These values are 1.96 and –1.96. The reject region consists of the area to the right of 1.96 and the area to the left of –1.96.

5. $Z = (1.88 - 1.84)\sqrt{64}/(.03) = 10.7$

6. Since 10.7 is in the reject region, H_0 is rejected.

7. At the .05 significance level, the data suggest that the vendor's assertion that the average weight is 1.84 is false.

Student's t Test

The t test is usually used for making inferences about a population mean when the population variance σ^2 is unknown and the sample size n is small. Student's t distribution applies to samples drawn from a normally distributed population. The use of the t distribution is never wrong for any sample size. However, a sample size of 30 is normally the crossover point between the t and Z tests. The test statistic formula for this is

$$t = \frac{\bar{X} - \mu_0}{s/\sqrt{n}}$$

where

$\bar{X}$ = sample mean

μ_0 = target value or population mean

s = sample standard deviation

n = number of test samples

For the t test the null and alternative hypotheses are the same as they were for the Z test. The test statistic t is compared with a critical value t_α or $t_{\alpha/2}$, which is based on a significance level α for a one-tail test or $\alpha/2$ for a two-tail test, and the number of degrees of freedom, (df). The degree of freedom is determined by the number of samples n and is given by:

$$df = n - 1$$

Procedure for Calculating t *Test*

1. Calculate the sample mean $\bar{X}$ and the sample standard deviation s

2. Find $\bar{X} - \mu_0$

3. Calculate the standard error $s/\sqrt{n}$

4. Divide the results of step 2 by step 3

EXAMPLE

A cutoff saw has been producing parts with a mean length of 4.125. A new blade is installed and we want to know whether the mean has decreased. We select a random sample of 20, measure the length of each part, and find that the average length is 4.123 and the sample standard deviation is .008. Assume that the population is normally distributed. Use a significance level of .10 to determine whether the mean length has decreased.

Since the population standard deviation is unknown, the t test will be used.

1. Condition is met.

2. H_0: $\mu = 4.125$, H_1: $\mu < 4.125$, which is a left-tail test.

3. From the problem statement, $\alpha = .10$.

4. The positive critical value is in the 19th row of the $t_{.10}$ column of the t-table. This value is 1.328. Since this is a left-tail test, the critical value is –1.328. The reject region consists of the area to the left of –1.328.

5. $t = \left(4.123 - 4.125\right)\sqrt{20}/\left(.008\right) = -1.1$

6. Since –1.1 is not in the reject region, H_0 is not rejected.

7. At the .10 significance level the data does not indicate that the average length has decreased.

One Population Proportion (p Test)

A p test is used when testing a claim about a population proportion and we have a fixed number of independent trials having constant probabilities, with each trial having two outcome possibilities (a binomial distribution). When $np < 5$ or $n(1 - p) < 5$, the binomial distribution is used to test hypotheses relating to proportion.

Procedure for Calculating p *Test*

1. Set conditions that $np \geq 5$ and $n(1 - p) \geq 5$ are to be met; then the binomial distribution of sample proportions can be approximated by a normal distribution.

2. The hypothesis tests for comparing a sample proportion p with a fixed value p_0 are given by the following:

$$H_0: p = p_0, \ H_0: p \leq p_0, \ H_0: p \geq p_0$$

$$H_1: p \neq p_0, \ H_1: p > p_0, \ H_1: p < p_0$$

The null hypothesis is denoted by H_0 and the alternative hypothesis is denoted by H_1.

3. Decide on α, the significance level.

4. Find the critical values in a standard normal table $-Z_\alpha$, Z_α, and $Z_{\alpha/2}$, (left-tail, right-tail, or two-tail test, respectively).

5. Calculate the test statistic using

$$Z = \frac{p' - p_0}{\sqrt{\dfrac{p_0(1 - p_0)}{n}}}$$

where

p' = sample proportion = x/n

p = population proportion

n = number of samples

x = number of items in the sample with the defined attribute

p_0 = the hypothesized proportion

6. Reject H_0 if the test statistic is in the reject region. If not, do not reject H_0.

7. State the conclusion

EXAMPLE

A vendor claims that at most two percent of a shipment of parts is defective. Receiving inspection chooses a random sample of 500 and finds 15 defectives. At the 0.05 significance level, do these data indicate that the vendor is wrong?

Here, $n = 500$, $x = 15$, $p' = 15 \div 500 = 0.03$, and $p_0 = 0.02$.

1. Compute $np_0 = 500 \times 0.02 = 10$ and $n(1 - p_0) = 500 \times 0.98 = 490$.

   Both values are ≥ 5 so conditions are met.

2. $H_0: p \leq 0.02$ and $H_1: p > 0.02$ (right-tail test).

3. $\alpha = 0.05$.

4. Critical value = 1.645, from a normal table.

5. $Z = \dfrac{0.03 - 0.02}{\sqrt{(0.02 \times 0.98) \div 500}} \approx 1.597$

6. Do not reject H_0.

7. At the 0.05 significance level, the data do not support a conclusion that the vendor is incorrect in asserting that at most two percent of the shipment is defective.

3. PAIRED-COMPARISON TESTS

> Define and describe paired-comparison
> parametric hypothesis tests. (Understand)
>
> **Body of Knowledge IV.B.3**

Two-Mean, Equal Variance *t* Test

In a two-mean, equal variance *t* test, the tests are between two sample means. ($\bar{X}$ versus $\bar{X}_2$), and σ_1, and σ_2 are unknown but considered equal.

$$H_0: \mu_1 = \mu_2, H_1: \mu_1 \neq \mu_2$$

$$t = \frac{\bar{X}_1 - \bar{X}_2}{s_p / \sqrt{\frac{1}{n_1} + \frac{1}{n_2}}}$$

where

s_p = pooled standard deviation

$$s_p = \sqrt{\frac{\left((n_1 - 1)s_1^2 + (n_2 - 1)s_2^2\right)}{n_1 + n_2 - 2}}$$

$$df = n_1 + n_2 - 2$$

Part IV.B.3

EXAMPLE

Two operators are machining parts in two CNCs and they want to test the difference between two sample means. Samples are taken in pairs and their differences are calculated. For this, a paired *t* test is used, where

$$H_0: \mu_1 = \mu_2, H_1: \mu_1 \neq \mu_2$$

	CNC 1	CNC 2
1	5.257	5.243
2	5.220	5.193
3	5.235	5.225
4	5.230	5.220
5	5.225	5.223
	$x_1 = 5.2334$	$x_2 = 5.2208$
	$s_1 = .0143$	$s_2 = .0179$

Continued

Continued

$$s_p = \sqrt{\frac{\left((n_1 - 1)s_1^2 + (n_2 - 1)s_2^2\right)}{n_1 + n_2 - 2}}, \ df = 5 + 5 - 2 = 8$$

$$s_p = \sqrt{\frac{4(.0143)^2 + 4(.0179)^2}{8}} = .0162$$

$$t = \frac{5.2334 - 5.2208}{.0162\sqrt{\frac{1}{5} + \frac{1}{5}}} = 1.230$$

The critical value for $t_{.025, 8} = 2.306$ (a two-sided test for $\alpha = 0.05$). Therefore, the null hypothesis H_0 can not be rejected.

Two-Mean, Unequal Variance *t* Test

In a two-mean, unequal variance *t* test the tests are between two sample means ($\bar{X}_1$ versus $\bar{X}_2$), and σ_1 and σ_2 are unknown but are not considered equal.

$$H_0: \mu_1 = \mu_2, \ H_1: \mu_1 \neq \mu_1$$

$$t = \frac{\bar{X}_1 - \bar{X}_2}{\sqrt{\frac{s_1^2}{n_1} + \frac{s_2^2}{n_2}}}$$

$$df = \frac{1}{\left(\dfrac{\dfrac{s_1^2}{n_1}}{\dfrac{s_1^2}{n_1} + \dfrac{s_2^2}{n_2}}\right) + \left(\dfrac{\dfrac{s_2^2}{n_2}}{\dfrac{s_1^2}{n_1} + \dfrac{s_2^2}{n_2}}\right)}{n_1 - 1} + \dfrac{}{n_2 - 1}}$$

Part IV.B.3

EXAMPLE

Use data from the prior example to perform an unequal variance test: $df = 7.627 \approx 8$. Round off df to increase the confidence level rather than reduce it:

$$t = \frac{5.2334 - 5.2208}{\sqrt{\frac{(.0143)^2}{5} + \frac{(.0179)^2}{5}}} = 1.230$$

The critical value for $t_{.025,8} = 2.306$ (two-sided test for $\alpha = 0.05$). The null hypothesis H_0 is rejected.

Paired *t* Test

In these tests, subjects are matched in pairs and the outcomes are compared within each matched pair:

$$t = \frac{\bar{d}}{\frac{s_d}{\sqrt{n}}}$$

In general, the paired *t* test is a more sensitive test than the comparison of two independent samples.

Note: The paired *t* test is applied when we have a before-and-after scenario or there is a dependency between the two sets of measurements. For example, measurement of samples before and after heat treatment, measurement before and after calibration of equipment, pre- and post-training skill assessment of an employee. It is important to know when to apply a paired *t* test.

Procedure for Paired **t** *Test*

1. Find the differences between each pair of data by subtracting one from the other.

2. Use this data and calculate the mean $\bar{d}$ and the standard deviation s of all the differences.

3. Let n be the number of paired differences.

4. Calculate the standard error $\frac{s}{\sqrt{n}}$ and save this data.

5. Divide the mean $\bar{d}$ by the standard error $\frac{s}{\sqrt{n}}$ from step 4.

EXAMPLE

Two operators are machining parts in a CNC and they want to compare the difference between two sample means. Samples are taken in pairs and their differences are calculated. A paired *t* test is used, where

$$H_0: \mu_1 = \mu_2, \; H_1: \mu_1 \neq \mu_2$$

	Operator 1	Operator 2	Difference (d)
1	5.257	5.243	0.014
2	5.220	5.193	0.027
3	5.235	5.225	0.010
4	5.230	5.220	0.010
5	5.225	5.223	0.002
			$\bar{d} = 0.0126$
			$S_d = 0.00915$

Continued

Continued

$$df = n - 1 = 4$$

$$t = \frac{\bar{d}}{\dfrac{s_d}{\sqrt{n}}} = 3.080$$

$t_{.025,\,4} = 2.776$ ($\alpha = 0.05$ for a two-sided test; a paired test is always a two-tail test). The null hypothesis H_0 is rejected.

F Test

The F statistic is the ratio of two sample variances (also called two chi-square distributions) and is represented as

$$F = \frac{(s_1)^2}{(s_2)^2}$$

where

s_1^2 and s_2^2 = sample variances of the two samples 1 & 2 under comparison.

σ_1^2 and σ_2^2 are population variances from which the sample may have been drawn.

Procedure for Calculating Two-Sample-Variance F *Test*

1. Set the conditions: populations are normal and samples are independent.

2. The hypothesis tests for comparing two population variances σ_1^2 and σ_2^2 are given by

   $H_0: \sigma_1^2 = \sigma_2^2,\ H_0: \sigma_1^2 \leq \sigma_2^2,\ H_0: \sigma_1^2 \geq \sigma_2^2$

   $H_1: \sigma_1^2 \neq \sigma_2^2,\ H_1: \sigma_1^2 > \sigma_2^2,\ H_1: \sigma_1^2 < \sigma_2^2$

   where H_0 represents the null hypothesis and H_1 represents the alternative hypothesis. The F distribution has a nonsymmetrical shape and depends on the number of degrees of freedom associated with s_1^2 and s_2^2. Number of degrees of freedom are represented by v_1 and v_2.

3. Find the critical values in an F table.

4. Calculate the test statistic using

$$F = \frac{(s_1)^2}{(s_2)^2}$$

Part IV.B.3

5. Reject the test hypothesis H_0 if it is in the reject region, otherwise do not reject H_0.

6. State the conclusion.

EXAMPLE

A pickle factory is studying the effect of aging on its product. They want to know if there is an improvement in consistency of crispness (strength) after aging for one month. The data collected is reported below (assume a 95 percent confidence level).

	Initial reading	After one month
Number of tests	8	6
Standard deviation	1800	600

Here

H_0: $\sigma_1^2 \leq \sigma_2^2$ and H_1: $\sigma_1^2 > \sigma_2^2$

$v_1 = 7$ and $v_2 = 5$

Since this is concerned with an improvement in variation, a one-tail test with α risk in the right tail could be used. Using the *F* table (Appendix F), the critical value of *F* is 4.88. The null hypothesis rejection area is equal to or greater than 4.88.

$$F = \frac{\left(s_1\right)^2}{\left(s_2\right)^2} = \frac{\left(1800\right)^2}{\left(600\right)^2} = 9$$

The null hypothesis is rejected in this case as the calculated *F* value is in the critical region. There is enough evidence to prove reduced variance and higher consistency of crispness after aging for one month.

---

4. SINGLE-FACTOR ANALYSIS OF VARIANCE (ANOVA)

Define terms related to one-way ANOVAs and interpret their results and data plots. (Apply)

Body of Knowledge IV.B.4

One-Way ANOVA

ANOVA is a statistical method for comparing several population means. We draw a simple random sample (SRS) from each population and use the data to test the null hypothesis that the population means are all equal.

A factor in ANOVA describes the cause of the variation in the data. When only one factor is being considered, the procedure is known as *one-way ANOVA*. This type of ANOVA has two parts, the variation among treatment means and the variation within treatments. To use one-way ANOVA, the following conditions must be present:

    a. The populations of interest must be normally distributed

    b. The samples must be independent of each other

    c. Each population must have the same variance

The basic idea here is to determine whether the variation caused by the factor is a sufficiently large multiple of the experimental error to reject the null hypothesis. The *F*-statistic measures that multiple. The experimental error is measured as the within-treatment variation.

Procedure for Calculating One-Way ANOVA

1. H_o: $\mu_1 = \mu_2 = \mu_3 = \ldots = \mu_k$, H_a: not all the means are equal; this is a right-tail test.

2. Determine the α value. This is similar to the use of α in confidence intervals. In hypothesis testing jargon, the value of α is referred to as the significance level.

3. Construct the ANOVA table:

Source of variation	Sum of squares	Degrees of freedom	Mean squares	F-statistic
Between treatment	SS_B	$k - 1$	$MS_B = SS_B \div (k - 1)$	$F = MS_B / MS_W$
Within treatment	SS_W	$N - k$	$MS_W = SS_W \div (N - k)$	
Total	SS_T	$N - 1$		

A fundamental property of this table is that the total row is the total of the values of the entries above it in the sum of squares column and the degrees of freedom column, where:

    N = number of readings

    n = number of readings per level (or treatment)

    k = number of levels (or treatments)

    T = grand total of readings $\Sigma y_i = \Sigma T_i$

    C = correction factor = $T^2 \div N$

    $y_i's$ = individual measurements

    SS_T = sum of squares total = $\Sigma y_i^2 - C$

    SS_B = sum of squares between treatments = $\Sigma T_i^2/n - C$

    SS_W = sum of squares within treatment = $SS_T - SS_B$

4. The test statistic is the *F*-value as defined in the table.

5. Find the critical value in an *F* table using $k - 1$ as the numerator degrees of freedom and $k(n - 1)$ as the denominator degrees of freedom.

6. Determine whether the null hypothesis should be rejected. Since this is a right-tail test, if the value of the test statistic is $\geq$ the critical value, then the null hypothesis is rejected and the alternative hypothesis is accepted. If the value of the test statistic is $<$ the critical value, the null hypothesis is not rejected.

7. State the conclusion in terms of the original problem.

EXAMPLE

A polyurethane casting process can be run at 200°F, 220°F, or 240°F. Does the temperature significantly affect the moisture content? Use $\alpha = 0.05$.

To answer the question, four batches were run at each of the temperatures. The twelve runs were executed in random order. The temperature results are:

240°F	220°F	200°F
10.8	11.4	14.3
10.4	11.9	12.6
11.2	11.6	13.0
9.9	12.0	14.2

The entries in the table are individual measurements, referred to as *y*-values, and are moisture content values in percent H_2O.

The hypothesis test:

1. Assume that the conditions have been tested and are satisfied.

2. H_0: $\mu_1 = \mu_2 = \mu_3$, H_a: not all the means are equal, this is a right-tail test.

3. $\alpha = .05$.

4. Construct the ANOVA table.

5. Calculate the average in each column.

240°F	220°F	200°F
10.8	11.4	14.3
10.4	11.9	12.6
11.2	11.6	13.0
9.9	12.0	14.2
$T_1 = 42.3$	$T_2 = 46.9$	$T_3 = 54.1$
$\bar{y}_1 = 10.575$	$\bar{y}_2 = 11.725$	$\bar{y}_3 = 13.525$

Continued

Continued

where

number of readings $N = 12$

number of readings per level (or treatment) $n = 4$

number of levels (or treatments) $k = 3$

$$\Sigma y_i^2 = 10.8^2 + 10.4^2 + 11.2^2 + 9.9^2 + 11.4^2 + 11.9^2 + 11.6^2 +$$
$$12.0^2 + 14.3^2 + 12.6^2 + 13.0^2 + 14.2^2 = 1732.27$$

Grand total of readings: $T = \Sigma y_i = \Sigma T_i = 42.3 + 46.9 + 54.1 = 143.3$

Correction factor: $C = T^2 \div N = 143.3^2 \div 12 = 1711.24$

Sum of squares total $= SS_T = \Sigma y^2 - C = 1732.27 - 1711.24 = 21.03$

Sum of squares between treatments $= SS_B = \Sigma T_i^2 / n - C$
$$= 42.3^2/4 + 46.9^2/4 + 54.1^2/4 - 1711.24$$
$$= 17.69$$

Sum of squares within treatment $= SS_W = SS_T - SS_B = 21.03 - 17.69 = 3.34$

These values fit into an ANOVA table as follows:

Source of variation	Sum of squares	Degrees of freedom	Mean square	F-statistic
Between treatment	$SS_B = 17.69$	$k - 1 = 2$	$17.69/2 = 8.85$	23.92
Within treatment	$SS_W = 3.3$	$N - k = 9$	$3.34/9 = 0.37$	
Total	$SS_T = 21.03$	$N - 1 = 11$		

6. The test statistic is defined as $F = MS_B/MS_W = 8.85/0.37 = 23.92$.

7. The critical values are in the F table located in Appendix F. The table is indexed by the degrees of freedom associated with the numerator and denominator of the fraction used to calculate F. In this case the numerator MS_B has 2 degrees of freedom and the denominator MS_W has 9 degrees of freedom. From the $F_{.05}$ table in column 2 and row 9, $F = 4.26$. Here there is only one rejection region, which is the shaded area on the right tail of the distribution. This is a right-tail test. The test statistic 23.92 exceeds the critical value 4.26 so the null hypothesis is rejected.

8. Thus the conclusion is that at the .05 significance level the data indicates that temperature does have an impact on moisture content.

Using Excel's FINV Function

One can generate critical F-statistics using Excel's FINV function, which is represented as

FINV(probability, deg_freedom1, deg_freedom2)

where

probability = the level of significance

deg_freedom1 = $v_1 = k - 1$

deg_freedom2 = $v_2 = N - k$

Figure 17.3 illustrates the FINV function used to determine the critical *F*-statistic with $\alpha = 0.05$, $v_1 = 3 - 1 = 2$, and $v_2 = 12 - 3 = 9$ from our previous example.

Cell A1 contains the Excel formula =FINV(0.05,2,9) with the result being 3.862. This value is very close to the one in the *F* distribution table (Appendix F), 4.2564.

Using Excel to Perform One-Way ANOVA

One can perform ANOVA using Excel; here are the steps:

1. Enter the data in each column of a blank spreadsheet.

2. Select Data Analysis from the Tools menu bar (Refer to *Installing Data Analysis* in the Excel help menu). See sharepoint for details.

3. Select ANOVA: Single Factor from the Data Analysis dialog box and click OK (see Figure 17.4).

4. Set up the ANOVA: Single Factor dialog box as shown in Figure 17.5.

5. Click OK; Figure 17.6 shows the final ANOVA results.

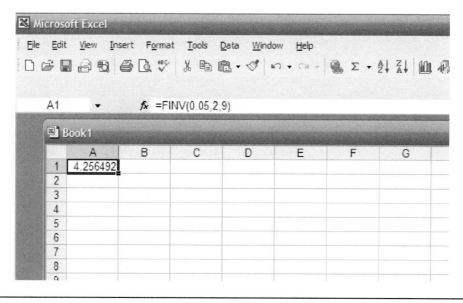

Figure 17.3 Excel's FINV function.

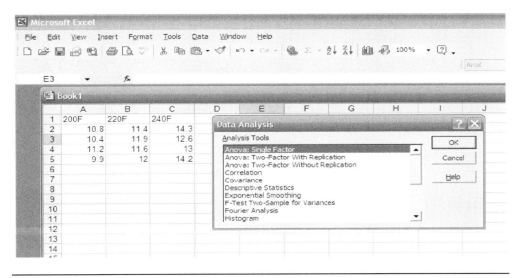

Figure 17.4   Setting up a one-way ANOVA in Excel.

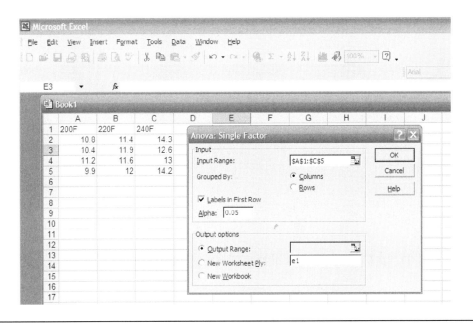

Figure 17.5   The ANOVA: Single Factor dialog box.

These results are consistent with what we found doing it the hard way in the previous sections. Notice that the p-value = 0.000254 for this test, meaning we can reject H_0 as this p-value $\leq \alpha$, which is 0.05.

D	E	F	G	H	I	J	K	L
	Anova: Single Factor							
	SUMMARY							
	Groups	*Count*	*Sum*	*Average*	*Variance*			
	200F	4	42.3	10.575	0.309167			
	220F	4	46.9	11.725	0.075833			
	240F	4	54.1	13.525	0.729167			
	ANOVA							
	Source of Variation	*SS*	*df*	*MS*	*F*	*P-value*	*F crit*	
	Between Groups	17.68667	2	8.843333	23.81152	0.000254	4.256492	
	Within Groups	3.3425	9	0.371389				
	Total	21.02917	11					

Figure 17.6 Final results of one-way ANOVA in Excel.

5. CHI SQUARE

Define and interpret chi square and use it to
determine statistical significance. (Analyze)

Body of Knowledge IV.B.5

Procedure for Chi Square (β^2) Test

1. Conditions:

   • All expected frequencies are at least 1

   • At most, 20 percent of the expected frequencies are less than 5

2. H_0: the distribution has not changed; H_a: the distribution has changed.

3. Determine α, the significance level.

4. Find the critical value in row $k - 1$ in the χ^2_α column of the χ^2 table, (Appendix H) where k = number of categories in the distribution. This is always a right-tail test, so the reject region is the area to the right of this critical value.

5. Calculate the test statistic using the formula

$$\chi^2 = \Sigma[(O - E)^2/E] \text{ (the sum of the last column in a } \chi^2 \text{ table)}$$

where O is the observed frequency and E is the expected frequency.

6. Reject H_0 if the test statistic is in the reject region. Otherwise do not reject.

7. State the conclusion.

EXAMPLE

Suppose that all rejected products have exactly one of four types of defects and that historically they have been distributed as follows:

Paint run	16%
Paint blister	28%
Decal crooked	42%
Door cracked	14%
Total	100%

Data on rejected parts for a randomly selected week in the current year are:

Paint run	27
Paint blister	60
Decal crooked	100
Door cracked	21

The question that one needs to answer is: is the distribution of defect/deformity types different from the historical distribution? This is often called the χ^2 *goodness-of-fit test* (pronounced 'chi square'). To get a feel for this test, construct a table that displays the number of defects that would be expected in each category if the sample exactly followed the historical percentages:

	Probability	Observed frequency	Expected frequency
Paint run	0.16	27	33.28
Paint blister	0.28	60	58.24
Decal crooked	0.42	100	87.36
Door cracked	0.14	21	29.12
Total			208.00

The expected frequency for paint run is found by calculating 16 percent of 208, and so on. It remains to be seen if the difference between the expected frequencies and observed frequencies is sufficiently large to conclude that the sample comes from a population that has a different distribution. Test this at the .05 significance level.

Continued

Continued

The test statistic is obtained by the following equation:

$$\chi^2 = \Sigma \frac{(O-E)^2}{E}$$

The null hypothesis is that the distribution hasn't changed. This hypothesis will be rejected if the total of the last column is too large. The results are as follows:

	Probability	Observed frequency (O)	Expected frequency (E)	(O − E)	$\frac{(O-E)^2}{E}$
Paint run	0.16	27	33.28	−6.28	1.19
Paint blister	0.28	65	58.24	6.76	0.78
Decal crooked	0.42	95	87.36	7.64	0.67
Door cracked	0.14	21	29.12	−8.12	2.26
Total			208.00		4.9

EXAMPLE

Using the data from the previous example:

1. The conditions are met.

2. H_0: The distribution of defect types has not changed.

   H_a: The distribution of defect types has changed.

3. $\alpha = .05$

4. From row 3 of the $\chi^2_{.05}$ column, the critical value is 7.815. The reject region is the area to the right of 7.815.

5. $\chi^2 = \Sigma[(O - E)^2/E] = 4.9$

6. Since the test statistic does not fall in the reject region, do not reject H_0.

7. At the .05 significance level, the data do not indicate that the distribution has changed.

Using Excel to Perform Chi-Square Distribution

One can generate critical chi-square scores using Excel's CHIINV function, which has the following characteristics:

CHIINV(probability, deg_freedom)

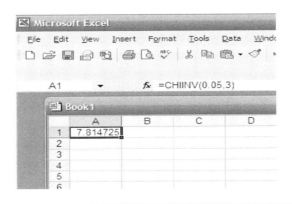

Figure 17.7   Excel's CHINV function.

where

probability = the level of significance α

deg_freedom = the number of degrees of freedom

For example, to determine the critical chi-square score for $\alpha = .05$ and df $= 3$ from the previous example, the CHIINV function is illustrated in Figure 17.7.

Cell A1 contains the Excel formula =CHIINV(0.05,3) with the result being 7.815. This is similar to the value in the chi-square distribution table (Appendix H).

Contingency Tables

Contingency tables are two-dimensional classification tables with rows and columns containing original frequencies or count data that can be analyzed to determine whether the two variables are independent or have significant association. When the totals of rows and columns are analyzed in a certain way, the chi-square procedure will test whether there is dependency between the two classifications. Also, a *contingency coefficient* can be calculated. If the chi-square test shows a significant dependency, the contingency coefficient will show the strength of the correlation.

Parametric and Nonparametric Tests

Parametric test implies a descriptive measure calculated using population data. Usually, an assumption is made when performing a hypothesis test that the data are a sample from a certain distribution, commonly referred to as the normal distribution. *Nonparametric test* implies that there is no assumption of a specific distribution for the population.

Nonparametric techniques of hypothesis testing are applicable for many quality engineering problems and projects. These tests are also called *distribution-free* as they make no assumption regarding the population distribution. They can be applied to *ranking tests*, in which data are not specific in any continuous data or attribute sense, but are simply ranks. Three powerful nonparametric techniques commonly used are the Kendall coefficient of concordance, Spearman rank correlation coefficient, and Kruskal-Wallis one-way analysis of variance. We will not go into detailed descriptions of these techniques as they are outside the scope of the Green Belt BoK.

Part V

Six Sigma—*Improve & Control*

Part V

Chapter 18

A. Design of Experiments (DOE)

1. BASIC TERMS

> Define and describe basic DOE terms such
> as independent and dependent variables,
> factors and levels, response, treatment, error,
> repetition, and replication. (Understand)
>
> **Body of Knowledge V.A.1**

Factor

A *factor* is the variable controlled by the experimenter, and could be viewed as a stimulus; one of the controlled or uncontrolled variables whose influence on a response is studied in an experiment.

Levels

A *level* refers to the settings or possible values of a factor in an experimental design throughout the progress of the experiment. The "levels" of a factor could be quantitative measures (that is, three different temperatures) or qualitative (that is, on or off, high–medium–low, one of four different operators).

Treatment

A *treatment* is a single level assigned to a single factor or experimental unit during the experimental run. Example: pressure at 200 psi. A treatment is also a specific combination of factor levels whose effect is to be compared with other treatments. A *treatment combination* is the set or series of levels for all factors in a given experimental run. Example: pressure—200 psi, temperature—70° F, feed—high.

Block

A *block* is a portion of the experimental material or environment that is common to itself and distinct from other portions (for example, samples from the same batch). Blocking will be explained later as an experimental design method.

Experimental Design

The *experimental design* or *pattern* is the formal experiment plan that includes the responses, factors, levels, blocks, treatments, and the use of planned grouping, randomization, and replication.

Experimental Error

The variation in the response variable when levels and factors are held constant. Experimental error must be subtracted to determine the true effect of an experiment.

Planned Grouping

Planned grouping is a practice done to promote uniformity within blocks and minimize the effect of unwanted variables. This will make the experiement more effective in determining assignable causes.

Randomization

Randomization organizes the experiment to have treatment combinations done in a chance manner, improving statistical validity.

Replication

Replication repeats observations or measurements to increase precision, reduce measurement errors, and balance unknown factors. It is the repetition of the set of all the treatment combinations to be compared in an experiment. Each of the repetitions is called a replicate or a replication, and is done to increase reliability.

Repetition

It is important to note the difference between replication and repetition in the context of DOE. Replication is a process of running the experimental trials in a random manner. In contrast, *repetition* is a process of running the experimental trials under the same setup of machine parameters. In other words, the variation due to machine setup can't be captured using repetition. Replication requires resetting of each trial condition; therefore the cost of the experiment and also the time taken to complete the experiment may be increased to some extent.

Variables

Dependent variables are variables dependent on another variable. In simple terms, the independent variable is said to cause an apparent change in, or simply affect, the dependent variable. In analysis, researchers usually want to explain why the dependent variable has a given value. In research, the values of a dependent variable in different settings are usually compared. It is important to remember that the dependent variable does not change unless the independent variable on which it relies also changes.

Independent variables are variables presumed to affect or determine a dependent variable. They can be changed as required, and their values do not represent a problem requiring explanation in an analysis but are simply taken as given. The independent variable in an experiment is most commonly an input and does not have interactions with other variables.

Response variables are variables that show the observed results of an experimental treatment. The response is the outcome of the experiment as a result of controlling the levels, interactions, and number of factors.

DOE Overview—Planning and Organizing Experiments

History of DOE

Design of experiments (DoE) is a structured, organized method that is used to determine the relationship between the different factors (*X*'s) affecting a process and the output of that process (*Y*). Sir Ronald A. Fisher, the renowned mathematician and geneticist, first developed this method in the 1920s and 1930s. Fisher started working as a statistician in 1919 at the Rothamsted Experimental Station. This research center in England was conducting a series of experiments to measure the effects of different fertilizers on various crops.

Key Point: The use of DOE in agriculture is one of the primary reasons that the United States maintains such a large lead in what farmers can produce compared to other parts of the world. Also, you may note that some of the terms that we still use in DOE have agricultural connotations.

Purpose

The objective of a designed experiment is to generate knowledge about a product or process. The experiment seeks to find the effect that a set of independent variables has on a set of dependent variables. The independent variables that the experimenter controls are called *control factors* or *signal factors* or sometimes just factors. The other factors are called *noise factors*.

In the terminology of experimental design, each outcome (observation of the variable of interest, which is the expression level in our case) is measured in correspondence with a set of levels of different factors that may influence it. The experimenter specifically wants to study how the outcome depends on their variation. Some other effects correspond to the inevitable variability in the experimental setting, and the researcher mainly wants to control for their presence in interpreting the results.

Design of experiments involves designing a set of experiments to identify optimal conditions, the factors that most influence the results, and details such as the existence of interactions and synergies between factors. A *data matrix* is a table organizing the data into columns for analysis. The columns of the matrix represent factors and the rows are the different experiments. Within the individual squares, the levels of each factor are shown, corresponding to the effect of that level.

DoE methods require well-structured data matrices. Analysis of variance (ANOVA) delivers accurate results even when the matrix that is analyzed is quite small. Experimental design is a strategy that can be applied to investigate a phenomenon in order to gain understanding or improve performance.

CHECKLIST

Building a design means carefully choosing a small number of experiments that are to be performed under controlled conditions. There are four interrelated steps in building a design:

❑ Define an objective

❑ Define the variables that will be controlled

❑ Define the variables that will be measured to describe the outcome of the experimental runs (response variables) and examine their precision

❑ Choose the design that is compatible with the objective, number of design variables, and precision of measurements

---

Planning Test Programs

Experiments should have carefully defined objectives, separation of the effects of factors, freedom from bias, and precision. Based on the background information, choose the factors and design the experimental program. Define the experiment by number of experimental factors, structure of experimental design, and the kind of information the experiment is primarily intended to provide.

Classification of Experimental Designs

- *Completely randomized* experiments are appropriate when only one factor is analyzed.

- *Factorials* are appropriate when investigating several factors at two or more levels and interaction is necessary.

- *Blocked factorials* reduce the number of runs and use blocking to run the experiment in subsets.

- *Fractional factorials* reduce the combinations of factors and levels required to be run while resulting in a close estimate to the full factorial.

- *Randomized blocks* investigate a single factor when material or environment can be blocked.

- *Latin square* and *Youden square* experiments are used to investigate a primary factor while controlling the interactions and affects of other variables. In Latin square, the number of rows, columns, and treatments must all be equal, and there must be no interactions between the row, the column, and the studied factor. For this reason, the Latin square is not a factorial design, which allows interactions between the several factors comprising the design. While Youden squares also have the same number of columns and treatments, a fairly wide choice in the number of rows is possible.

- *Response surface* provides contour diagrams or maps of how the factors influence the response and direction for optimization of variable settings.

- *Mixture designs* are factorial experiments that express factor levels in percentages adding up to 100 percent. With mixtures, the property of interest depends on the proportions of the mixture components and not on the amounts.

Experimental Objectives

When preparing to conduct an experiment, the first consideration is "What question are we seeking to answer?" Examples of experimental objectives include:

Find the inspection procedure that provides optimum precision.

Find the combination of mail and media ads that produces the most sales.

Find the cake recipe that produces the most consistent taste in the presence of oven temperature variation.

Find the combination of valve dimensions that produces the most linear output.

Sometimes the design of experiments objective derives from a question. The objective must be related to the enterprise goals and objectives. The objective must also be measurable and the measurement system must be reasonably simple and easy to operate. Once the DoE objective and a measurement system have been determined, the factors and levels are selected as the things (factors) the experimenters would change and the various values (levels) they would recommend. From these recommendations, the list of factors and the levels for each factor are determined. A practical guideline for selecting levels is "Be bold but not foolish."

The next step is to choose the appropriate design given affordability and time available. Establish a budget of time and other resources. It is usually best to begin with more modest screening designs whose purpose is to determine the variables and levels that need further study.

DOE Design Principles

Randomization. Randomization allows us to spread the effect of variables through the error term. Randomization is a method of designing and organizing the experiment that attempts to lessen the effects of special cause variation by randomly assigning when the test will be run.

Suppose there are eight treatments with five replications per treatment. This produces 40 tests. The purpose of randomization is to spread out the variation caused by noise variables. The 40 tests may be randomized in several ways.

Number the tests from 1 to 40 and randomize those numbers to obtain the order in which tests are performed. This is referred to as a completely randomized design.

Suppose time of day is a noise factor such that products made before noon are different from those made after noon. With the completely randomized design, each run will likely have parts from both morning and afternoon.

Blocking. Blocking attempts to mitigate the effect of variables that we are trying to eliminate or avoid. Blocking is a method of designing and organizing the experiment that attempts to lessen the effects of special cause variation by grouping the experiments in batches of tests or runs.

This is called a *randomized block* design. For example, random selection might put runs 1, 4, 5, and 8 during first shift and 2, 3, 6, and 7 during second shift. Another method that may be used to nullify the impact of the shift change would be to do the first three replicates of each run during the first shift and the remaining two replicates of each run during the second shift.

Replication. This is the repetition of the set of all the treatment combinations to be compared in an experiment in a random order.

Other Principal Items

- Sample size is determined by the type of experiment chosen.

- Interaction occurs when one or more factors have an influence on the behavior of another factor.

- Confounding occurs when a factor interaction cannot be separately determined from a major factor in an experiment.

- Screening experiments can be used to screen out insignificant factors.

Experimentation (DOE)

A planned experiment (often called design of experiments or DOE) can be very useful in understanding the variation, through testing and optimizing, of a process. The purpose of running a DOE is to determine better ways or understand the other factors in the process. There is a basic process that these designed experiments tend to follow.

A planned experiment on your operation can be very useful. During DOE, a list of exact activities will be defined for each trial. Confirmation tests determine if the experiment has successfully identified better process conditions.

Part V.A.1

CHECKLIST

Experimentation

- ❏ Map the current process
- ❏ Brainstorm the causes of variation
- ❏ Use a cause-and-effect diagram to list and categorize sources of variation
- ❏ Brainstorm the key factors causing variation
- ❏ Determine variation levels usable in the process
- ❏ Define the experiment
- ❏ Run the experiment by operating the process using the various factors
- ❏ Collect samples from each run of the experiment
- ❏ Calculate which factors actually affect the process
- ❏ Run the process to confirm improvements
- ❏ Update operation sheets to show the new parameters of operation

Getting good results from DOE involves a number of steps. It is important to set objectives and select process variables and an experimental design appropriate for the objectives. After executing the design, a quick confirmation can check that the data are consistent with the experimental assumptions. The final stage is to analyze and interpret the results, and present the results for further actions or decisions.

CHECKLIST

DOE steps: important practical considerations

- ❏ Check performance of gages/measurement devices first
- ❏ Keep experiments as simple as possible
- ❏ Check that all planned runs are feasible
- ❏ Watch for process drifts and shifts
- ❏ Avoid unplanned changes
- ❏ Allow some time and backup material for unexpected events
- ❏ Obtain buy-in from all parties involved
- ❏ Maintain effective ownership of each step in the experimental plan
- ❏ Preserve all raw data—not just summary averages
- ❏ Record everything that happens
- ❏ Reset equipment to original state after experiment

Experimental objectives can be summarized under four categories:

- *Comparative.* Conclude if a factor is significant

- *Screening.* Select a few important main effects

- *Response surface.* Find optimal settings and weak points of processes

- *Mixture.* Determine the best proportions of a mixture

Once the objectives are set, the experimentation plan can be developed.

CHECKLIST

Typical DOE checklist

❑ Define objective of experiment

❑ Learn facts about the process

❑ Brainstorm a list of dependent and independent variables

❑ Run "dabbling experiments" to debug equipment

❑ Assign levels to each independent variable

❑ Select or develop a DOE plan

❑ Run experiments in random order and analyze periodically

❑ Draw conclusions and verify with replication

It is recommended to apply an iterative approach to DOE. Rather than limiting observations to a single experiment, it is common to perform two, three, or more experiments to get the final answer. Since each experiment provides a different answer, the experimenter can logically move through stages of experimentation.

There are additional assumptions that must be in place in order for the experiment to be valid and successful:

a. Measurement system capability

- Confirm the measurement system before embarking on the experiment

- Confirm the measurement system throughout the life of the experiment

b. Process stability

- Experiment should start and end at standard process set points under identifiable operating conditions

- Baseline needs to be established to reveal whether the process drifted during experimentation

c. Residuals

- Residuals are estimates of experimental error (observed response–predicted response)

- Should be normally and independently distributed with a mean of zero and constant variance

Application of DoE

The operator will work with engineering, supervisors, and Six Sigma practitioners (those specially training using Six Sigma problem-solving techniques) to look for variation. The operators know the machines best and will be able to give valuable insights on what might happen if different settings are used on the machines. During the DOE, a list of exact settings will be designed for each trial. There are typically eight or more test runs (trials) made for each DOE, and the operator will be asked to run the machine at the designed settings and take random parts from the machine for testing. Once the sample parts are tested and the measures recorded, the person who designed the DOE will probably use a computer to calculate the optimal setting based on the measurements that came from the samples.

A confirmation test should then be run using the new settings to see if the experiment has identified a better working condition for the machine. If proven out, the new setting should become part of the operation and the operator will then need to update the documentation in his or her area to reflect the new process settings and parameters.

Another variation on this same theme is the SDCA (standardize, do, check, act) cycle. This is most commonly used once a process has been improved to update control plans and process sheets to lock in the improvements and standardize the changes throughout the organization. SDCA is the outcome of applying sound recommendations based on the correct interpretation of valid effects obtained from proper design of experiments.

Key Point: DOE is best used for optimizing a process versus as a problem-solving tool.

2. MAIN EFFECTS

> Interpret main effects and interaction plots. (Apply)
>
> **Body of Knowledge V.A.2**

Main Effects

Main effects are defined as an estimate of the effect of a factor independent of any other means.

The first step in calculating main effects, sometimes called *average main effects,* is to average the results for each level of each factor. This is accomplished by averaging the results of the runs for that level.

For example, $F_{.01}$ (feed at the .01 in./min. level) is calculated by averaging the results of four runs in which feed was set at the .01 level. Results of the four runs are 10, 4, 6 and 2.

Run	F	Response
1	–	10
2	–	4
3	–	6
4	–	2
5	I	7
6	+	6
7	+	6
8	+	3

These were runs 1, 2, 3, and 4, so

$$F_{.01} = (10 + 4 + 6 + 2) \div 4 = 5.5$$

Similarly,

$$F_{.04} = (7 + 6 + 6 + 3) \div 4 = 5.5$$

Runs numbered 1, 2, 5, and 6 had S at 1300 rev/min, so

$$S_{1300} = (10 + 4 + 7 + 6) \div 4 = 6.75$$

and

$$S_{1800} = (6 + 2 + 6 + 3) \div 4 = 4.25$$
$$C_{100} = (10 + 6 + 7 + 6) \div 4 = 7.25$$
$$C_{140} = (4 + 2 + 6 + 3) \div 4 = 3.75$$

The main effects may be graphed as shown in Figure 18.1.

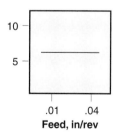 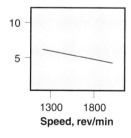 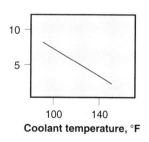

Figure 18.1 Main effects graphs.

Part V.A.2

Since the better surface finish (the quality characteristic of interest in this case) has the lowest "score," the team would choose the level of each factor that produces the lowest result. The team would suggest using a speed of 1800 rev/min and coolant temp of 140° F. What feed rate should be recommended? Since both $F_{.01}$ and $F_{.04}$ are 5.5, the feed rate doesn't impact surface finish in this range. The team would recommend a feed rate of .04 since it will result in a faster operation.

Factors with the greater difference between the "high" and "low" results are the factors with the greatest impact on the quality characteristic of interest. Most authors refer to the main effect as the "high level" result minus the "low level" result for the factor. For example:

$$\text{Main effect of factor } F = F_{.04} - F_{.01} = 5.5 - 5.5 = 0$$

$$\text{Similarly, main effect of } S = S_{1800} - S_{1300} = 4.25 - 6.75 = -2.50$$

$$\text{and } C = C_{140} - C_{100} = 3.75 - 7.25 = -3.50$$

Using this definition of main effect, the larger the absolute value of the main effect, the more influence that factor has on the quality characteristic. It is possible that the perceived difference between "high" and "low" results is not statistically significant. This would occur if the experimental error is so large that it would be impossible to determine whether the difference between the high and low values is due to a real difference in the dependent variable or due to experimental error. This may be determined by using ANOVA procedures.

LEARNING

The α-risk is the probability that the analysis will show that there is a significant difference when there is not. The β-risk is the probability that the analysis will show that there is no significant difference when there is. The power of the experiment is defined as $1 - \beta$, so the higher the power of the experiment, the lower the β-risk. In general, a higher number of replications or a larger sample size provides a more precise estimate of experimental error, which in turn reduces the β-risk.

Interaction Effects

Interactions occur when the effect of one input factor on the output depends on the level of another input factor. The preferred DOE approach screens a large number of factors with highly fractional experiments. Once suspected factors have been reduced, interactions are explored or additional levels are examined.

To assess the interaction effects, return to the original experimental design matrix, replacing each high level with "+" and each low level with "–" as shown in Table 18.1.

To find an entry in the column labeled "F × S," multiply the entries in the F and S columns, using the multiplication rule, "If the signs are the same, the result is positive; otherwise, the result is negative." Fill in the other interaction columns the same way. To fill in the F × S × C column, multiply the F × S column by the C column (see Table 18.2).

Table 18.1   A 2^3 full-factorial design using + and − format.

Run	F	S	C	F × S	F × C	S × C	F × S × C
1	−	−	−				
2	−	−	+				
3	−	+	−				
4	−	+	+				
5	+	−	−				
6	+	−	+				
7	+	+	−				
8	+	+	+				

Table 18.2   A 2^3 full-factorial design showing interaction columns.

Run	F	S	C	F × S	F × C	S × C	F × S × C	Response
1	−	−	−	+	+	+	−	10
2	−	−	+	+	−	−	+	4
3	−	+	−	−	+	−	+	6
4	−	+	+	−	−	+	−	2
5	+	−	−	−	−	+	+	7
6	+	−	+	−	+	−	−	6
7	+	+	−	+	−	−	−	6
8	+	+	+	+	+	+	+	3

To calculate the effect of the interaction between factors F and S, first find $F \times S_+$ by averaging the results of the runs that have a "+" in the F × S column:

$$F \times S_+ = (10 + 4 + 6 + 3) \div 4 = 5.75$$

Similarly,

$$F \times S_- = (6 + 2 + 7 + 6) \div 4 = 5.25$$

The effect of the F × S interaction is

$$5.75 - 5.25 = 0.50$$

Similar calculations show that

$$F \times C = 1.50, S \times C = 0, \text{ and } F \times S \times C = -1$$

The presence of interactions indicates that the main effects aren't additive.

Table 18.3   Half fraction of 2^3 (also called a 2^{3-1} design).

Run #	A	B	C
1	–	–	+
2	–	+	–
3	+	–	–
4	+	+	+

The design shown in Table 18.3 uses only four of the eight possible runs; therefore, the experiment itself will consume only half the resources as the one shown in Table 18.2. It still has three factors at two levels each. It is traditional to call this a 2^{3-1} design because it has two levels and three factors but only $2^{3-1} = 2^2 = 4$ runs. It is also called a half fraction of the full-factorial because it has half the number of runs as in the 2^3 full-factorial design.

Balanced Designs

An experimental design is called balanced when each setting of each factor appears the same number of times with each setting of every other factor.

The logical next question is, "Why use a full-factorial design when a fractional design uses a fraction of the resources?" To see the answer, review the following example.

EXAMPLE

Columns have been added to the design in Table 18.3 with two- and three-level interactions as shown in Table 18.4 using the multiplication rule.

Table 18.4   Half fraction of 2^3 design with interaction columns to be filled in by the reader.

Run #	A	B	C	A × B	A × C	B × C	A × B × C
1	–	–	+	+	–	–	+
2	–	+	–	–	+	–	+
3	+	–	–	–	–	+	+
4	+	+	+	+	+	+	+

Effects and Confounding

An experimental design uses effects to determine whether or not setting a factor at a particular level has a significant impact on the process. This should allow the assignable causes to be traceable and capable of further analysis or action.

Note that the A × B interaction column has the same configuration as the C column (see Table 18.4). Isn't that scary? This means that when the C main effect is calculated, it is not clear whether the effect is due to factor C or the interaction between A × B or, more likely, a combination of these two causes. Statisticians say that the main effect C is confounded with the interaction effect A × B.

Suppose the team has completed a number of full-factorial designs and determined that factors A, B, and C do not interact significantly in the ranges involved. Then there would be no significant confounding and the fractional factorial would be an appropriate design.

Design and Analysis of One-Factor Experiments

One-factor experiments are completely randomized when no tests are omitted and the order is completely random. A randomized block experiment involves taking a factor in each treatment and making exactly one measurement. Results are analyzed and evaluated with ANOVA, and significant values exceed the F statistic derived from the samples.

Examples of one-factor experiments are Latin square and Graeco-Latin squares, which do not incorporate interactions among factors.

EXAMPLE

A process can be run at 180° F, 200° F, or 220° F. Does the temperature significantly affect the moisture content?

Produce four batches at each of the temperatures.

Temperature, °F		
180	200	220
#1	#5	#9
#2	#6	#10
#3	#7	#11
#4	#8	#12

The 12 tests could be completely randomized. A completely randomized design would have a chart like the following to show the testing order, where test #3 is done first, and so on:

Temperature, °F		
180	200	220
#3	#11	#8
#7	#5	#1
#12	#9	#2
#6	#4	#10

Continued

Continued

If the team decided to produce one batch at each temperature each day for four days, they would randomize the order of the temperatures each day, thus using a randomized block design. The test order chart would then look like the following:

Day	Temperature, °F		
	180	200	220
1	#3	#1	#2
2	#1	#3	#2
3	#1	#2	#3
4	#2	#1	#3

The team might decide to block for two noise variables: the day the test was performed and the machine the test was performed on. In this case, a Latin square design could be used. However, these designs require that the number of levels of each of the noise factors is equal to the number of treatments. Since they have decided to test at three temperatures, they must use three days and three machines. This design is shown in Table 18.5.

Assume that the team decides on the completely randomized design and runs the 12 tests with the following results:

Temperature, °F		
180	200	220
10.8	11.4	14.3
10.4	11.9	12.6
11.2	11.6	13.0
9.9	12.0	14.2

The averages of the three columns are 10.6, 11.7, and 13.5, respectively. A dot plot of these data is shown in Figure 18.2.

Figure 18.2 suggests that an increase in temperature does cause an increase in moisture. How much spread is significant? That question is best answered by using analysis of variance (ANOVA) procedures, where the main effect is compared to the F statistic.

Table 18.5 Latin square design.

Day	Machine #1	Machine #2	Machine #3
1	180	200	220
2	200	220	180
3	220	180	200

Continued

Continued

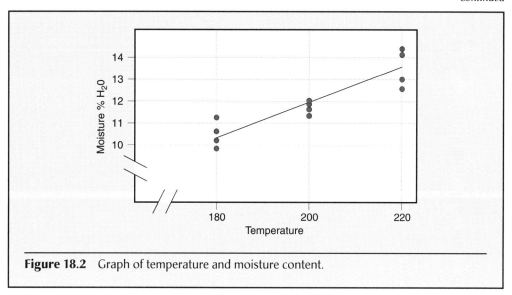

Figure 18.2   Graph of temperature and moisture content.

Design and Analysis of Full-Factorial Experiments

Full-factorial experiments look at every possible combination in order to complete a full study of interactions. Full-factorial results can be retained and converted into different experimental designs.

EXAMPLE

A 2^2 full-factorial completely randomized experiment is conducted, with the results shown in Table 18.6.

The first step is to find the mean response for each run and calculate the interaction column as shown in Table 18.7.

The main effect of factor A is

$$(24.7 + 37.3) \div 2 - (28.4 + 33) \div 2 = 0.3$$

Table 18.6   A 2^2 full-factorial completely randomized experiment with results.

Run #	A	B	Response, y			$\bar{y}$
1	–	–	28.3	28.6	28.2	28.4
2	–	+	33.5	32.7	32.9	33.0
3	+	–	24.6	24.6	24.8	24.7
4	+	+	37.2	37.6	37.0	37.3

Continued

Part V.A.2

Continued

Table 18.7 A 2^2 full-factorial completely randomized experiment with results.

Run #	A	B	A x B	Response, y			$\bar{y}$
1	–	–	+	28.3	28.6	28.2	28.4
2	–	+	–	33.5	32.7	32.9	33.0
3	+	–	–	24.6	24.6	24.8	24.7
4	+	+	+	37.2	37.6	37.0	37.3

The main effect of factor B is

$$(33.0 + 37.3) \div 2 - (28.4 + 24.7) \div 2 = 8.6$$

The interaction effect A × B is

$$(28.4 + 37.3) \div 2 - (33.0 + 24.7) \div 2 = 4.0$$

The next issue is whether these effects are statistically significant or merely the result of experimental error. The larger the effect, the more likely that the effect is significant. The definitive answer to the question can be found by conducting a two-way ANOVA on the data. The calculations are quite cumbersome, so software packages are often employed.

Using a hypothesis testing model, the null hypothesis would be that the source of variation is not statistically significant. In this case, the P-values for the sources of variation are small enough to reject the null hypothesis and declare these factors, B and the A × B interaction, to be statistically significant at the 0.05 significance level. What the ANOVA test really does is compare the between-treatment variation with the within-treatment variation.

Full versus fractional factorial must be understood to ensure that the experiment is properly designed. Full-factorial is an experimental design that contains all levels of all factors. No possible treatments are omitted. Fractional factorial is a balanced experimental design that contains fewer than all combinations of all levels of all factors. The following examples will show how the same experiment can be displayed as either a full-factorial or a fractional factorial.

FULL-FACTORIAL EXAMPLE

Suppose you are cooking steak for 100 people, and the current approval rating is 75 percent acceptable. You want to know the effect of different methods and approaches to see how the overall approval or "yield" is affected.

Continued

Continued

Assuming:

Cooking method: (+) is grill and (–) is fry

Meat: (+) is sirloin and (–) is ribeye

Marinade: (+) is red wine and rosemary (–) is soya sauce and garlic

Experiment	Cooking method	Meat	Marinade	% approval
1	–	–	–	66
2	+	–	–	88
3	–	+	–	58
4	+	+	–	84
5	–	–	+	67
6	+	–	+	91
7	–	+	+	63
8	+	+	+	84
			Average	75.125

Next we find the effect of setting the different factors to their respective levels:

Cooking method: $[(88 + 84 + 91 + 84) - (66 + 58 + 67 + 63)]/4 = 23.25$

Meat: $[(58 + 84 + 63 + 84) - (66 + 88 + 67 + 91)]/4 = -5.75$

Marinade: $[(67 + 91 + 63 + 84) - (66 + 88 + 58 + 84)]/4 = 2.25$

When the steak is grilled instead of fried, we gain 23 percent approval. The interaction effects can be checked with interaction columns.

Exp.	Cook	Meat	Mar.	Cook × Meat	Meat × Mar.	Cook × Mar.	Cook × Meat × Mar.	% approval
1	–	–	–	+	+	+	–	66
2	+	–	–	–	+	–	+	88
3	–	+	–	–	–	+	+	58
4	+	+	–	+	–	–	–	84
5	–	–	+	+	–	–	+	67
6	+	–	+	–	–	+	–	91
7	–	+	+	–	+	–	–	63
8	+	+	+	+	+	+	+	84

Cook × Meat interactions: $[(66 + 84 + 67 + 84) - (88 + 58 + 91 + 63)]/4 = 1.25$

Continued

Part V.A.2

Continued

Meat × Mar. interactions: [(66 + 88 + 63 + 84) – (58 + 84 + 67 + 91)]/4 = 0.25

Cook × Mar. interactions: [(66 + 58 + 91 + 84) – (88 + 84 + 67 + 63)]/4 = –0.75

Cook × Meat × Mar. interactions: [(88 + 58 + 67 + 84) – (66 + 84 + 91 + 63)]/4 = –1.75

In this example, the interactions have minimal effects on approval or yield.

FRACTIONAL FACTORIAL EXAMPLE

This design can identify a similar outcome with fewer experiments.

Experiment	Cooking method	Meat	Marinade	% approval
2	+	–	–	88
3	–	+	–	58
5	–	–	+	67
8	+	+	+	84
			Average	76.67

Cooking method: [(88 + 84) – (58 + 67)]/2 = 23.5

Meat: [(58 + 84) – (88 + 67)]/2 = –6.5

Marinade: [(67 + 84) – (88 + 58)]/2 = 2.5

Although the results are not the same as a full-factorial, similar conclusions can be derived.

Since we already know from the full-factorial that the interaction effects are not significant, we can draw valid conclusions from the main effects of a fractional factorial. However, when the interaction effects are present, so are the risks of confounding.

To summarize, a full-factorial experiment assesses all of the factors and levels, and ensures that main effects and interaction effects of an experiment are accurately revealed.

Design and Analysis of Two-Level Fractional Factorial Experiments

Fractional factorial experiments save time and money by not examining every possible combination. This method is used for quick exploratory tests, when interactions are insignificant, and many tests are needed rapidly.

In contrast, full-factorial experiments require a large number of runs, especially if several factors or several levels are involved. Recall that the formula for the number of runs in a full-factorial experiment is

$$\text{number of runs} = L^F$$

where

L = number of levels

F = number of factors

If runs are replicated, the number of tests will be multiples of these values. Because of the extensive resource requirements of full-factorial experiments, fractional factorial experimental designs were developed. The example below shows a full-factorial experiment run with 50 percent of the runs in a balanced design, so that the factors could be shown in their different levels equally.

EXAMPLE

A fractional factorial design can identify a similar outcome with fewer experiments.

Experiment	Cooking method	Meat	Marinade	% approval
2	+	−	−	88
3	−	+	−	58
5	−	−	+	67
8	+	+	+	84
			Average	76.67

Cooking method: [(88 + 84) − (58 + 67)]/2 = 23.5

Meat: [(58 + 84) − (88 + 67)]/2 = −6.5

Marinade: [(67 + 84) − (88 + 58)]/2 = 2.5

Although the results are not the same as a full-factorial, similar conclusions can be derived. The effects were achieved with less time and fewer resources.

Two-Level Fractional Factorial Experiment Procedure

The procedure can be summarized into three basic stages:

- Select a process; identify the output factors of concern and the input factors and levels to be investigated

- Select a design, conduct the experiment under predetermined conditions, and analyze the data

- Analyze the data and draw conclusions

Part V.A.2

EXAMPLE

Step 1: Select a process; identify outputs and input factors

a. Development and delivery of computer software to a customer

b. Success is based on deployment without issues or with post-release maintenance issues

c. Study the effect of seven variables at two levels (can be both variable-quantitative or attribute-qualitative)

Input factors	Level 1 (–)	Level 2 (+)
A. Requirements	20 high-level requirements	Defined 400+ business, functional, technical, and user requirements
B. Risk analysis	Minimal checklist	Formal
C. Architecture	Agile	Structured
D. Design and coding	Prototyping	Staged delivery
E. System integration	Freeware and shareware	Prequalified components
F. Product testing	Exploratory and random checks	Unit–integration–system–user acceptance tests
G. Quality assurance	Final inspection only	Series of five progressive go/no-go gates requiring approval

EXAMPLE

Step 2: Experiment

Assuming that no interactions are evaluated or considered, the seven factors can be evaluated at two levels. *Pass* refers to the condition of having no critical or major issues obtained after product release, and *score* refers to a level of customer satisfaction with the software.

Test	A	B	C	D	E	F	G	Pass	Score
1	+	+	–	+	–	–	+	Yes +	85
2	+	+	–	–	+	+	–	No –	57
3	+	–	+	+	–	+	–	No –	82
4	+	–	+	–	+	–	+	Yes +	100
5	–	+	+	+	+	–	–	No –	69
6	–	+	+	–	–	+	+	Yes +	87
7	–	–	–	+	+	+	+	No –	72
8	–	–	–	–	–	–	–	No –	44
							Average		74.5

EXAMPLE

Step 3: Analyze the data and draw conclusions

Test	\multicolumn{7}{c}{Input factors}							\multicolumn{2}{c}{Outputs (results)}	
	A	B	C	D	E	F	G	Pass	Score
1	+85	+85	−85	+85	−85	−85	+85	Yes +	85
2	+57	+57	−57	−57	+57	+57	−57	No −	57
3	+82	−82	+82	+82	−82	+82	−82	No −	82
4	+100	−100	+100	−100	+100	−100	+100	Yes +	100
5	−69	+69	+69	+69	+69	−69	−69	No −	69
6	−87	+87	+87	−87	−87	+87	+87	Yes +	87
7	−72	−72	−72	+72	+72	+72	+72	No −	72
8	−44	−44	−44	−44	−44	−44	−44	No −	44
							Average		74.5

Find the differences and divide by 4 to find the effect.

Difference	52	0	80	20	0	0	92
Effect	13	0	20	5	0	0	23

For brevity, focus on C and G, which are the largest contributors.

C (architecture): structured architecture will improve satisfaction by 20%

G (quality assurance): quality assurance measures will improve satisfaction by 23%

Two-Level Fractional Factorial Experiment Conclusions

ANOVA is the appropriate statistical method for assessing the significance of the experimental effects. The ANOVA outcomes summarized in Table 18.8 indicate that at certain levels of confidence, changing the levels of two of the factors significantly affects the process outcomes.

Based on the F value for significance, only factors G and C are significant effects influencing the overall process.

Through these examples, fractional factorial experiments have been shown to be a cost-effective alternative to full-factorial experiments. They can also be specifically designed in their own right as a way to quickly interpret the main effects of an experiment.

Part V.A.2

Table 18.8 ANOVA outcomes.

Factor	Effect	Sum of squares	F value significance
G	23	66.1	$85.29 < 85$ 95% confidence
C	20	50	$65.42 < 57$ 90% confidence
A	13	21.2	$27.22 < 57$ Not important
D	5	3.1	Error term value

Chapter 19

B. Statistical Process Control (SPC)

1. OBJECTIVES AND BENEFITS

> Describe the objectives and benefits of SPC,
> including controlling process performance,
> identifying special and common causes, etc.
> (Analyze)
>
> Body of Knowledge V.B.1

Statistical Process Control

The basis of the *control* portion of a Six Sigma program is the correct application and interpretation of control charts, which is generally categorized as statistical process control (SPC).

Definitions

control process—A feedback loop through which we measure actual performance, compare it with a standard, and act on the difference.

statistical process control (SPC)—The application of statistical techniques for measuring and analyzing (and hopefully improving) the variation in processes.

statistical quality control (SQC)—The application of statistical techniques for measuring and improving the quality of processes.

statistical process display (SPD)—The misapplication of statistical techniques to pretend that information is being used to run a process, when in reality it is only for show (usually for a customer) instead of an actual application to improve a process.

SPC Theory

SPC originated in the 1920s, when Dr. Walter Shewhart of Bell Telephone Laboratories discovered that variation in manufacturing could be attributed to inherent (random) variation and intermittent (assignable) variation. SPC has evolved since that time to become a core competency among inspectors, quality specialists, and Six Sigma practitioners.

Tactics

- $\bar{X}$ and R charts are the most common type of control chart, and are calculated for each subgroup (generally four to 10 samples) and plotted in order of production on separate charts.

- After an assignable cause of variation is discovered and removed, new control limits calculated from 25 new subgroup averages and ranges often give a substantially narrower process capability, becoming the economic limit to improvement.

- In 1953, Rath and Strong developed *pre-control* for IBM, which is a simple algorithm. The tolerance band is divided into a target zone bounded by two cautionary zones. A pair of individual samples is measured periodically, and if both fall within the cautionary zone or either falls outside tolerance, the process is adjusted immediately. Pre-control requires no calculations or charting

- Factorial experiments and multi-vari analysis are other innovations in diagnostic techniques.

Objectives and Benefits

The goal of any quality activity is to meet the needs of the customer. Statistical process control (SPC) consists of a set of tools and activities that contribute to this goal through the following objectives:

- Determine process capability

- Monitor processes in real time

- Identify whether processes are operating as expected

- Identify whether processes have changed and corrective action is required

- Make statistically valid decisions

- Center the process

- Determine when and when not to take action on the process

- Determine the type of action to take (that is, actions to eliminate special causes, actions to improve the overall process)

- Quantify and reduce variation

- Improve understanding of products and processes

- Improve product and process design

- Monitor continual improvement and confirm that changes were effective

The statistical process control (SPC) tools achieve these objectives by collecting and analyzing data.

Statistical Process Control: Errors

- Controlling process performance involves sampling coordinated activity and modifying the process behavior.

- Control charts are used to separate assignable causes from random variation.

- Type I errors occur when a behavior treated as a special cause has no effect in the process.

- Type II errors occur when special causes affecting the process are not addressed.

- Tampering or impulsively modifying the process to reduce variation will actually contribute to increasing variation.

To use SPC effectively, create a data collection plan and collect as much data as possible. Historical data may be available, but used with caution. Place the collected data on a histogram and calculate the mean and standard deviation. The histogram provides a visual picture of the variation and center of the process, and the mean and standard deviation provide numerical values for comparison. Other charts that are often used include scatter diagrams, run charts, and control charts. These and other statistical process control tools are available in various SPC software packages and in some spreadsheets.

Key Point: Any process (machinery, office, sports team, household, and so on) can be monitored using basic SPC techniques. If you have some control of the process, you can then make changes to see if you actually improve the variation (range) or move the target (average).

Process Capability: Special versus Common Causes

Every process has variation. Process improvement requires reducing the amount of variation that is currently present. Variation can be physical or mechanical (that is, tool, machine, maintenance, equipment, environment) or procedural (operator, accuracy, legibility, workload).

Process Capability (Learning)

- The specification limits should reflect the voice of the customer.

- The process variation reflects the voice of the process.

- Process capability is measured by capability index (C_p) and process performance (C_{pk}).

Process variation has two main categories: special and common. Variation must be traceable to its sources, making it necessary to distinguish between common and special causes.

Part V.B.1

The *common causes* of variation are those that are inherent to the process and generally are not controllable by process operators. Common cause variation is also known as *natural variation* and refers to the many sources of variation within a process. Common causes reside in processes within statistical control, and can be characterized by location (process average), spread (piece-to-piece variability), and shape (distribution) for predictability.

Special causes of variation include unusual events that the operator, when properly alerted, can usually remove or adjust. Special causes are sometimes called *assignable causes.* Unless all the special causes of variation are identified and mitigated, the process output will be unpredictably influenced with random results.

The principal purpose of control charts is to recognize the presence of special causes so that appropriate action can be taken. While both special and common causes can be detected with statistical techniques, common causes are more difficult to isolate and remove. A process is considered to be in statistical control when only common causes remain after special causes have been removed.

Tactics

A principal problem is the separation of special and common causes. If you adjust a process in response to common cause variation, the result is usually more variation rather than less. This is sometimes called overadjustment or overcontrol. If you fail to respond to the presence of a special cause of variation this cause is likely to produce additional process variation. This is referred to as underadjustment or undercontrol.

Key Point: Consider trying this test: Using a stopwatch, start the timer as you turn on the ignition of your primary means of transportation going to work or school. Turn off the timer once you arrive at your designation. Record your times for a period of time and identify what is causing the variation in times. What are the common causes and what are the special causes?

Special Cause Examples

Figures 19.1 through 19.3 represent the effects of special causes on a process, resulting in excessive averages and variations.

Common Cause Example

Figure 19.4 represents the effects of common causes resulting in changes within the tolerance levels for average and varation.

Process Behavior Charts (Control Charts)

Key Point: The idea behind the name change is that we want to study the process in question, not the people! How is the process behaving and is there something that we should or can do about it?

The foundations for process behavior charts (control charts) were laid by Walter Shewhart (called the father of modern day quality control) in the late 1920s. Today, there are over 30 different charts that can be used; however, we typically only use six or seven on a regular basis. These charts display the process variation while

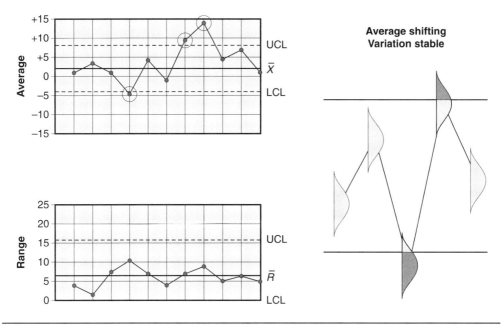

Figure 19.1   Average shifting, variation stable.

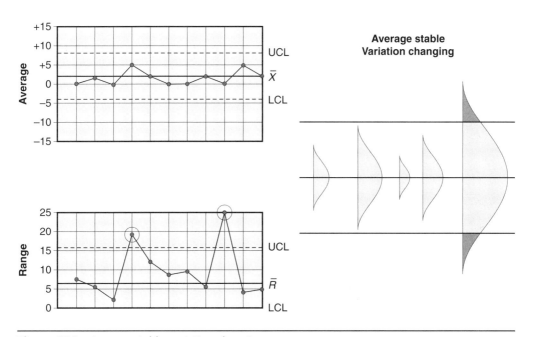

Figure 19.2   Average stable, variation changing.

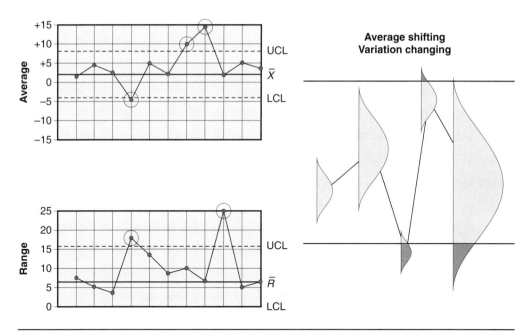

Figure 19.3   Average shifting, variation changing.

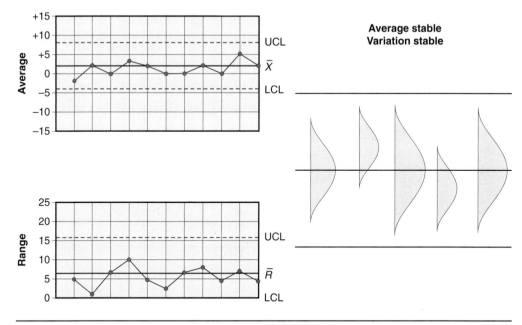

Figure 19.4   Average stable, variation stable.

work is being done. This allows the operator to ensure that the process is stable and continuing to operate within the process boundaries (not necessarily specification limits) that have been established for that process. If something does start to deteriorate or change in the process, the process behavior chart will give the operator an early warning indicator that something needs to be adjusted or changed to bring the process back into control.

Process Behavior Charts (Statistical Process Control)

- Typically only six or seven types are used on a regular basis

- Create a picture of the process variation while work is being done

- Ensure that the process is stable and continuing to operate within the process boundaries established for that process

- Provide an early warning to adjust or change the process to bring it back into control

- Variable data is continuous and comes from scales or measures

- Attribute data is discrete and comes from indicators

- Ensure that the measurements from the process are recorded, calculated, and plotted appropriately

- Refer to an upper control limit or lower control limit value from a table

- Being in statistical control refers to being between upper and lower control limits

Control charts are used to attain a state of statistical control, monitor a process, and determine process capability. Control charts can monitor process stability and achieve parts per million defect levels. Reduction of variation is achieved through other techniques, referencing control charts.

A state of statistical control means that only random causes are present in the process. It does not mean that products meet specifications. Conversely, a process not in statistical control may still produce product conforming to specifications.

- Control charts attain statistical control using 25 subgroups, a log of process changes during data collection, computed trial control limits from the data, charting the data for each subgroup, eliminating assignable causes of excessive variation, and continuing the control measures.

- The mean and standard deviation are estimated based on the sample data. Averages are more sensitive to change than individual readings.

- Control limits based on the statistical variation of the process can be established at ±3 standard deviations from the mean.

- The operating characteristic (OC) curve is a plot of the true value of a process parameter against the probability that a single sample will fall within the control limits (see Figure 19.5). It shows the ability of the chart to detect process changes.

Part V.B.1

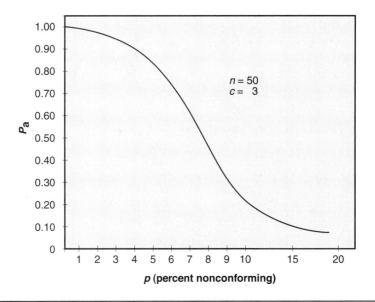

Figure 19.5   An operating characteristic (OC) curve.

Figure 19.6 is an example of an $\bar{X}$ and R control chart.

Setting Up Control Charts

- Choose the characteristic to be charted based on what is defective and controlled or adjustable by the worker.

- Identify the process variables and conditions contributing to product characteristics.

- Consider attribute data (that is, percent defective) and variables data (that is, numerical measurements) to diagnose causes and determine action. Charts for attributes require discrete measurements (that is, pass/fail, counts) and will be useful provided that the defective rate is high enough to show on a chart with a reasonable subgroup size. Variables charts require measurements on a continuous scale (that is, length, weight, and so on.)

- Determine the earliest point in the process where testing can be done to get information on assignable causes. The earlier the cause can be identified, the more likely the consequences can be effectively contained and mitigated.

- Choose the type of control chart used.

- Decide on the central line and the basis for calculating control limits.

- Choose the rational subgroup and the appropriate strategy (subgroup frequency, size, and so on).

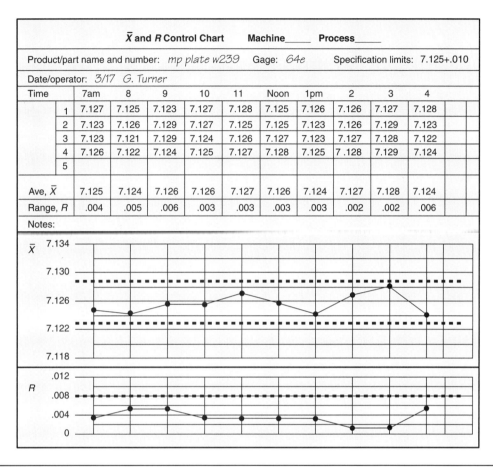

X̄ and R Control Chart				Machine_____		Process_____				

Product/part name and number: *mp plate w239*   Gage: *64e*   Specification limits: 7.125+.010

Date/operator: *3/17 G. Turner*

Time		7am	8	9	10	11	Noon	1pm	2	3	4		
	1	7.127	7.125	7.123	7.127	7.128	7.125	7.126	7.126	7.127	7.128		
	2	7.123	7.126	7.129	7.127	7.125	7.125	7.123	7.126	7.129	7.123		
	3	7.123	7.121	7.129	7.124	7.126	7.127	7.123	7.127	7.128	7.122		
	4	7.126	7.122	7.124	7.125	7.127	7.128	7.125	7.128	7.129	7.124		
	5												
Ave, X̄		7.125	7.124	7.126	7.126	7.127	7.126	7.124	7.127	7.128	7.124		
Range, R		.004	.005	.006	.003	.003	.003	.003	.002	.002	.006		

Notes:

Figure 19.6 X̄ and R control chart example with data plotted.

- Provide the system for collecting data.

- Calculate the control limits and provide specific instructions on interpretation of results and actions to be taken.

By identifying and resolving the special causes, the Six Sigma Green Belt can facilitate bringing the process into statistical control. At this point, the process results are predictable and the suitability of the process to achieve customer specifications is revealed. From here out, continual improvement can be realized.

Control charts can also be used for maintaining statistical control. After the expected process level and dispersion are attained, the expected range of variation will become the standard against which subsequent samples are compared to detect the presence of significant causes of variation. Use of the expected range of variation (sometimes referred to as "natural control limits") as a standard will help detect significant changes in the process.

Part V.B.1

Control charts maintain statistical control and provide traceable evidence through three key actions:

- *Collection.* Run the process and collect the data for plotting on a graph or chart.

- *Control.* Calculate control limits to support analysis and establish process variability.

- *Capability.* Establish the ability of the process to meet customer specifications.

Advantages of Control Charts

- Data able to be collected at the process by the operator

- Increase yield by revealing and containing problems at the stage the problem is identified

- Provide consistency between operators, shifts, or facilities

- Determine whether problems require local or management action

Selection of Variable

When a control chart is to be used, a variable must be selected for monitoring. Sometimes that variable is the most critical dimension of the product.

In some cases the variable of choice is a "leading indicator" of special causes—one that detects special causes before others do. Contractual requirements with a customer sometimes specify the variable(s) to be monitored via control chart. If the root cause of the special variation is known, an input variable may be monitored. Often the variable to be monitored is the one that is the most difficult to hold, as determined by capability analyses. It is possible to monitor several variables on separate control charts, especially if computerized charting is employed. The selection of the variable to be charted depends on experience and judgment.

Selection of Variables

a. Key process input variables (KPIVs) may be analyzed to determine their effect on a process.

b. Key process output variables (KPOVs) determine process capability and process monitoring using control charting.

c. Design of experiments and analysis of variance (ANOVA) methods may also identify variables significant to process control.

Variables that are critical to quality should be selected for control charts based on:

- Importance to customer perception

- Objectivity (counted or measured)

- Clear indicators to suggest whether quality is being achieved

- Quality function deployment identifies the customer needs and wants

Characteristics for Analysis

- Concentrate on characteristics that are most promising for process improvement

- Consider the needs of the customer or end user

- Address current and potential problem areas

- For mature systems, investigate relationships, interactions, and correlations

2. RATIONAL SUBGROUPING

Define and describe how rational subgrouping is used. (Understand)

Body of Knowledge V.B.2

Rational Subgrouping

The method used to select samples for a control chart must be logical, or "rational." Processes must not be out of control (otherwise use a simple run chart), so that the samples used will be valid. A rational subgroup is a sample set that is sufficient to determine common-cause scenarios. Normally the average of a subgroup is used.

Rational Subgrouping

- The division of observations into rational subgroups is key.

- Success of control charting depends on the selection of subgroups.

- Selection should result in groups as homogenous as possible.

- The first subgroup should reflect product all produced as nearly as possible at one time.

- One subgroup should be representative of all of the production over a given period of time.

- More useful information is derived from smaller groups (that is, five subgroups of five than one subgroup of 25). Larger subgroups provide too much opportunity for process change within the subgroup.

- Attributes control charts are based on Poisson or binomial distributions and require 50 or more samples within subgroups.

Part V.B.2

Choosing the rational subgroup requires care to make sure the same process is producing each item.

In the case of the $\bar{X}$ and R chart, the $\bar{X}$ chart should detect any process shift while the R chart should capture only common cause variation. That means there should be a high probability of variation between successive samples while the variation within the sample is kept small. Therefore, samples frequently consist of parts that are produced successively by the same process to minimize the *within-sample variation*. The next sample is chosen some time later so that any process shifts that have occurred will be displayed on the chart as *between-sample variation*.

The choice of sample size depends to some extent on the resources available to do the measuring. The traditional charts have room for five readings per sample, but fewer of the spaces may be used if necessary. In general, the larger the sample size, the more sensitive the chart. Sensitivity also depends on the type of charting technique, with variables charts being more sensitive to special causes than attributes charts.

For variables charts, data is reported from a particular characteristic of a process output in small subgroups of two to five sequential pieces taken methodically (for example, every 20 minutes, three times per shift)

For attributes charts, larger subgroup sizes (that is, 50 to 200) are required in order to observe detectable process shifts. Subgroup sizes need not be exactly repeated, but should not vary by more than 20 percent. In the event that sample sizes change, control limits should be recalculated. Quantity and frequency of collection is dependent on the process, and should support the sufficient data collection necessary to view the full range of process variation.

Rational Subgrouping Approach

- Select the size, frequency, and number of subgroups based on the control chart using the groups.

- Choose subgroups to minimize piece-to-piece variation within the subgroup.

- Ensure that sample sizes remain constant for all subgroups under review.

- Collect subgroups frequently enough to reveal potential opportunities for variation due to shifts, operators, materials, timing, and so on.

- Major sources of variation should have an opportunity to appear through the subgroup selection.

- A quantity of 25 or more subgroups containing 100 or more individual readings should provide stability and indicate process location and spread for further analysis.

- Where possible, apply existing data that was recently collected and which is consistent with the subgroup approach.

Sampling without considering rational subgrouping will incorporate the variations from the different streams:

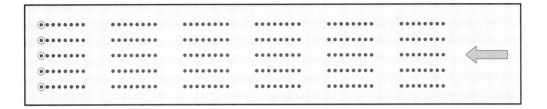

Rational subgrouping applied to enhance randomness and reduce "piece-to-piece" variation:

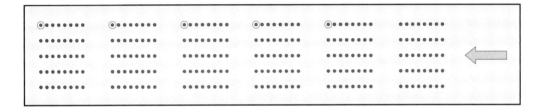

3. SELECTION AND APPLICATION OF CONTROL CHARTS

Identify, select, construct, and apply the following types of control charts: $\bar{X}$ and R, $\bar{X}$ and s, individuals and moving range (ImR/XmR), median ($\tilde{X}$), p, np, c, and u. (Apply)

Body of Knowledge V.B.3

Key Point: There are many other forms of control charts/process behavior charts that have been developed over the years for specific applications. The ones mentioned here are the more common ones.

Variables Charts

The variables chart is so named because the data to be plotted result from measurement on a variable or continuous scale. This type of measurement occurs when for each pair of values there are an infinite number of possible values between them. Variable data is always quantitative and continuous, therefore smaller sample groups (four to six units) are usable for charting. Generally, 25 subgroups are used before constructing the control chart for history and trending.

Common variables charts are: $\bar{X}$ and R chart, $\bar{X}$ and s, individuals and moving range, and median charts.

Control Charts for Variables

- Plot specific measurements of process characteristics
- $\bar{X}$ and R charts (data is readily available)
- Run charts (single-point data)
- $M\bar{X}$–MR charts (limited data, moving average, moving range)
- XmR charts (limited data, individual moving range)
- $\bar{X}$ and s charts (sigma is available)
- Median charts
- Short run charts

Best results are obtained from the following preparation steps:

- Ensure a responsive environment with candid and forthcoming people committed to quality and improvement.
- Define the process elements (that is, people, equipment, material, methods, environment), relationships (upstream, downstream, serial, parallel), and documentation/records.
- Define the measurement system.

Benefits for Analysis of Variables

- Focus on measurable characteristics.
- Measurement value is more powerful than a "yes/no" or "pass/fail" statement
- Reduce total inspection costs with better data
- Reduce turnaround time for corrective actions
- Processes can be analyzed even within specification limits

Control Limits

Control limits are calculated based on data from the process. Formulas for control limits are given in Appendix C. Several constants are needed in the formulas. The values of these constants can be found in Appendix D.

When calculating control limits, it is prudent to collect as much data as practical. Many authorities specify at least 25 samples. It is very important that sample size be held constant.

$\bar{X}$ and R Control Charts

Constructing $\bar{X}$ and R charts:

- Determine sample size and frequency
- Calculate average and range, and the averages of both measures
- Calculate the control limits based on the subgroup sample size (Appendix D)
- Plot the data and analyze the chart

Control limits for $\bar{X}$ and R control charts are given by the following formulas:

Upper control limit for the averages chart: $\text{UCL}_{\bar{x}} = \bar{\bar{X}} + A_2\bar{R}$

Lower control limit for the averages chart: $\text{LCL}_{\bar{x}} = \bar{\bar{X}} - A_2\bar{R}$

Upper control limit for the range chart: $\text{UCL}_R = D_4\bar{R}$

Lower control limit for the range chart: $\text{LCL}_R = D_3\bar{R}$

where

$\bar{\bar{X}}$ = averages of the sample averages (the process average)

$\bar{R}$ = average of the ranges

A_2, D_3, and D_4 are constants depending on sample size from Appendix D.

EXAMPLE

Data are collected from a face-and-plunge operation done on a lathe. The dimension being measured is the groove inside diameter (ID), which has a tolerance of $7.125 \pm .010$. Four parts are measured every hour. These values have been entered in Figure 19.7.

The next step is to calculate the average ($\bar{X}$) and range (R) for each sample. These values have been entered in Figure 19.7. Next, calculate the average of the averages ($\bar{\bar{X}}$) and the average range ($\bar{R}$). These values are 7.126 and .0037, respectively. Following are the control limit calculations:

$\text{UCL}_{\bar{x}} = \bar{\bar{X}} + A_2\bar{R} = 7.126 + .729 \times .0037 \approx 7.129$

$\text{LCL}_{\bar{x}} = \bar{\bar{X}} - A_2\bar{R} = 7.126 - .729 \times .0037 \approx 7.123$

$\text{UCL}_R = D_4\bar{R} = 2.282 \times .0037 \approx .008$

There is no lower control limit for the R chart because D_3 is undefined for this sample size.

Continued

Continued

$\bar{X}$ and *R* Control Chart		Machine_____	Process_____						

Product/part name and number: *mp plate w239*   Gage: *64e*   Specification limits: 7.125±.010

Date/operator: *3/17   G. Turner*

Time		7am	8	9	10	11	Noon	1pm	2	3	4		
	1	7.127	7.125	7.123	7.127	7.128	7.125	7.126	7.126	7.127	7.128		
	2	7.123	7.126	7.129	7.127	7.125	7.125	7.123	7.126	7.129	7.123		
	3	7.123	7.121	7.129	7.124	7.126	7.127	7.123	7.127	7.128	7.122		
	4	7.126	7.122	7.124	7.125	7.127	7.128	7.125	7.128	7.129	7.124		
	5												
Ave, $\bar{X}$		7.125	7.124	7.126	7.126	7.127	7.126	7.124	7.127	7.128	7.124		
Range, *R*		.004	.005	.006	.003	.003	.003	.003	.002	.002	.006		

Notes:

$\bar{X}$

R

Figure 19.7   Measurement data entered in an $\bar{X}$ and *R* control chart.

In these calculations, the values of A_2, D_3, and D_4, are found in the Foundation Tools folder on the CD-ROM. The row for subgroup size four is used because each hourly sample has four readings. The next step is to choose a scale on the average and range charts that includes the control limits. The control limits are then drawn, usually with a dashed line, and the average lines are drawn on each chart, usually with solid lines. Finally, the points are plotted and connected with a broken line. The final chart is shown in Figure 19.8.

Continued

Continued

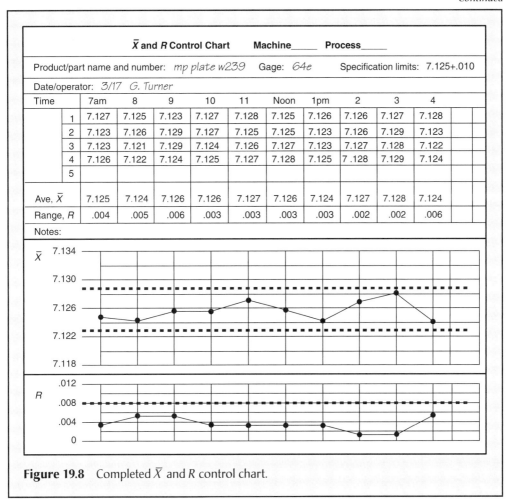

Figure 19.8   Completed $\bar{X}$ and R control chart.

$\bar{X}$ and s Control Charts

The $\bar{X}$ and s control chart is very similar to the $\bar{X}$ and R chart except that each value in the range row is replaced by the sample standard deviation s. Calculation of control limits also is very similar. Instead of using $\bar{R}$, these formulas use $\bar{s}$ and the appropriate constants from Appendix D.

Upper control limit for the averages chart: $\text{UCL}_{\bar{x}} = \bar{\bar{X}} + A_3\bar{s}$

Lower control limit for the averages chart: $\text{LCL}_{\bar{x}} = \bar{\bar{X}} + A_3\bar{s}$

Upper control limit for the standard deviation chart: $\text{UCL}_s = B_4\bar{s}$

Lower control limit for the standard deviation chart: $\text{LCL}_s = B_3\bar{s}$

An example of an $\bar{X}$ and s control chart is shown in Figure 19.9, using the same data that were used in Figure 19.8.

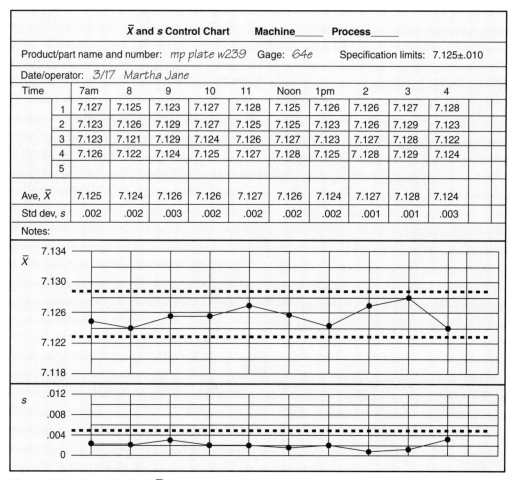

Figure 19.9   Example of an $\bar{X}$ and *s* control chart.

The formula calculations:

$$\mathrm{UCL}_{\bar{X}} = \bar{\bar{X}} + A_3\bar{s} = 7.126 + (1.628)(.0020) \approx 7.129$$

$$\mathrm{LCL}_{\bar{X}} = \bar{\bar{X}} + A_3\bar{s} = 7.126 - (1.628)(.0020) \approx 7.123$$

Control limits for the standard deviation chart:

$$\mathrm{UCL}_s = B_4\bar{s} = (2.266)(.0020) \approx .005$$

$$\mathrm{LCL}_s = B_3\bar{s} = 0(.0020) = 0$$

Individuals and Moving Range Control Charts

Recall that larger sample sizes produce more sensitive charts. In some situations, however, a sample size of one must be used. If the sample size is one, an individuals and moving range (also known as ImR or XmR) chart is appropriate. An example of an ImR chart is shown in Figure 19.10. The data are entered in the row numbered 1. The moving range is calculated by taking the absolute value of the

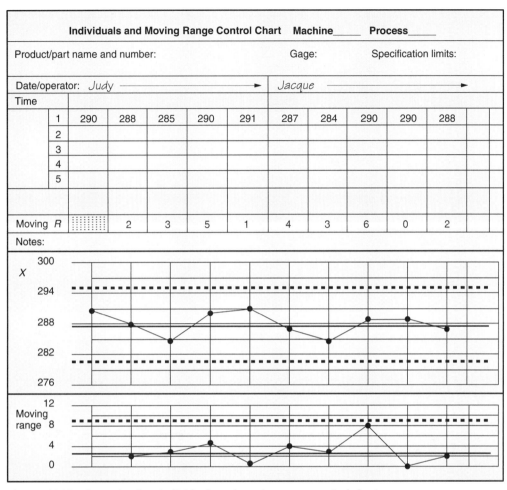

Figure 19.10   Example of an individuals and moving range control chart.

difference between each measurement and the previous one. This value is entered in the row labeled "Moving *R*."

The control limit formulas for the ImR control chart are given in Appendix C and repeated here:

$$UCL_X = \bar{X} + E_2\bar{R}$$

$$LCL_X = \bar{X} - E_2\bar{R}$$

$$UCL_R = D_4\bar{R}$$

$$LCL_R = D_3\bar{R}$$

The values of E_2, D_3, and D_4 are also found in Appendix D. The sample size is two because two subsequent subgroups are compared in each moving range.

The measurements in Figure 19.10 have an average of 288.3 and an average range of 2.889.

Part V.B.3

$$UCL_x = 288.3 + (2.660)(2.889) \approx 296$$

$$LCL_x = 288.3 - (2.660)(2.889) \approx 280.6$$

$$UCL_r = 3.267 \, (2.889) \approx 9.439$$

$$LCL_r = 0 \, (\, 2.889) = 0$$

These control limits are drawn and the measurements and ranges are then plotted.

Median Control Charts

Median charts plot the median of the sample rather than the average. This chart is often used when outliers are expected. All data points in the sample are plotted, and the user connects the middle point in successive samples. Figure 19.11 illustrates a median chart. To detect ranges that are outside range control limits, a paper or plastic gage is constructed that has a length equal to the distance between range control limits. The user of the chart places the gage over the plotted points

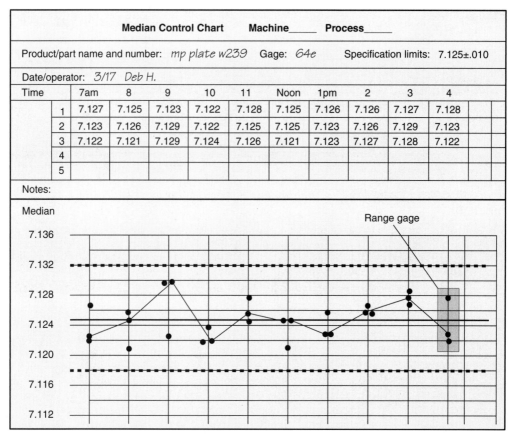

Figure 19.11   Example of a median control chart with associated range gage. The range gage is also shown in position over the points plotted for the 4 PM sample, showing that they are within the range control limits.

for a particular sample. If the gage can't cover all the points, the range exceeds control limits. Trends and other anomalies in the range are difficult to detect using the median chart.

The control limits for the median chart are calculated in the usual way:

$$\text{UCL} = \bar{X}' + A'_2 \bar{R} = 7.125 + (1.880)(.0036) \approx 7.132$$

$$\text{LCL} = \bar{X}' - A'_2 \bar{R} = 7.125 - (1.880)(.0036) \approx 7.118$$

$$\text{UCL}_r = D_4 \bar{R} = (2.574)(.0036) \approx .009$$

$$\text{LCL}_r = D_3 \bar{R} = 0$$

where

A'_2 is the special A_2 constant for use with median charts

x' is the sample median

Attribute Control Charts

Attribute charts are used for count data. For attribute control charts, if every item is in one of two categories, such as good or bad, "defectives" are counted. If each item may have several flaws, "defects" are counted. Attribute data are generally qualitative, but can be counted, recorded, and analyzed. Examples are nonconformities, nonconforming units, and percent nonconforming. Larger sample sizes are required for analysis (50 to 200) to fit binomial or Poisson distributions.

Control Charts for Attributes

- p charts (Defectives—sample size varies)
- np charts (Defectives—sample size fixed)
- c charts (Defects—sample size fixed)
- u charts (Defects—sample size varies)
- Short run charts for p, np, c, u

Constructing attribute charts follows a process similar to that for variables charts, except for the use of the much larger sample size:

- Follow trends and cycles to evaluate process changes
- Use subgroup size greater than 50
- Calculate the control limits using the formulas
- Plot the data and analyze the chart

p Control Charts

The p chart measures the proportion of defective parts or pieces within the group under review. This could be for a single characteristic or multiple characteristics. Pieces either conform or are rejected. The rejected portion is expressed as a decimal fraction of the sample size.

The *p* chart is used to chart binary data where each item is in one of two categories. This would be the appropriate chart for plotting numbers of defectives, for instance. In the following example, each blood sample is in one of two categories, so the *p* chart is appropriate, although neither category is defective.

EXAMPLE

A test for the presence of the Rh factor in 12 samples of donated blood yields the data shown on the *p* chart in Figure 19.12.

p Chart							Machine/process: *Blood analysis*								

Product: *Donated blood*　　　　　　　　　Defective = *Rh negative*

Date: 2002 *Sept.* 8　8　8　　8　9　9　12　12　12　12　12　12　12
Operator　　*Emily* ---------------------------------- *Dana* ----------------------------

Defectives, *np*	# 14	18	13	17	15	15	16	11	14	13	14	17			
Sample size:	125	111	133	120	118	137	108	110	124	128	144	138			
Fraction, *p*	.11	.16	.10	.14	.13	.11	.15	.10	.11	.10	.10	.12			

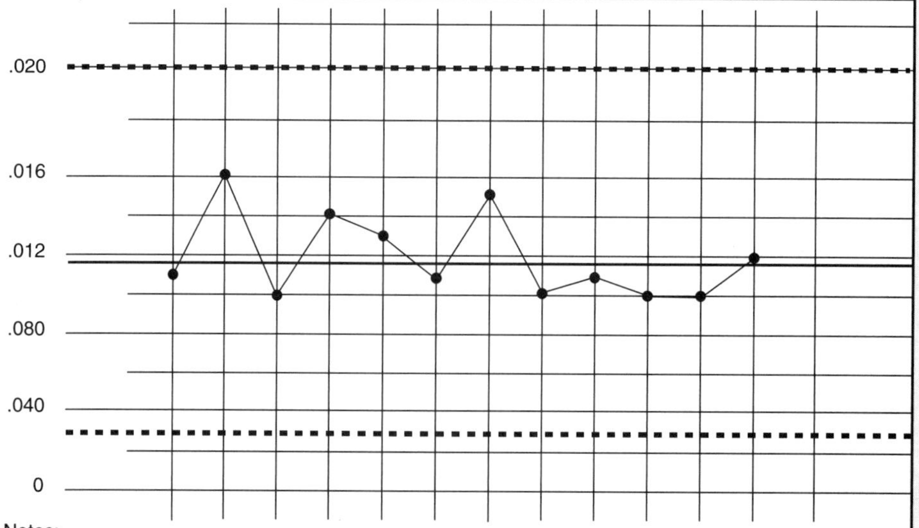

Notes:

Figure 19.12　Example of a *p* chart.

Continued

Continued

Control limits for the *p* chart are given by the following formulas:

$$UCL_p = \bar{p} + 3\sqrt{\frac{\bar{p}(1-\bar{p})}{\bar{n}}}$$

$$LCL_p = \bar{p} - 3\sqrt{\frac{\bar{p}(1-\bar{p})}{\bar{n}}}$$

where

$$\bar{n} = \frac{\text{Sum of the sample sizes}}{\text{Number of samples}}$$

$$\bar{p} = \frac{\text{Sum of the discrepancies}}{\text{Sum of the sample sizes}} = \frac{\sum \text{discrepancies}}{\sum n}$$

Note: when the formula for LCL produces a negative number, no LCL is used.

The control limit formulas use the average sample size. Some software packages recompute control limits each time the sample size changes. While technically correct, this is somewhat difficult when charts are being plotted by hand. As a compromise, the Automotive Industry Action Group (AIAG) recommends recalculating control limits whenever the sample is more than 25 percent above or below the average sample size. In the example in Figure 19.12:

$$\bar{n} = \frac{\text{Sum of the sample sizes}}{\text{Number of samples}} = 1496 \div 12 = 124.7$$

$$\bar{p} = \frac{\text{Sum of the discrepancies}}{\text{Sum of the sample sizes}} = \frac{\sum \text{discrepancies}}{\sum n} = 177 \div 1496 = 0.118$$

$$\sqrt{\frac{\bar{p}(1-\bar{p})}{\bar{n}}} = \sqrt{\frac{.118(.882)}{124.7}} \approx .029$$

$$UCL = \bar{p} + 3\sqrt{\frac{\bar{p}(1-\bar{p})}{\bar{n}}} = 0.118 + 3 \times 0.029 \approx 0.205$$

$$LCL = \bar{p} - 3\sqrt{\frac{\bar{p}(1-\bar{p})}{\bar{n}}} = 0.118 - 3 \times 0.029 \approx 0.030$$

np Control Charts

The *np* chart measures the number of rejected items in a sample with an integer rather than a proportion. The *np* chart is most useful when sample sizes are constant and the integer number is more meaningful and relevant than the proportional decimal amount.

If defectives are being counted and the sample size remains constant, the *np* chart can be used instead of the *p* chart.

Part V.B.3

EXAMPLE

Packages containing 1000 light bulbs are randomly selected and all 1000 bulbs are light-tested. The data have been entered in the *np* chart shown in Figure 19.13. Note that this

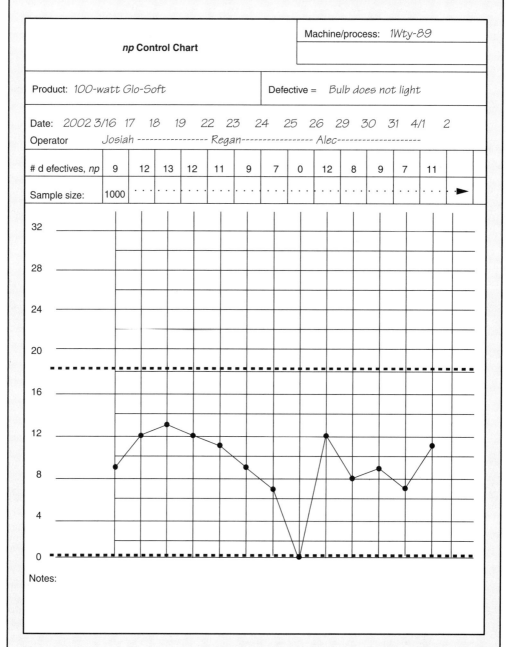

Figure 19.13   Example of an *np* control chart.

Continued

Part V.B.3

Continued

chart is slightly simpler to use than the *p* chart because the number of defectives is plotted rather than the fraction of the sample.

The formulas for control limits:

$$\text{UCL}_{np} = \overline{np} + 3\sqrt{\overline{np}\left(1 - \frac{\overline{np}}{n}\right)}$$

$$\text{LCL}_{np} = \overline{np} - 3\sqrt{\overline{np}\left(1 - \frac{\overline{np}}{n}\right)}$$

where

np = average number of defectives

n = sample size

Note: When the formula for LCL produces a negative number, no LCL is used.

For the example shown in Figure 37.9,

$$\overline{np} = 120\sqrt{13} \approx 9.23 \text{ and } n = 1000.$$
$$\text{UCL}np = 9.23 + 3(3.02) \approx 18.29$$
$$\text{LCL}np = 9.23 - 3(3.02) \approx 0.17$$

u Control Chart

The *u* chart is appropriate to use when defects rather than defectives are counted. The *u* chart measures the number of defects or problems on a per unit basis. The example in Figure 19.14 shows the results of inspecting panes of glass in which defects include bubbles, scratches, chips, inclusions, waves, and dips. The number of defects is counted and recorded for each sample, and the fraction (# defects ÷ sample size) is calculated and plotted.

The formulas for the control limits for the *u* chart:

$$\text{UCL}_u = \overline{u} + \frac{3\sqrt{\overline{u}}}{\sqrt{\overline{n}}}$$

$$\text{LCL}_u = \overline{u} - \frac{3\sqrt{\overline{u}}}{\sqrt{\overline{n}}}$$

where

$$\overline{u} = \frac{\sum \text{defects}}{\sum \text{sample sizes}}$$

$\overline{n}$ = average sample size

Note: When the formula for LCL produces a negative number, no LCL is used.

The control limit formulas use the average sample size $\bar{n}$. Some software packages recalculate control limits each time the sample size changes. While technically correct, this is somewhat difficult when charts are being plotted by hand. As a compromise, the Automotive Industry Action Group (AIAG) recommends recalculating control limits whenever the sample is more than 25 percent above or below the average sample size.

For the example in Figure 19.14:

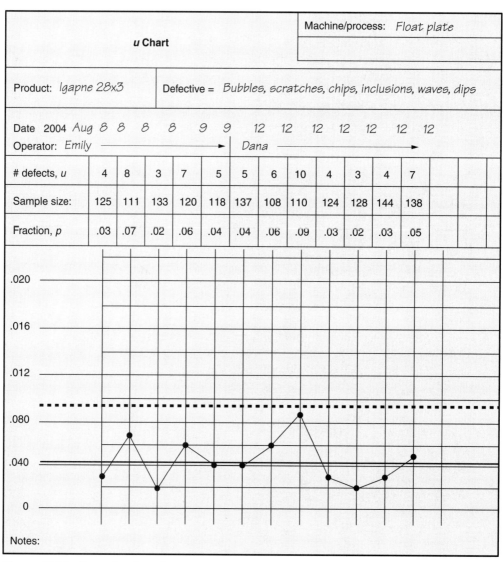

Figure 19.14 Example of a *u* chart.

$$\bar{u} = 66 \div 1496 \approx .044$$

$$\bar{n} = 1496 \div 12 \approx 124.7$$

$$UCL_u = \bar{u} + \frac{3\sqrt{\bar{u}}}{\sqrt{\bar{n}}} = .044 + 3\left(.210 \div 11.167\right) \approx 0.100$$

$$LCL_u = \bar{u} - \frac{3\sqrt{\bar{u}}}{\sqrt{\bar{n}}} = .044 - 3\left(.210 \div 11.167\right) \approx -0.012 \approx 0$$

c Control Charts

The c chart measures the number of defects within a sample. When defects are counted and the sample size is constant, the c chart may be used instead of the u chart. This is relevant for processes that have a continuous flow or where there are many different potential sources of variation or deficiencies. Note that this chart is slightly simpler to use than the u chart because the number of defects is plotted rather than the fraction of the sample. An example of a c chart is given in Figure 19.15.

The formulas for control limits for the c chart:

$$UCL_c = \bar{c} + 3\sqrt{\bar{c}}$$
$$LCL_c = \bar{c} - 3\sqrt{\bar{c}}$$

where

$\bar{c}$ = average number of defects

Note: When the formula for LCL produces a negative number, no LCL is used.
For the example in Figure 19.15:

$$\bar{c} = 217 \div 13 \approx 16.7$$

$$UCL = 16.7 + \left(3 \times 4.1\right) = 29$$

$$LCL = 16.7 - \left(3 \times 4.1\right) = 4.4$$

Key Point: The use of short run techniques involves setting a target value for the particular item being run on the machinery and measuring/charting the plus and minus values from the target value. By doing this, you can develop a true process behavior chart for the process (for example, the way a particular machine is operating) instead of a particular component.

Part V.B.3

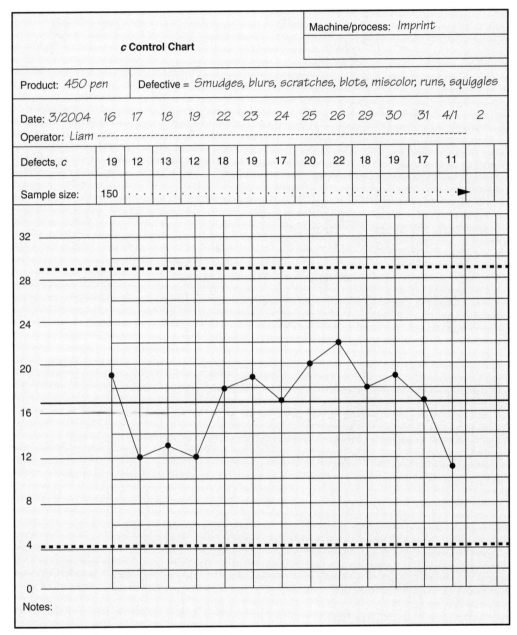

	c Control Chart								Machine/process: *Imprint*				

Product: *450 pen*	Defective = *Smudges, blurs, scratches, blots, miscolor, runs, squiggles*

Date: *3/2004*	*16*	*17*	*18*	*19*	*22*	*23*	*24*	*25*	*26*	*29*	*30*	*31*	*4/1*	*2*
Operator: *Liam*														

Defects, *c*	19	12	13	12	18	19	17	20	22	18	19	17	11		
Sample size:	150														

Notes:

Figure 19.15   Example of a *c* control chart.

4. ANALYSIS OF CONTROL CHARTS

> Interpret control charts and distinguish
> between common and special causes using
> rules for determining statistical control.
> (Analyze)
>
> **Body of Knowledge V.B.4**

Analysis of Control Charts

A critical tool in the analysis of charted data is the process log. Entries in the log should include all changes in the process and its environment.

Each of the control limit formulas uses data from the process. The upper and lower limits are placed at $\pm 3\sigma$ from the average. The control chart compares each new point with the distribution that was used as the basis for the control limits. The control limits enclose the vast majority of the points from the distribution, 99.72 percent if it is a normal distribution. When a point falls outside the control limits the probability is quite high that the process has changed.

In reality the "out of statistical control" condition is often very subtle and would perhaps not be detected without the control chart. This, in fact, is the one of the main values of the control chart: it detects changes in a process that would not otherwise be noticed. This may permit adjustment or other action on the process before serious damage is done.

On the other side of the coin, one of the hazards of using a control chart without proper training is the tendency to react to a point that is not right on target by adjusting the process, even though the chart does not indicate that the process has changed. If an adjustment is made whenever a point is not exactly on target it may tend to destabilize a stable process.

In the ideal situation, a process should not need adjustment except when the chart indicates that it is out of statistical control. Dr. W. E. Deming, one of the authorities in the field, states, "The function of a control chart is to minimize the net economic loss from . . . overadjustment and underadjustment."[1]

Analyzing for Causes

- Finding common causes is more difficult because common cause variation is the intrinsic variation in the process itself.

- An improvement in common cause variation means modifying the very heart of the process.

Control Chart Interpretation

- *Specials* are any points above the UCL or below the LCL

- Run violation occurs when seven or more consecutive points are on one side of the centerline

- A 1 in 20 violation is more than 1 point in 20 in the outer 33 percent of the control chart

- Trend violation is an upward or downward movement of five or more consecutive points or drifts of seven or more points

Process Control

- A process is in control when both the average and variation are stable

- Trends can be corrected with equipment repair, rotation, or replacement

- Jumps reflect abrupt changes in material, method, or performance, and can be corrected with consistency

- Recurring cycles reflect wear and fatigue and can be overcome with tighter controls and reduced cycle times

- Points near or outside limits could indicate overadjustment or material variation and can be corrected with test and inspection and reduction of operator controls

- Lack of variability suggests that control limits are too loose or there may be a measurement issue (that is, fudging, tampering)

Process change can be determined by studying charts and identifying process shifts. Statistical indicators of process change are available. Two of the most widely used are Minitab and the AIAG SPC Manual.

- The eight rules used by the software package Minitab:

  - One point more than 3σ from the centerline (either side)

  - Nine points in a row on the same side of the centerline

  - Six points in a row all increasing or all decreasing

  - Fourteen points in a row alternating up and down

  - Two out of three points more than 2σ from the centerline (same side)

  - Four out of five points more than 1σ from the centerline (same side)

  - Fifteen points in a row within 1σ of the centerline (either side)

  - Eight points in a row more than 1σ from the centerline (either side)

- The six rules listed by the Automotive Industry Action Group (AIAG) in their SPC Manual:

  - Points beyond the control limits

  - Seven points in a row on one side of the average

  - Seven points in a row that are consistently increasing (equal to or greater than the preceding points) or consistently decreasing

  - Over 90 percent of the plotted points are in the middle third of the control limit region (for 25 or more subgroups)

- Fewer than 40 percent of the plotted points are in the middle third of the control limit region (for 25 or more subgroups)

- Obvious nonrandom patterns such as cycles

Each of these rules are illustrated in Figures 19.16 through 19.29. Any points that violate the rule are circled.

If, for instance, an increase in values represents a safety hazard, it would not be necessary to wait for the specified number of successively increasing points to take action. Control limits are somewhat arbitrary and could conceivably be adjusted based on the economic trade-off between the costs of not taking action when an out-of-control condition occurs and taking action when an out-of-control condition has not occurred. Deming stated (in a private conversation in October 1985), however, that moving the control limits up and down can be a source of additional problems and it would be better in most cases to put that energy into reducing variation.

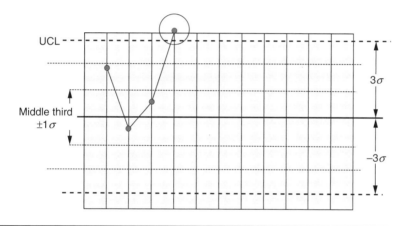

Figure 19.16   One point more than 3σ from the centerline (either side).

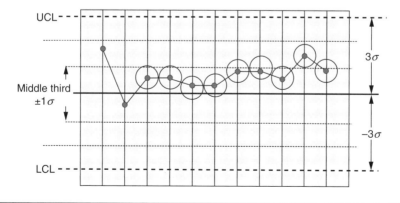

Figure 19.17   Nine points in a row on the same side of the centerline.

Part V.B.4

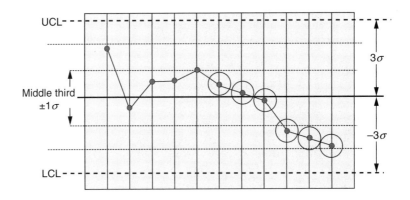

Figure 19.18 Six points in a row all increasing or decreasing.

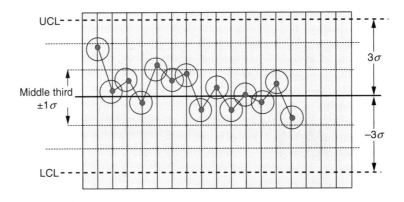

Figure 19.19 Fourteen points in a row alternating up and down.

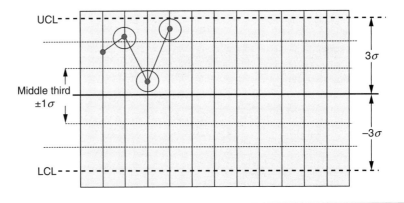

Figure 19.20 Two out of three points more than 2σ from the centerline (same side).

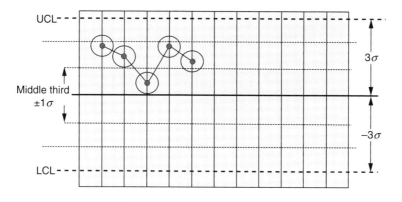

Figure 19.21   Four out of five points more than 1σ from the centerline (same side).

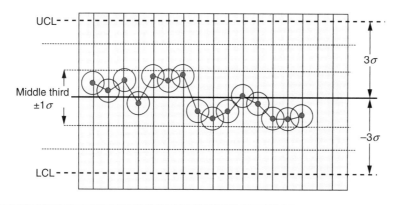

Figure 19.22   Fifteen points in a row within 1σ of the centerline (either side).

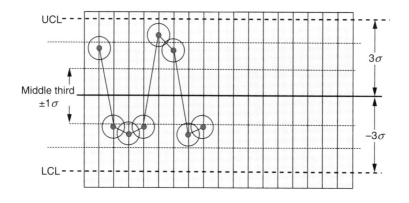

Figure 19.23   Eight points in a row more than 1σ from the centerline (either side).

Part V.B.4

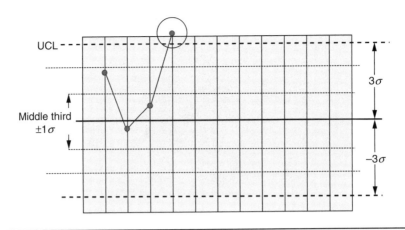

Figure 19.24 Points beyond the control limits.

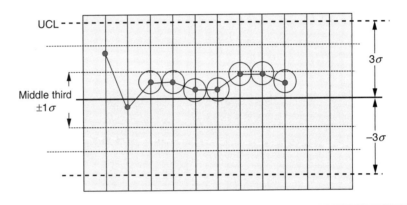

Figure 19.25 Seven points in a row more on one side of the average.

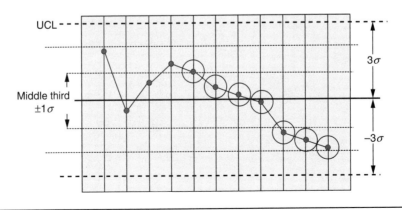

Figure 19.26 Seven points in a row that are consistently increasing or consistently decreasing.

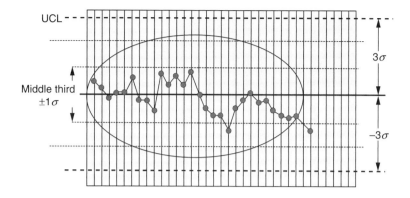

Figure 19.27   Over 90 percent of the plotted points are in the middle third of the control limit region (for 25 or more subgroups).

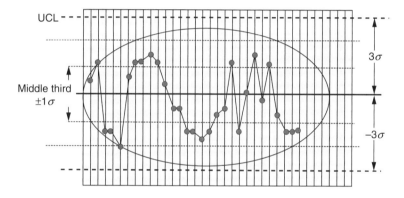

Figure 19.28   Fewer than 40 percent of the plotted points are in the middle third of the control limit region (for 25 or more subgroups).

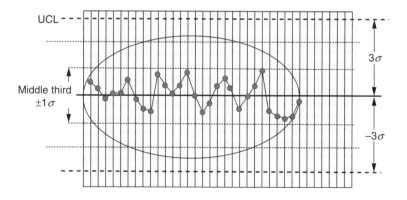

Figure 19.29   Obvious nonrandom patterns such as cycles.

Part V.B.4

Ensure that each point is calculated and plotted correctly. For variables charts, the range section should be analyzed first. Increases in the range values represent increased variation between the readings within an individual sample. Possible causes include bearings, tooling, or fixtures. Changes in the averages chart represent some sort of shift in the process. Frequent causes are tool wear, changes in raw materials, and changes in measurement systems or process parameters such as machine settings, voltages, pneumatic pressure, or other settings.

It will be more useful if we can relate the violation to possible causes. Only when the causes of the deviation are assignable can continual improvement occur.

It is useful to construct a list of things to check when certain chart characteristics occur. Such a list can come from a discussion among experienced personnel as well as from data from a process log.

In most cases, "out of control" conditions reflect process readings at or beyond the control limits. These can be traced to several causes including inaccurate control point calculations, declining process performance, or errors in the measurement system. Nonrandom patterns or trends likely indicate the presence of a special cause (for example, novice operator, worn machine). In this case, the points associated with the special causes should be excluded when recalculating control limits, which should be consequently more restrictive.

In some cases the events on the "out of control" lists represent improved situations; particularly if the readings centralize to the mean and do not come close to reaching or exceeding control limits. The process should be investigated to determine what changed and to see whether this change can be perpetuated. If a log is maintained for the process it may be possible to find changes that correspond to the time that the improvement occurred.

In the event of "false signals," a common cause may be incorrectly linked to a special cause, forcing a process modification. Modifying the process in this way will actually increase process variation and make the process less stable and more likely to fall out of control. Special causes should be confirmed and validated. Experience is the best teacher when it comes to chart interpretation, and efforts should be made to document a body of knowledge about each process.

SOURCES OF VARIABILITY

- Long-term variation (product spread or process spread)
- Lot-to-lot variation
- Stream-to-stream variation (assuming lots have multiple streams)
- Time-to-time variation
- Piece-to-piece variation
- Within-piece variation (assumes complexity of the piece)
- Inherent error of measurement
- Inherent process capability

The null hypothesis is that the process hasn't changed, and as each point is plotted the chart is examined to determine whether there is sufficient evidence to reject the null hypothesis and conclude that the process has changed.

Key Point: When reading a process behavior chart, always start with the variables section (range) first to determine whether the process is changing internally and then look at the target value (averages) to understand other forces on the process.

Chapter 20

C. Implement and Validate Solutions

> Use various improvement methods such as
> brainstorming, main effects analysis, multi-
> vari studies, FMEA, measurement system
> capability re-analysis, and post-improvement
> capability analysis to identify, implement, and
> validate solutions through F-test, t-test, etc.
> (Create)
>
> **Body of Knowledge V.C**

REVISIT SIX SIGMA CONCEPTS

DMAIC

- *Define.* Identify the issue causing decreased customer satisfaction

- *Measure.* Collect data from the process

- *Analyze.* Study the process and data for clues to what is going on

- *Improve.* Act on the data to improve the process

- *Control.* Monitor the system to sustain the gains

SIPOC Process Identification (Checklist)

- Supplier
- Input
- Process
- Output
- Customer

Improve and Control Tools and Methods

- Management involvement
- Team meetings
- Employee involvement
- PDSA
- Continual improvement
- Cycle time analysis
- Sampling plans
- Self-directed teams
- Process improvement
- Organizational change
- Variation reduction
- Cleanliness
- Failure mode and effects analysis (FMEA)
- Cost of quality
- Improvement teams
- Lean office
- Lessons learned
- Mistake-proofing (poka-yoke)

Improve Tools and Methods

- Organizational change
- Cleanliness
- Systems thinking
- Problem solving
- Brainstorm alternatives
- Flowcharts
- Experiments

Control Tools and Methods

- SDCA (standardize, do, check, analyze)
- FMEA

- Standard operating procedures
- Long-term measurement systems analysis
- Process behavior charts
- Lean office
- Process capability

Six Sigma Road Map (Checklist)

- Use a problem-solving methodology to plan improvements
- Follow DMAIC method to deploy the improvement
- Monitor the process using process behavior charts
- Update standard operating procedures and lessons learned
- Start over again for continual improvement—PDSA/SDCA.

IMPLEMENTATION CONCEPTS

Having obtained the necessary data, the following techniques can be used for implementation.

Cycle Time Analysis

- Yield can be defined as the total number of units handled correctly (no rework or rechecking) through the process steps.
- Four basic principles of cycle time analysis are *eliminate, combine, simplify,* and *change.*
- Rolled throughput yield is a measure to track the overall quality output of the process, and to evaluate the success of improvements to the process.

Flowchart

- Create a picture of the steps in a process as it is supposed to operate
- Create the boundaries that you intend to flowchart
- Determine the various steps in the process
- Build the sequence of the process
- Draw the flowchart using the appropriate symbols
- Verify that the flowchart is complete and appropriate for the given operation

Failure Mode and Effects Analysis (FMEA)

- FMEA is a matrix of process issues, effects, measures, and mitigations that characterizes the risks of a process or system.

- A number scale has been developed.

- Severity measures how critical the problem is.

- Frequency measures the likelihood of occurrence.

- Detection measures the possibility of detecting an issue before it moves downstream.

- Risk priority number (RPN) is the factor of the three measures, and prioritizes the risks for mitigation.

- See Chapter 9 (page 100) for detailed information and an example.

Lessons Learned (SLACK)

- *Summary.* This is an overview of the observations.

- *Lessons learned.* This is the extract of problems and opportunities observed.

- *Action.* Actions are derived from lessons learned to implement improvement steps.

- *Commitment.* This describes the individual or functional area responsible for actions.

- *Knowledge base.* This is the reference for control plans, SOPs, or other documentation.

Measurement System Analysis

- Steps are taken to determine the effectiveness of measurement processes

- Determine how well people are using the existing measurement process

- Confirms efficiency and effectiveness

Process Improvement

- Making a system work better to satisfy customer wants and needs.

- Reduce variability due to variation, instability, and off-target conditions.

- Instability indicates the lack of a stable operating process.

- Off-target conditions are a design issue possibly related to an obsolete or inappropriate set of process steps.

Standardization

- Process of locking in the gains made during the improvement process

- SDCA (standardize, do, check, adjust)

- Done after control plans and process documentation have been updated

- Process is updated, confirmed, and validated as being suitable

- Standard operating procedures are a step-by-step description of how to complete tasks

MAIN EFFECTS

Main effects are defined as the estimate of the effect of a factor independent of any other means.

The first step in calculating main effects, sometimes called average main effects, is to average the results for each level of each factor.

The significance of main effects to a successful Six Sigma program is the ability to determine the consequence of setting a factor at a particular level for the duration of a particular process. Understanding the main effect of a design of experiments initiative will allow the Six Sigma team to capture the necessary information to confirm or refute the proposal to modify the process in that way.

When main effects can not be determined with significance, then that also eliminates that particular factor or attribute from further action, saving potential waste and misuse of resources. An example of a reject main effect is that the color of the baseball cap worn by the pitcher will determine the accuracy of the pitch thrown. Since cap color (red, blue, black, and so on) can be removed from consideration, the baseball team does not have to waste effort selecting the color with the hope of improving its pitching. This is similar to a software organization who attempts to solve their product development deficiencies solely by investing in automated testing and defect management, and devoting effort away from influential factors like requirements gathering and code reviews for testing and tracking existing defects instead of defect prevention.

MULTI-VARI STUDIES

When the goal is to ferret out the cause of variation, it is often useful to get a better handle on the variation itself. For example, if the varying characteristic is surface finish, it would be helpful to know:

Is the surface finish consistent on a particular part?

Is the surface finish consistent from part to consecutive part?

Is the surface finish consistent over time?

A multi-vari study answers these questions, providing a big step toward identifying the cause of the variation. Multi-vari analysis is a graphical technique that attempts to display variation in categories that will aid in identifying causes.

Typical categories are positional, cyclical, and temporal. Positional variation is often called within-part variation and refers to variation of a characteristic on the same product. Cyclical variation covers part-to-part variation. Temporal variation occurs as change over time.

Reanalysis of the measurement system is required: change in process, change in customer specifications, new measuring devices, annual ISO validation, and most importantly continued process improvement.

The total observed variation in a process is made up of two components: process variation and measurement variation. Process improvement efforts typically result in reduced process variation; however, the current measurement system could become incapable of achieving the desired level of process control.

Measurement variation can be calculated by performing a gage repeatability and reproducibility (GR&R) analysis, as described in Chapter 14.

VALIDATION OF SIX SIGMA OUTCOMES

Validation is defined simply as confirming that an entity is suitable for use to fulfill a specified purpose in its designated environment by the intended user. Any change that is implemented as a result of a Six Sigma initiative (design of experiments, control charts, lean tools, and so on) must be validated to determine whether:

- The change has been implemented

- The change was effective

It serves no value—beyond academic pursuits—to investigate a problem only to have the solution remain idle and the problem recurring. Solutions must be communicated, applied, incorporated into training and regular processes, and monitored. In some cases, the solution may solve the problem under analysis but inadvertently create a problem elsewhere.

For example, a robust software solution that defines a specific user interface to support usability may create additional performance requirements beyond the capabilities of a typical client environment. Or the modified material changed to address one special cause may be incompatible with a downstream process.

Validating solutions confirms (or refutes) the suitability of the Six Sigma recommendation and truly establishes the checkpoint for control and a baseline for continual improvement. Success and efficiencies are gained methodically and incrementally and rely on "small victories" to act as building blocks to quality.

Successful companies depend on the consistent achievement of small gains to not only contribute to profitability but also to create positive momentum and a consistent track record of tangible improvements. Validations confirm those improvements and provide the knowledge base with which to govern future improvement efforts.

Validation methods include document reviews, process audits, reviews of control charts and process records, observations, and interviews with the participants and stakeholders of a particular process to get objective evidence supporting the *validity* of the Six Sigma change.

Part V.C

Chapter 21

D. Control Plan

Assist in developing a control plan to
document and hold the gains, and assist
in implementing controls and monitoring
systems. (Apply)

Body of Knowledge V.D

Control plans make the operator aware of items in the system for controlling parts and processes during full production. The control plan is a document (updated as needed) that explains how to control the work flow in your process. It should have, as a minimum, the following basic information:

- A flowchart or other graphical representation of the process with the desired outcomes displayed.

- Any special or safety characteristics must be clearly displayed on the control plan.

- A description of the direct relationship between any highlighted characteristics and their controlling process setting or parameters.

- Identification of any gages or test equipment needed for the operations.

- Identification of appropriate sample sizes and frequencies of all testing.

- Any reactions to failure mode and effects analysis (FMEA) conditions should be spelled out to prevent nonconforming products or out-of-control conditions.

- The operators should easily understand reaction plans.

- Verify accuracy with the next operation in the process.

The control plan should outline the steps to be followed during each phase of the process to ensure that all process outputs will be in a state of control. Operators need to feel comfortable working with the paperwork in their area. A simple plan based on the template in Figure 21.1 should be adequate to track the necessary data on a single page or sheet. Examples are shown as Figures 21.2 and 21.3.

Sample Control Plan Layout				
Plant	Operation	Date control limits calculated	Part number	Specification
Machine	Characteristic	Sample size/ frequency	Part name	Control item
Averages chart				Actions on special causes
Ranges chart				Action instructions
Readings				Subgroup size
Sum of readings				
Process Log				
Date/time	Material change	Methods/ equipment change	Operator change	Comments

Figure 21.1   A sample control plan template.

Deming was well known for his constant harping on managers to fix the process, not the people. Studies have shown that 80 percent of the time, the real issue is something in the system. Operators need to use data collection tools to demonstrate that they are following the control plan so that any issue that may arise can be shown to be due to system operation.

Control plans provide a structured approach for the design, selection, and implementation of value-added control methods for the total system. The scope of control plans includes dynamic control plans, quality process sheets, and standard operating procedures. In whatever form, control plans are dynamic documents that explain how to control the process work flow.

Part V.D

Soft Start-Up Valve Control Plan

Control plan number: CP714				Control plan revision level: C					Revision date: 12/01/07	
Part/assembly number/rev: 714647-H & 714648-J				Product line: Soft start air dump valve					Originator: J. Hausner	
						Methods				
							Sample		Control method	Reaction plan code
Sta #	Process description	Machine tools/ equipment	Print no.	Characteristic specification	Evaluation measurement equipment		Size	Freq.		
14	Machine needle bleed port on cover	Drill press	714648	0.060" min diameter	0.60 (minus) gage pin S/N 15-50-2118		1	1 per hour	Check sheet	A
18	Pressure gage torque	Torque driver	714647 714648	20 +/- 5 IN LB	Torque gage S/N 15-50-2019		5	1 per shift	$\bar{X}$ chart	E, F
23	Body-cover screw torque	Torque driver	714647 714648	60 +/- 15 IN LB	Torque gage S/N 15-50-2120		3 per screw	2 per shift	Separate $\bar{X}$ charts	E, F
27	Solenoid assembly torque	Torque driver	209647 209648	14 +/- 7 IN LB	Torque gage S/N 15-50-2019		5	1 per shift	$\bar{X}$ chart	E, F
29	Final air test	Test tank	209647 209648	Functional test and leak check	Visual: ref. QA spec 203795 Functional: ref. assy instruction		1	100%	Go/no-go	A, B, C, D
All	All	All	209647 209648	Workmanship	Visual		1	100%	Go/no-go	See note 2

Note 1: At all times, quarantine one hour worth of product before releasing to shipping. In the event of a final test failure, the last hour of production should be set aside for possible retest. This should be done on all final test failures with the exception of porosity.

Note 2: Compare suspect unit to visual accept/reject standards. If unit is unacceptable, stop the line and follow standard four-step reaction plan: (A) contain suspect units; (B) diagnose the root cause and implement corrective action; (C) verify that the corrective action is effective; (D) disposition suspect material (sort, scrap, rework, use as-is).

Figure 21.2   An example control plan—first page.

Soft Start-Up Valve Control Plan

Control plan number: CP714	Key contact: J. Hausner	Control plan revision level: C	Revision date: 12/01/07
Part/assembly number/rev: 714647-H & 714648-J	Part name/description: Soft start air dump valve HG & HJ series	Product line: Airlogic control valve series	Originator: J. Hausner

Failure mode	Reaction plan	Code
Valve fails to open	Containment: Segregate nonconforming unit and previous hour of production for MRB. Disposition: Verify that wire leads and power supply are hooked up correctly. Verify needle port diameter > 0.060". If port diameter is under spec, switch to 100% inspection for the next 50 units and notify the product engineer (PE) if another failure is found. Replace drill bit if hole is not drilled through or burrs are present. Verify that piston ring is installed and free of nicks. Verify that needle valve is open at least one complete turn. Verify that the solenoid port resistor is installed. Try another solenoid. If other tests fail, check diameter of diaphragm. Contact the PE if additional diagnosis is required. Verification: Verify that corrective action eliminates problem. Disposition: Scrap nonconforming components. Rework assemblies as necessary and retest 100% of the previous hour of production.	
Valve fails to close	Containment: Segregate nonconforming product for MRB. Diagnosis: Verify that wire leads and power supply are hooked up correctly. Verify that flow control is open. Verify that diaphragm is installed correctly and check for voids in the seal bead. Verify that the dump hole is drilled completely through bonnet. Check that the fluid resistor is in place. Try another solenoid. If solenoid sticks open, quarantine current batch and switch to a new batch of solenoids. Contact PE if further diagnosis is required to determine cause. Verification: Verify that corrective action eliminates problem. Notify PE if another failure is found on the next 50 units. Disposition: Scrap nonconforming components. Rework assembly and retest.	
Body–bonnet leak	Containment: Segregate nonconforming product for MRB. Diagnosis: Verify torque. For torque adjustments, see Reaction Code "E" below. Ensure that diaphragm is installed correctly and that there are no voids present on the bead. Verify that the bead grooves on the bonnet and body are free of nicks or porosity and the diameters are within tolerance. Verify that the milled slot on the body is within tolerance. Contact PE if further diagnosis is required. Verification: Verify that corrective action eliminates problem. Disposition: Scrap nonconforming components. Rework assembly and retest. Contact line lead or PE if there are two or more consecutive failures or three failures within one hour.	
Leak at fittings	Containment: Segregate nonconforming product for MRB. Diagnosis: Verify that fittings are installed correctly and have the correct torque applied. Verify that the threads on the fitting and assembly are free of nicks or porosity. Contact PE if further diagnosis is required. Verification: Verify that corrective action eliminates problem. Notify PE if another failure is found on the next 50 units. Disposition: Scrap nonconforming components.	
Torque out of spec	Containment: Segregate nonconforming product for MRB. Diagnosis: Verify torque using another torque gage. For torque adjustments, take at least 10 samples and adjust torque gun if average is more than one standard deviation away from the nominal. Notify maintenance if average is close to nominal and there are any observations out of spec. Contact PE for further diagnosis. Verification: Measure a minimum of three subgroups and verify that the process is near nominal and in control. Disposition: If undertorqued, retorque assembly. If overtorqued, replace screw(s) and retorque.	
SPC out of control, but parts in spec	Refer to QA/SPC procedure 231573. Comply with SPC procedure requirements. Document the root cause and corrective action in a note on the control chart.	

Figure 21.3   An example control plan—second page.

CHECKLIST

Control Plan

❑   Offer a flowchart or graphical representation

❑   Display special characteristics

❑   Describe relationships between characteristics and controlled process settings or parameters

❑   Identify gages or test equipment

❑   Identify sample sizes and frequency of testing

❑   Specify reactions or troubleshooting solutions to FMEA conditions to prevent nonconforming products or out-of-control conditions

❑   Confirm understanding by operators

❑   Ensure that all actions are traceable to the control plan

---

Another variation on this same theme is the SDCA (standardize, do, check, act) cycle. This is most commonly used once a process has been improved to update the control plans and process sheets to lock in the improvements and standardize the changes throughout the organization.

Dynamic Control Planning

The dynamic control plan (DCP) combines necessary information into one document to help plan, monitor, control, study, and maintain your process. Some of the documents include: standard operating procedures (SOP), control plans, failure mode and effects analysis (FMEA), gage control plan, quality planning sheets (QPS), and others.

The DCP is often called a living document where the operators have the right and responsibility to update the DCP any time that things change; the documents need to be updated to communicate to others so they know that something is different in the process.

The basic DCP includes a matrix (sometimes referred to as the DCP critical path) of the following items:

- DCP launch

- Team structure

- Question log

- Support information

- Pre-launch or preliminary controls

- Process failure mode and effects analysis (PFMEA)

- Control plan

- Illustrations and instructions

- Implement and maintain

When starting a DCP process, everyone needs to know what is going to happen and management must be committed to support the efforts. The team's focus for the DCP is to maintain the control plan and the control planning process. Teams should also remember to maintain a log to keep a process history that can be used in the lessons learned database as well as for detailed study of the process when designed experiments are to be used.

Supporting information includes any number of items including but not limited to: blueprints, engineering specifications, prototype plans, FMEAs (design and process), special or critical characteristic identification, process sheets, flowcharts, statistical information, and so on. All this information should be available to the operators involved prior to any new line being started in the plant or prior to launching a new product or process so that activities will work out better and quicker to get things running smoothly. The process FMEA and the control plan (see Table 21.1) are the primary focuses of the DCP process and include any number of illustrations and instructions, with some of these being enlarged and posted on the job site to allow for ease of use in running the operation.

It is the responsibility of the operators and supervisors to ensure that, once started, this process is maintained and updated regularly to ensure quality of products and services. If problems occur, the records and documentation contribute to helping fix the process.

Table 21.1   FMECA and control plan.

Failure mode effect and criticality analysis (FMECA)							Control plan	
Failure mode	Failure effect	Critical	Priority	Ease to detect	Risk priority	Action	Mitigation	Validation
Run-time error	System shutdown	5	5	2	50	Restore system	Graceful shutdown with frequent data saving	Validated in process
Bar code mismatch	Invalid sample accepted	4	4	4	64	Reject sample	Insert bar code checking safeguards	Validated in process
Timing error	Expiry of sample	4	4	3	48	Dispose sample	Set alarm	Validated in process
Power outage	System shutdown	5	5	1	25	Restore system	Graceful shutdown at 30 percent power, run on cable	Validated in process

---

CHECKLIST

Dynamic Control Planning

- ❏ Constantly updated document indicating how to plan, monitor, control, study, and maintain the process
- ❏ Changes must be communicated to all necessary parties
- ❏ Helps to ensure that the process runs smoothly

Dynamic Control Plan

- ❏ Team structure
- ❏ Support information
- ❏ Preliminary controls
- ❏ Process failure mode and effects summary
- ❏ Control plan
- ❏ Illustrations and instructions
- ❏ Procedures for implementation and maintenance

Gage Control Plan

Gage R&R (repeatability and reproducibility) is used to measure the accuracy of the gaging system. The prerequisite is that the process is in control. Special studies are available for variables, attributes, and destructive data.

A *gage control plan* is followed to look at the tools for monitoring and checking the process. Maintaining your tools is important to safety and the quality of your processes. The gage control plan can be a type of FMEA for the tools you use, and should look at maintenance, calibration, and proper handling of the instruments.

The gage control plan, as the control plan, provides for a written method to describe the system that controls the proper usage of the equipment to help ensure that measurement variation is as low as possible given the current set of conditions. The gage control plan is not meant to replace the gage or test equipment instruction sheets, but to guide the operator in what to do if certain circumstances occur. Figure 21.4 shows a gage R&R data sheet.

The gage repeatability and reproducibility reports (see Figure 21.5) support the conclusions of a gage control plan. The parameters in a gage control plan can include: proper storage and care of the gage or test equipment, calibration requirements, handling requirements, and indication of what parts or processes the gage or test equipment is used for. For more details, refer to Part III, *Measure*.

Standard Operating Procedures

When the process is updated, confirmed, and validated as being suitable, standard operating procedures (SOPs) can be developed. Standard operating procedures

Part V.D

Appraiser/ trial #		Part										Average
		1	2	3	4	5	6	7	8	9	10	
1. A	1	0.65	1.00	0.85	0.85	0.55	1.00	0.95	0.85	1.00	0.60	0.83
2.	2	0.60	1.00	0.80	0.95	0.45	1.00	0.95	0.80	1.00	0.70	0.825
3.	3											
4. Average		0.625	1.000	0.825	0.900	0.500	1.000	0.950	0.825	1.000	0.650	$\bar{X}_a$ = 0.8275
5. Range		0.05	0.00	0.05	0.10	0.10	0.00	0.00	0.05	0.00	0.10	$\bar{R}_a$ = 0.045
6. B	1	0.55	1.05	0.80	0.80	0.40	1.00	0.95	0.75	1.00	0.55	0.785
7.	2	0.55	0.95	0.75	0.75	0.40	1.05	0.90	0.70	0.95	0.50	0.75
8.	3											
9. Average		0.550	1.000	0.775	0.775	0.400	1.025	0.925	0.725	0.975	0.525	$\bar{X}_b$ = 0.7675
10. Range		0.00	0.10	0.05	0.05	0.00	0.05	0.05	0.05	0.05	0.05	$\bar{R}_b$ = 0.045
11. C	1	0.50	1.05	0.80	0.80	0.45	1.00	0.95	0.80	1.05	0.85	0.825
12.	2	0.55	1.00	0.80	0.80	0.50	1.05	0.95	0.80	1.05	0.80	0.83
13.	3											
14. Average		0.525	1.025	0.800	0.800	0.475	1.025	0.950	0.800	1.050	0.825	$\bar{X}_c$ = 0.8275
15. Range		0.05	0.05	0.00	0.00	0.05	0.05	0.00	0.00	0.00	0.05	$\bar{R}_c$ = 0.030
16. Part average ($\bar{X}_p$)		0.567	1.008	0.800	0.825	0.458	1.017	0.942	0.783	1.008	0.667	$\bar{\bar{X}}$ = 0.8075 R_p = 0.559
17. $[\bar{R}_a = 0.045] + [\bar{R}_b = 0.045] + [\bar{R}_c = 0.03]/[\text{# of appraisers} = 3] =$												$\bar{\bar{R}}$ = 0.04
18. $[\text{Max } \bar{X} = 0.8275] - [\text{Min } \bar{X} = 0.7675] = \bar{X}_{\text{DIFF}}$												0.06
19. $[\bar{\bar{R}} = 0.04] \times [D_4{}^* = 3.27] = \text{UCL}_R$												0.13
20. $[\bar{\bar{R}} = 0.04] \times [D3^* = 0.00] = \text{LCL}_R$												0.00

*D_4 = 3.27 for two trials and 2.58 for three trials; D_3 = 0 for up to seven trials. UCL$_R$ represents the limit of individual Rs. Circle those that are beyond this limit. Identify the cause and correct. Repeat these readings using the same appraiser and unit as originally used or discard values and re-average and recompute R and the limiting value from the remaining observations.

Figure 21.4 A gage repeatability and reproducibility data sheet.

are a step-by-step description of how to complete tasks. Documented evidence will go a long way in preventing finger-pointing or faultfinding and the operator being blamed for something out of their control. Standard operating procedures create consistency and establish the proper methods for completing a process.

Standardization is the process of locking in the gains made during the improvement process. Following the SDCA (standardize, do, check, adjust) process, standardization is done after control plans and process documentation have been updated.

Many different terms are used for SOPs, such as work instructions, level three ISO 9001 documentation, operating guides, job aids, or standard job practices.

Part no. and name: Gasket   Gage name: Thickness gage   Date: 4/12/07
Characteristics: Thickness   Gage no.:   X – 2934   Performed by:
Specification: 0.6–1.0 mm   Gage type: 0.0–10.1 mm   _____

From data sheet: $\bar{\bar{R}} = 0.04$ $\bar{X}_{DIFF} = 0.06$ $R_p = 0.559$

Measurement Unit Analysis			% Total Variation (TV)	
Repeatability – Equipment variation (EV)			%EV	= 100 [EV/TV]
EV $= \bar{\bar{R}} \times K_1$				
$= 0.04 \times 4.56$	**Trials**	K_1		= 100 [0.18/0.93]
$= 0.18$	2	4.56		
	3	3.05		= 18.7%
Reproducibility – Appraiser variation (AV)			%AV	= 100 [AV/TV]
AV =				= 100 [0.16/0.93]
=				= 16.8%
= 0.16	**Appraisers**	**2** | **3**	n = number of parts	
	K_2	3.65 | 2.70	r = number of trials	
Repeatability & reproducibility (R&R)			%R&R	= 100 [R&R/TV]
R&R =				= 100 [0.24/0.93]
=	**Parts**	K_1		
= 0.24	2	3.65		= 25.2%
Part variation (PV)	3	2.70	%PV	= 100 [PV/TV]
	4	2.30		
PV $= R_p \times K_3$	5	2.08		= 100 [0.90/0.93]
$= 0.56 \times 1.62$	6	1.93		
	7	1.82		= 96.8%
$= 0.90$	8	1.74		
Total variation (TV)	9	1.67		
	10	1.62		
TV =				
=				
= 0.93				

All calculations are based upon predicting 5.15 sigma (99.0% of the area under the normal distribution curve).

K_1 is $5.15/d_2$, where d_2 is dependent on the number of trials (m) and the number of parts times the number of appraisers (g), which is assumed to be greater than 15. d_2 values are from Table 2, p. 29.

AV – If a negative value is calculated under the square root sign, the appraiser variation (AV) defaults to zero (0).

K_2 is $5.15/d_2^*$, where d_2^* is dependent on the number of appraisers (m) and (g) is 1, since there is only one range calculation.

K_3 is $5.15/d_2^*$, where d_2^* is dependent on the number of parts (m) and (g) is 1, since there is only one range calculation.

d_2^* is obtained from Table D$_3$, "Quality Control and Industrial Statistics," A. J. Duncan. (See Appendix, reference 4.)

Figure 21.5   Gage repeatability and reproducibility report example.

SOPs should give the details and address things such as What is the job? Where does the SOP apply? When does the SOP apply? and Who is responsible?

Operators are responsible for following the SOPs as written. If at any time deviations are taken, then the operator needs to document what was done and why. This will be a big help if at a later date a problem arises and an investigation is done.

The SOP should be a living document; if something changes in the system, then the operator should ensure that the SOP is updated. When something changes in the process and a new desirable level is achieved, the operator should update all documents relating to that process.

CONTINUAL IMPROVEMENT

Continual improvement (CI) is a process of keeping an open mind and looking for ways to make the things that you do better, cheaper, or faster. As the industrial revolution progressed into the early 1900s, Frederick Taylor developed a method of work specialization that is still used by many organizations today. It was during this time that workers first stopped checking their own work and specialized inspectors were employed in inspection teams. This process progressed and developed for several decades and professional organizations developed around doing inspection better.

During the late 1920s, Walter Shewhart developed the first control chart and statistical process control (SPC) was born (we now call this *process behavior charting*). Many organizations continued to rely on inspectors, but the use of charting that could bring operators back into looking at the quality of their work became a requirement in the United States during World War II. It was in 1951 when Armand Feigenbaum first published the book *Total Quality Control* and the TQM age started.

During the 1960s and 1970s, the use of quality circles and employee involvement became the next evolution in continual improvement. This was followed by a major resurgence of SPC during the 1980s. During the 1990s, the International Organization for Standardization (ISO) quality management system (ISO 9000) and the Malcolm Baldrige National Quality Award became the preferred strategies for continual improvement.

Other terms that have been used of late include: value analysis/value engineering, lean manufacturing/lean office, kaizen, poka-yoke, and others. Six Sigma has become the latest wave of the ongoing continual improvement movement and is bringing many fields of study back into the hands of the people doing the work.

Some people refer to these various methods as continuous improvement as they feel that we should always be making geometric strides in everything we do. Unfortunately nature and human beings do not work that way. Even in evolution, sometimes things have to step back or level off every now and then. As we learn new things, sometimes humans have to relearn old knowledge to gain new. Thus Deming changed the term *continuous* to *continual*.

Part V.D

Within this change, Deming also developed the *system of profound knowledge.* This concept involves: an appreciation for a system, knowledge about variation, theory of knowledge, and psychology. By using each of these concepts, continual improvement can and will become a reality in our organizations. Our goal is to always maintain and improve the quality of the products or services we provide to customers, both internal and external.

When the PDSA and SDCA cycles are used together, the operator will see a complete system for identifying processes, improving those processes, and application of lessons learned. The two cycles working together with the other tools in this book will help the operator continually improve the work that is done with an eye toward satisfying the customer.

PROCESS IMPROVEMENT

Process improvement is the act of making the system work better to satisfy customer wants and needs. It is a vital element in order for continual improvement to become a reality. We are looking at reducing overall variability, not just the variation. Variability is made up of three components: instability, variation, and off-target.

In dealing with variability, most practitioners have traditionally only dealt with the variation question. Variation is very important and we use the tools covered in this book to help reduce variation as much as possible. The other two components are also very important. Without knowledge of these two, instability and off-target, we could miss some very important factors and even cause major problems in the shop.

Instability is the lack of a stable operating process. Common cause and special cause variation are unchecked and not responded to. Without a stable process, capability values are not worth calculating and customers can, and do, see any number of issues come and go without rhyme or reason. The best method for monitoring a process is process behavior charts, but far too often either they are not kept up to date or not used at all. Operators should play a big role in monitoring the processes to ensure that the jobs they perform are stable and in control.

Off-target is often the responsibility of the engineers who design the parts and production. The operator can only monitor whether the process is centered within the engineering specifications and/or control limits. Even though today we talk about the Taguchi loss function and how processes should be centered on the customers' wants and needs, many jobs we work in today were designed years ago when engineers put the target wherever it made the most economic sense for the company instead of the customer. So the operator should monitor the process and be ready to give up-to-date information to engineers when processes are to be redesigned so that the new thinking becomes a reality on the shop floor.

LEAN TOOLS FOR CONTROL

One of the principal problems in any organization is the control of its processes. In addition to the techniques of SPC, the Green Belt may employ tools grouped under the name "lean thinking."

CHECKLIST

Lean Operation

- ❏ Specify value by specific product
- ❏ Identify the value stream for each product
- ❏ Make value flow without interruption or delay
- ❏ Let the customer pull value through the process steps
- ❏ Pursue perfection and prevent rework

Lean is the application of tools for the removal of waste and variation in a process, which ultimately allows for outcomes that will be delivered more efficiently and be closer to the specifications and expectations set by the customer.

Lean tools for control include:

- *5S:* sort (*seiri*), straighten (*seiton*), shine (*seiso*), standardize (*sieketsu*), and sustain (*shitsuke*); used to create order and organization.

- *Visual factory* applies visual displays and visual controls to allow anyone to promptly know the status of the process and interpret whether the process is operating properly.

- *Kaizen* pursues low-cost gradual improvement of processes either on an ongoing basis or as a dedicated endeavor known as a *kaizen blitz*.

- *Kanban* is a signal for a particular action including "obtain inventory," "produce part," or "move material from the upstream point to the downstream process." Kanban also ensures that no defective pieces are allowed to pass or be transferred.

- *Poka-yoke* is mistake-proofing by design and can include sizing devices, limit switches, color signals, and alarms.

- *Total productive maintenance* manages operations with preventive maintenance, load balancing, and streamlined flow control.

- *Standard work* applies capacity resource planning to determine the most efficient combinations of operations.

Mistake-Proofing (Error-Proofing or Poka-Yoke)

Poka-yoke activities, by devising methods that make erroneous events impossible, further enable process control by automatically eliminating another source of variation. Example: A newly assigned press operator stacked finished parts on a pallet with the incorrect orientation. The next operator didn't notice the difference, resulting in several hundred spoiled products. A fixture for the pallet now makes it impossible to stack misoriented parts.

Part V.D

Mistake-proofing (poka-yoke) is achieved by limiting or restricting ways to complete a task to ensure accuracy and compliance (for example, electric plug design intended to ensure correct connection).

Poka-yoke tries either to ensure that there is only one way (or limited ways) to perform any given task in a process or to make any mistake very obvious as soon as it happens. These efforts help to reduce variation in the process and help prevent nonconformance issues from occurring downstream in the process or when a customer uses the product or service. Have you noticed that when you try to plug an electrical appliance into an electrical outlet that the plug can only go in one way (this is true for either two- or three-prong plugs)! This is an example of mistake-proofing that allows the electronics industry to help ensure proper usage of appliances in a home (see Figure 21.6).

Our jobs can be looked at in the same way. Is it currently possible to put a part in the machine more than one way? Can the process be done in a different order from what the process sheets say? Can a part be accidentally put in upside down or backwards? If any of these issues or any number of others exists, we should help ensure that things are being done more consistently to help reduce the variation in the process.

We may need to get the quality office or engineering group involved in some changes to our processes; however, some we can do with the help of our natural work groups. If there are groups of parts that come through your area that are very similar, look over the paperwork that accompanies the production. Is everything arranged logically for your work space? Is the paperwork aligned to show similar steps in the same order of production (since different engineers may have designed the processes, the process sequence may not be the same)? If you could change anything about your work area, what would it be? Tell your supervisor or team the ideas that you have.

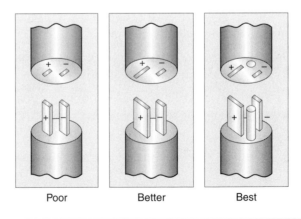

| Poor | Better | Best |

Figure 21.6   Example of poka-yoke in electrical plug design.

The originator of this method is a Japanese engineer named Shigeo Shingo, and there is now a yearly prize in the United States for the best example of mistake-proofing submitted to the judges.

5S

A process is impacted by its environment, as is the ability of personnel to respond to process change. Improvements in the general state of the work area, including access to hand tools, and so on, are an aid to process control. Especially critical here is the cleanliness, lighting, and general housekeeping status of any area where measurements are conducted, since process control data are filtered through the measurement system. Example: a process thought to be incapable was greatly improved by regular cleaning of the surface plate on which the micrometer stand was mounted.

Visual Factory

Failing to follow work instructions in detail is a common source of process variation, so easily accessible and clearly illustrated work instructions are critical. This is especially true in situations where cross-trained personnel flex into various workstations and mixed-model schedules are employed. Good lines, signs, and labels help ensure that the right component is at the right place and time, further reducing variation. If the process operator's attention must be turned away from the process to manage material replenishment, poorer process control may result. Example: a component was installed upside down at least partly because the work instructions, although clear, were installed at the previous location of the assembly step.

Kaizen

Process control can be enhanced through kaizen events that reduce non-value-added activities. The resulting work is more productive and permits a closer process focus by all involved. Example: fan blades previously retrieved from a large box for each unit are now hung from an arm of a "Christmas tree" located near the operator. A *kaizen event* is a radical change to an existing situation. It is referred to in Japanese as *kaikakku*. *Kaizen* is the gradual improvement of the current situation. North Americans interchangeably use kaizen event or *kaizen blitz* for kaikakku.

Kanban

A system is best controlled when material and information flow into and out of the process in a smooth and rational manner. If process inputs arrive before they are needed, unnecessary confusion, inventory, and costs generally occur. If process outputs are not synchronized with downstream processes, the results are often delays, disappointed customers, and associated costs. A properly administered kanban system improves system control by assuring timely movement of products and information.

Total Productive Maintenance

Total productive maintenance aims to remove deficiencies from machines to minimize or eliminate defects and downtime. This extends beyond preventive maintenance to include management of people, processes, systems, and the environment. In any situation where mechanical devices are used, the working state of those devices has an impact on the control of the process. If equipment deteriorates even subtly, the process output may be affected, often in unsuspected ways.

Standard Work

Standard work is a term used to systematize how a part is processed, and includes man–machine interactions and studies of human motion. Operations are safely carried out with all tasks organized in the best-known sequence and by using the most effective combination of resources. Finding better ways of producing an ever more consistent product is the essence of process control. Standard work contributes to this effort by assuring that product flowing into a process has minimal variation and that there is a reduction in the variation caused by the process.

Key Point: There are many tools and techniques that can be used to help improve a given process or situation. One key is stay open-minded, take initial readings or measurements of the process, and use whatever is available to try to improve and monitor the process. The sheer fact that you are focusing on an issue will go a long way to highlighting to everyone involved that management is actually watching this area. Things will sometimes magically start improving when people are focused on the issues.

Part VI
Appendices

Appendix A
ASQ Code of Ethics

FUNDAMENTAL PRINCIPLES

ASQ requires its members and certification holders to conduct themselves ethically by:

    I.   Being honest and impartial in serving the public, their employers, customers, and clients.

    II.   Striving to increase the competence and prestige of the quality profession, and

    III.   Using their knowledge and skill for the enhancement of human welfare.

Members and certification holders are required to observe the tenets set forth below:

RELATIONS WITH THE PUBLIC

Article 1 – Hold paramount the safety, health, and welfare of the public in the performance of their professional duties.

RELATIONS WITH EMPLOYERS AND CLIENTS

Article 2 – Perform services only in their areas of competence.

Article 3 – Continue their professional development throughout their careers and provide opportunities for the professional and ethical development of others.

Article 4 – Act in a professional manner in dealings with ASQ staff and each employer, customer or client.

Article 5 – Act as faithful agents or trustees and avoid conflict of interest and the appearance of conflicts of interest.

RELATIONS WITH PEERS

Article 6 – Build their professional reputation on the merit of their services and not compete unfairly with others.

Article 7 – Assure that credit for the work of others is given to those to whom it is due.

Ref: http://www.asq.org/about-asq/who-we-are/ethics.html

Appendix B

Six Sigma Green Belt Certification Body of Knowledge

Included in this body of knowledge are explanations (subtext) and cognitive levels for each topic or subtopic in the test. These details will be used by the Examination Development Committee as guidelines for writing test questions and are designed to help candidates prepare for the exam by identifying specific content within each topic that can be tested. Except where specified, the subtext is not intended to limit the subject or be all-inclusive of what might be covered in an exam but is intended to clarify how topics are related to the role of the Certified Six Sigma Green Belt. The descriptor in parentheses at the end of each subtext entry refers to the highest cognitive level at which the topic will be tested. A complete description of cognitive levels is provided at the end of this document.

I. Overview: Six Sigma and the Organization (15 Questions)

    A. *Six Sigma and organizational goals.*

        1. *Value of Six Sigma.* Recognize why organizations use Six Sigma, how they apply its philosophy and goals, and the origins of Six Sigma (Juran, Deming, Shewhart, etc.). Describe how process inputs, outputs, and feedback impact the larger organization. (Understand)

        2. *Organizational drivers and metrics.* Recognize key drivers for business (profit, market share, customer satisfaction, efficiency, product differentiation) and how key metrics and scorecards are developed and impact the entire organization. (Understand)

        3. *Organizational goals and Six Sigma projects.* Describe the project selection process including knowing when to use Six Sigma improvement methodology (DMAIC) as opposed to other problem-solving tools, and confirm that the project supports and is linked to organizational goals. (Understand)

    B. *Lean principles in the organization.*

        1. *Lean concepts and tools.* Define and describe concepts such as value chain, flow, pull, perfection, etc., and tools commonly used to eliminate waste, including kaizen, 5S, error-proofing, value-stream mapping, etc. (Understand)

2. *Value-added and non-value-added activities.* Identify waste in terms of excess inventory, space, test inspection, rework, transportation, storage, etc., and reduce cycle time to improve throughput. (Understand)

3. *Theory of constraints.* Describe the theory of constraints. (Understand)

C. *Design for Six Sigma (DFSS) in the organization.*

1. *Quality function deployment (QFD).* Describe how QFD fits into the overall DFSS process. (Understand) (Note: the application of QFD is covered in II.A.6.)

2. *Design and process failure mode and effects analysis (DFMEA & PFMEA).* Define and distinguish between design FMEA (DFMEA) and process (PFMEA) and interpret associated data. (Analyze) (Note: the application of FMEA is covered in II.D.2.)

3. *Road maps for DFSS.* Describe and distinguish between DMADV (define, measure, analyze, design, verify) and IDOV (identify, design, optimize, verify), identify how they relate to DMAIC and how they help close the loop on improving the end product/process during the design (DFSS) phase. (Understand)

II. Six Sigma—*Define* (25 Questions)

A. *Process management for projects.*

1. *Process elements.* Define and describe process components and boundaries. Recognize how processes cross various functional areas and the challenges that result for process improvement efforts. (Analyze)

2. *Owners and stakeholders.* Identify process owners, internal and external customers, and other stakeholders in a project. (Apply)

3. *Identify customers.* Identify and classify internal and external customers as applicable to a particular project, and show how projects impact customers. (Apply)

4. *Collect customer data.* Use various methods to collect customer feedback (e.g., surveys, focus groups, interviews, observation) and identify the key elements that make these tools effective. Review survey questions to eliminate bias, vagueness, etc. (Apply)

5. *Analyze customer data.* Use graphical, statistical, and qualitative tools to analyze customer feedback. (Analyze)

6. *Translate customer requirements.* Assist in translating customer feedback into project goals and objectives, including critical to quality (CTQ) attributes and requirements statements. Use voice of the customer analysis tools such as quality function deployment (QFD) to translate customer requirements into performance measures. (Apply)

B. *Project management basics.*

1. *Project charter and problem statement.* Define and describe elements of a project charter and develop a problem statement, including baseline and improvement goals. (Apply)

2. *Project scope.* Assist with the development of project definition/scope using Pareto charts, process maps, etc. (Apply)

3. *Project metrics.* Assist with the development of primary and consequential metrics (e.g., quality, cycle time, cost) and establish key project metrics that relate to the voice of the customer. (Apply)

4. *Project planning tools.* Use project tools such as Gantt charts, critical path method (CPM), and program evaluation and review technique (PERT) charts, etc. (Apply)

5. *Project documentation.* Provide input and select the proper vehicle for presenting project documentation (e.g., spreadsheet output, storyboards, etc.) at phase reviews, management reviews, and other presentations. (Apply)

6. *Project risk analysis.* Describe the purpose and benefit of project risk analysis, including resources, financials, impact on customers and other stakeholders, etc. (Understand)

7. *Project closure.* Describe the objectives achieved and apply the lessons learned to identify additional opportunities. (Apply)

C. *Management and planning tools.* Define, select, and use 1) affinity diagrams, 2) interrelationship digraphs, 3) tree diagrams, 4) prioritization matrices, 5) matrix diagrams, 6) process decision program charts (PDPC), and 7) activity network diagrams. (Apply)

D. *Business results for projects.*

1. *Process performance.* Calculate process performance metrics such as defects per unit (DPU), rolled throughput yield (RTY), cost of poor quality (COPQ), defects per million opportunities (DPMO) sigma levels, and process capability indices. Track process performance measures to drive project decisions. (Analyze)

2. *Failure mode and effects analysis (FMEA).* Define and describe failure mode and effects analysis (FMEA). Describe the purpose and use of scale criteria and calculate the risk priority number (RPN). (Analyze)

E. *Team dynamics and performance.*

1. *Team stages and dynamics.* Define and describe the stages of team evolution, including forming, storming, norming, performing, adjourning, and recognition. Identify and help resolve negative dynamics such as overbearing, dominant, or reluctant participants, the unquestioned acceptance of opinions as facts, groupthink,

feuding, floundering, the rush to accomplishment, attribution, discounts, plops, digressions, tangents, etc. (Understand)

2. *Six Sigma and other team roles and responsibilities.* Describe and define the roles and responsibilities of participants on Six Sigma and other teams, including Black Belt, Master Black Belt, Green Belt, champion, executive, coach, facilitator, team member, sponsor, process owner, etc. (Apply)

3. *Team tools.* Define and apply team tools such as brainstorming, nominal group technique, multi-voting, etc. (Apply)

4. *Communication.* Use effective and appropriate communication techniques for different situations to overcome barriers to project success. (Apply)

III. Six Sigma—*Measure* (30 Questions)

A. *Process analysis and documentation.*

1. *Process modeling.* Develop and review process maps, written procedures, work instructions, flowcharts, etc. (Analyze)

2. *Process inputs and outputs.* Identify process input variables and process output variables (SIPOC), and document their relationships through cause-and-effect diagrams, relational matrices, etc. (Analyze)

B. *Probability and statistics.*

1. *Drawing valid statistical conclusions.* Distinguish between enumerative (descriptive) and analytical (inferential) studies, and distinguish between a population parameter and a sample statistic. (Apply)

2. *Central limit theorem and sampling distribution of the mean.* Define the central limit theorem and describe its significance in the application of inferential statistics for confidence intervals, control charts, etc. (Apply)

3. *Basic probability concepts.* Describe and apply concepts such as independence, mutually exclusive, multiplication rules, etc. (Apply)

C. *Collecting and summarizing data.*

1. *Types of data and measurement scales.* Identify and classify continuous (variables) and discrete (attributes) data. Describe and define nominal, ordinal, interval, and ratio measurement scales. (Analyze)

2. *Data collection methods.* Define and apply methods for collecting data such as check sheets, coded data, etc. (Apply)

3. *Techniques for assuring data accuracy and integrity.* Define and apply techniques such as random sampling, stratified sampling, sample homogeneity, etc. (Apply)

4. *Descriptive statistics.* Define, compute, and interpret measures of dispersion and central tendency, and construct and interpret frequency distributions and cumulative frequency distributions. (Analyze)

5. *Graphical methods.* Depict relationships by constructing, applying, and interpreting diagrams and charts such as stem-and-leaf plots, box-and-whisker plots, run charts, scatter diagrams, Pareto charts, etc. Depict distributions by constructing, applying, and interpreting diagrams such as histograms, normal probability plots, etc. (Create)

D. *Probability distributions.* Describe and interpret normal, binomial, and Poisson, chi square, Student's t, and F distributions. (Apply)

E. *Measurement system analysis.* Calculate, analyze, and interpret measurement system capability using repeatability and reproducibility (GR&R), measurement correlation, bias, linearity, percent agreement, and precision/tolerance (P/T). (Evaluate)

F. *Process capability and performance.*

1. *Process capability studies.* Identify, describe, and apply the elements of designing and conducting process capability studies, including identifying characteristics, identifying specifications and tolerances, developing sampling plans, and verifying stability and normality. (Evaluate)

2. *Process performance vs. specification.* Distinguish between natural process limits and specification limits, and calculate process performance metrics such as percent defective. (Evaluate)

3. *Process capability indices.* Define, select, and calculate C_p and C_{pk}, and assess process capability. (Evaluate)

4. *Process performance indices.* Define, select, and calculate P_p, P_{pk}, C_{pm}, and assess process performance. (Evaluate)

5. *Short-term vs. long-term capability.* Describe the assumptions and conventions that are appropriate when only short-term data are collected and when only attributes data are available. Describe the changes in relationships that occur when long-term data are used, and interpret the relationship between long- and short-term capability as it relates to a 1.5 sigma shift. (Evaluate)

6. *Process capability for attributes data.* Compute the sigma level for a process and describe its relationship to P_{pk}. (Apply)

IV. Six Sigma—*Analyze* (15 Questions)

A. *Exploratory data analysis.*

1. *Multi-vari studies.* Create and interpret multi-vari studies to interpret the difference between positional, cyclical, and temporal variation;

apply sampling plans to investigate the largest sources of variation. (Create)

2. *Simple linear correlation and regression.* Interpret the correlation coefficient and determine its statistical significance (p-value); recognize the difference between correlation and causation. Interpret the linear regression equation and determine its statistical significance (p-value). Use regression models for estimation and prediction. (Evaluate)

B. *Hypothesis testing.*

1. *Basics.* Define and distinguish between statistical and practical significance and apply tests for significance level, power, type I and type II errors. Determine appropriate sample size for various tests. (Apply).

2. *Tests for means, variances, and proportions.* Define, compare, and contrast statistical and practical significance. (Apply)

3. *Paired-comparison tests.* Define and describe paired-comparison parametric hypothesis tests. (Understand)

4. *Single-factor analysis of variance (ANOVA).* Define terms related to one-way ANOVAs and interpret their results and data plots. (Apply)

5. *Chi square.* Define and interpret chi square and use it to determine statistical significance. (Analyze)

V. Six Sigma—*Improve & Control* (15 Questions)

A. *Design of experiments (DOE).*

1. *Basic terms.* Define and describe basic DOE terms such as independent and dependent variables, factors and levels, response, treatment, error, repetition, and replication. (Understand)

2. *Main effects.* Interpret main effects and interaction plots. (Apply)

B. *Statistical process control (SPC).*

1. *Objectives and benefits.* Describe the objectives and benefits of SPC, including controlling process performance, identifying special and common causes, etc. (Analyze)

2. *Rational subgrouping.* Define and describe how rational subgrouping is used. (Understand)

3. *Selection and application of control charts.* Identify, select, construct, and apply the following types of control charts: $\bar{X}$ and R, $\bar{X}$ and s, individuals and moving range (ImR/XmR), median ($\tilde{X}$), p, np, c, and u. (Apply)

4. *Analysis of control charts.* Interpret control charts and distinguish between common and special causes using rules for determining statistical control. (Analyze)

C. *Implement and validate solutions.* Use various improvement methods such as brainstorming, main effects analysis, multi-vari studies, FMEA, measurement system capability reanalysis, and post-improvement capability analysis to identify, implement, and validate solutions through F-test, t-test, etc. (Create)

D. *Control plan.* Assist in developing a control plan to document and hold the gains, and assist in implementing controls and monitoring systems. (Apply)

SIX LEVELS OF COGNITION BASED ON BLOOM'S TAXONOMY (REVISED)

In addition to *content* specifics, the subtext detail also indicates the intended *complexity level* of the test questions for that topic. These levels are based on the Revised "Levels of Cognition" (from Bloom's Taxonomy, 2001) and are presented below in rank order, from least complex to most complex.

Remember

Be able to remember or recognize terminology, definitions, facts, ideas, materials, patterns, sequences, methodologies, principles, etc. (Also commonly referred to as recognition, recall, or rote knowledge.)

Understand

Be able to read and understand descriptions, communications, reports, tables, diagrams, directions, regulations, etc.

Apply

Be able to apply ideas, procedures, methods, formulas, principles, theories, etc., in job-related situations.

Analyze

Be able to break down information into its constituent parts and recognize the parts' relationship to one another and how they are organized; identify sublevel factors or salient data from a complex scenario.

Evaluate

Be able to make judgments regarding the value of proposed ideas, solutions, methodologies, etc., by using appropriate criteria or standards to estimate accuracy, effectiveness, economic benefits, etc.

Create

Be able to put parts or elements together in such a way as to show a pattern or structure not clearly there before; able to identify which data or information from a complex set is appropriate to examine further or from which supported conclusions can be drawn.

Appendix C
Control Limit Formulas

VARIABLES CHARTS

$\bar{x}$ and R chart:

    Averages chart : $\bar{\bar{x}} \pm A_2 \bar{R}$ *Range chart* : $LCL = D_3 \bar{R}$ $UCL = D_4 \bar{R}$

$\bar{x}$ and s chart:

    Averages chart : $\bar{\bar{x}} \pm A_3 \bar{s}$ *Standard deviation chart* : $LCL = B_3 \bar{s}$ $UCL = B_4 \bar{s}$

Individuals and moving range chart (two-value moving window):

    Individuals chart : $\bar{x} \pm 2.66 \bar{R}$ *Moving range* : $UCL = 3.267 \bar{R}$

Moving average and moving range (two-value moving window):

    Moving average : $\bar{\bar{x}} \pm 1.88 \bar{R}$ *Moving range* : $UCL = 3.267 \bar{R}$

Median chart:

    Median chart : $\bar{x}' \pm A_2' \bar{R}$ *Range chart* : $LCL = D_3 \bar{R}$ $UCL = D_4 \bar{R}$

ATTRIBUTE CHARTS

Variable sample size:		Constant sample size:	
p chart:	$\bar{p} \pm 3 \sqrt{\dfrac{\bar{p}(1-\bar{p})}{\bar{n}}}$	np chart:	$n\bar{p} \pm 3 \sqrt{n\bar{p}(1-\bar{p})}$
u chart:	$\bar{u} \pm 3 \sqrt{\dfrac{\bar{u}}{\bar{n}}}$	c chart:	$\bar{c} \pm 3 \sqrt{\bar{c}}$
D chart:	$\bar{D} \pm 3 \sigma_D$	U chart:	$\bar{U} \pm 3 \sigma_U$

Appendix D

Constants for Control Charts

Subgroup size										A_2 for median	
N	A_2	d_2	D_3	D_4	A_3	c_4	B_3	B_4	E_2	charts	A_4
2	1.880	1.128	–	3.267	2.659	0.798	–	3.267	2.660	1.880	2.224
3	1.023	1.693	–	2.574	1.954	0.886	–	2.568	1.772	1.187	1.091
4	0.729	2.059	–	2.282	1.628	0.921	–	2.266	1.457	0.796	0.758
5	0.577	2.326	–	2.114	1.427	0.940	–	2.089	1.290	0.691	0.594
6	0.483	2.534	–	2.004	1.287	0.952	0.030	1.970	1.184	0.548	0.495
7	0.419	2.704	0.076	1.924	1.182	0.959	0.118	1.882	1.109	0.508	0.429
8	0.373	2.847	0.136	1.864	1.099	0.965	0.185	1.815	1.054	0.433	0.380
9	0.337	2.970	0.184	1.816	1.032	0.969	0.239	1.761	1.010	0.412	0.343
10	0.308	3.078	0.223	1.777	0.975	0.973	0.284	1.716	0.975	0.362	0.314

Appendix E

Areas under Standard Normal Curve

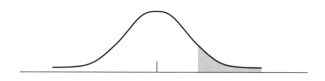

z	0.00	0.01	0.02	0.03	0.04
0.0	0.50000000000	0.49601064369	0.49202168628	0.48803352659	0.48404656315
0.1	0.46017216272	0.45620468746	0.45224157398	0.44828321335	0.44432999519
0.2	0.42074029056	0.41683383652	0.41293557735	0.40904588486	0.40516512830
0.3	0.38208857781	0.37828047818	0.37448416528	0.37069998106	0.36692826396
0.4	0.34457825839	0.34090297377	0.33724272685	0.33359782060	0.32996855366
0.5	0.30853753873	0.30502573090	0.30153178755	0.29805596539	0.29459851622
0.6	0.27425311775	0.27093090378	0.26762889347	0.26434729212	0.26108629969
0.7	0.24196365222	0.23885206809	0.23576249778	0.23269509230	0.22964999716
0.8	0.21185539858	0.20897008787	0.20610805359	0.20326939183	0.20045419326
0.9	0.18406012535	0.18141125489	0.17878637961	0.17618554225	0.17360878034
1.0	0.15865525393	0.15624764502	0.15386423037	0.15150500279	0.14916995033
1.1	0.13566606095	0.13349951324	0.13135688104	0.12923811224	0.12714315056
1.2	0.11506967022	0.11313944644	0.11123243745	0.10934855243	0.10748769707
1.3	0.09680048459	0.09509791780	0.09341750899	0.09175913565	0.09012267246
1.4	0.08075665923	0.07926984145	0.07780384053	0.07635850954	0.07493369953
1.5	0.06680720127	0.06552171209	0.06425548782	0.06300836446	0.06178017671
1.6	0.05479929170	0.05369892815	0.05261613845	0.05155074849	0.05050258347
1.7	0.04456546276	0.04363293652	0.04271622079	0.04181513761	0.04092950898
1.8	0.03593031911	0.03514789358	0.03437950245	0.03362496942	0.03288411866
1.9	0.02871655982	0.02806660666	0.02742894970	0.02680341888	0.02618984494
2.0	0.02275013195	0.02221559443	0.02169169377	0.02117826964	0.02067516287
2.1	0.01786442056	0.01742917794	0.01700302265	0.01658580668	0.01617738337
2.2	0.01390344751	0.01355258115	0.01320938381	0.01287372144	0.01254546144
2.3	0.01072411002	0.01044407706	0.01017043867	0.00990307556	0.00964186995
2.4	0.00819753592	0.00797626026	0.00776025355	0.00754941142	0.00734363096
2.5	0.00620966533	0.00603655808	0.00586774172	0.00570312633	0.00554262344
2.6	0.00466118802	0.00452711113	0.00439648835	0.00426924341	0.00414530136
2.7	0.00346697380	0.00336416041	0.00326409582	0.00316671628	0.00307195922
2.8	0.00255513033	0.00247707500	0.00240118247	0.00232740021	0.00225567669
2.9	0.00186581330	0.00180714378	0.00175015693	0.00169481002	0.00164106123

Continued

Continued

z	0.00	0.01	0.02	0.03	0.04
3.0	0.00134989803	0.00130623845	0.00126387343	0.00122276869	0.00118289074
3.1	0.00096760321	0.00093543672	0.00090425520	0.00087403152	0.00084473917
3.2	0.00068713794	0.00066367486	0.00064095298	0.00061895109	0.00059764850
3.3	0.00048342414	0.00046647986	0.00045008724	0.00043422992	0.00041889195
3.4	0.00033692927	0.00032481440	0.00031310568	0.00030179062	0.00029085709
3.5	0.00023262908	0.00022405335	0.00021577340	0.00020777983	0.00020006352
3.6	0.00015910859	0.00015309850	0.00014730151	0.00014171061	0.00013631902
3.7	0.00010779973	0.00010362962	0.00009961139	0.00009573989	0.00009201013
3.8	0.00007234804	0.00006948340	0.00006672584	0.00006407163	0.00006151716
3.9	0.00004809634	0.00004614806	0.00004427448	0.00004247293	0.00004074080
4.0	0.00003167124	0.00003035937	0.00002909907	0.00002788843	0.00002672560
4.1	0.00002065751	0.00001978296	0.00001894362	0.00001813816	0.00001736529
4.2	0.00001334575	0.00001276853	0.00001221512	0.00001168457	0.00001117599
4.3	0.00000853991	0.00000816273	0.00000780146	0.00000745547	0.00000712414
4.4	0.00000541254	0.00000516853	0.00000493505	0.00000471165	0.00000449794
4.5	0.00000339767	0.00000324138	0.00000309198	0.00000294918	0.00000281271
4.6	0.00000211245	0.00000201334	0.00000191870	0.00000182833	0.00000174205
4.7	0.00000130081	0.00000123858	0.00000117922	0.00000112260	0.00000106859
4.8	0.00000079333	0.00000075465	0.00000071779	0.00000068267	0.00000064920
4.9	0.00000047918	0.00000045538	0.00000043272	0.00000041115	0.00000039061
5.0	0.00000028665	0.00000027215	0.00000025836	0.00000024524	0.00000023277
5.1	0.00000016983	0.00000016108	0.00000015277	0.00000014487	0.00000013737
5.2	0.00000009964	0.00000009442	0.00000008946	0.00000008476	0.00000008029
5.3	0.00000005790	0.00000005481	0.00000005188	0.00000004911	0.00000004647
5.4	0.00000003332	0.00000003151	0.00000002980	0.00000002818	0.00000002664
5.5	0.00000001899	0.00000001794	0.00000001695	0.00000001601	0.00000001512
5.6	0.00000001072	0.00000001012	0.00000000955	0.00000000901	0.00000000850
5.7	0.00000000599	0.00000000565	0.00000000533	0.00000000502	0.00000000473
5.8	0.00000000332	0.00000000312	0.00000000294	0.00000000277	0.00000000261
5.9	0.00000000182	0.00000000171	0.00000000161	0.00000000151	0.00000000143
6.0	0.00000000099	0.00000000093	0.00000000087	0.00000000082	0.00000000077

Continued

95% Conf. Int.

Continued

z	0.05	0.06	0.07	0.08	0.09
0.0	0.48006119416	0.47607781735	0.47209682982	0.46811862799	0.46414360741
0.1	0.44038230763	0.43644053711	0.43250506832	0.42857628410	0.42465456527
0.2	0.40129367432	0.39743188680	0.39358012680	0.38973875244	0.38590811880
0.3	0.36316934882	0.35942356678	0.35569124520	0.35197270758	0.34826827346
0.4	0.32635522029	0.32275811025	0.31917750878	0.31561369652	0.31206694942
0.5	0.29115968679	0.28773971885	0.28433884905	0.28095730890	0.27759532475
0.6	0.25784611081	0.25462691467	0.25142889510	0.24825223045	0.24509709367
0.7	0.22662735238	0.22362729244	0.22064994634	0.21769543759	0.21476388416
0.8	0.19766254312	0.19489452125	0.19215020210	0.18942965478	0.18673294304
0.9	0.17105612631	0.16852760747	0.16602324606	0.16354305933	0.16108705951
1.0	0.14685905638	0.14457229966	0.14230965436	0.14007109009	0.13785657203
1.1	0.12507193564	0.12302440305	0.12100048442	0.11900010746	0.11702319602
1.2	0.10564977367	0.10383468112	0.10204231507	0.10027256795	0.09852532905
1.3	0.08850799144	0.08691496195	0.08534345082	0.08379332242	0.08226443868
1.4	0.07352925961	0.07214503697	0.07078087699	0.06943662333	0.06811211797
1.5	0.06057075800	0.05937994059	0.05820755564	0.05705343324	0.05591740252
1.6	0.04947146803	0.04845722627	0.04745968180	0.04647865786	0.04551397732
1.7	0.04005915686	0.03920390329	0.03836357036	0.03753798035	0.03672695570
1.8	0.03215677480	0.03144276298	0.03074190893	0.03005403896	0.02937898004
1.9	0.02558805952	0.02499789515	0.02441918528	0.02385176434	0.02329546775
2.0	0.02018221541	0.01969927041	0.01922617223	0.01876276643	0.01830889985
2.1	0.01577760739	0.01538633478	0.01500342297	0.01462873078	0.01426211841
2.2	0.01222447266	0.01191062542	0.01160379152	0.01130384424	0.01101065832
2.3	0.00938670553	0.00913746753	0.00889404263	0.00865631903	0.00842418640
2.4	0.00714281074	0.00694685079	0.00675565261	0.00656911914	0.00638715476
2.5	0.00538614595	0.00523360816	0.00508492575	0.00494001576	0.00479879660
2.6	0.00402458854	0.00390703257	0.00379256235	0.00368110801	0.00357260095
2.7	0.00297976324	0.00289006808	0.00280281463	0.00271794492	0.00263540208
2.8	0.00218596145	0.00211820504	0.00205235899	0.00198837585	0.00192620913
2.9	0.00158886965	0.00153819521	0.00148899875	0.00144124192	0.00139488724

Continued

95% Confidence Interval

$1 - \alpha = .95$

$\alpha = .05$

$\frac{\alpha}{2} = .025$ (find in body of table)

$z \rightarrow 1.96$

Continued

z	0.05	0.06	0.07	0.08	0.09
3.0	0.00114420683	0.00110668496	0.00107029385	0.00103500297	0.00100078248
3.1	0.00081635231	0.00078884569	0.00076219469	0.00073637526	0.00071136397
3.2	0.00057702504	0.00055706107	0.00053773742	0.00051903543	0.00050093691
3.3	0.00040405780	0.00038971236	0.00037584092	0.00036242915	0.00034946312
3.4	0.00028029328	0.00027008769	0.00026022918	0.00025070689	0.00024151027
3.5	0.00019261558	0.00018542740	0.00017849061	0.00017179710	0.00016533898
3.6	0.00013112015	0.00012610762	0.00012127523	0.00011661698	0.00011212703
3.7	0.00008841729	0.00008495668	0.00008162377	0.00007841418	0.00007532364
3.8	0.00005905891	0.00005669351	0.00005441768	0.00005222823	0.00005012211
3.9	0.00003907560	0.00003747488	0.00003593632	0.00003445763	0.00003303665
4.0	0.00002560882	0.00002453636	0.00002350657	0.00002251785	0.00002156866
4.1	0.00001662376	0.00001591238	0.00001522998	0.00001457545	0.00001394772
4.2	0.00001068853	0.00001022135	0.00000977365	0.00000934467	0.00000893366
4.3	0.00000680688	0.00000650312	0.00000621233	0.00000593397	0.00000566753
4.4	0.00000429351	0.00000409798	0.00000391098	0.00000373215	0.00000356116
4.5	0.00000268230	0.00000255768	0.00000243862	0.00000232488	0.00000221623
4.6	0.00000165968	0.00000158105	0.00000150600	0.00000143437	0.00000136603
4.7	0.00000101708	0.00000096796	0.00000092113	0.00000087648	0.00000083391
4.8	0.00000061731	0.00000058693	0.00000055799	0.00000053043	0.00000050418
4.9	0.00000037107	0.00000035247	0.00000033476	0.00000031792	0.00000030190
5.0	0.00000022091	0.00000020963	0.00000019891	0.00000018872	0.00000017903
5.1	0.00000013024	0.00000012347	0.00000011705	0.00000011094	0.00000010515
5.2	0.00000007605	0.00000007203	0.00000006821	0.00000006459	0.00000006116
5.3	0.00000004398	0.00000004161	0.00000003937	0.00000003724	0.00000003523
5.4	0.00000002518	0.00000002381	0.00000002250	0.00000002127	0.00000002010
5.5	0.00000001428	0.00000001349	0.00000001274	0.00000001203	0.00000001135
5.6	0.00000000802	0.00000000757	0.00000000714	0.00000000673	0.00000000635
5.7	0.00000000446	0.00000000421	0.00000000396	0.00000000374	0.00000000352
5.8	0.00000000246	0.00000000231	0.00000000218	0.00000000205	0.00000000193
5.9	0.00000000134	0.00000000126	0.00000000119	0.00000000112	0.00000000105
6.0	0.00000000072	0.00000000068	0.00000000064	0.00000000060	0.00000000056

Appendix F

F Distributions

$F_{0.1}$

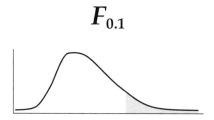

F distribution $F_{0.1}$

	Numerator degrees of freedom										
	1	2	3	4	5	6	7	8	9	10	11
1	39.86	49.50	53.59	55.83	57.24	58.20	58.91	59.44	59.86	60.19	60.47
2	8.53	9.00	9.16	9.24	9.29	9.33	9.35	9.37	9.38	9.39	9.40
3	5.54	5.46	5.39	5.34	5.31	5.28	5.27	5.25	5.24	5.23	5.22
4	4.54	4.32	4.19	4.11	4.05	4.01	3.98	3.95	3.94	3.92	3.91
5	4.06	3.78	3.62	3.52	3.45	3.40	3.37	3.34	3.32	3.30	3.28
6	3.78	3.46	3.29	3.18	3.11	3.05	3.01	2.98	2.96	2.94	2.92
7	3.59	3.26	3.07	2.96	2.88	2.83	2.78	2.75	2.72	2.70	2.68
8	3.46	3.11	2.92	2.81	2.73	2.67	2.62	2.59	2.56	2.54	2.52
9	3.36	3.01	2.81	2.69	2.61	2.55	2.51	2.47	2.44	2.42	2.40
10	3.29	2.92	2.73	2.61	2.52	2.46	2.41	2.38	2.35	2.32	2.30
11	3.23	2.86	2.66	2.54	2.45	2.39	2.34	2.30	2.27	2.25	2.23
12	3.18	2.81	2.61	2.48	2.39	2.33	2.28	2.24	2.21	2.19	2.17
13	3.14	2.76	2.56	2.43	2.35	2.28	2.23	2.20	2.16	2.14	2.12
14	3.10	2.73	2.52	2.39	2.31	2.24	2.19	2.15	2.12	2.10	2.07
15	3.07	2.70	2.49	2.36	2.27	2.21	2.16	2.12	2.09	2.06	2.04
16	3.05	2.67	2.46	2.33	2.24	2.18	2.13	2.09	2.06	2.03	2.01
17	3.03	2.64	2.44	2.31	2.22	2.15	2.10	2.06	2.03	2.00	1.98
18	3.01	2.62	2.42	2.29	2.20	2.13	2.08	2.04	2.00	1.98	1.95
19	2.99	2.61	2.40	2.27	2.18	2.11	2.06	2.02	1.98	1.96	1.93
20	2.97	2.59	2.38	2.25	2.16	2.09	2.04	2.00	1.96	1.94	1.91
21	2.96	2.57	2.36	2.23	2.14	2.08	2.02	1.98	1.95	1.92	1.90
22	2.95	2.56	2.35	2.22	2.13	2.06	2.01	1.97	1.93	1.90	1.88
23	2.94	2.55	2.34	2.21	2.11	2.05	1.99	1.95	1.92	1.89	1.87
24	2.93	2.54	2.33	2.19	2.10	2.04	1.98	1.94	1.91	1.88	1.85
25	2.92	2.53	2.32	2.18	2.09	2.02	1.97	1.93	1.89	1.87	1.84
26	2.91	2.52	2.31	2.17	2.08	2.01	1.96	1.92	1.88	1.86	1.83
27	2.90	2.51	2.30	2.17	2.07	2.00	1.95	1.91	1.87	1.85	1.82
28	2.89	2.50	2.29	2.16	2.06	2.00	1.94	1.90	1.87	1.84	1.81
29	2.89	2.50	2.28	2.15	2.06	1.99	1.93	1.89	1.86	1.83	1.80
30	2.88	2.49	2.28	2.14	2.05	1.98	1.93	1.88	1.85	1.82	1.79
40	2.84	2.44	2.23	2.09	2.00	1.93	1.87	1.83	1.79	1.76	1.74
60	2.79	2.39	2.18	2.04	1.95	1.87	1.82	1.77	1.74	1.71	1.68
100	2.76	2.36	2.14	2.00	1.91	1.83	1.78	1.73	1.69	1.66	1.64

Continued

(left margin label: Denominator degrees of freedom)

F distribution $F_{0.1}$ *(continued)*

		Numerator degrees of freedom									
	12	**13**	**14**	**15**	**16**	**17**	**18**	**19**	**20**	**21**	**22**
1	60.71	60.90	61.07	61.22	61.35	61.46	61.57	61.66	61.74	61.81	61.88
2	9.41	9.41	9.42	9.42	9.43	9.43	9.44	9.44	9.44	9.44	9.45
3	5.22	5.21	5.20	5.20	5.20	5.19	5.19	5.19	5.18	5.18	5.18
4	3.90	3.89	3.88	3.87	3.86	3.86	3.85	3.85	3.84	3.84	3.84
5	3.27	3.26	3.25	3.24	3.23	3.22	3.22	3.21	3.21	3.20	3.20
6	2.90	2.89	2.88	2.87	2.86	2.85	2.85	2.84	2.84	2.83	2.83
7	2.67	2.65	2.64	2.63	2.62	2.61	2.61	2.60	2.59	2.59	2.58
8	2.50	2.49	2.48	2.46	2.45	2.45	2.44	2.43	2.42	2.42	2.41
9	2.38	2.36	2.35	2.34	2.33	2.32	2.31	2.30	2.30	2.29	2.29
10	2.28	2.27	2.26	2.24	2.23	2.22	2.22	2.21	2.20	2.19	2.19
11	2.21	2.19	2.18	2.17	2.16	2.15	2.14	2.13	2.12	2.12	2.11
12	2.15	2.13	2.12	2.10	2.09	2.08	2.08	2.07	2.06	2.05	2.05
13	2.10	2.08	2.07	2.05	2.04	2.03	2.02	2.01	2.01	2.00	1.99
14	2.05	2.04	2.02	2.01	2.00	1.99	1.98	1.97	1.96	1.96	1.95
15	2.02	2.00	1.99	1.97	1.96	1.95	1.94	1.93	1.92	1.92	1.91
16	1.99	1.97	1.95	1.94	1.93	1.92	1.91	1.90	1.89	1.88	1.88
17	1.96	1.94	1.93	1.91	1.90	1.89	1.88	1.87	1.86	1.86	1.85
18	1.93	1.92	1.90	1.89	1.87	1.86	1.85	1.84	1.84	1.83	1.82
19	1.91	1.89	1.88	1.86	1.85	1.84	1.83	1.82	1.81	1.81	1.80
20	1.89	1.87	1.86	1.84	1.83	1.82	1.81	1.80	1.79	1.79	1.78
21	1.87	1.86	1.84	1.83	1.81	1.80	1.79	1.78	1.78	1.77	1.76
22	1.86	1.84	1.83	1.81	1.80	1.79	1.78	1.77	1.76	1.75	1.74
23	1.84	1.83	1.81	1.80	1.78	1.77	1.76	1.75	1.74	1.74	1.73
24	1.83	1.81	1.80	1.78	1.77	1.76	1.75	1.74	1.73	1.72	1.71
25	1.82	1.80	1.79	1.77	1.76	1.75	1.74	1.73	1.72	1.71	1.70
26	1.81	1.79	1.77	1.76	1.75	1.73	1.72	1.71	1.71	1.70	1.69
27	1.80	1.78	1.76	1.75	1.74	1.72	1.71	1.70	1.70	1.69	1.68
28	1.79	1.77	1.75	1.74	1.73	1.71	1.70	1.69	1.69	1.68	1.67
29	1.78	1.76	1.75	1.73	1.72	1.71	1.69	1.68	1.68	1.67	1.66
30	1.77	1.75	1.74	1.72	1.71	1.70	1.69	1.68	1.67	1.66	1.65
40	1.71	1.70	1.68	1.66	1.65	1.64	1.62	1.61	1.61	1.60	1.59
60	1.66	1.64	1.62	1.60	1.59	1.58	1.56	1.55	1.54	1.53	1.53
100	1.61	1.59	1.57	1.56	1.54	1.53	1.52	1.50	1.49	1.48	1.48

Denominator degrees of freedom

Continued

F distribution $F_{0.1}$ (continued)

					Numerator degrees of freedom						
	23	24	25	26	27	28	29	30	40	60	100
1	61.94	62.00	62.05	62.10	62.15	62.19	62.23	62.26	62.53	62.79	63.01
2	9.45	9.45	9.45	9.45	9.45	9.46	9.46	9.46	9.47	9.47	9.48
3	5.18	5.18	5.17	5.17	5.17	5.17	5.17	5.17	5.16	5.15	5.14
4	3.83	3.83	3.83	3.83	3.82	3.82	3.82	3.82	3.80	3.79	3.78
5	3.19	3.19	3.19	3.18	3.18	3.18	3.18	3.17	3.16	3.14	3.13
6	2.82	2.82	2.81	2.81	2.81	2.81	2.80	2.80	2.78	2.76	2.75
7	2.58	2.58	2.57	2.57	2.56	2.56	2.56	2.56	2.54	2.51	2.50
8	2.41	2.40	2.40	2.40	2.39	2.39	2.39	2.38	2.36	2.34	2.32
9	2.28	2.28	2.27	2.27	2.26	2.26	2.26	2.25	2.23	2.21	2.19
10	2.18	2.18	2.17	2.17	2.17	2.16	2.16	2.16	2.13	2.11	2.09
11	2.11	2.10	2.10	2.09	2.09	2.08	2.08	2.08	2.05	2.03	2.01
12	2.04	2.04	2.03	2.03	2.02	2.02	2.01	2.01	1.99	1.96	1.94
13	1.99	1.98	1.98	1.97	1.97	1.96	1.96	1.96	1.93	1.90	1.88
14	1.94	1.94	1.93	1.93	1.92	1.92	1.92	1.91	1.89	1.86	1.83
15	1.90	1.90	1.89	1.89	1.88	1.88	1.88	1.87	1.85	1.82	1.79
16	1.87	1.87	1.86	1.86	1.85	1.85	1.84	1.84	1.81	1.78	1.76
17	1.84	1.84	1.83	1.83	1.82	1.82	1.81	1.81	1.78	1.75	1.73
18	1.82	1.81	1.80	1.80	1.80	1.79	1.79	1.78	1.75	1.72	1.70
19	1.79	1.79	1.78	1.78	1.77	1.77	1.76	1.76	1.73	1.70	1.67
20	1.77	1.77	1.76	1.76	1.75	1.75	1.74	1.74	1.71	1.68	1.65
21	1.75	1.75	1.74	1.74	1.73	1.73	1.72	1.72	1.69	1.66	1.63
22	1.74	1.73	1.73	1.72	1.72	1.71	1.71	1.70	1.67	1.64	1.61
23	1.72	1.72	1.71	1.70	1.70	1.69	1.69	1.69	1.66	1.62	1.59
24	1.71	1.70	1.70	1.69	1.69	1.68	1.68	1.67	1.64	1.61	1.58
25	1.70	1.69	1.68	1.68	1.67	1.67	1.66	1.66	1.63	1.59	1.56
26	1.68	1.68	1.67	1.67	1.66	1.66	1.65	1.65	1.61	1.58	1.55
27	1.67	1.67	1.66	1.65	1.65	1.64	1.64	1.64	1.60	1.57	1.54
28	1.66	1.66	1.65	1.64	1.64	1.63	1.63	1.63	1.59	1.56	1.53
29	1.65	1.65	1.64	1.63	1.63	1.62	1.62	1.62	1.58	1.55	1.52
30	1.64	1.64	1.63	1.63	1.62	1.62	1.61	1.61	1.57	1.54	1.51
40	1.58	1.57	1.57	1.56	1.56	1.55	1.55	1.54	1.51	1.47	1.43
60	1.52	1.51	1.50	1.50	1.49	1.49	1.48	1.48	1.44	1.40	1.36
100	1.47	1.46	1.45	1.45	1.44	1.43	1.43	1.42	1.38	1.34	1.29

Denominator degrees of freedom

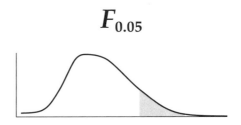

$$F_{0.05}$$

F distribution $F_{0.05}$

					Numerator degrees of freedom						
	1	**2**	**3**	**4**	**5**	**6**	**7**	**8**	**9**	**10**	**11**
1	161.4	199.5	215.7	224.6	230.2	234.0	236.8	238.9	240.5	241.9	243.0
2	18.51	19.00	19.16	19.25	19.30	19.33	19.35	19.37	19.38	19.40	19.40
3	10.13	9.55	9.28	9.12	9.01	8.94	8.89	8.85	8.81	8.79	8.76
4	7.71	6.94	6.59	6.39	6.26	6.16	6.09	6.04	6.00	5.96	5.94
5	6.61	5.79	5.41	5.19	5.05	4.95	4.88	4.82	4.77	4.74	4.70
6	5.99	5.14	4.76	4.53	4.39	4.28	4.21	4.15	4.10	4.06	4.03
7	5.59	4.74	4.35	4.12	3.97	3.87	3.79	3.73	3.68	3.64	3.60
8	5.32	4.46	4.07	3.84	3.69	3.58	3.50	3.44	3.39	3.35	3.31
9	5.12	4.26	3.86	3.63	3.48	3.37	3.29	3.23	3.18	3.14	3.10
10	4.96	4.10	3.71	3.48	3.33	3.22	3.14	3.07	3.02	2.98	2.94
11	4.84	3.98	3.59	3.36	3.20	3.09	3.01	2.95	2.90	2.85	2.82
12	4.75	3.89	3.49	3.26	3.11	3.00	2.91	2.85	2.80	2.75	2.72
13	4.67	3.81	3.41	3.18	3.03	2.92	2.83	2.77	2.71	2.67	2.63
14	4.60	3.74	3.34	3.11	2.96	2.85	2.76	2.70	2.65	2.60	2.57
15	4.54	3.68	3.29	3.06	2.90	2.79	2.71	2.64	2.59	2.54	2.51
16	4.49	3.63	3.24	3.01	2.85	2.74	2.66	2.59	2.54	2.49	2.46
17	4.45	3.59	3.20	2.96	2.81	2.70	2.61	2.55	2.49	2.45	2.41
18	4.41	3.55	3.16	2.93	2.77	2.66	2.58	2.51	2.46	2.41	2.37
19	4.38	3.52	3.13	2.90	2.74	2.63	2.54	2.48	2.42	2.38	2.34
20	4.35	3.49	3.10	2.87	2.71	2.60	2.51	2.45	2.39	2.35	2.31
21	4.32	3.47	3.07	2.84	2.68	2.57	2.49	2.42	2.37	2.32	2.28
22	4.30	3.44	3.05	2.82	2.66	2.55	2.46	2.40	2.34	2.30	2.26
23	4.28	3.42	3.03	2.80	2.64	2.53	2.44	2.37	2.32	2.27	2.24
24	4.26	3.40	3.01	2.78	2.62	2.51	2.42	2.36	2.30	2.25	2.22
25	4.24	3.39	2.99	2.76	2.60	2.49	2.40	2.34	2.28	2.24	2.20
26	4.23	3.37	2.98	2.74	2.59	2.47	2.39	2.32	2.27	2.22	2.18
27	4.21	3.35	2.96	2.73	2.57	2.46	2.37	2.31	2.25	2.20	2.17
28	4.20	3.34	2.95	2.71	2.56	2.45	2.36	2.29	2.24	2.19	2.15
29	4.18	3.33	2.93	2.70	2.55	2.43	2.35	2.28	2.22	2.18	2.14
30	4.17	3.32	2.92	2.69	2.53	2.42	2.33	2.27	2.21	2.16	2.13
40	4.08	3.23	2.84	2.61	2.45	2.34	2.25	2.18	2.12	2.08	2.04
60	4.00	3.15	2.76	2.53	2.37	2.25	2.17	2.10	2.04	1.99	1.95
100	3.94	3.09	2.70	2.46	2.31	2.19	2.10	2.03	1.97	1.93	1.89

Denominator degrees of freedom

Continued

F distribution $F_{0.05}$ *(continued)*

		12	13	14	15	16	17	18	19	20	21	22

		Numerator degrees of freedom										
		12	**13**	**14**	**15**	**16**	**17**	**18**	**19**	**20**	**21**	**22**
	1	243.9	244.7	245.4	245.9	246.5	246.9	247.3	247.7	248.0	248.3	248.6
	2	19.41	19.42	19.42	19.43	19.43	19.44	19.44	19.44	19.45	19.45	19.45
	3	8.74	8.73	8.71	8.70	8.69	8.68	8.67	8.67	8.66	8.65	8.65
	4	5.91	5.89	5.87	5.86	5.84	5.83	5.82	5.81	5.80	5.79	5.79
	5	4.68	4.66	4.64	4.62	4.60	4.59	4.58	4.57	4.56	4.55	4.54
	6	4.00	3.98	3.96	3.94	3.92	3.91	3.90	3.88	3.87	3.86	3.86
	7	3.57	3.55	3.53	3.51	3.49	3.48	3.47	3.46	3.44	3.43	3.43
	8	3.28	3.26	3.24	3.22	3.20	3.19	3.17	3.16	3.15	3.14	3.13
	9	3.07	3.05	3.03	3.01	2.99	2.97	2.96	2.95	2.94	2.93	2.92
	10	2.91	2.89	2.86	2.85	2.83	2.81	2.80	2.79	2.77	2.76	2.75
	11	2.79	2.76	2.74	2.72	2.70	2.69	2.67	2.66	2.65	2.64	2.63
Denominator degrees of freedom	12	2.69	2.66	2.64	2.62	2.60	2.58	2.57	2.56	2.54	2.53	2.52
	13	2.60	2.58	2.55	2.53	2.51	2.50	2.48	2.47	2.46	2.45	2.44
	14	2.53	2.51	2.48	2.46	2.44	2.43	2.41	2.40	2.39	2.38	2.37
	15	2.48	2.45	2.42	2.40	2.38	2.37	2.35	2.34	2.33	2.32	2.31
	16	2.42	2.40	2.37	2.35	2.33	2.32	2.30	2.29	2.28	2.26	2.25
	17	2.38	2.35	2.33	2.31	2.29	2.27	2.26	2.24	2.23	2.22	2.21
	18	2.34	2.31	2.29	2.27	2.25	2.23	2.22	2.20	2.19	2.18	2.17
	19	2.31	2.28	2.26	2.23	2.21	2.20	2.18	2.17	2.16	2.14	2.13
	20	2.28	2.25	2.22	2.20	2.18	2.17	2.15	2.14	2.12	2.11	2.10
	21	2.25	2.22	2.20	2.18	2.16	2.14	2.12	2.11	2.10	2.08	2.07
	22	2.23	2.20	2.17	2.15	2.13	2.11	2.10	2.08	2.07	2.06	2.05
	23	2.20	2.18	2.15	2.13	2.11	2.09	2.08	2.06	2.05	2.04	2.02
	24	2.18	2.15	2.13	2.11	2.09	2.07	2.05	2.04	2.03	2.01	2.00
	25	2.16	2.14	2.11	2.09	2.07	2.05	2.04	2.02	2.01	2.00	1.98
	26	2.15	2.12	2.09	2.07	2.05	2.03	2.02	2.00	1.99	1.98	1.97
	27	2.13	2.10	2.08	2.06	2.04	2.02	2.00	1.99	1.97	1.96	1.95
	28	2.12	2.09	2.06	2.04	2.02	2.00	1.99	1.97	1.96	1.95	1.93
	29	2.10	2.08	2.05	2.03	2.01	1.99	1.97	1.96	1.94	1.93	1.92
	30	2.09	2.06	2.04	2.01	1.99	1.98	1.96	1.95	1.93	1.92	1.91
	40	2.00	1.97	1.95	1.92	1.90	1.89	1.87	1.85	1.84	1.83	1.81
	60	1.92	1.89	1.86	1.84	1.82	1.80	1.78	1.76	1.75	1.73	1.72
	100	1.85	1.82	1.79	1.77	1.75	1.73	1.71	1.69	1.68	1.66	1.65

Continued

F distribution $F_{0.05}$ *(continued)*

					Numerator degrees of freedom						
	23	**24**	**25**	**26**	**27**	**28**	**29**	**30**	**40**	**60**	**100**
1	248.8	249.1	249.3	249.5	249.6	249.8	250.0	250.1	251.1	252.2	253.0
2	19.45	19.45	19.46	19.46	19.46	19.46	19.46	19.46	19.47	19.48	19.49
3	8.64	8.64	8.63	8.63	8.63	8.62	8.62	8.62	8.59	8.57	8.55
4	5.78	5.77	5.77	5.76	5.76	5.75	5.75	5.75	5.72	5.69	5.66
5	4.53	4.53	4.52	4.52	4.51	4.50	4.50	4.50	4.46	4.43	4.41
6	3.85	3.84	3.83	3.83	3.82	3.82	3.81	3.81	3.77	3.74	3.71
7	3.42	3.41	3.40	3.40	3.39	3.39	3.38	3.38	3.34	3.30	3.27
8	3.12	3.12	3.11	3.10	3.10	3.09	3.08	3.08	3.04	3.01	2.97
9	2.91	2.90	2.89	2.89	2.88	2.87	2.87	2.86	2.83	2.79	2.76
10	2.75	2.74	2.73	2.72	2.72	2.71	2.70	2.70	2.66	2.62	2.59
11	2.62	2.61	2.60	2.59	2.59	2.58	2.58	2.57	2.53	2.49	2.46
12	2.51	2.51	2.50	2.49	2.48	2.48	2.47	2.47	2.43	2.38	2.35
13	2.43	2.42	2.41	2.41	2.40	2.39	2.39	2.38	2.34	2.30	2.26
14	2.36	2.35	2.34	2.33	2.33	2.32	2.31	2.31	2.27	2.22	2.19
15	2.30	2.29	2.28	2.27	2.27	2.26	2.25	2.25	2.20	2.16	2.12
16	2.24	2.24	2.23	2.22	2.21	2.21	2.20	2.19	2.15	2.11	2.07
17	2.20	2.19	2.18	2.17	2.17	2.16	2.15	2.15	2.10	2.06	2.02
18	2.16	2.15	2.14	2.13	2.13	2.12	2.11	2.11	2.06	2.02	1.98
19	2.12	2.11	2.11	2.10	2.09	2.08	2.08	2.07	2.03	1.98	1.94
20	2.09	2.08	2.07	2.07	2.06	2.05	2.05	2.04	1.99	1.95	1.91
21	2.06	2.05	2.05	2.04	2.03	2.02	2.02	2.01	1.96	1.92	1.88
22	2.04	2.03	2.02	2.01	2.00	2.00	1.99	1.98	1.94	1.89	1.85
23	2.01	2.01	2.00	1.99	1.98	1.97	1.97	1.96	1.91	1.86	1.82
24	1.99	1.98	1.97	1.97	1.96	1.95	1.95	1.94	1.89	1.84	1.80
25	1.97	1.96	1.96	1.95	1.94	1.93	1.93	1.92	1.87	1.82	1.78
26	1.96	1.95	1.94	1.93	1.92	1.91	1.91	1.90	1.85	1.80	1.76
27	1.94	1.93	1.92	1.91	1.90	1.90	1.89	1.88	1.84	1.79	1.74
28	1.92	1.91	1.91	1.90	1.89	1.88	1.88	1.87	1.82	1.77	1.73
29	1.91	1.90	1.89	1.88	1.88	1.87	1.86	1.85	1.81	1.75	1.71
30	1.90	1.89	1.88	1.87	1.86	1.85	1.85	1.84	1.79	1.74	1.70
40	1.80	1.79	1.78	1.77	1.77	1.76	1.75	1.74	1.69	1.64	1.59
60	1.71	1.70	1.69	1.68	1.67	1.66	1.66	1.65	1.59	1.53	1.48
100	1.64	1.63	1.62	1.61	1.60	1.59	1.58	1.57	1.52	1.45	1.39

Denominator degrees of freedom

$$F_{0.01}$$

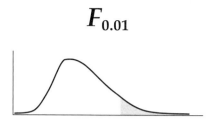

F distribution $F_{0.01}$

	Numerator degrees of freedom										
	1	**2**	**3**	**4**	**5**	**6**	**7**	**8**	**9**	**10**	**11**
1	4052	4999	5404	5624	5764	5859	5928	5981	6022	6056	6083
2	98.5	99	99.16	99.25	99.3	99.33	99.36	99.38	99.39	99.4	99.41
3	34.12	30.82	29.46	28.71	28.24	27.91	27.67	27.49	27.34	27.23	27.13
4	21.2	18	16.69	15.98	15.52	15.21	14.98	14.8	14.66	14.55	14.45
5	16.26	13.27	12.06	11.39	10.97	10.67	10.46	10.29	10.16	10.05	9.963
6	13.75	10.92	9.78	9.148	8.746	8.466	8.26	8.102	7.976	7.874	7.79
7	12.25	9.547	8.451	7.847	7.46	7.191	6.993	6.84	6.719	6.62	6.538
8	11.26	8.649	7.591	7.006	6.632	6.371	6.178	6.029	5.911	5.814	5.734
9	10.56	8.022	6.992	6.422	6.057	5.802	5.613	5.467	5.351	5.257	5.178
10	10.04	7.559	6.552	5.994	5.636	5.386	5.2	5.057	4.942	4.849	4.772
11	9.646	7.206	6.217	5.668	5.316	5.069	4.886	4.744	4.632	4.539	4.462
12	9.33	6.927	5.953	5.412	5.064	4.821	4.64	4.499	4.388	4.296	4.22
13	9.074	6.701	5.739	5.205	4.862	4.62	4.441	4.302	4.191	4.1	4.025
14	8.862	6.515	5.564	5.035	4.695	4.456	4.278	4.14	4.03	3.939	3.864
15	8.683	6.359	5.417	4.893	4.556	4.318	4.142	4.004	3.895	3.805	3.73
16	8.531	6.226	5.292	4.773	4.437	4.202	4.026	3.89	3.78	3.691	3.616
17	8.4	6.112	5.185	4.669	4.336	4.101	3.927	3.791	3.682	3.593	3.518
18	8.285	6.013	5.092	4.579	4.248	4.015	3.841	3.705	3.597	3.508	3.434
19	8.185	5.926	5.01	4.5	4.171	3.939	3.765	3.631	3.523	3.434	3.36
20	8.096	5.849	4.938	4.431	4.103	3.871	3.699	3.564	3.457	3.368	3.294
21	8.017	5.78	4.874	4.369	4.042	3.812	3.64	3.506	3.398	3.31	3.236
22	7.945	5.719	4.817	4.313	3.988	3.758	3.587	3.453	3.346	3.258	3.184
23	7.881	5.664	4.765	4.264	3.939	3.71	3.539	3.406	3.299	3.211	3.137
24	7.823	5.614	4.718	4.218	3.895	3.667	3.496	3.363	3.256	3.168	3.094
25	7.77	5.568	4.675	4.177	3.855	3.627	3.457	3.324	3.217	3.129	3.056
26	7.721	5.526	4.637	4.14	3.818	3.591	3.421	3.288	3.182	3.094	3.021
27	7.677	5.488	4.601	4.106	3.785	3.558	3.388	3.256	3.149	3.062	2.988
28	7.636	5.453	4.568	4.074	3.754	3.528	3.358	3.226	3.12	3.032	2.959
29	7.598	5.42	4.538	4.045	3.725	3.499	3.33	3.198	3.092	3.005	2.931
30	7.562	5.39	4.51	4.018	3.699	3.473	3.305	3.173	3.067	2.979	2.906
40	7.314	5.178	4.313	3.828	3.514	3.291	3.124	2.993	2.888	2.801	2.727
60	7.077	4.977	4.126	3.649	3.339	3.119	2.953	2.823	2.718	2.632	2.559
100	6.895	4.824	3.984	3.513	3.206	2.988	2.823	2.694	2.59	2.503	2.43

(Denominator degrees of freedom — left column)

Continued

F distribution $F_{0.01}$ *(continued)*

	Numerator degrees of freedom										
	12	13	14	15	16	17	18	19	20	21	22
1	6107	6126	6143	6157	6170	6181	6191	6201	6208.7	6216.1	6223.1
2	99.42	99.42	99.43	99.43	99.44	99.44	99.44	99.45	99.448	99.451	99.455
3	27.05	26.98	26.92	26.87	26.83	26.79	26.75	26.72	26.69	26.664	26.639
4	14.37	14.31	14.25	14.2	14.15	14.11	14.08	14.05	14.019	13.994	13.97
5	9.888	9.825	9.77	9.722	9.68	9.643	9.609	9.58	9.5527	9.5281	9.5058
6	7.718	7.657	7.605	7.559	7.519	7.483	7.451	7.422	7.3958	7.3721	7.3506
7	6.469	6.41	6.359	6.314	6.275	6.24	6.209	6.181	6.1555	6.1324	6.1113
8	5.667	5.609	5.559	5.515	5.477	5.442	5.412	5.384	5.3591	5.3365	5.3157
9	5.111	5.055	5.005	4.962	4.924	4.89	4.86	4.833	4.808	4.7855	4.7651
10	4.706	4.65	4.601	4.558	4.52	4.487	4.457	4.43	4.4054	4.3831	4.3628
11	4.397	4.342	4.293	4.251	4.213	4.18	4.15	4.123	4.099	4.0769	4.0566
12	4.155	4.1	4.052	4.01	3.972	3.939	3.91	3.883	3.8584	3.8363	3.8161
13	3.96	3.905	3.857	3.815	3.778	3.745	3.716	3.689	3.6646	3.6425	3.6223
14	3.8	3.745	3.698	3.656	3.619	3.586	3.556	3.529	3.5052	3.4832	3.463
15	3.666	3.612	3.564	3.522	3.485	3.452	3.423	3.396	3.3719	3.3498	3.3297
16	3.553	3.498	3.451	3.409	3.372	3.339	3.31	3.283	3.2587	3.2367	3.2165
17	3.455	3.401	3.353	3.312	3.275	3.242	3.212	3.186	3.1615	3.1394	3.1192
18	3.371	3.316	3.269	3.227	3.19	3.158	3.128	3.101	3.0771	3.055	3.0348
19	3.297	3.242	3.195	3.153	3.116	3.084	3.054	3.027	3.0031	2.981	2.9607
20	3.231	3.177	3.13	3.088	3.051	3.018	2.989	2.962	2.9377	2.9156	2.8953
21	3.173	3.119	3.072	3.03	2.993	2.96	2.931	2.904	2.8795	2.8574	2.837
22	3.121	3.067	3.019	2.978	2.941	2.908	2.879	2.852	2.8274	2.8052	2.7849
23	3.074	3.02	2.973	2.931	2.894	2.861	2.832	2.805	2.7805	2.7582	2.7378
24	3.032	2.977	2.93	2.889	2.852	2.819	2.789	2.762	2.738	2.7157	2.6953
25	2.993	2.939	2.892	2.85	2.813	2.78	2.751	2.724	2.6993	2.677	2.6565
26	2.958	2.904	2.857	2.815	2.778	2.745	2.715	2.688	2.664	2.6416	2.6211
27	2.926	2.872	2.824	2.783	2.746	2.713	2.683	2.656	2.6316	2.609	2.5886
28	2.896	2.842	2.795	2.753	2.716	2.683	2.653	2.626	2.6018	2.5793	2.5587
29	2.868	2.814	2.767	2.726	2.689	2.656	2.626	2.599	2.5742	2.5517	2.5311
30	2.843	2.789	2.742	2.7	2.663	2.63	2.6	2.573	2.5487	2.5262	2.5055
40	2.665	2.611	2.563	2.522	2.484	2.451	2.421	2.394	2.3689	2.3461	2.3252
60	2.496	2.442	2.394	2.352	2.315	2.281	2.251	2.223	2.1978	2.1747	2.1533
10	2.368	2.313	2.265	2.223	2.185	2.151	2.12	2.092	2.0666	2.0431	2.0214

Continued

F distribution $F_{0.01}$ *(continued)*

		23	24	25	26	27	28	29	30	40	60	100

Numerator degrees of freedom

	23	24	25	26	27	28	29	30	40	60	100
1	6228.7	6234.3	6239.9	6244.5	6249.2	6252.9	6257.1	6260.4	6286.4	6313	6333.9
2	99.455	99.455	99.459	99.462	99.462	99.462	99.462	99.466	99.477	99.484	99.491
3	26.617	26.597	26.579	26.562	26.546	26.531	26.517	26.504	26.411	26.316	26.241
4	13.949	13.929	13.911	13.894	13.878	13.864	13.85	13.838	13.745	13.652	13.577
5	9.4853	9.4665	9.4492	9.4331	9.4183	9.4044	9.3914	9.3794	9.2912	9.202	9.13
6	7.3309	7.3128	7.296	7.2805	7.2661	7.2528	7.2403	7.2286	7.1432	7.0568	6.9867
7	6.092	6.0743	6.0579	6.0428	6.0287	6.0156	6.0035	5.992	5.9084	5.8236	5.7546
8	5.2967	5.2793	5.2631	5.2482	5.2344	5.2214	5.2094	5.1981	5.1156	5.0316	4.9633
9	4.7463	4.729	4.713	4.6982	4.6845	4.6717	4.6598	4.6486	4.5667	4.4831	4.415
10	4.3441	4.3269	4.3111	4.2963	4.2827	4.27	4.2582	4.2469	4.1653	4.0819	4.0137
11	4.038	4.0209	4.0051	3.9904	3.9768	3.9641	3.9522	3.9411	3.8596	3.7761	3.7077
12	3.7976	3.7805	3.7647	3.7501	3.7364	3.7238	3.7119	3.7008	3.6192	3.5355	3.4668
13	3.6038	3.5868	3.571	3.5563	3.5427	3.53	3.5182	3.507	3.4253	3.3413	3.2723
14	3.4445	3.4274	3.4116	3.3969	3.3833	3.3706	3.3587	3.3476	3.2657	3.1813	3.1118
15	3.3111	3.294	3.2782	3.2636	3.2499	3.2372	3.2253	3.2141	3.1319	3.0471	2.9772
16	3.1979	3.1808	3.165	3.1503	3.1366	3.1238	3.1119	3.1007	3.0182	2.933	2.8627
17	3.1006	3.0835	3.0676	3.0529	3.0392	3.0264	3.0145	3.0032	2.9204	2.8348	2.7639
18	3.0161	2.999	2.9831	2.9683	2.9546	2.9418	2.9298	2.9185	2.8354	2.7493	2.6779
19	2.9421	2.9249	2.9089	2.8942	2.8804	2.8675	2.8555	2.8442	2.7608	2.6742	2.6023
20	2.8766	2.8594	2.8434	2.8286	2.8148	2.8019	2.7898	2.7785	2.6947	2.6077	2.5353
21	2.8183	2.801	2.785	2.7702	2.7563	2.7434	2.7313	2.72	2.6359	2.5484	2.4755
22	2.7661	2.7488	2.7328	2.7179	2.704	2.691	2.6789	2.6675	2.5831	2.4951	2.4218
23	2.7191	2.7017	2.6857	2.6707	2.6568	2.6438	2.6316	2.6202	2.5355	2.4471	2.3732
24	2.6764	2.6591	2.643	2.628	2.614	2.601	2.5888	2.5773	2.4923	2.4035	2.3291
25	2.6377	2.6203	2.6041	2.5891	2.5751	2.562	2.5498	2.5383	2.453	2.3637	2.2888
26	2.6022	2.5848	2.5686	2.5535	2.5395	2.5264	2.5142	2.5026	2.417	2.3273	2.2519
27	2.5697	2.5522	2.536	2.5209	2.5069	2.4937	2.4814	2.4699	2.384	2.2938	2.218
28	2.5398	2.5223	2.506	2.4909	2.4768	2.4636	2.4513	2.4397	2.3535	2.2629	2.1867
29	2.5121	2.4946	2.4783	2.4631	2.449	2.4358	2.4234	2.4118	2.3253	2.2344	2.1577
30	2.4865	2.4689	2.4526	2.4374	2.4233	2.41	2.3976	2.386	2.2992	2.2079	2.1307
40	2.3059	2.288	2.2714	2.2559	2.2415	2.228	2.2153	2.2034	2.1142	2.0194	1.9383
60	2.1336	2.1154	2.0984	2.0825	2.0677	2.0538	2.0408	2.0285	1.936	1.8363	1.7493
100	2.0012	1.9826	1.9651	1.9489	1.9337	1.9194	1.9059	1.8933	1.7972	1.6918	1.5977

Denominator degrees of freedom

Appendix G

Binomial Distribution

Probability of x or fewer occurrences in a sample of size n

Binomial distribution

n	x	0.01	0.02	0.03	0.04	0.05	0.06	0.07	0.08	0.09	0.10	0.15	0.20	0.25	0.30	0.35	0.40	0.45	0.50
2	0	0.980	0.960	0.941	0.922	0.903	0.884	0.865	0.846	0.828	0.810	0.723	0.640	0.563	0.490	0.423	0.360	0.303	0.250
2	1	1.000	1.000	0.999	0.998	0.998	0.996	0.995	0.994	0.992	0.990	0.978	0.960	0.938	0.910	0.878	0.840	0.798	0.750
3	0	0.970	0.941	0.913	0.885	0.857	0.831	0.804	0.779	0.754	0.729	0.614	0.512	0.422	0.343	0.275	0.216	0.166	0.125
3	1	1.000	0.999	0.997	0.995	0.993	0.990	0.986	0.982	0.977	0.972	0.939	0.896	0.844	0.784	0.718	0.648	0.575	0.500
3	2	1.000	1.000	1.000	1.000	1.000	1.000	1.000	0.999	0.999	0.999	0.997	0.992	0.984	0.973	0.957	0.936	0.909	0.875
4	0	0.961	0.922	0.885	0.849	0.815	0.781	0.748	0.716	0.686	0.656	0.522	0.410	0.316	0.240	0.179	0.130	0.092	0.063
4	1	0.999	0.998	0.995	0.991	0.986	0.980	0.973	0.966	0.957	0.948	0.890	0.819	0.738	0.652	0.563	0.475	0.391	0.313
4	2	1.000	1.000	1.000	1.000	1.000	0.999	0.999	0.998	0.997	0.996	0.988	0.973	0.949	0.916	0.874	0.821	0.759	0.688
4	3	1.000	1.000	1.000	1.000	1.000	1.000	1.000	1.000	1.000	1.000	0.999	0.998	0.996	0.992	0.985	0.974	0.959	0.938
5	0	0.951	0.904	0.859	0.815	0.774	0.734	0.696	0.659	0.624	0.590	0.444	0.328	0.237	0.168	0.116	0.078	0.050	0.031
5	1	0.999	0.996	0.992	0.985	0.977	0.968	0.958	0.946	0.933	0.919	0.835	0.737	0.633	0.528	0.428	0.337	0.256	0.188
5	2	1.000	1.000	1.000	0.999	0.999	0.998	0.997	0.995	0.994	0.991	0.973	0.942	0.896	0.837	0.765	0.683	0.593	0.500
5	3	1.000	1.000	1.000	1.000	1.000	1.000	1.000	1.000	1.000	1.000	0.998	0.993	0.984	0.969	0.946	0.913	0.869	0.813
5	4	1.000	1.000	1.000	1.000	1.000	1.000	1.000	1.000	1.000	1.000	1.000	1.000	0.999	0.998	0.995	0.990	0.982	0.969
6	0	0.941	0.886	0.833	0.783	0.735	0.690	0.647	0.606	0.568	0.531	0.377	0.262	0.178	0.118	0.075	0.047	0.028	0.016
6	1	0.999	0.994	0.988	0.978	0.967	0.954	0.939	0.923	0.905	0.886	0.776	0.655	0.534	0.420	0.319	0.233	0.164	0.109
6	2	1.000	1.000	0.999	0.999	0.998	0.996	0.994	0.991	0.988	0.984	0.953	0.901	0.831	0.744	0.647	0.544	0.442	0.344
6	3	1.000	1.000	1.000	1.000	1.000	1.000	1.000	0.999	0.999	0.999	0.994	0.983	0.962	0.930	0.883	0.821	0.745	0.656
6	4	1.000	1.000	1.000	1.000	1.000	1.000	1.000	1.000	1.000	1.000	1.000	0.998	0.995	0.989	0.978	0.959	0.931	0.891
6	5	1.000	1.000	1.000	1.000	1.000	1.000	1.000	1.000	1.000	1.000	1.000	1.000	1.000	0.999	0.998	0.996	0.992	0.984
7	0	0.932	0.868	0.808	0.751	0.698	0.648	0.602	0.558	0.517	0.478	0.321	0.210	0.133	0.082	0.049	0.028	0.015	0.008
7	1	0.998	0.992	0.983	0.971	0.956	0.938	0.919	0.897	0.875	0.850	0.717	0.577	0.445	0.329	0.234	0.159	0.102	0.063
7	2	1.000	1.000	0.999	0.998	0.996	0.994	0.990	0.986	0.981	0.974	0.926	0.852	0.756	0.647	0.532	0.420	0.316	0.227
7	3	1.000	1.000	1.000	1.000	1.000	1.000	0.999	0.999	0.998	0.997	0.988	0.967	0.929	0.874	0.800	0.710	0.608	0.500
7	4	1.000	1.000	1.000	1.000	1.000	1.000	1.000	1.000	1.000	1.000	0.999	0.995	0.987	0.971	0.944	0.904	0.847	0.773
7	5	1.000	1.000	1.000	1.000	1.000	1.000	1.000	1.000	1.000	1.000	1.000	1.000	0.999	0.996	0.991	0.981	0.964	0.938
7	6	1.000	1.000	1.000	1.000	1.000	1.000	1.000	1.000	1.000	1.000	1.000	1.000	1.000	1.000	0.999	0.998	0.996	0.992

Continued

Binomial distribution *(continued)*

n	x	0.01	0.02	0.03	0.04	0.05	0.06	0.07	0.08	0.09	0.10	0.15	0.20	0.25	0.30	0.35	0.40	0.45	0.50
8	0	0.923	0.851	0.784	0.721	0.663	0.610	0.560	0.513	0.470	0.430	0.272	0.168	0.100	0.058	0.032	0.017	0.008	0.004
8	1	0.997	0.990	0.978	0.962	0.943	0.921	0.897	0.870	0.842	0.813	0.657	0.503	0.367	0.255	0.169	0.106	0.063	0.035
8	2	1.000	1.000	0.999	0.997	0.994	0.990	0.985	0.979	0.971	0.962	0.895	0.797	0.679	0.552	0.428	0.315	0.220	0.145
8	3	1.000	1.000	1.000	1.000	1.000	0.999	0.999	0.998	0.997	0.995	0.979	0.944	0.886	0.806	0.706	0.594	0.477	0.363
8	4	1.000	1.000	1.000	1.000	1.000	1.000	1.000	1.000	1.000	1.000	0.997	0.990	0.973	0.942	0.894	0.826	0.740	0.637
8	5	1.000	1.000	1.000	1.000	1.000	1.000	1.000	1.000	1.000	1.000	1.000	0.999	0.996	0.989	0.975	0.950	0.912	0.855
8	6	1.000	1.000	1.000	1.000	1.000	1.000	1.000	1.000	1.000	1.000	1.000	1.000	1.000	0.999	0.996	0.991	0.982	0.965
8	7	1.000	1.000	1.000	1.000	1.000	1.000	1.000	1.000	1.000	1.000	1.000	1.000	1.000	1.000	1.000	0.999	0.998	0.996
9	0	0.914	0.834	0.760	0.693	0.630	0.573	0.520	0.472	0.428	0.387	0.232	0.134	0.075	0.040	0.021	0.010	0.005	0.002
9	1	0.997	0.987	0.972	0.952	0.929	0.902	0.873	0.842	0.809	0.775	0.599	0.436	0.300	0.196	0.121	0.071	0.039	0.020
9	2	1.000	0.999	0.998	0.996	0.992	0.986	0.979	0.970	0.960	0.947	0.859	0.738	0.601	0.463	0.337	0.232	0.150	0.090
9	3	1.000	1.000	1.000	1.000	0.999	0.999	0.998	0.996	0.994	0.992	0.966	0.914	0.834	0.730	0.609	0.483	0.361	0.254
9	4	1.000	1.000	1.000	1.000	1.000	1.000	1.000	1.000	0.999	0.999	0.994	0.980	0.951	0.901	0.828	0.733	0.621	0.500
9	5	1.000	1.000	1.000	1.000	1.000	1.000	1.000	1.000	1.000	1.000	0.999	0.997	0.990	0.975	0.946	0.901	0.834	0.746
9	6	1.000	1.000	1.000	1.000	1.000	1.000	1.000	1.000	1.000	1.000	1.000	1.000	0.999	0.996	0.989	0.975	0.950	0.910
9	7	1.000	1.000	1.000	1.000	1.000	1.000	1.000	1.000	1.000	1.000	1.000	1.000	1.000	1.000	0.999	0.996	0.991	0.980
9	8	1.000	1.000	1.000	1.000	1.000	1.000	1.000	1.000	1.000	1.000	1.000	1.000	1.000	1.000	1.000	1.000	0.999	0.998
10	0	0.904	0.817	0.737	0.665	0.599	0.539	0.484	0.434	0.389	0.349	0.197	0.107	0.056	0.028	0.013	0.006	0.003	0.001
10	1	0.996	0.984	0.965	0.942	0.914	0.882	0.848	0.812	0.775	0.736	0.544	0.376	0.244	0.149	0.086	0.046	0.023	0.011
10	2	1.000	0.999	0.997	0.994	0.988	0.981	0.972	0.960	0.946	0.930	0.820	0.678	0.526	0.383	0.262	0.167	0.100	0.055
10	3	1.000	1.000	1.000	1.000	0.999	0.998	0.996	0.994	0.991	0.987	0.950	0.879	0.776	0.650	0.514	0.382	0.266	0.172
10	4	1.000	1.000	1.000	1.000	1.000	1.000	1.000	0.999	0.999	0.998	0.990	0.967	0.922	0.850	0.751	0.633	0.504	0.377
10	5	1.000	1.000	1.000	1.000	1.000	1.000	1.000	1.000	1.000	1.000	0.999	0.994	0.980	0.953	0.905	0.834	0.738	0.623

Appendix H

Chi-Square Distribution

Chi-square distribution

df	$\chi^2_{0.995}$	$\chi^2_{0.99}$	$\chi^2_{0.975}$	$\chi^2_{0.95}$	$\chi^2_{0.90}$	$\chi^2_{0.10}$	$\chi^2_{0.05}$	$\chi^2_{0.025}$	$\chi^2_{0.01}$	$\chi^2_{0.005}$
1	0.000	0.000	0.001	0.004	0.016	2.706	3.841	5.024	6.635	7.879
2	0.010	0.020	0.051	0.103	0.211	4.605	5.991	7.378	9.210	10.597
3	0.072	0.115	0.216	0.352	0.584	6.251	7.815	9.348	11.345	12.838
4	0.207	0.297	0.484	0.711	1.064	7.779	9.488	11.143	13.277	14.860
5	0.412	0.554	0.831	1.145	1.610	9.236	11.070	12.832	15.086	16.750
6	0.676	0.872	1.237	1.635	2.204	10.645	12.592	14.449	16.812	18.548
7	0.989	1.239	1.690	2.167	2.833	12.017	14.067	16.013	18.475	20.278
8	1.344	1.647	2.180	2.733	3.490	13.362	15.507	17.535	20.090	21.955
9	1.735	2.088	2.700	3.325	4.168	14.684	16.919	19.023	21.666	23.589
10	2.156	2.558	3.247	3.940	4.865	15.987	18.307	20.483	23.209	25.188
11	2.603	3.053	3.816	4.575	5.578	17.275	19.675	21.920	24.725	26.757
12	3.074	3.571	4.404	5.226	6.304	18.549	21.026	23.337	26.217	28.300
13	3.565	4.107	5.009	5.892	7.041	19.812	22.362	24.736	27.688	29.819
14	4.075	4.660	5.629	6.571	7.790	21.064	23.685	26.119	29.141	31.319
15	4.601	5.229	6.262	7.261	8.547	22.307	24.996	27.488	30.578	32.801
16	5.142	5.812	6.908	7.962	9.312	23.542	26.296	28.845	32.000	34.267
17	5.697	6.408	7.564	8.672	10.085	24.769	27.587	30.191	33.409	35.718
18	6.265	7.015	8.231	9.390	10.865	25.989	28.869	31.526	34.805	37.156
19	6.844	7.633	8.907	10.117	11.651	27.204	30.144	32.852	36.191	38.582
20	7.434	8.260	9.591	10.851	12.443	28.412	31.410	34.170	37.566	39.997
21	8.034	8.897	10.283	11.591	13.240	29.615	32.671	35.479	38.932	41.401
22	8.643	9.542	10.982	12.338	14.041	30.813	33.924	36.781	40.289	42.796
23	9.260	10.196	11.689	13.091	14.848	32.007	35.172	38.076	41.638	44.181
24	9.886	10.856	12.401	13.848	15.659	33.196	36.415	39.364	42.980	45.558
25	10.520	11.524	13.120	14.611	16.473	34.382	37.652	40.646	44.314	46.928
26	11.160	12.198	13.844	15.379	17.292	35.563	38.885	41.923	45.642	48.290
27	11.808	12.878	14.573	16.151	18.114	36.741	40.113	43.195	46.963	49.645
28	12.461	13.565	15.308	16.928	18.939	37.916	41.337	44.461	48.278	50.994

Continued

Chi-square distribution *(continued)*

df	$\chi^2_{0.995}$	$\chi^2_{0.99}$	$\chi^2_{0.975}$	$\chi^2_{0.95}$	$\chi^2_{0.90}$	$\chi^2_{0.10}$	$\chi^2_{0.05}$	$\chi^2_{0.025}$	$\chi^2_{0.01}$	$\chi^2_{0.005}$
29	13.121	14.256	16.047	17.708	19.768	39.087	42.557	45.722	49.588	52.335
30	13.787	14.953	16.791	18.493	20.599	40.256	43.773	46.979	50.892	53.672
31	14.458	15.655	17.539	19.281	21.434	41.422	44.985	48.232	52.191	55.002
32	15.134	16.362	18.291	20.072	22.271	42.585	46.194	49.480	53.486	56.328
33	15.815	17.073	19.047	20.867	23.110	43.745	47.400	50.725	54.775	57.648
34	16.501	17.789	19.806	21.664	23.952	44.903	48.602	51.966	56.061	58.964
35	17.192	18.509	20.569	22.465	24.797	46.059	49.802	53.203	57.342	60.275
40	20.707	22.164	24.433	26.509	29.051	51.805	55.758	59.342	63.691	66.766
45	24.311	25.901	28.366	30.612	33.350	57.505	61.656	65.410	69.957	73.166
50	27.991	29.707	32.357	34.764	37.689	63.167	67.505	71.420	76.154	79.490
55	31.735	33.571	36.398	38.958	42.060	68.796	73.311	77.380	82.292	85.749
60	35.534	37.485	40.482	43.188	46.459	74.397	79.082	83.298	88.379	91.952
65	39.383	41.444	44.603	47.450	50.883	79.973	84.821	89.177	94.422	98.105
70	43.275	45.442	48.758	51.739	55.329	85.527	90.531	95.023	100.425	104.215
75	47.206	49.475	52.942	56.054	59.795	91.061	96.217	100.839	106.393	110.285
80	51.172	53.540	57.153	60.391	64.278	96.578	101.879	106.629	112.329	116.321
85	55.170	57.634	61.389	64.749	68.777	102.079	107.522	112.393	118.236	122.324
90	59.196	61.754	65.647	69.126	73.291	107.565	113.145	118.136	124.116	128.299
95	63.250	65.898	69.925	73.520	77.818	113.038	118.752	123.858	129.973	134.247
100	67.328	70.065	74.222	77.929	82.358	118.498	124.342	129.561	135.807	140.170

Appendix I

Exponential Distribution

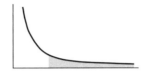

Exponential distribution

X	Area to left of X	Area to right of X
0	0.00000	1.00000
0.1	0.09516	0.90484
0.2	0.18127	0.81873
0.3	0.25918	0.74082
0.4	0.32968	0.67032
0.5	0.39347	0.60653
0.6	0.45119	0.54881
0.7	0.50341	0.49659
0.8	0.55067	0.44933
0.9	0.59343	0.40657
1	0.63212	0.36788
1.1	0.66713	0.33287
1.2	0.69881	0.30119
1.3	0.72747	0.27253
1.4	0.75340	0.24660
1.5	0.77687	0.22313
1.6	0.79810	0.20190
1.7	0.81732	0.18268
1.8	0.83470	0.16530
1.9	0.85043	0.14957
2	0.86466	0.13534
2.1	0.87754	0.12246
2.2	0.88920	0.11080
2.3	0.89974	0.10026
2.4	0.90928	0.09072
2.5	0.91792	0.08208
2.6	0.92573	0.07427

Continued

Exponential distribution *(continued)*

X	Area to left of X	Area to right of X
2.7	0.93279	0.06721
2.8	0.93919	0.06081
2.9	0.94498	0.05502
3	0.95021	0.04979
3.1	0.95495	0.04505
3.2	0.95924	0.04076
3.3	0.96312	0.03688
3.4	0.96663	0.03337
3.5	0.96980	0.03020
3.6	0.97268	0.02732
3.7	0.97528	0.02472
3.8	0.97763	0.02237
3.9	0.97976	0.02024
4	0.98168	0.01832
4.1	0.98343	0.01657
4.2	0.98500	0.01500
4.3	0.98643	0.01357
4.4	0.98772	0.01228
4.5	0.98889	0.01111
4.6	0.98995	0.01005
4.7	0.99090	0.00910
4.8	0.99177	0.00823
4.9	0.99255	0.00745
5	0.99326	0.00674
5.1	0.99390	0.00610
5.2	0.99448	0.00552
5.3	0.99501	0.00499
5.4	0.99548	0.00452
5.5	0.99591	0.00409
5.6	0.99630	0.00370
5.7	0.99665	0.00335
5.8	0.99697	0.00303
5.9	0.99726	0.00274
6	0.99752	0.00248

Appendix J

Poisson Distribution

Probability of x or fewer occurrences of an event

Poisson distribution

$\lambda\downarrow x\rightarrow$	0	1	2	3	4	5	6	7	8	9	10	11	12	13	14	15	16	17
0.005	0.995	1.000	1.000	1.000	1.000	1.000	1.000	1.000	1.000	1.000	1.000	1.000	1.000	1.000	1.000	1.000	1.000	1.000
0.01	0.990	1.000	1.000	1.000	1.000	1.000	1.000	1.000	1.000	1.000	1.000	1.000	1.000	1.000	1.000	1.000	1.000	1.000
0.02	0.980	1.000	1.000	1.000	1.000	1.000	1.000	1.000	1.000	1.000	1.000	1.000	1.000	1.000	1.000	1.000	1.000	1.000
0.03	0.970	1.000	1.000	1.000	1.000	1.000	1.000	1.000	1.000	1.000	1.000	1.000	1.000	1.000	1.000	1.000	1.000	1.000
0.04	0.961	0.999	1.000	1.000	1.000	1.000	1.000	1.000	1.000	1.000	1.000	1.000	1.000	1.000	1.000	1.000	1.000	1.000
0.05	0.951	0.999	1.000	1.000	1.000	1.000	1.000	1.000	1.000	1.000	1.000	1.000	1.000	1.000	1.000	1.000	1.000	1.000
0.06	0.942	0.998	1.000	1.000	1.000	1.000	1.000	1.000	1.000	1.000	1.000	1.000	1.000	1.000	1.000	1.000	1.000	1.000
0.07	0.932	0.998	1.000	1.000	1.000	1.000	1.000	1.000	1.000	1.000	1.000	1.000	1.000	1.000	1.000	1.000	1.000	1.000
0.08	0.923	0.997	1.000	1.000	1.000	1.000	1.000	1.000	1.000	1.000	1.000	1.000	1.000	1.000	1.000	1.000	1.000	1.000
0.09	0.914	0.996	1.000	1.000	1.000	1.000	1.000	1.000	1.000	1.000	1.000	1.000	1.000	1.000	1.000	1.000	1.000	1.000
0.1	0.905	0.995	1.000	1.000	1.000	1.000	1.000	1.000	1.000	1.000	1.000	1.000	1.000	1.000	1.000	1.000	1.000	1.000
0.15	0.861	0.990	0.999	1.000	1.000	1.000	1.000	1.000	1.000	1.000	1.000	1.000	1.000	1.000	1.000	1.000	1.000	1.000
0.2	0.819	0.982	0.999	1.000	1.000	1.000	1.000	1.000	1.000	1.000	1.000	1.000	1.000	1.000	1.000	1.000	1.000	1.000
0.25	0.779	0.974	0.998	1.000	1.000	1.000	1.000	1.000	1.000	1.000	1.000	1.000	1.000	1.000	1.000	1.000	1.000	1.000
0.3	0.741	0.963	0.996	1.000	1.000	1.000	1.000	1.000	1.000	1.000	1.000	1.000	1.000	1.000	1.000	1.000	1.000	1.000
0.35	0.705	0.951	0.994	1.000	1.000	1.000	1.000	1.000	1.000	1.000	1.000	1.000	1.000	1.000	1.000	1.000	1.000	1.000
0.4	0.670	0.938	0.992	0.999	1.000	1.000	1.000	1.000	1.000	1.000	1.000	1.000	1.000	1.000	1.000	1.000	1.000	1.000
0.5	0.607	0.910	0.986	0.998	1.000	1.000	1.000	1.000	1.000	1.000	1.000	1.000	1.000	1.000	1.000	1.000	1.000	1.000
0.6	0.549	0.878	0.977	0.997	1.000	1.000	1.000	1.000	1.000	1.000	1.000	1.000	1.000	1.000	1.000	1.000	1.000	1.000
0.7	0.497	0.844	0.966	0.994	0.999	1.000	1.000	1.000	1.000	1.000	1.000	1.000	1.000	1.000	1.000	1.000	1.000	1.000
0.8	0.449	0.809	0.953	0.991	0.999	1.000	1.000	1.000	1.000	1.000	1.000	1.000	1.000	1.000	1.000	1.000	1.000	1.000
0.9	0.407	0.772	0.937	0.987	0.998	1.000	1.000	1.000	1.000	1.000	1.000	1.000	1.000	1.000	1.000	1.000	1.000	1.000
1	0.368	0.736	0.920	0.981	0.996	0.999	1.000	1.000	1.000	1.000	1.000	1.000	1.000	1.000	1.000	1.000	1.000	1.000
1.2	0.301	0.663	0.879	0.966	0.992	0.998	1.000	1.000	1.000	1.000	1.000	1.000	1.000	1.000	1.000	1.000	1.000	1.000
1.4	0.247	0.592	0.833	0.946	0.986	0.997	0.999	1.000	1.000	1.000	1.000	1.000	1.000	1.000	1.000	1.000	1.000	1.000
1.6	0.202	0.525	0.783	0.921	0.976	0.994	0.999	1.000	1.000	1.000	1.000	1.000	1.000	1.000	1.000	1.000	1.000	1.000
1.8	0.165	0.463	0.731	0.891	0.964	0.990	0.997	0.999	1.000	1.000	1.000	1.000	1.000	1.000	1.000	1.000	1.000	1.000
2	0.135	0.406	0.677	0.857	0.947	0.983	0.995	0.999	1.000	1.000	1.000	1.000	1.000	1.000	1.000	1.000	1.000	1.000

Continued

Poisson distribution *(continued)*

$\lambda\downarrow x\rightarrow$	0	1	2	3	4	5	6	7	8	9	10	11	12	13	14	15	16	17
2.2	0.111	0.355	0.623	0.819	0.928	0.975	0.993	0.998	1.000	1.000	1.000	1.000	1.000	1.000	1.000	1.000	1.000	1.000
2.4	0.091	0.308	0.570	0.779	0.904	0.964	0.988	0.997	0.999	1.000	1.000	1.000	1.000	1.000	1.000	1.000	1.000	1.000
2.6	0.074	0.267	0.518	0.736	0.877	0.951	0.983	0.995	0.999	1.000	1.000	1.000	1.000	1.000	1.000	1.000	1.000	1.000
2.8	0.061	0.231	0.469	0.692	0.848	0.935	0.976	0.992	0.998	0.999	1.000	1.000	1.000	1.000	1.000	1.000	1.000	1.000
3	0.050	0.199	0.423	0.647	0.815	0.916	0.966	0.988	0.996	0.999	1.000	1.000	1.000	1.000	1.000	1.000	1.000	1.000
3.2	0.041	0.171	0.380	0.603	0.781	0.895	0.955	0.983	0.994	0.998	1.000	1.000	1.000	1.000	1.000	1.000	1.000	1.000
3.4	0.033	0.147	0.340	0.558	0.744	0.871	0.942	0.977	0.992	0.997	0.999	1.000	1.000	1.000	1.000	1.000	1.000	1.000
3.6	0.027	0.126	0.303	0.515	0.706	0.844	0.927	0.969	0.988	0.996	0.999	1.000	1.000	1.000	1.000	1.000	1.000	1.000
3.8	0.022	0.107	0.269	0.473	0.668	0.816	0.909	0.960	0.984	0.994	0.998	0.999	1.000	1.000	1.000	1.000	1.000	1.000
4	0.018	0.092	0.238	0.433	0.629	0.785	0.889	0.949	0.979	0.992	0.997	0.999	1.000	1.000	1.000	1.000	1.000	1.000
4.5	0.011	0.061	0.174	0.342	0.532	0.703	0.831	0.913	0.960	0.983	0.993	0.998	0.999	1.000	1.000	1.000	1.000	1.000
5	0.007	0.040	0.125	0.265	0.440	0.616	0.762	0.867	0.932	0.968	0.986	0.995	0.998	0.999	1.000	1.000	1.000	1.000
5.5	0.004	0.027	0.088	0.202	0.358	0.529	0.686	0.809	0.894	0.946	0.975	0.989	0.996	0.998	0.999	1.000	1.000	1.000
6	0.002	0.017	0.062	0.151	0.285	0.446	0.606	0.744	0.847	0.916	0.957	0.980	0.991	0.996	0.999	0.999	1.000	1.000
6.5	0.002	0.011	0.043	0.112	0.224	0.369	0.527	0.673	0.792	0.877	0.933	0.966	0.984	0.993	0.997	0.999	1.000	1.000
7	0.001	0.007	0.030	0.082	0.173	0.301	0.450	0.599	0.729	0.830	0.901	0.947	0.973	0.987	0.994	0.998	0.999	1.000
7.5	0.001	0.005	0.020	0.059	0.132	0.241	0.378	0.525	0.662	0.776	0.862	0.921	0.957	0.978	0.990	0.995	0.998	0.999
8	0.000	0.003	0.014	0.042	0.100	0.191	0.313	0.453	0.593	0.717	0.816	0.888	0.936	0.966	0.983	0.992	0.996	0.998
8.5	0.000	0.002	0.009	0.030	0.074	0.150	0.256	0.386	0.523	0.653	0.763	0.849	0.909	0.949	0.973	0.986	0.993	0.997
9	0.000	0.001	0.006	0.021	0.055	0.116	0.207	0.324	0.456	0.587	0.706	0.803	0.876	0.926	0.959	0.978	0.989	0.995
9.5	0.000	0.001	0.004	0.015	0.040	0.089	0.165	0.269	0.392	0.522	0.645	0.752	0.836	0.898	0.940	0.967	0.982	0.991
10	0.000	0.000	0.003	0.010	0.029	0.067	0.130	0.220	0.333	0.458	0.583	0.697	0.792	0.864	0.917	0.951	0.973	0.986
10.5	0.000	0.000	0.002	0.007	0.021	0.050	0.102	0.179	0.279	0.397	0.521	0.639	0.742	0.825	0.888	0.932	0.960	0.978

Appendix K

Values of the t Distribution

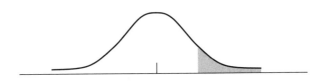

Values of t distribution

ν	$t_{0.100}$	$t_{0.050}$	$t_{0.025}$	$t_{0.010}$	$t_{0.005}$	ν
1	3.078	6.314	12.706	31.821	63.656	1
2	1.886	2.920	4.303	6.965	9.925	2
3	1.638	2.353	3.182	4.541	5.841	3
4	1.533	2.132	2.776	3.747	4.604	4
5	1.476	2.015	2.571	3.365	4.032	5
6	1.440	1.943	2.447	3.143	3.707	6
7	1.415	1.895	2.365	2.998	3.499	7
8	1.397	1.860	2.306	2.896	3.355	8
9	1.383	1.833	2.262	2.821	3.250	9
10	1.372	1.812	2.228	2.764	3.169	10
11	1.363	1.796	2.201	2.718	3.106	11
12	1.356	1.782	2.179	2.681	3.055	12
13	1.350	1.771	2.160	2.650	3.012	13
14	1.345	1.761	2.145	2.624	2.977	14
15	1.341	1.753	2.131	2.602	2.947	15
16	1.337	1.746	2.120	2.583	2.921	16
17	1.333	1.740	2.110	2.567	2.898	17
18	1.330	1.734	2.101	2.552	2.878	18
19	1.328	1.729	2.093	2.539	2.861	19
20	1.325	1.725	2.086	2.528	2.845	20
21	1.323	1.721	2.080	2.518	2.831	21
22	1.321	1.717	2.074	2.508	2.819	22
23	1.319	1.714	2.069	2.500	2.807	23
24	1.318	1.711	2.064	2.492	2.797	24
25	1.316	1.708	2.060	2.485	2.787	25
26	1.315	1.706	2.056	2.479	2.779	26
27	1.314	1.703	2.052	2.473	2.771	27
28	1.313	1.701	2.048	2.467	2.763	28

Continued

Values of t distribution *(continued)*

v	$t_{0.10}$	$t_{0.05}$	$t_{0.025}$	$t_{0.01}$	$t_{0.005}$	v
29	1.311	1.699	2.045	2.462	2.756	29
30	1.310	1.697	2.042	2.457	2.750	30
31	1.309	1.696	2.040	2.453	2.744	31
32	1.309	1.694	2.037	2.449	2.738	32
33	1.308	1.692	2.035	2.445	2.733	33
34	1.307	1.691	2.032	2.441	2.728	34
35	1.306	1.690	2.030	2.438	2.724	35
40	1.303	1.684	2.021	2.423	2.704	40
45	1.301	1.679	2.014	2.412	2.690	45
50	1.299	1.676	2.009	2.403	2.678	50
55	1.297	1.673	2.004	2.396	2.668	55
60	1.296	1.671	2.000	2.390	2.660	60
70	1.294	1.667	1.994	2.381	2.648	70
80	1.292	1.664	1.990	2.374	2.639	80
90	1.291	1.662	1.987	2.368	2.632	90
100	1.290	1.660	1.984	2.364	2.626	100
200	1.286	1.653	1.972	2.345	2.601	200
400	1.284	1.649	1.966	2.336	2.588	400
600	1.283	1.647	1.964	2.333	2.584	600
800	1.283	1.647	1.963	2.331	2.582	800
999	1.282	1.646	1.962	2.330	2.581	999

Endnotes

Introduction

1. *ASQ Certified Six Sigma Green Belt Guidelines* booklet.
2. Bloom's Taxonomy.
3. *ASQ CSSGB Guidelines.*

Chapter 1

1. W. E. Deming, *Out of the Crisis* (Cambridge, MA: MIT Press, 1982, 1986).
2. R. T. Westcott, ed., *Certified Manager of Quality/Organizational Excellence Handbook* (Milwaukee: ASQ Quality Press, 2006).
3. Ibid.
4. J. M. Juran, *Managerial Breakthrough: A New Concept of the Manager's Job* (New York: McGraw-Hill, 1964).

Chapter 2

1. M. Rother and J. Schook, *Learning to See* (Brookline, MA: the Lean Enterprise Institute, 1999).
2. E. M. Goldratt, *Critical Chain* (Great Barrington, MA: The North River Press, 1997).

Chapter 3

1. D. Woodford, *Design for Six Sigma—IDOV Methodology.* http://www.isixsigma.com/ library/content/c020819a.asp. 2002.
2. F. Breyfogle, *Implementing Six Sigma,* 2nd ed. (New York: John Wiley & Sons, 2003).

Chapter 4

1. E. J. Rice, "Automotive Excellence: Know the History of Training to Promote Learning," *ASQ Automotive Division* 3, no. 4 (Fall 1997): 12–15.
2. W. E. Deming, *The New Economics for Industry, Government, Education* (Cambridge: MIT, Center for Advanced Engineering Study, 1993).

Chapter 5

1. H. Kerzner, *Project Management: A Systems Approach to Planning, Schedule, and Controls,* 8th ed. (New York: John Wiley & Sons, 2003).

Chapter 7

1. D. W. Benbow and T. M. Kubiak, *The Certified Six Sigma Black Belt Handbook* (Milwaukee: ASQ Quality Press, 2005).
2. Ibid.
3. Ibid.

Chapter 8

1. B. W. Tuckman, "Developmental Sequence in Small Groups," *Psychological Bulletin* 63, no. 6 (November–December, 1965): 384–99.

Chapter 9

1. K. Ishikawa, *Guide to Quality Control* (Tokyo: Asian Productivity Organization, 1976).
2. Automotive Industry Action Group (AIAG), *Potential Failure Mode and Effects Analysis (FMEA) Reference Manual*, 3rd ed. (DaimlerChrysler Corporation, Ford Motor Company, General Motors Corporation, 2001).
3. N. R. Tague, *The Quality Toolbox*, 2nd ed. (Milwaukee: ASQ Quality Press, 2004).
4. Ibid.
5. D. H. Stamatis, *Total Quality Service: Principles, Practices, and Implementation* (Boca Raton, FL: CRC Press, 1996).
6. J. M. Juran and A. B. Godfrey, *Juran's Quality Handbook*, 5th ed. (New York: McGraw-Hill, 1999).

Chapter 11

1. http://www.animatedsoftware.com/statglos/sgcltheo.htm.

Chapter 12

1. Copyright Minitab Help, revised to match example.

Chapter 13

1. www.richland.edu/james/lecture/m170/ch12-int.html.
2. www.andrews.edu/~calkins/math/webtexts/prod12.htm.

Chapter 14

1. Copyright © 2000–2005 Minitab Inc.
2. Copyright © 2000–2005 Minitab Inc.
3. AIAG, *Measurement System Analysis*, 3rd ed. (DaimlerChrysler Corporation, Ford Motor Company, General Motors Corporation, 2002).

Chapter 15

1. Formula and some definitions from Minitab Help.

Chapter 19

1. W. E. Deming, *Quality, Productivity, and Competitive Position* (Cambridge, MA: Massachusetts Institute of Technology, 1982).

The Six Sigma Acronym List

For use in Certified Six Sigma exams and other Six Sigma activities.

5M&P—materials, methods, machines, measurement, Mother Nature and people

5S—sort (seiri), straighten (seiton), shine (seiso), standardize (seiketsu), sustain (shitsuke)

8D—eight disciplines of problem solving

14 points—Doctor Deming's 14 management practices

AIAG—Automotive Industry Action Group

AND—activity network diagram

ANOM—analysis of means—advanced statistical tool used in hypothesis testing

ANOVA—analysis of variance—advanced statistical tool used in hypothesis testing

AOQ—average outgoing quality

AOQL—average outgoing quality limit

AQL—acceptable quality level

AQP—advanced quality planning

AQL—acceptable quality level

ARL—average run length

ASN—average sample number

ASQ—American Society for Quality

ASQC—American Society for Quality Control (ASQ name before 1997)

AV—appraiser variation (used on GR&R form)

BB—Black Belt—a person who has received training (typically four weeks over a four-month period of time) in the advanced tools and methodology of Six Sigma.

BIB—balanced incomplete block design (used in design of experiments)

BIC—best in class

BOK—body of knowledge

BOM—bill of materials

BPR—business process reengineering

Cmk—Machine capability index (Calculated using continuous uninterupted samples. Also known as short-term capability.)

C$_p$—process capability measurement—compares engineering specification divided by process six standard deviations

C$_{pk}$—process capability measurement—compares engineering specification to process mean divided by three standard deviations

C/O—changeover time—the amount of time required to change tools in a process to produce a different part

C/T—cycle time—the amount of time to perform a particular process

C&E—cause and effect (also known as Ishikawa diagram or fishbone diagram)

CAPA—corrective and preventive action

CBT—computer based training

CCR—critical customer requirement

CE—concurrent engineering

CI—continuous improvement

CMM—coordinate measuring machine

COPQ—cost of poor quality—measure of waste in operation

COQ—cost of quality—see COPQ

CP—control plan

CPM—critical path method

CSSBB—ASQ Certified Six Sigma Black Belt

CSSGB—ASQ Certified Six Sigma Green Belt

CTC—critical to customer

CTQ—critical to quality—identification of items or issues that are important to the customer

CTS—critical to satisfaction

CUSUM—cumulative sum control chart

DCCDI—define–customer–concept–design–implement

DCOV—define–characterize–optimize–verify

DCP—dynamic control plan

df—degrees of freedom

DFA—design for assembly

DFD—design for disassembly

DFE—design for ergonomics

DFM—design for manufacturing

DFMA—design for manufacturing and assembly

DFMEA—design failure mode and effects analysis

DFSS—design for Six Sigma

DFX—design for X

DMADOV—define–measure–analyze–optimize–verify

DMADV—define–measure–analyze–design–verify

DMAIC—define–measure–analyze–improve–control

DMEDI—define–measure–explore–develop–implement

DOE—design of experiment(s)—an advanced statistical tool

DPMO—deficiencies (defects) per million opportunities—measure of bad issues

DPM—deficiencies (defects) per million units—measure of bad issues

DPO—deficiencies (defects) per opportunity—measure of issues that are possible

DPU—deficiencies (defects) per unit—measure of bad issues on a product or in a service

DVP—design verification plan

DVT—design verification test

ECO—engineer change order

EDA—exploratory data analysis

EOQ—economic order quantity

ETA—event tree analysis

EV—equipment variation (used on GR&R form)

EVOP—evolutionary operation—advanced statistical tool

EWMA—exponentially weighted moving average

F Test—advanced statistical tool used in hypothesis testing

FAI—first article inspection

FEA—finite element analysis

FIFO—first in first out

FMEA—failure mode and effects analysis—tool to evaluate risks in a process

FMECA—failure mode effects and criticality analysis

FTA—fault tree analysis

GB—Green Belt—a persons who has receive training (typically five to ten days) in the basic tools and methodology of Six Sigma.

GD&T—geometric dimensioning and tolerancing—engineering nomenclature used on blue prints

GLD—generalized lambda distribution

GLM—general linear model, $Y = XB + U$

GMP—good manufacturing practices

GPC—gage performance curve (used in MSA)

GR&R—gage repeatability and reproducibility—method of checking the measurement system

GRR—gage repeatability and reproducibility (used on GR&R form)

GUM—*Guide to the Expression of Uncertainty of Measurement*

HALT—highly accelerated life test

HASS—highly accelerated stress screening

HOQ—house of quality

ICOV—identify–characterize–optimize–validate

ID—interrelationship digraph

IDDOV—identify–define–develop–optimize–verify

IDEA—identify–design–evaluate–affirm

IDOV—identify–design–optimize–verify

IMR—individual moving range (used in control charts or process behavior charts)

IPO—input–process–output

IPS—innovative problem solving (used in TRIZ)

IQR—intraquartile range (from box plot)

ISSSP—International Society of Six Sigma Practitioners

JIS—Japan Industrial Standard

JIT—just in time—providing parts or services as needed by the customer, neither late nor early, but just in time

JUSE—Union of Japanese Scientists and Engineers

KC—key characteristic

KCC—key control characteristic

KISS—keep it simple and specific, or keep it simple statistician

KPI—key performance indicator

KPIV—key process input variable—important issues on the inputs of SIPOC

KPOV—key process output variable—important issues on the outputs of SIPOC

LCL—lower control limit—measure used in control charts

LIFO—last in first out

LQ—limiting quality

LQL—limiting quality level

LSD—least significant difference

LSL—lower specification limit—engineering limit

LTPD—lot tolerance percentage defective

MBB—Master Black Belt

MBNQA—Malcolm Baldrige National Quality Award

MBWA—manage by walking around

MCF—mean cumulative function (expected number of repairs per system before time t)

MIL-STD—USA Military Standard

MRB—management review board

MRP—material requirements planning

MS—mean squares

MS (RES)—residual mean square

MSA—measurement system analysis—analyzing the measurement system to establish how good it is (GR&R is one of the measures)

MSE—error mean square

MTBF—mean time between failures

MTTF—mean time to failure

MTTR—mean time to recover/repair

MTTR—mean time to repair

NA—needs assessment

ndc—number of distinct categories (used on the GR&R form)

NDT—nondestructive testing

NGT—nominal group technique

NIST—USA National Institute of Standards and Technology

NPI—new product introduction

NPR—number of problem reports

NPV—net present value

NTF—no trouble found

NVA—non-value-added

OC—operating characteristic

OCAP—out of control action plan

OCC—operating characteristic curve

OEE—overall equipment effectiveness—a measure of machine availability, machine performance, and the machine quality rating

OEM—original equipment manufacturer

OFI—opportunity for improvement

OJT—on-the-job training

OTD—on-time-delivery

P_p—long-term process capability measurement—compares engineering specification divided by process six standard deviations (also any time a process is *not* stable)

P_{pk}—long-term process capability measurement—compares engineering specification to process mean divided by three standard deviations (also any time a process is *not* stable)

P/T—precision/tolerance

P&L—profit and loss

PDCA—plan–do–check–act (sometimes called the Deming cycle or Shewhart cycle)

PDPC—process decision program chart (management and planning tool)

PDSA—plan, do, study, and act—a process improvement model

PE—professional engineer

PERT—program evaluation review technique

PFMEA—potential failure modes and effects analysis—tool to evaluate shop floor risks

PFMEA—process failure mode and effects analysis

PM—preventive maintenance

PM—program management

PMP—project management professional

PPAP—potential product approval process

PPCC—normal probability plot correlation coefficient

PPM—parts per million

PRAT—production reliability acceptance test

PV—part variation (used on GR&R form)

Q&R—quality and reliability

QA—quality assurance

QAI—Quality Assurance Institute

QAR—quality assurance representative

QC—quality control

QCT—quality, cost, timing

QFD—quality function deployment

QI—quality improvement

QLA—quality level agreement

QLF—quality loss function

QMS—quality management system

QRB—quality review board

QS-9000—Quality Systems Requirements 9000 (Automotive Industry)

QuEST—quality excellence for suppliers of telecommunications

R&M—reliability and maintenance

R&R—repeatability and reproducibility (see also GR&R)

RAM—reliability, availability, and maintainability

RCM—reliability centered maintenance

REG—regression

RES—residual

RFQ—request for quote

RMS—root mean square

ROE—return on equity

ROI—return on investment

RONA—return on net assets

RPN—risk priority number (found on FMEAs)

RQL—rejectable quality level

RSM—response surface methodology—advanced statistical tool used in analyzing quantitative variables/factors over some specified process

RTY—rolled throughput yield

SBP—strategic business plan

SDCA—standardize–do–check–act—a process stability model

SDWT—self-directed work team

SE—standard error

SIPOC—supplier, input, process, output, and customer—a model that represents the overall system or transformation that is occurring

SKSP—skip lot sampling plan

SLACK—summary, learning objectives, application, context, knowledge base

SMART—specific, meaningful, agreed to, realistic, time phased

SME—subject matter expert

SMED—single-minute exchange of dies

SN—signal-to-noise ratio

SOP—standard operating procedure

SoPK—system of profound knowledge (Dr. W. Edwards Deming)

SOW—statement of work

SPC—statistical process control—method of monitoring a process using statistical tools

SQA—supplier quality assurance

SQC—statistical quality control

SQP—strategic quality plan

SS—Six Sigma

SS—sum of squares

SSA—Six Sigma Academy: for-profit group formed by Motorola to teach Six Sigma

SSBoK—Six Sigma Body of Knowledge

SSE—error sum of squares

SSI—interaction sum of squares

SSOS—Six Sigma operating system: an adaptation of the DMAIC model

SSR—residual sum of squares

SST—total sum of squares

STD—standard deviation

SWOT—strengths, weaknesses, opportunities, threats

t Test—advanced statistical tool used in hypothesis testing.

TBD—to be determined

TDR—technical design review(s)

TNA—training needs assessment

TOC—theory of constraints

TPM—total productive maintenance

TPS—Toyota Production System

TQ—total quality

TQC—total quality control

TQM—total quality management

TRIZ—theory of inventive problem solving (Russian acronym)

TV—total variation (used on GR&R form)

UCL—upper control limit—measure used on control charts

USL—upper specification limit—engineering limit

VA—value added

VA/VE—value analysis/value engineering

VDA—verband der automobilindustrie (German)

VOC—voice of the customer—collection of data from customers

VOP—voice of the process—collection of data from the system or process

WBS—work breakdown structure

WI—work instructions

WIIFM—what's in it for me

WIP—work in progress

X—cause or process variable

Y—effect or process output

YRR—one-year return rate

ZD—zero defects

Glossary

acceptance number—The maximum number of defects or defectives allowable in a sampling lot for the lot to be acceptable.

acceptance quality limit (AQL)—In a continuing series of lots, a quality level that, for the purpose of sampling inspection, is the limit of a satisfactory process average.

acceptance sampling—Inspection of a sample from a lot to decide whether to accept that lot. There are two types: attributes sampling and variables sampling. In attributes sampling, the presence or absence of a characteristic is noted in each of the units inspected. In variables sampling, the numerical magnitude of a characteristic is measured and recorded for each inspected unit; this involves reference to a continuous scale of some kind.

acceptance sampling plan—A specific plan that indicates the sampling sizes and associated acceptance or nonacceptance criteria to be used. In attributes sampling, for example, there are single, double, multiple, sequential, chain, and skip-lot sampling plans. In variables sampling, there are single, double, and sequential sampling plans. For detailed descriptions of these plans, see the standard ANSI/ISO/ASQ A3534-2-1993: *Statistics—Vocabulary and Symbols—Statistical Quality Control*.

accuracy—The closeness of agreement between a test result or measurement result and the accepted/true value.[2]

activity based costing—An accounting system that assigns costs to a product based on the amount of resources used to design, order, or make it.

activity network diagram—A diagram that links tasks with direct arrows showing the path through the task list. Tasks are linked when a task is dependent on a preceding task.[3] (AKA *arrow diagram*.)

Advanced Product Quality Planning (APQP)—High-level automotive process for product realization, from design through production part approval.

affinity diagram—A management tool for organizing information (usually gathered during a brainstorming activity).

American National Standards Institute (ANSI)—A private, nonprofit organization that administers and coordinates the U.S. voluntary standardization and conformity assessment system. It is the U.S. member body in the International Organization for Standardization, known as ISO.

American Society for Quality (ASQ)—A professional, not-for-profit association that develops, promotes, and applies quality related information and technology for the private sector, government, and academia. ASQ serves more than 108,000 individuals and 1,100 corporate members in the United States and 108 other countries.

analysis of means (ANOM)—A statistical procedure for troubleshooting industrial processes and analyzing the results of experimental designs with factors at fixed levels. It provides a graphical display of data. Ellis R. Ott developed the procedure in 1967 because he observed that nonstatisticians had difficulty understanding analysis of variance. Analysis of means is easier for quality practitioners to use because it is an extension of the control chart. In 1973, Edward G. Schilling further extended the concept, enabling analysis of means to be used with nonnormal distributions and attributes data in which the normal approximation to the binomial distribution does not apply. This is referred to as analysis of means for treatment effects.

analysis of variance (ANOVA)—A basic statistical technique for determining the proportion of influence a factor or set of factors has on total variation. It subdivides the total variation of a data set into meaningful component parts associated with specific sources of variation to test a hypothesis on the parameters of the model or to estimate variance components. There are three models: fixed, random, and mixed.

analytical (inferential) studies—A set of techniques used to arrive at a conclusion about a population based upon the information contained in a sample taken from that population.[1]

arrow diagram—A planning tool to diagram a sequence of events or activities (nodes) and their interconnectivity. It is used for scheduling and especially for determining the critical path through nodes. (AKA *activity network diagram*.)

assignable cause—A name for the source of variation in a process that is not due to chance and therefore can be identified and eliminated. Also called "special cause."

attribute (discrete) data—Go/no-go information. The control charts based on attribute data include percent chart, number of affected units chart, count chart, count per unit chart, quality score chart, and demerit chart.

attributes, method of—Method of measuring quality that consists of noting the presence (or absence) of some characteristic (attribute) in each of the units under consideration and counting how many units do (or do not) possess it. Example: go/no-go gauging of a dimension.

audit—The on-site verification activity, such as inspection or examination, of a product, process, or quality system, to ensure compliance to requirements.

An audit can apply to an entire organization or might be specific to a product, function, process, or production step.

Automotive Industry Action Group (AIAG)—A global automotive trade association with about 1600 member companies that focuses on common business processes, implementation guidelines, education, and training.

average chart—A control chart in which the subgroup average, x-bar, is used to evaluate the stability of the process level.

average outgoing quality (AOQ)—The expected average quality level of an outgoing product for a given value of incoming product quality.

average outgoing quality limit (AOQL)—The maximum average outgoing quality over all possible levels of incoming quality for a given acceptance sampling plan and disposal specification.

average run length (ARL)—On a control chart, the number of subgroups expected to be inspected before a shift in magnitude takes place.

average sample number (ASN)—The average number of sample units inspected per lot when reaching decisions to accept or reject.

average total inspection (ATI)—The average number of units inspected per lot, including all units in rejected lots. Applicable when the procedure calls for 100 percent inspection of rejected lots.

B

balanced scorecard—A management system that provides feedback on both internal business processes and external outcomes to continuously improve strategic performance and results.

Baldrige Award—See *Malcolm Baldrige National Quality Award*.

baseline measurement—The beginning point, based on an evaluation of output over a period of time, used to determine the process parameters prior to any improvement effort; the basis against which change is measured.

batch and queue—Producing more than one piece and then moving the pieces to the next operation before they are needed.

Bayes's theorem—A formula to calculate conditional probabilities by relating the conditional and marginal probability distributions of random variables.

benchmarking—A technique in which a company measures its performance against that of best-in-class companies, determines how those companies achieved their performance levels, and uses the information to improve its own performance. Subjects that can be benchmarked include strategies, operations, and processes.

benefit–cost analysis—An examination of the relationship between the monetary cost of implementing an improvement and the monetary value of the benefits achieved by the improvement, both within the same time period.

bias—The influence in a sample of a factor that causes the data population or process being sampled to appear different from what it actually is, typically in a specific direction.[3]

binomial distribution—A discrete distribution that is applicable whenever an experiment consists of n independent Bernoulli trials and the probability of an outcome, say, success, is constant throughout the experiment.[1]

Black Belt (BB)—Full-time team leader responsible for implementing process improvement projects—define, measure, analyze, improve, and control (DMAIC) or define, measure, analyze, design, and verify (DMADV)—within a business to drive up customer satisfaction and productivity levels.

block diagram—A diagram that shows the operation, interrelationships, and interdependencies of components in a system. Boxes, or blocks (hence the name), represent the components; connecting lines between the blocks represent interfaces. There are two types of block diagrams: a functional block diagram, which shows a system's subsystems and lower-level products and their interrelationships and which interfaces with other systems; and a reliability block diagram, which is similar to the functional block diagram but is modified to emphasize those aspects influencing reliability.

brainstorming—A technique teams use to generate ideas on a particular subject. Each person on the team is asked to think creatively and write down as many ideas as possible. The ideas are not discussed or reviewed until after the brainstorming session.

breakthrough improvement—A dynamic, decisive movement to a new, higher level of performance.

business process reengineering (BPR)—The concentration on improving business processes to deliver outputs that will achieve results meeting the firm's objectives, priorities, and mission.

C

***c* chart**—See *count chart*.

calibration—The comparison of a measurement instrument or system of unverified accuracy to a measurement instrument or system of known accuracy to detect any variation from the required performance specification.

capability—The total range of inherent variation in a stable process determined by using data from control charts.

cause—An identified reason for the presence of a defect, problem, or effect.

causation—The relationship between two variables. The changes in variable x cause changes in y. For example, a change in outdoor temperature causes changes in natural gas consumption for heating. If we can change x, we can bring about a change in y.

cause-and-effect diagram—A tool for analyzing process dispersion. It is also referred to as the "Ishikawa diagram," because Kaoru Ishikawa developed it, and the "fishbone diagram," because the completed diagram resembles a fish skeleton. The diagram illustrates the main causes and subcauses leading to an effect (symptom). The cause-and-effect diagram is one of the "seven tools of quality."

centerline—A line on a graph that represents the overall average (mean) operating level of the process.

central limit theorem—A theorem that states that irrespective of shape of the distribution of a population, the distribution of sample means is approximately normal when the sample size is large.[1]

central tendency—The tendency of data gathered from a process to cluster toward a middle value somewhere between the high and low values of measurement.

certification—The result of a person meeting the established criteria set by a certificate granting organization.

Certified Six Sigma Black Belt (CSSBB)—An ASQ certification.

Certified Six Sigma Green Belt (CSSGB)—An ASQ certification.

chain reaction—A chain of events described by W. Edwards Deming: improve quality, decrease costs, improve productivity, increase market share with better quality and lower price, stay in business, provide jobs, and provide more jobs.

chain sampling plan—In acceptance sampling, a plan in which the criteria for acceptance and rejection apply to the cumulative sampling results for the current lot and one or more immediately preceding lots.

champion—A business leader or senior manager who ensures that resources are available for training and projects, and who is involved in periodic project reviews; also an executive who supports and addresses Six Sigma organizational issues.

change agent—An individual from within or outside an organization who facilitates change in the organization; might be the initiator of the change effort, but not necessarily.

changeover—A process in which a production device is assigned to perform a different operation or a machine is set up to make a different part—for example, a new plastic resin and new mold in an injection molding machine.

changeover time—The time required to modify a system or workstation, usually including both teardown time for the existing condition and setup time for the new condition.

characteristic—The factors, elements, or measures that define and differentiate a process, function, product, service, or other entity.

chart—A tool for organizing, summarizing, and depicting data in graphic form.

charter—A written commitment approved by management stating the scope of authority for an improvement project or team.

check sheet—A simple data recording device. The check sheet is custom-designed by the user, which allows him or her to readily interpret the results. The check sheet is one of the "seven tools of quality."

checklist—A tool for ensuring that all important steps or actions in an operation have been taken. Checklists contain items important or relevant to an issue or situation. Checklists are often confused with check sheets.

chi square distribution—Probability distribution of sum of squares of n independent normal variables.[1] ("goodness of fit")

classification of defects—The listing of possible defects of a unit, classified according to their seriousness. Note: Commonly used classifications: class A, class B, class C, class D; or critical, major, minor, and incidental; or critical, major, and minor. Definitions of these classifications require careful preparation and tailoring to the product(s) being sampled to ensure accurate assignment of a defect to the proper classification. A separate acceptance sampling plan is generally applied to each class of defects.

common causes—Causes of variation that are inherent in a process over time. They affect every outcome of the process and everyone working in the process. (AKA *chance causes*.) Also see *special causes*.

compliance—The state of an organization that meets prescribed specifications, contract terms, regulations, or standards.

conformance—An affirmative indication or judgment that a product or service has met the requirements of a relevant specification, contract, or regulation.

conformity assessment—All activities concerned with determining that relevant requirements in standards or regulations are fulfilled, including sampling, testing, inspection, certification, management system assessment and registration, accreditation of the competence of those activities, and recognition of an accreditation program's capability.

constraint—Anything that limits a system from achieving higher performance or throughput; also, the bottleneck that most severely limits the organization's ability to achieve higher performance relative to its purpose or goal.

consumer—The external customer to whom a product or service is ultimately delivered; also called end user.

continuous (variable) data—Data that vary with discontinuity across an interval. The values of continuous data are often represented by floating point numbers. In sampling, continuous data are often referred to as variable data.[3]

continuous flow production—A method in which items are produced and moved from one processing step to the next, one piece at a time. Each process makes only the one piece that the next process needs, and the transfer batch size is one. Also referred to as one-piece flow and single-piece flow.

continuous improvement (CI)—Sometimes called continual improvement. The ongoing improvement of products, services, or processes through incremental and breakthrough improvements.

continuous quality improvement (CQI)—A philosophy and attitude for analyzing capabilities and processes and improving them repeatedly to achieve customer satisfaction.

continuous sampling plan—In acceptance sampling, a plan, intended for application to a continuous flow of individual units of product, that involves acceptance and rejection on a unit-by-unit basis and employs alternate periods of 100 percent inspection and sampling. The relative amount of 100 percent inspection depends on the quality of submitted product. Continuous sampling plans usually require that each t period of 100 percent inspection be continued until a specified number i of consecutively inspected units is found clear of defects. Note: For single-level continuous sampling plans, a single d sampling rate (for example, inspect one unit in five or one unit in 10) is used during sampling. For multilevel continuous sampling plans, two or more sampling rates can be used. The rate at any given time depends on the quality of submitted product.

control chart—A chart with upper and lower control limits on which values of some statistical measure for a series of samples or subgroups are plotted. The chart frequently shows a central line to help detect a trend of plotted values toward either control limit.

control limits—The natural boundaries of a process within specified confidence levels, expressed as the upper control limit (UCL) and the lower control limit (LCL).

control plan (CP)—Written description of the systems for controlling part and process quality by addressing the key characteristics and engineering requirements.

corrective action—A solution meant to reduce or eliminate an identified problem.

corrective action recommendation (CAR)—The full cycle corrective action tool that offers ease and simplicity for employee involvement in the corrective action/process improvement cycle.

correlation (statistical)—A measure of the relationship between two data sets of variables.

cost of poor quality (COPQ)—The costs associated with providing poor-quality products or services. There are four categories: internal failure costs (costs associated with defects found before the customer receives the product or service), external failure costs (costs associated with defects found after the customer receives the product or service), appraisal costs (costs incurred to determine the degree of conformance to quality requirements), and prevention costs (costs incurred to keep failure and appraisal costs to a minimum).

cost of quality (COQ)—Another term for COPQ. It is considered by some to be synonymous with COPQ but is considered by others to be unique. While the two concepts emphasize the same ideas, some disagree as to which concept came first and which categories are included in each.

count chart—A control chart for evaluating the stability of a process in terms of the count of events of a given classification occurring in a sample; known as a "*c* chart."

count per unit chart—A control chart for evaluating the stability of a process in terms of the average count of events of a given classification per unit occurring in a sample.

C_p—The ratio of tolerance to six sigma, or the upper specification limit (USL) minus the lower specification limit (LSL) divided by six sigma. It is sometimes referred to as the engineering tolerance divided by the natural tolerance and is only a measure of dispersion.

C_{pk} **index**—Equals the lesser of the USL minus the mean divided by three sigma (or the mean) minus the LSL divided by three sigma. The greater the C_{pk} value, the better.

C_{pm}—Used when a target value within the specification limits is more significant than overall centering.[3]

critical path method (CPM)—An activity-oriented project management technique that uses arrow-diagramming techniques to demonstrate both the time and the cost required to complete a project. It provides one time estimate: normal time. *process w/ longest duration (days), not simply steps.*

critical to quality (CTQ)—A characteristic of a product or service that is essential to ensure customer satisfaction.[2]

cumulative sum control chart (CUSUM)—A control chart on which the plotted value is the cumulative sum of deviations of successive samples from a target value. The ordinate of each plotted point represents the algebraic sum of the previous ordinate and the most recent deviations from the target.

customer relationship management (CRM)—A strategy for learning more about customers' needs and behaviors to develop stronger relationships with them. It brings together information about customers, sales, marketing effectiveness, responsiveness, and market trends. It helps businesses use technology and human resources to gain insight into the behavior of customers and the value of those customers.

customer satisfaction—The result of delivering a product or service that meets customer requirements.

cycle time—The time required to complete one cycle of an operation. If cycle time for every operation in a complete process can be reduced to equal takt time, products can be made in single-piece flow. Also see *takt time.*

cyclical variation—Looks at the piece-to-piece changes in consecutive order. Patterns are identified in groups, batches, or lots of units.[3]

D

D chart—See *demerit chart*.

data—A set of collected facts. There are two basic kinds of numerical data: measured or variable data, such as "16 ounces," "4 miles," and "0.75 inches"; and counted or attribute data, such as "162 defects."

decision matrix—A matrix teams use to evaluate problems or possible solutions. For example, a team might draw a matrix to evaluate possible solutions, listing them in the far left vertical column. Next, the team selects criteria to rate the possible solutions, writing them across the top row. Then, each possible solution is rated on a scale of 1 to 5 for each criterion, and the rating is recorded in the corresponding grid. Finally, the ratings of all the criteria for each possible solution are added to determine its total score. The total score is then used to help decide which solution deserves the most attention.

defect—A product's or service's nonfulfillment of an intended requirement or reasonable expectation for use, including safety considerations. There are four classes of defects: class 1, very serious, leads directly to severe injury or catastrophic economic loss; class 2, serious, leads directly to significant injury or significant economic loss; class 3, major, is related to major problems with respect to intended normal or reasonably foreseeable use; and class 4, minor, is related to minor problems with respect to intended normal or reasonably foreseeable use.

defective—A defective unit; a unit of product that contains one or more defects with respect to the quality characteristic(s) under consideration.

demerit chart—A control chart for evaluating a process in terms of a demerit (or quality score); in other words, a weighted sum of counts of various classified nonconformities.

Deming cycle—Another term for the plan–do–study–act cycle. Walter Shewhart created it (calling it the plan–do–check–act cycle), but W. Edwards Deming popularized it, calling it plan–do–study–act.

dependability—The degree to which a product is operable and capable of performing its required function at any randomly chosen time during its specified operating time, provided that the product is available at the start of that period. (Nonoperation related influences are not included.) Dependability can be expressed by the ratio: time available divided by (time available + time required).

design for Six Sigma (DFSS)—Used for developing a new product or process, or for processes that need total overhaul. A process often used in DFSS is called DMADV: define, measure, analyze, design, verify.[4] See also *DMADV*.

design of experiments (DoE)—A branch of applied statistics dealing with planning, conducting, analyzing, and interpreting controlled tests to evaluate the factors that control the value of a parameter or group of parameters.

design record—Engineering requirements, typically contained in various formats; examples include engineering drawings, math data, and referenced specifications.

deviation—In numerical data sets, the difference or distance of an individual observation or data value from the center point (often the mean) of the set distribution.

dissatisfiers—The features or functions a customer expects that either are not present or are present but not adequate; also pertains to employees' expectations.

distribution (statistical)—The amount of potential variation in the outputs of a process, typically expressed by its shape, average, or standard deviation.

DMADV—A data-driven quality strategy for designing products and processes; it is an integral part of a Six Sigma quality initiative. It consists of five interconnected phases: define, measure, analyze, design, and verify.

DMAIC—A data-driven quality strategy for improving processes and an integral part of a Six Sigma quality initiative. DMAIC is an acronym for define, measure, analyze, improve, and control.

Dodge-Romig sampling plans—Plans for acceptance sampling developed by Harold F. Dodge and Harry G. Romig. Four sets of tables were published in 1940: single sampling lot tolerance tables, double sampling lot tolerance tables, single sampling average outgoing quality limit tables, and double sampling average outgoing quality limit tables.

downtime—Lost production time during which a piece of equipment is not operating correctly due to breakdown, maintenance, power failures, or similar events.

E

effect—The result of an action being taken; the expected or predicted impact when an action is to be taken or is proposed.

effectiveness—The state of having produced a decided on or desired effect.

efficiency—The ratio of the output to the total input in a process.

efficient—A term describing a process that operates effectively while consuming minimal resources (such as labor and time).

eight wastes—Taiichi Ohno originally enumerated seven wastes (muda) and later added underutilized people as the eighth waste commonly found in physical production. The eight are: 1. overproduction ahead of demand; 2. waiting for the next process, worker, material, or equipment; 3. unnecessary transport of materials (for example, between functional areas of facilities, or to or from a stockroom or warehouse); 4. overprocessing of parts due to poor tool and product design; 5. inventories more than the absolute minimum; 6. unnecessary movement by employees during the course of their work (such as to look for parts, tools, prints, or help); 7. production of defective parts; 8. underutilization of employees' brainpower, skills, experience, and talents.

eighty–twenty (80–20)—A term referring to the Pareto principle, which was first defined by J. M. Juran in 1950. The principle suggests that most effects come from relatively few causes; that is, 80 percent of the effects come from 20 percent of the possible causes. Also see *Pareto chart*.

enumerative (descriptive) studies—A group of methods used for organizing, summarizing, and representing data using tables, graphs, and summary statistics.[1]

error detection—A hybrid form of error-proofing. It means a bad part can be made but will be caught immediately, and corrective action will be taken to prevent another bad part from being produced. A device is used to detect and stop the process when a bad part is made. This is used when error-proofing is too expensive or not easily implemented.

error-proofing—Use of process or design features to prevent the acceptance or further processing of nonconforming products. Also known as mistake-proofing.

experimental design—A formal plan that details the specifics for conducting an experiment, such as which responses, factors, levels, blocks, treatments, and tools are to be used.

external customer—A person or organization that receives a product, service, or information but is not part of the organization supplying it. Also see *internal customer*.

external failure—Nonconformance identified by the external customers.

F

F **distribution**—A continuous probability distribution of the ratio of two independent chi-square random variables.[1]

failure—The inability of an item, product, or service to perform required functions on demand due to one or more defects.

failure cost—The cost resulting from the occurrence of defects. One element of cost of quality or cost of poor quality.

failure mode analysis (FMA)—A procedure to determine which malfunction symptoms appear immediately before or after a failure of a critical parameter in a system. After all possible causes are listed for each symptom, the product is designed to eliminate the problems.

failure mode and effects analysis (FMEA)—A systematized group of activities to recognize and evaluate the potential failure of a product or process and its effects, identify actions that could eliminate or reduce the occurrence of the potential failure, and document the process.

first in, first out (FIFO)—Use of material produced by one process in the same order by the next process. A FIFO queue is filled by the supplying process and emptied by the customer process. When a FIFO lane gets full, production is stopped until the next (internal) customer has used some of that inventory.

first-pass yield (FPY)—Also referred to as the quality rate, the percentage of units that completes a process and meets quality guidelines without being scrapped, rerun, retested, returned, or diverted into an offline repair area. FPY is calculated by dividing the units entering the process minus the defective units by the total number of units entering the process.

first-time quality (FTQ)—Calculation of the percentage of good parts at the beginning of a production run.

fishbone diagram—See *cause-and-effect diagram.*

fitness for use—A term used to indicate that a product or service fits the customer's defined purpose for that product or service.

five S (5S)—Five Japanese terms beginning with "s" used to create a workplace suited for visual control and lean production. *Seiri* means to separate needed tools, parts, and instructions from unneeded materials and to remove the unneeded ones. *Seiton* means to neatly arrange and identify parts and tools for ease of use. *Seiso* means to conduct a cleanup campaign. *Seiketsu* means to conduct seiri, seiton, and seiso daily to maintain a workplace in perfect condition. *Shitsuke* means to form the habit of always following the first four S's.

five whys—A technique for discovering the root causes of a problem and showing the relationship of causes by repeatedly asking the question, "Why?"

flow—The progressive achievement of tasks along the value stream so a product proceeds from design to launch, order to delivery, and raw to finished materials in the hands of the customer with no stoppages, scrap, or backflows.

flowchart—A graphical representation of the steps in a process. Flowcharts are drawn to better understand processes. One of the "seven tools of quality."

force-field analysis—A technique for analyzing what aids or hinders an organization in reaching an objective. An arrow pointing to an objective is drawn down the middle of a piece of paper. The factors that will aid the objective's achievement, called the driving forces, are listed on the left side of the arrow. The factors that will hinder its achievement, called the restraining forces, are listed on the right side of the arrow.

G

gage repeatability and reproducibility (GR&R)—The evaluation of a gauging instrument's accuracy by determining whether its measurements are repeatable (there is close agreement among a number of consecutive measurements of the output for the same value of the input under the same operating conditions) and reproducible (there is close agreement among repeated measurements of the output for the same value of input made under the same operating conditions over a period of time).

Gantt chart—A type of bar chart used in process planning and control to display planned and finished work in relation to time.

geometric dimensioning and tolerancing (GD&T)—A set of rules and standard symbols to define part features and relationships on an engineering drawing depicting the geometric relationship of part features and allowing the maximum tolerance that permits full function of the product.

go/no-go—State of a unit or product. Two parameters are possible: go (conforms to specifications) and no-go (does not conform to specifications).

Green Belt (GB)—An employee who has been trained in the Six Sigma improvement method at a Green Belt level and will lead a process improvement or quality improvement team as part of his or her full-time job.

H

Hawthorne effect—The concept that every change results (initially, at least) in increased productivity.

heijunka—A method of leveling production, usually at the final assembly line, that makes just-in-time production possible. It involves averaging both the volume and sequence of different model types on a mixed-model production line. Using this method avoids excessive batching of different types of product and volume fluctuations in the same product.

histogram—A graphic summary of variation in a set of data. The pictorial nature of a histogram lets people see patterns that are difficult to detect in a simple table of numbers. One of the "seven tools of quality."

hoshin kanri—The selection of goals, projects to achieve the goals, designation of people and resources for project completion, and establishment of project metrics.

hoshin planning—Breakthrough planning. A Japanese strategic planning process in which a company develops up to four vision statements that indicate where the company should be in the next five years. Company goals and work plans are developed based on the vision statements. Periodic submitted audits are then conducted to monitor progress. Also see *value stream*.

house of quality—A product planning matrix, somewhat resembling a house, that is developed during quality function deployment and shows the relationship of customer requirements to the means of achieving these requirements.

I

in-control process—A process in which the statistical measure being evaluated is in a state of statistical control; in other words, the variations among the observed sampling results can be attributed to a constant system of chance causes (common causes). Also see *out-of-control process*.

incremental improvement—Improvement implemented on a continual basis.

indicators—Established measures to determine how well an organization is meeting its customers' needs and other operational and financial performance expectations.

inputs—The products, services, and material obtained from suppliers to produce the outputs delivered to customers.

inspection—Measuring, examining, testing, and gauging one or more characteristics of a product or service and comparing the results with specified requirements to determine whether conformity is achieved for each characteristic.

inspection cost—The cost associated with inspecting a product to ensure that it meets the internal or external customer's needs and requirements; an appraisal cost.

inspection lot—A collection of similar units or a specific quantity of similar material offered for inspection and acceptance at one time.

inspection, normal—Inspection used in accordance with a sampling plan under ordinary circumstances.

inspection, 100 percent—Inspection of all the units in the lot or batch.

internal customer—The recipient (person or department) within an organization of another person's or department's output (product, service, or information). Also see *external customer.*

internal failure—A product failure that occurs before the product is delivered to external customers.

International Organization for Standardization—A network of national standards institutes from 157 countries working in partnership with international organizations, governments, industry, business, and consumer representatives to develop and publish international standards; acts as a bridge between public and private sectors.

interrelationship diagram—A management tool that depicts the relationship among factors in a complex situation; also called a *relations diagram.*

Ishikawa diagram—See *cause-and-effect diagram.*

J

just-in-time (JIT) manufacturing—An optimal material requirement planning system for a manufacturing process in which there is little or no manufacturing material inventory on hand at the manufacturing site and little or no incoming inspection.

K

kaizen—A Japanese term that means gradual unending improvement by doing little things better and setting and achieving increasingly higher standards. Masaaki Imai made the term famous in his book, *Kaizen: The Key to Japan's Competitive Success.*

kanban—A Japanese term for one of the primary tools of a just-in-time system. It maintains an orderly and efficient flow of materials throughout the entire manufacturing process. It is usually a printed card that contains specific information such as part name, description, and quantity.

key performance indicator (KPI)—A statistical measure of how well an organization is doing in a particular area. A KPI could measure a company's financial performance or how it is holding up against customer requirements.

key process characteristic—A process parameter that can affect safety or compliance with regulations, fit, function, performance, or subsequent processing of product.

key product characteristic—A product characteristic that can affect safety or compliance with regulations, fit, function, performance, or subsequent processing of product.

L

leadership—An essential part of a quality improvement effort. Organization leaders must establish a vision, communicate that vision to those in the organization, and provide the tools and knowledge necessary to accomplish the vision.

lean—Producing the maximum sellable products or services at the lowest operational cost while optimizing inventory levels.

lean enterprise—A manufacturing company organized to eliminate all unproductive effort and unnecessary investment, both on the shop floor and in office functions.

lean manufacturing/production—An initiative focused on eliminating all waste in manufacturing processes. Principles of lean manufacturing include zero waiting time, zero inventory, scheduling (internal customer pull instead of push system), batch to flow (cut batch sizes), line balancing, and cutting actual process times. The production systems are characterized by optimum automation, just-in-time supplier delivery disciplines, quick changeover times, high levels of quality, and continuous improvement.

lean migration—The journey from traditional manufacturing methods to one in which all forms of waste are systematically eliminated.

linearity—Refers to measurements being statistically different from one end of the measurement space to the other. For example, a measurement process may be very capable of measuring small parts but much less accurate measuring large parts, or one end of a long part can be measured more accurately than the other.[3]

lot—A defined quantity of product accumulated under conditions considered uniform for sampling purposes.

lot, batch—A definite quantity of some product manufactured under conditions of production that are considered uniform.

lot quality—The value of percentage defective or of defects per hundred units in a lot.

lot size (also referred to as *N*)—The number of units in a lot.

lower control limit (LCL)—Control limit for points below the central line in a control chart.

M

maintainability—The probability that a given maintenance action for an item under given usage conditions can be performed within a stated time interval when the maintenance is performed under stated conditions using stated procedures and resources.

Malcolm Baldrige National Quality Award (MBNQA)—An award established by the U.S. Congress in 1987 to raise awareness of quality management and recognize U.S. companies that have implemented successful quality management systems. Awards can be given annually in six categories: manufacturing, service, small business, education, healthcare, and nonprofit. The award is named after the late Secretary of Commerce Malcolm Baldrige, a proponent of quality management. The U.S. Commerce Department's National Institute of Standards and Technology manages the award, and ASQ administers it.

Master Black Belt (MBB)—Six Sigma or quality expert responsible for strategic implementations in an organization. An MBB is qualified to teach other Six Sigma facilitators the methods, tools, and applications in all functions and levels of the company, and is a resource for using statistical process control in processes.

matrix diagram—A planning tool for displaying the relationships among various data sets.

mean—A measure of central tendency; the arithmetic average of all measurements in a data set.

mean time between failures (MTBF)—The average time interval between failures for repairable product for a defined unit of measure; for example, operating hours, cycles, and miles.

measure—The criteria, metric, or means to which a comparison is made with output.

measurement—The act or process of quantitatively comparing results with requirements.

median—The middle number or center value of a set of data in which all the data are arranged in sequence.

metric—A standard for measurement.

MIL-STD-105E—A military standard that describes the sampling procedures and tables for inspection by attributes. (See the "Standards and Specifications" section of the CD-ROM for a copy.)

mistake-proofing—Use of production or design features to prevent the manufacture or passing downstream of a nonconforming product; also known as error-proofing.

mode—The value occurring most frequently in a data set.

muda—Japanese for *waste*; any activity that consumes resources but creates no value for the customer.

multivariate control chart—A control chart for evaluating the stability of a process in terms of the levels of two or more variables or characteristics.

multi-voting—Typically used after brainstorming, multi-voting narrows a large list of possibilities to a smaller list of the top priorities (or to a final selection) by allowing items to be ranked in importance by participants. Multi-voting is preferable to straight voting because it allows an item that is favored by all, but not the top choice of any, to rise to the top.[4]

N

n—The number of units in a sample.

N—The number of units in a population.

nominal group technique (NGT)—A technique, similar to brainstorming, to generate ideas on a particular subject. Team members are asked to silently write down as many ideas as possible. Each member is then asked to share one idea, which is recorded. After all the ideas are recorded, they are discussed and prioritized by the group.

nonconformity—The nonfulfillment of a specified requirement.

nondestructive testing and evaluation (NDT, NDE)—Testing and evaluation methods that do not damage or destroy the product being tested.

nonlinear parameter estimation—A method whereby the arduous and labor-intensive task of multiparameter model calibration can be carried out automatically under the control of a computer.

nonparametric tests—All tests involving ranked data (data that can be put in order). Nonparametric tests are often used in place of their parametric counterparts when certain assumptions about the underlying population are questionable. For example, when comparing two independent samples, the Wilcoxon Mann-Whitney test (see entry) does not assume that the difference between the samples is normally distributed, whereas its parametric counterpart, the two-sample *t*-test, does. Nonparametric tests can be, and often are, more powerful in detecting population differences when certain assumptions are not satisfied.

non-value-added—A term that describes a process step or function that is not required for the direct achievement of process output. This step or function is identified and examined for potential elimination. Also see *value-added*.

normal distribution (statistical)—The charting of a data set in which most of the data points are concentrated around the average (mean), thus forming a bell-shaped curve.

O

operating characteristic curve (OC curve)—A graph to determine the probability of accepting lots as a function of the lots' or processes' quality level when using various sampling plans. There are three types: type A curves, which give the probability of acceptance for an individual lot coming from finite production (will not continue in the future); type B curves, which give the probability of acceptance for lots coming from a continuous process; and type C curves, which (for a continuous sampling plan) give the long-run percentage of product accepted during the sampling phase.

operations—Work or steps to transform raw materials to finished product.

out of spec—A term that indicates a unit does not meet a given requirement or specification.

out-of-control process—A process in which the statistical measure being evaluated is not in a state of statistical control. In other words, the variations among the observed sampling results can not be attributed to a constant system of chance causes. Also see *in-control process*.

outputs—Products, materials, services, or information provided to customers (internal or external), from a process.

P

p **chart**—See *percent chart*.

paired-comparison tests—Examples are two-mean, equal variance *t* test; two-mean, unequal variance *t* test; paired *t* test; and *F* test.

Pareto chart—A graphical tool for ranking causes from most significant to least significant. It is based on the Pareto principle, which was first defined by Joseph M. Juran in 1950. The principle, named after 19th century economist Vilfredo Pareto, suggests that most effects come from relatively few causes; that is, 80 percent of the effects come from 20 percent of the possible causes. One of the "seven tools of quality."

parts per million (ppm)—A method of stating the performance of a process in terms of actual nonconforming material, which can include rejected, returned, or suspect material in the calculation.

percent chart—A control chart for evaluating the stability of a process in terms of the percentage of the total number of units in a sample in which an event of a given classification occurs. Also referred to as a proportion chart.

plan–do–check–act (PDCA) cycle—A four-step process for quality improvement. In the first step (plan), a way to effect improvement is developed. In the second step (do), the plan is carried out, preferably on a small scale. In the third step (check), a study takes place between what was predicted and what was observed in the previous step. In the last step (act), action is taken on the causal system to effect the desired change. The plan–do–check–act cycle is sometimes referred to as the Shewhart cycle, because Walter A. Shewhart discussed the concept in his book *Statistical Method from the Viewpoint of Quality Control*, and as the Deming cycle, because W. Edwards Deming introduced the concept in Japan. The Japanese subsequently called it the Deming cycle. Also called the plan–do–study–act (PDSA) cycle.

point of use—A technique that ensures people have exactly what they need to do their jobs—work instructions, parts, tools, and equipment—where and when they need them.

Poisson distribution—A discrete probability distribution that expresses the probability of a number of events occurring in a fixed time period if these events occur with a known average rate and are independent of the time since the last event.

poka-yoke—Japanese term that means mistake-proofing. A poka-yoke device is one that prevents incorrect parts from being made or assembled or easily identifies a flaw or error.

positional variation—Type of variation frequently within-piece, but can also include machine-to-machine variation, line-to-line or plant-to-plant variation, within-batch variation, and test positioning variation.[3]

P_p (process performance index)—An index describing process performance in relation to specified tolerance.[2]

P_{pk} (minimum process performance index)—The smaller of upper process performance index and lower process performance index.[2]

practical significance—At least as important as the question of statistical significance, practical or economic significance determines whether an observed sample difference is large enough to be of practical interest.

precision—The aspect of measurement that addresses repeatability or consistency when an identical item is measured several times.

prevention cost—The cost incurred by actions taken to prevent a nonconformance from occurring; one element of cost of quality or cost of poor quality.

preventive action—Action taken to remove or improve a process to prevent potential future occurrences of a nonconformance.

prioritization matrix—An L-shaped matrix that uses pairwise comparisons of a list of options to a set of criteria in order to choose the best option(s). First, the importance of each criterion is decided. Then each criterion is considered separately, with each option rated for how well it meets the criterion. Finally, all the ratings are combined for a final ranking of options. Numerical calculations ensure a balance between the relative importance of the criteria and the relative merits of the options.[4]

probability (statistical)—The likelihood of occurrence of an event, action, or item.

procedure—The steps in a process and how these steps are to be performed for the process to fulfill a customer's requirements; usually documented.

process—A set of interrelated work activities characterized by a set of specific inputs and value-added tasks that make up a procedure for a set of specific outputs.

process average quality—Expected or average value of process quality.

process capability—A statistical measure of the inherent process variability of a given characteristic. The most widely accepted formula for process capability is six sigma.

process capability index—The value of the inherent tolerance specified for the characteristic divided by the process capability. The several types of process capability indices include the widely used C_{pk} and C_p.

process control—The method for keeping a process within boundaries; the act of minimizing the variation of a process.

process decision program charts (PDPC)—A variant of tree diagrams, a PDPC can be used as a simple alternative to FMEA.[3]

process flow diagram—A depiction of the flow of materials through a process, including any rework or repair operations; also called a process flow chart.

process improvement—The application of the plan–do–check–act cycle (see entry) to processes to produce positive improvement and better meet the needs and expectations of customers.

process management—The pertinent techniques and tools applied to a process to implement and improve process effectiveness, hold the gains, and ensure process integrity in fulfilling customer requirements.

process map—A type of flowchart depicting the steps in a process and identifying responsibility for each step and key measures.

process owner—The person who coordinates the various functions and work activities at all levels of a process, has the authority or ability to make changes in the process as required, and manages the entire process cycle to ensure performance effectiveness.

process performance management—The overseeing of process instances to ensure their quality and timeliness; can also include proactive and reactive actions to ensure a good result.

process quality—The value of percentage defective or of defects per hundred units in product from a given process. Note: The symbols "p" and "c" are commonly used to represent the true process average in fraction defective or defects per unit, and "$100p$" and "$100c$" the true process average in percentage defective or in defects per hundred units.

production part approval process (PPAP)—A "Big Three" automotive process that defines the generic requirements for approval of production parts, including production and bulk materials. Its purpose is to determine during an actual production run at the quoted production rates whether all customer engineering design record and specification requirements are properly understood by the supplier and that the process has the potential to produce product consistently meeting these requirements.

program evaluation and review technique (PERT) charts—Developed during the Nautilus submarine program in the 1950s, a PERT chart resembles an activity network diagram in that it shows task dependencies. It calculates best, average, and worst expected completion times.[3]

project management—The application of knowledge, skills, tools, and techniques to a broad range of activities to meet the requirements of a particular project.

project team—Manages the work of a project. The work typically involves balancing competing demands for project scope, time, cost, risk, and quality, satisfying stakeholders with differing needs and expectations, and meeting identified requirements.

proportion chart—See *percent chart*.

pull system—An alternative to scheduling individual processes, in which the customer process withdraws the items it needs from a supermarket (see entry) and the supplying process produces to replenish what was withdrawn; used to avoid push. Also see *kanban*.

Q

quality—A subjective term for which each person or sector has its own definition. In technical usage, quality can have two meanings: 1. the characteristics of a product or service that bear on its ability to satisfy stated or implied needs; 2. a product or service free of deficiencies. According to Joseph M. Juran, quality means "fitness for use"; according to Philip Crosby, it means "conformance to requirements."

quality assurance/quality control (QA/QC)—Two terms that have many interpretations because of the multiple definitions for the words "assurance" and "control." For example, "assurance" can mean the act of giving confidence, the state of being certain, or the act of making certain; "control" can mean an evaluation to indicate needed corrective responses, the act of guiding, or the state of a process in which the variability is attributable to a constant system of chance causes. (For a detailed discussion on the multiple definitions, see ANSI/ISO/ASQ A3534-2, *Statistics—Vocabulary and Symbols—Statistical Quality Control*.) One definition of quality assurance is: all the planned and systematic activities implemented within the quality system that can be demonstrated to provide confidence that a product or service will fulfill requirements for quality. One definition for quality control is: the operational techniques and activities used to fulfill requirements for quality. Often, however, "quality assurance" and "quality control" are used interchangeably, referring to the actions performed to ensure the quality of a product, service, or process.

quality audit—A systematic, independent examination and review to determine whether quality activities and related results comply with plans and whether these plans are implemented effectively and are suitable to achieve the objectives.

quality costs—See *cost of poor quality.*

quality function deployment (QFD)—A structured method in which customer requirements are translated into appropriate technical requirements for each stage of product development and production. The QFD process is often referred to as listening to the voice of the customer. *(matrix diagrams)*

quality loss function—A parabolic approximation of the quality loss that occurs when a quality characteristic deviates from its target value. The quality loss function is expressed in monetary units: the cost of deviating from the target increases quadratically the farther the quality characteristic moves from the target. The formula used to compute the quality loss function depends on the type of quality characteristic being used. The quality loss function was first introduced in this form by Genichi Taguchi.

quality management (QM)—The application of a quality management system in managing a process to achieve maximum customer satisfaction at the lowest overall cost to the organization while continuing to improve the process.

quality management system (QMS)—A formalized system that documents the structure, responsibilities, and procedures required to achieve effective quality management.

queue time—The time a product spends in a line awaiting the next design, order processing, or fabrication step.

quick changeover—The ability to change tooling and fixtures rapidly (usually within minutes) so multiple products can be run on the same machine.

R

random cause—A cause of variation due to chance and not assignable to any factor.

random sampling—A commonly used sampling technique in which sample units are selected so all combinations of n units under consideration have an equal chance of being selected as the sample.

range (statistical)—The measure of dispersion in a data set (the difference between the highest and lowest values).

range chart (*R* chart)—A control chart in which the subgroup range R evaluates the stability of the variability within a process.

rational subgrouping—Subgrouping wherein the variation is presumed to be only from random causes.[2]

regression analysis—A statistical technique for determining the best mathematical expression describing the functional relationship between one response and one or more independent variables.

relations diagram—See *interrelationship diagram.*

reliability—The probability of a product's performing its intended function under stated conditions without failure for a given period of time.

repeatability—The variation in measurements obtained when one measurement device is used several times by the same person to measure the same characteristic on the same product.

reproducibility—The variation in measurements made by different people using the same measuring device to measure the same characteristic on the same product.

requirements—The ability of an item to perform a required function under stated conditions for a stated period of time.

risk management—Using managerial resources to integrate risk identification, risk assessment, risk prioritization, development of risk handling strategies, and mitigation of risk to acceptable levels.

risk priority number (RPN)—The product of the severity, occurrence, and detection values determined. The higher the RPN, the more significant the failure mode.

robustness—The condition of a product or process design that remains relatively stable, with a minimum of variation, even though factors that influence operations or usage, such as environment and wear, are constantly changing.

root cause—A factor that caused a nonconformance and should be permanently eliminated through process improvement.

run chart—A chart showing a line connecting numerous data points collected from a process running over time.

S

sample—In acceptance sampling, one or more units of product (or a quantity of material) drawn from a lot for purposes of inspection to reach a decision regarding acceptance of the lot.

sample size [*n*]—The number of units in a sample.

sample standard deviation chart (*s* chart)—A control chart in which the subgroup standard deviation s is used to evaluate the stability of the variability within a process.

scatter diagram—A graphical technique to analyze the relationship between two variables. Two sets of data are plotted on a graph, with the *y*-axis being used for the variable to be predicted and the *x*-axis being used for the variable to make the prediction. The graph will show possible relationships (although two variables might appear to be related, they might not be; those who know most about the variables must make that evaluation). One of the "seven tools of quality."

seven tools of quality—Tools that help organizations understand their processes to improve them. The tools are the cause-and-effect diagram, check sheet, control chart, flowchart, histogram, Pareto chart, and scatter diagram.

seven wastes—See *eight wastes*.

Shewhart cycle—See *plan–do–check–act cycle*.

sigma—One standard deviation in a normally distributed process.

single-piece flow—A process in which products proceed one complete product at a time, through various operations in design, order taking, and production without interruptions, backflows, or scrap.

SIPOC diagram—A tool used by Six Sigma process improvement teams to identify all relevant elements (suppliers, inputs, process, outputs, customers) of a process improvement project before work begins.

Six Sigma—A method that provides organizations tools to improve the capability of their business processes. This increase in performance and decrease in process variation lead to defect reduction and improvement in profits, employee morale, and quality of products or services. Six Sigma quality is a term generally used to indicate that a process is well controlled (±6σ from the centerline in a control chart).

Six Sigma quality—A term generally used to indicate process capability in terms of process spread measured by standard deviations in a normally distributed process.

special causes—Causes of variation that arise because of special circumstances. They are not an inherent part of a process. Special causes are also referred to as assignable causes. Also see *common causes*.

specification—A document that states the requirements to which a given product or service must conform.

stages of team growth—Four stages that teams move through as they develop maturity: forming, storming, norming, and performing.

standard deviation (statistical)—A computed measure of variability indicating the spread of the data set around the mean.

standard work—A precise description of each work activity, specifying cycle time, takt time, the work sequence of specific tasks, and the minimum inventory of parts on hand needed to conduct the activity. All jobs are organized around human motion to create an efficient sequence without waste. Work organized in such a way is called standard(ized) work. The three elements that make up standard work are takt time, working sequence, and standard in-process stock.

standard work instructions—A lean manufacturing tool that enables operators to observe a production process with an understanding of how assembly tasks are to be performed. It ensures that the quality level is understood and serves as an excellent training aid, enabling replacement or temporary individuals to easily adapt and perform the assembly operation.

statistical process control (SPC)—The application of statistical techniques to control a process; often used interchangeably with the term statistical quality control.

statistical quality control (SQC)—The application of statistical techniques to control quality. Often used interchangeably with the term "statistical process control," although statistical quality control includes acceptance sampling, which statistical process control does not.

statistical significance—Level of accuracy expected of an analysis of data. Most frequently it is expressed as either a "95 percent level of significance" or "five percent confidence level."[5]

strengths, weaknesses, opportunities, threats (SWOT) analysis—A strategic technique used to assess an organization's competitive position.

Student's *t* distribution—A continuous distribution of the ratio of two independent random variables—a standard normal and a chi-square.[1]

supplier—A source of materials, service, or information input provided to a process.

supplier quality assurance—Confidence that a supplier's product or service will fulfill its customers' needs. This confidence is achieved by creating a relationship between the customer and supplier that ensures that the product will be fit for use with minimal corrective action and inspection. According to Joseph M. Juran, nine primary activities are needed: 1. define product and program quality requirements; 2. evaluate alternative suppliers; 3. select suppliers; 4. conduct joint quality planning; 5. cooperate with the supplier during the execution of the contract; 6. obtain proof of conformance to requirements; 7. certify qualified suppliers; 8. conduct quality improvement programs as required; 9. create and use supplier quality ratings.

supply chain—The series of suppliers to a given process.

system—A group of interdependent processes and people that together perform a common mission.

T

Taguchi methods—The American Supplier Institute's trademarked term for the quality engineering methodology developed by Genichi Taguchi. In this engineering approach to quality control, Taguchi calls for off-line quality control, online quality control, and a system of experimental design to improve quality and reduce costs.

takt time—The rate of customer demand, takt time is calculated by dividing production time by the quantity of product the customer requires in that time. Takt is the heartbeat of a lean manufacturing system. Also see *cycle time.*

team—A group of individuals organized to work together to accomplish a specific objective. Also see *stages of team growth.*

temporal variation—The time-to-time or shift-to-shift variation—that is, variation across time.[3]

theory of constraints (TOC)—A lean management philosophy that stresses removal of constraints to increase throughput while decreasing inventory and operating expenses. TOC's set of tools examines the entire system for continuous improvement. The current reality tree, conflict resolution diagram, future reality tree, prerequisite tree, and transition tree are the five tools used in TOC's ongoing improvement process. Also called *constraints management.*

throughput—The rate at which the system generates money through sales, or the conversion rate of inventory into shipped product.

tolerance—The maximum and minimum limit values a product can have and still meet customer requirements.

total productive maintenance (TPM)—A series of methods, originally pioneered by Nippondenso (a member of the Toyota group), to ensure that every machine in a production process is always able to perform its required tasks so production is never interrupted.

total quality management (TQM)—A term coined by the Naval Air Systems Command to describe its Japanese-style management approach to quality improvement. Since then, TQM has taken on many meanings. Simply put, it is a management approach to long-term success through customer satisfaction. TQM is based on all members of an organization participating in improving processes, products, services, and the culture in which they work. The methods for implementing this approach are found in the teachings of such quality leaders as Philip B. Crosby, W. Edwards Deming, Armand V. Feigenbaum, Kaoru Ishikawa, and Joseph M. Juran.

Toyota production system (TPS)—The production system developed by Toyota Motor Corp. to provide best quality, lowest cost, and shortest lead time through eliminating waste. TPS is based on two pillars: just-in-time and jidoka. TPS is maintained and improved through iterations of standardized work and kaizen.

tree diagram—A management tool that depicts the hierarchy of tasks and subtasks needed to complete an objective. The finished diagram bears a resemblance to a tree.

trend—The graphical representation of a variable's tendency, over time, to increase, decrease, or remain unchanged.

trend control chart—A control chart in which the deviation of the subgroup average, x-bar, from an expected trend in the process level is used to evaluate the stability of a process.

TRIZ—A Russian acronym for a theory of innovative problem solving.

t **test**—A method to assess whether the means of two groups are statistically different from each other.

type I error—An incorrect decision to reject something (such as a statistical hypothesis or a lot of products) when it is acceptable.

type II error—An incorrect decision to accept something when it is unacceptable.

U

u **chart**—Count-per-unit chart.

unit—An object for which a measurement or observation can be made; commonly used in the sense of a "unit of product," the entity of product inspected to determine whether it is defective or nondefective.

upper control limit (UCL)—Control limit for points above the central line in a control chart.

V

validation—The act of confirming that a product or service meets the requirements for which it was intended.

validity—The ability of a feedback instrument to measure what it was intended to measure; also, the degree to which inferences derived from measurements are meaningful.

value stream—All activities, both value-added and non-value-added, required to bring a product from raw material state into the hands of the customer, bring a customer requirement from order to delivery, and bring a design from concept to launch. Also see *hoshin planning*.

value stream mapping—A pencil and paper tool used in two stages. First, follow a product's production path from beginning to end and draw a visual representation of every process in the material and information flows. Second, draw a future state map of how value should flow. The most important map is the future state map.

value-added—A term used to describe activities that transform input into a customer (internal or external)–usable output.

variable (attributes) data—Measurement information. Control charts based on variable data include average (x-bar) chart, range (R) chart, and sample standard deviation (s) chart.

variation—A change in data, characteristic, or function caused by one of four factors: special causes, common causes, tampering, or structural variation.

verification—The act of determining whether products and services conform to specific requirements.

voice of the customer—The expressed requirements and expectations of customers relative to products or services, as documented and disseminated to the providing organization's members.

W

waste—Any activity that consumes resources and produces no added value to the product or service a customer receives. Also known as *muda*.

Wilcoxon Mann-Whitney test—Used to test the null hypothesis that two populations have identical distribution functions against the alternative hypothesis that the two distribution functions differ only with respect to location (median), if at all. It does not require the assumption that the differences between the two samples are normally distributed. In many applications, it is used in place of the two-sample *t* test when the normality assumption is questionable. This test can also be applied when the observations in a sample of data are ranks, that is, ordinal data, rather than direct measurements.

X

x-bar chart—Average chart.

Z

zero defects—A performance standard and method Philip B. Crosby developed; states that if people commit themselves to watching details and avoiding errors, they can move closer to the goal of zero defects.

Endnotes

Source: Except where noted, definitions reproduced with permission of ASQ, http://www.asq.org/glossary/index.html. The glossary was compiled by *Quality Progress* magazine editorial staff members Dave Nelsen, Assistant Editor, and Susan E. Daniels, Editor at Large. Volunteers James Bossert, R. Dan Reid, and James Rooney reviewed the content.

1. Reproduced by permission of Bhisham C. Gupta and H. Fred Walker, *Applied Statistics for the Six Sigma Green Belt* (Milwaukee: ASQ Quality Press, 2005).
2. Reproduced by permission of the ASQ Statistics Division, *Glossary and Tables for Statistical Quality Control*, 4th ed. (Milwaukee: ASQ Quality Press, 2004).
3. Reproduced by permission of Kim H. Pries, *Six Sigma for the Next Millennium* (Milwaukee: ASQ Quality Press, 2006).
4. Reproduced by permission of Nancy R. Tague, *The Quality Toolbox*, 2nd ed. (Milwaukee: ASQ Quality Press, 2005).
5. Reproduced by permission of Donald L. Siebels, *The Quality Improvement Glossary*. (Milwaukee: ASQ Quality Press, 2004).

References

AIAG. *Potential Failure Mode and Effects Analysis (FMEA) Reference Manual,* 3rd ed. DaimlerChrysler Corporation, Ford Motor Company, General Motors Corporation, 2001.

AIAG. *Measurement System Analysis Reference Manual,* 3rd ed. DaimlerChrysler Corporation, Ford Motor Company, General Motors Corporation, 2001.

AT&T. *Statistical Quality Control Handbook.* Milwaukee: ASQC Quality Press, 1985.

Barrentine, L. *Concepts for R&R Studies,* 2nd ed. Milwaukee: ASQ Quality Press, 2003.

Benbow, D. W., and T. M. Kubiak. *The Certified Six Sigma Black Belt Handbook.* Milwaukee: ASQ Quality Press, 2005.

Berger, R., D. Benbow, A. Elshennawy, and H. F. Walker. *Certified Quality Engineer Handbook,* 2nd ed. Milwaukee: ASQ Quality Press, 2006.

Breyfogle, F. W. *Implementing Six Sigma.* New York: John Wiley & Sons, 1999.

Chowdhury, S. *Design for Six Sigma: The Revolutionary Process for Achieving Extraordinary Profit.* Chicago: Dearborn Trade Publishing, 2002.

Day, R. G. *Quality Function Deployment.* Milwaukee: ASQC Quality Press, 1993.

Deming, W. E. *Out of the Crisis.* Cambridge, MA: MIT Press, 2000.

eStats: Engineering Statistics Handbook by NIST. www.itl.nist.gov/div898/handbook/index.htm

Galloway, D. *Mapping Work Processes.* Milwaukee: ASQC Quality Press, 1994.

Gould, L. "Building Better Vehicles via Axiomatic Design." *Automotive Design and Production* (June 2000).

Juran, J. M. *Juran's Quality Control Handbook,* 5th ed. New York: McGraw Hill, 1999.

Kubiak, T. M. "An Integrated Approach System," *Quality Progress* (July 2003).

Munro, R. A. *Six Sigma for the Office.* Milwaukee: ASQ Quality Press, 2003.

Munro, R. A. *Six Sigma for the Shop Floor.* Milwaukee: ASQ Quality Press, 2002.

Rantanen, K., and E. Domb. *Simplified TRIZ: New Problem-Solving Applications for Engineers and Manufacturing Professionals.* Boca Raton, FL: St. Lucie Press, 2002.

Tague, N. R. *The Quality Toolbox.* Milwaukee: ASQ Quality Press, 2004.

Wader, M. *Lean Tools—Pocket Guide to Implementing Lean Practices.* Surfside, FL: QSU, 2003.

Westcott, R. *Certified Manager of Quality/Organizational Excellence Handbook.* Milwaukee: ASQ Quality Press, 2005.

Wheeler, D. *Understanding Statistical Process Control,* 2nd ed. Knoxville, TN: SPC Press, 1992.

Womack, J. P., and D. T. Jones. *Lean Thinking.* New York: Free Press, 2003.

Selected Web Sites/Organizations

Deming Prize. www.juse.or.jp/e/deming/

GOAL/QPC. www.goalqpc.com/
http://qualitypress.asq.org/perl/catalog.cgi?item=H0822
Juran Institute. www.juran.com/
Leader to Leader Institute (Drucker). www.pfdf.org/
Malcolm Baldrige Award Criteria, 2007. www.quality.nist.gov/
Minitab. www.minitab.com/
NIST. www.nist.gov/
Shainin Red X. www.shainin.com/SLLCWEB/Cert/RX_01.cfm
Shingo Prize. www.shingoprize.org/
Sixsigmaforum.com
The W. Edwards Deming Institute. www.deming.org/
www.animatedsoftware.com/statglos/sgcltheo.htm
www.qualitytrainingportal.com/resources/fmea/index.htm.
www.todaysengineer.org/2005/Mar/team_dynamics.asp.

Index

A

activity network diagram (AND), 91
advanced quality planning (AQP), 91–92
affinity diagram, 92
AIAG (Automotive Industry Action Group), 216, 324
    GR&R reference, 204–5
    SPC Manual, process change rules, 328–29
alternative hypothesis, 248–49
American National Standards Institute (ANSI), 216
American Society for Quality
    certification process, xxiii–xxxvi
        examination process, xxvi–xxix
        test development process, xxiii–xxv
        test maintenance, xxv–xxvi
    Code of Ethics (Appendix A), 358–59
analysis of variance (ANOVA)
    in design of experiments, 297
    single-factor (one-way), 264–69
    using Excel to perform, 268–69
    using Excel's FINV function, 267–68
analytical statistical studies, 142–43
analyze, phase of DMAIC, 15, 223–74
assignable cause, 302
attribute(s) data, 110
    process capability for, 219–22
attributes control charts, 110–11, 319
auditing, 92–94
average main effects, 285

B

balanced design, in design of experiments, 288
balanced scorecard, 19, 66
bell curve, 182
benchmarking, 94–95
between-sample variation, 310
bias, in measurement system analysis, 200
binomial distribution, 176–79
    normal approximations of, 179
block, in design of experiments, 277

blocking, in design of experiments, 281
Bloom's Taxonomy, of levels of cognition, xxvii–xxviii
box plot, 163–66
box-and-whisker plot, 163–66
brainstorming, 84–87, 95–97, 114, 135–36
business results, for projects, 66–69
business systems, 8–9

C

c control chart, 325
causation, versus correlation, 172, 233
cause-and-effect diagram, 97–98, 134–35
cause-and-effect diagram with addition of cards (CEDAC), 134, 135–36
causes, analyzing for, 327
center, of sample, 159
central limit theorem, 143–46
Certified Six Sigma Green Belt Body of Knowledge, comparison to Certified Six Sigma Black Belt Body of Knowledge, xxx–xxxv
check sheet, 99
chi-square distribution, 184–85
    using Excel to perform, 272–73
chi square test, 270–74
combinations, in probability, 151–52
common cause variation, 166, 301
communication, flow, in organizations, 89–90
complementation rule, 148
compound events probability, 148
conditional probability, 148–49
confidence interval
    for the mean, 252–53
    for proportion, 254–55
    for regression line, 240–42
    for variation, 254
confounding, and effects, in design of experiments, 288–89
contingency coefficient, 273
contingency tables, 273
continual improvement (CI), 351–52
continuous data, 153–154